BROCAS
A POW'S LIFE IN LETTERS

Brocas
A POW's Life in Letters
Researched and edited by Paddy Jackson

Text © 2022 Paddy Jackson

Design and Layout by Maïa Gaffney-Hyde.
Set in Plantin.

ISBN: 978-1-7391137-0-4

Printed and bound in Estonia by Tallinna Raamatutrükikoda.

Brocas

A POW'S
LIFE IN LETTERS

During the Great War
from August 1914 – November 1918

RESEARCHED AND EDITED BY

PADDY JACKSON

Dedication

This book is dedicated to the late Isabelle Lady Burrows,
Brocas's mother whose courage, wisdom, stamina, and foresight
have made this book possible.

Brocas in Holland in 1918 from a cricket team
photograph. Source: Graves family archive

Montagu 'Brocas' Burrows CB DSO MC
31 October 1894 – 17 January 1967

Epitaph

'Brocas was endowed with a fine physique, good looks, a fine intelligence and a wonderful joie de vivre, he used them all in a full enjoyment of a full and varied life which he communicated to those with whom he was working or playing. When Brocas was around there was never a dull moment. He was never happier than at home with his wife and family...

...There have, of course, been many better cricketers, but Brocas was a very good man to have on any side and one of whom it can be truly said that he played cricket cheerfully and unselfishly to the enjoyment of himself, his own side, his opponents, and any spectators present.'

The Cricketer, spring 1967

'No one however sympathetic, who has been deprived of his freedom, can have the least conception how awful it is.'

— *Lieutenant J. E. T. Younger diary of 1 January 1917*
Source: Younger family archive

Acknowledgments

This 'project' began with an unsolicited phone call to Richard Burrows, whose father's name was referred to by Ian Fairweather in one of his letters as a fellow prisoner in a recently published book *Ian Fairweather – A Life in Letters*. He spelt the name as Brokus Burroughs, which meant that nothing emerged from any searches while researching my dad's prisoner of war experience during the Great War. By chance I spotted a Brocas Burrows on an ICRC (International Committee of the Red Cross) POW record for Torgau prison camp in 1914. The 'penny dropped' and the rest as they say is history. Unashamedly, I have adopted the format and style of the Fairweather book which seemed fitting because of their shared POW experience.

The Burrows family have preserved a remarkable archive, and within it a complete bound set of Brocas's letters written in the prison camps. Also, in the collection is an exercise book with a complete list of all the food and other items sent to him in parcels by the family. This reads like a social history of the officer class of this time and is also an important source of information regarding various escape attempts. Together with photos and the letters they are the basis of this story.

First thanks must go to Brocas's son, Richard, and daughter Jennifer, for their support, encouragement, and making available the full archive of letters, photographs and miscellaneous documents without which this book would not have been possible. Also, to Jennifer in particular, for contributing substantially the 'Prelude' and final chapter 'Life After the War', for without this context and personal knowledge this book about her father would be resoundingly incomplete.

Secondly to Graham Conway for invaluable help in researching the families and genealogy of many of the individuals mentioned in the letters. Adrian Graves for making available the Graves family archives for his grandfather Cecil Graves. Catherine Ashmore likewise for the Crutchley family archive of her grandfather Gerald Crutchley. Jane Hunter-Blair for the 'War Book 1914' compiled by the mother of

Lieutenant David Hunter-Blair. Ian Skeet for information regarding his grandfather Lieutenant 'Hasler' Skeet. Nick and Nichola Jee for information regarding Captain Henry Cohu Randall and Miss Marie Randall. Catherine Harris for information regarding Captain Victor Richard Tahourdin. Janet Merret and William Seymour for the POW diary of Captain Wilfred Laurence Edmund Radclyffe Dugmore. Dr Clair Roberts for sources and information regarding Lieutenant Ian Fairweather, a remarkable man who some have described as Australia's greatest modernist painter. The Scots may have a view on that. Michael Younger for the POW diary of John Edward Talbot Younger, his grandfather, and for POW paintings and other illustrations and anecdotes. Major Philip Watson for advice on the details and process of writing this book and taking it to publication.

To Maïa Gaffney-Hyde a special thanks for her skill, unstinting patience, meticulous attention to detail, and her general help and guidance in laying out and type-setting this book. Mark Pilkington of Strange Attractor Press for arranging publication. To you the reader, for your interest and please, if you are a relative, descendant of any of the protagonists, or a researcher who can add anything to this story then please don't hesitate to contact the author. You may just promote a second edition.

Lastly to my wife and our girls for unstinting and often unwitting support and for keeping life on track while I was immersed on the computer throughout a tough period of covid lock downs and restrictions.

Thank you all, and the many others who have helped along the way who I may have unwittingly forgotten to mention.

Contents

Prelude

Our 'Brocas' was christened Montagu 'Brocas' Burrows.

He was born at Kinnersley Manor, Reigate, Surrey on 31 October 1894 and died 17 January 1967 aged 72.

The name Brocas has an interesting provenance. When Lord Edward, soon to become Edward I, was Governor of Aquitaine, he made the acquaintance of Arnald de Brocas, a Gascon noble who was with him in Sicily when, on their return from a crusading pilgrimage to the Holy Land in 1272, they heard of the death of Henry III. Edward hurried back to England faithfully followed by Arnald and his three sons. Arnald was killed at the battle of Bannockburn in 1314 and his three sons and their descendants fought alongside the monarchs of the time and were rewarded with knighthoods, land and money. Sir Bernard Brocas who died in 1396 has a magnificent tomb in Westminster Abbey but his son was not so lucky. He was put to death in the Tower in 1400 for conspiracy in favour of Richard II. Shakespeare, *Richard II* Act V Scene VI – 'My Lord, I have from Oxford sent to London the heads of Brocas and Sir Bennet Seely. Two of the dangerous consorted traitors that sought thy dire overthrow.'

The Brocas crest is a severed head. Legend says it is that of the King of Morocco, but who chopped it off and when is a matter for speculation. An old family tree says the perpetrator was Sir John Brocas who died in 1365. The same source claims that the first Sir Bernard Brocas came over with William the Conqueror, a claim made by many families who feel that antiquity is much to be desired, but there is no proof to substantiate this. However, on a grave in a churchyard in Northern France, the inscription reads: 'Here lies Francois Beranger Edouard Bernard, Comte de Brocas de Lanauze, born Courmelois (Marne) 12 July 1880, died Lisbon 9 April 1964.' Last of the surname from 1066-1964. So perhaps this man's ancestor went over with the Normans, was ennobled after the battle and then went home, and his descendant was probably Arnald de Brocas.

Sir Bernard Brocas became hereditary Master of the Royal Buckhounds in 1363, which remained in the family until 1633 when Thomas Brocas sold the office for £3,000 to Lord Rockingham. Sir Pexall Brocas was the black sheep. Beside forgery and other misdemeanours, he was forced to do penance in the centre of Oxford for fathering between 70 and 100 illegitimate children. According to the account, the culprit was attended by 'thirty men in scarlet that waited upon him to the Lord Mayor, when he went to demand a dinner after doing penance.' Full of years and dishonour, Sir Pexall died in 1630. Hodge was his jester, the last private family to have one.

The last male Brocas in England died in the mid nineteenth century and the last female, Blanche, in 1862. Jane Brocas born 1641 married Sir William Gardiner and her four times great granddaughter, Mary Anna daughter of Sir James Whalley Smythe Gardiner, married Brocas's grandfather Professor Montagu Burrows in 1849.

Brocas's grandfather, Montagu Burrows (1819-1905) was the son of Lieutenant General Montagu Burrows (1775-1848). He attended the Royal Naval College at Portsmouth in 1832 and then served on anti-piracy patrols on the East Indies Station and was decorated for his service at the bombardment of Acre. Promoted to commander in 1852, he decided to study at Oxford and was placed on half pay. There he obtained first class honours in 1856 and 1857. For the next five years he tutored students and then in 1862 was chosen as the first Chichele Professor of Modern History. He wrote more than 12 books, among them the much-praised *The Life of Edward Lord Hawke*. When he died in 1905, he was given a university funeral with the distinction of having his naval sword displayed on his coffin, while naval flags at Portsmouth were dipped for a Fellow of All Souls. In 1901 he took part in the weird ceremony of the Mallard. According to legend, when the foundations of the college were being dug in 1438, an enormous mallard flew out of a drain. Since then, every hundred years, on All Souls' Day, the fellows march round the precincts of the college carrying lighted torches, behind an elected Lord Mallard carrying a pole topped by a mallard duck. Afterwards they sip wine from a chalice – in earlier times it was the blood of the mallard. Each participant received a medal with the Lord Mallard and the mallard on one side and the retinue with torches on the reverse. Having married into the Gardiner family, Burrows was delighted to discover a fifteenth century oak chest more than 4-foot-long containing over 600 documents and papers relating to the Brocas family dating from between 1271-1872. His meticulous study of these resulted in *The Family of Brocas of Beaurepaire and Roche Court*, some 500 pages, including a family tree and published in 1886.

Montagu and Mary Anna had four living children – two more died in infancy. Emily, born in 1853, married the Bishop of Hong Kong and was caught up in the Boxer Rebellion where she nursed her cousin John Jellicoe, saving his life after he had been shot through the lung when his ship was attacked by the Boxers. Just as well or the Battle of Jutland might have had a less favourable outcome as Sir John Jellicoe was admiral of the fleet. Soon after, in November 1916 he was appointed First Sea Lord. He retired in 1919 and in 1925 was created Earl Jellicoe and Viscount Brocas of Southampton.

Brocas's father, Stephen, born 1856, became Director of Education in Ceylon and while there wrote a guide to the hidden temples of that country which is still in use today. He was made CIE (Companion of the Indian Empire) and later knighted for the good work he had done there, for helping Indian students settle into Oxford life and, with his friend Baden Powell in the scout movement, being the first to suggest that less able bodied could become members. Baden Powell gave him the 'Silver Wolf,' which is the highest award given to those who work for the scouts. He was known as the Saint for all his good work and according to all the letters he received, was great fun and loved by all who knew him. In her autobiography, *An Oxford Childhood*, Carola Oman says that when he lectured to children in 1909 you could hear a pin drop he had such infectious cheerfulness. He and his Australian wife, Isabella Cruickshank, Brocas's mother, had four children, but when in Ceylon, two died in infancy. According to his mother the climate was terribly unhealthy so the survivors, Brocas and his sister Agnes, known as 'Duchess', were sent back to England to be cared for by their nurse Nana Pugh, and grandparents, until Stephen's tour of duty ended in 1906. This was the first time that 'Brocas' was used as a Christian name.

Brocas went to Summerfield Preparatory School and then to Eton. According to Carola Oman, he was very good looking but would not be seen talking to a 'tug' [scholar] who were all despised by the hearty parties. Although bright, he was not a distinguished scholar like his cousin Bernard, son of Stephen's elder brother Edward. He was a member of the 1912 cricket first eleven. The team members were: D G Wigan, G H B Chance, G L Davies, G Hamilton-Fletcher (Gareth),

L C Leggatt, E F Campbell, R E Naylor, J H Amory, G S Rawstorne (George), Hon G Freeman-Thomas and M B Burrows (Brocas). All joined up at the start of the war and Davies, Hamilton-Fletcher, Leggatt, Naylor and Freeman-Thomas were killed in action between 1914 and 1917. Brocas left Eton in 1913 and joined his parents at their house in Oxford to prepare for joining Balliol College in September of that year. During the summer, he and his father spent long periods studying Aristotle and his ilk in preparation for the entrance exam. Bernard's father had died in 1910 just before he was born and so Stephen took charge of his education. Bernard never forgave him for sending him to Trinity instead of Balliol. The reasoning being that the seriously intellectual college would encourage Brocas to concentrate on academic work instead of sport and also encourage Bernard to do the opposite!

It will be seen that Brocas's love of sport never deserted him throughout his life but that he also possessed great energy, intellect, and wisdom as witnessed by his ability to master many languages. These would be an undoubted asset as he rose through the ranks of the army during an illustrious career that began with over four years internment during the Great War, the subject of this book. He also possessed a sharp wit and sense of humour which was combined with a calm determination to prevail and succeed. That he never found time to write his autobiography is unfortunate and would have entertained where many a 'stuffy' general failed to do so. Hopefully he would have approved of this book and felt that it is a faithful account of this most challenging time which laid the foundations of his life thereafter. Surely another story for another time by a more knowledgeable political historian?

His letters leave many questions unanswered but there is enough to correctly fill this volume and provide a brief insight into the social history of the officer class of this time, as well as the positive aspects of life as a POW, or as a 'KG' as referred to by Brocas. It should be borne in mind that letters both to and from POWs were heavily censored by German authorities both in practice and by the self-censorship of the writers themselves as they sought to avoid contravening the rules as to what was, or was not admissible, for fear of the letters simply disappearing from the system.

His father, the only parent then in Holland, in a letter home to his wife on 26 February 1918 wrote:

I had a long talk with two senior officers (Major Chetwynd-Stapylton and Captain Picton-Warlow). They could not have spoken more warmly about the 'boy'. They said that he was of the best, that by means of strenuous exercise, keenness about every sort of amusement, and hard work at language he had kept himself more fit than any other officer they knew, old or young, that he was popular with all classes, and had been the life and soul of every camp he was in.

This is a fitting final tribute and summary of Brocas's understated life as a 'KG' to which his letters and a few of his fathers' letters bear witness.

My one regret is that I never met Brocas, nor had the opportunity to share a joke and a pint and ask more about his escape attempts. What happened to Miloradovitch, to his autograph book, etc.? I am however, indebted to his son Richard and daughter Jennifer for all their help, and allowing access to their astonishing family archive which has made this book possible.

Preface

On a blazing hot late summer day, 24 August 1914, at Audregnies in Belgium, after fighting a desperate rear-guard action all day, 2nd Lieutenant Ian Fairweather, 1st Battalion Cheshire Regiment, was captured by the advancing German army along with over 300 of his regiment. Some were wounded and captured, some were wounded and escaped capture, a further 56 lay dead. In a cornfield among the recently harvested stooks a dangerously wounded fellow officer, Captain Eric Archer Jackson, was covered with straw by a colleague, left for dead and lay on the battlefield for over a day, fighting for his life. Against all the odds he survived and like the 2nd lieutenant would spend the rest of the war in German POW camps. Both would become persistent but unsuccessful escapers and, although they were moved from camp to camp, they were never in the same camp at the same time and their paths probably never crossed again until now. Ian Fairweather however, spent nearly all his captivity in the same camps as Brocas, not as close friends, but as co escape-minded conspirators. But again, after the war and until now, their paths probably never crossed again.

On 5 April 1960, while living on Bribie Island, Northern Australia, and scratching a living as a reclusive artist that same former 2nd lieutenant wrote a letter to his sister; Letter number 131 in a book 'Ian Fairweather – A Life in Letters'. He was reminiscing, and when remembering several of his fellow prisoners of war in Germany, he pondered the fate of one 'Brokus Burroughs.' This chance reference, and hours of research, have spawned this narrative. Borne out of the trials of incarceration and forged by their shared experience of internment, Montagu Brocas Burrows and Ian Fairweather would ultimately achieve a greatness, although by markedly different routes, which both would have appreciated of each other. The duality by which the letters they wrote, and the way they have been preserved so carefully by others, is however remarkable. So too this story which by pure chance has unfolded to be now cast in print. Well Brocas, a little late, this is your story and Ian, your small part in it.

The letters Brocas wrote are faithfully reproduced, the grammar, punctuation and spellings are as written and transcribed by his sister (Agnes, known as Duchess) and are only altered where an obvious mistake occurs such as mis-spelling of a name or place. There is the possibility of small errors due to the trying circumstances in which they were written. Also included are a few of the many letters his father wrote home from Holland in 1918 and extracts from others to which the same rules have been applied.

Brocas's letters indicate a broad appreciation of international events and wider circumstances associated with internment. They reveal a sharp wit, intelligence and energy maintained at a high level despite the deprivation resulting from his confinement. He was an active sportsman and took key roles in amateur dramatic performances. He learnt and became proficient in Russian, mastered French, German, and Italian and dabbled in Hindustani. He appears to have been positive and optimistic throughout and, being so strongly motivated, undoubtedly helped many others to survive over a thousand dark days as a 'KG' (Kriegsgefangener).

This narrative focuses on two main threads in the letters. Firstly, the support of his family and friends back home, both practically with parcels (Appendix I) and mentally with letters, which, whether typical or not, was critical to his survival and a successful life thereafter. Secondly, the means by which Brocas and his parents in particular, communicated in code and by concealment to circumvent the censorship imposed by the Germans as he and the family sought to facilitate his escape. Brocas mentions many names of fellow POWs, some of whom were with him throughout. Where possible these have been identified and outline details included (Appendix II). There is a brief chapter describing each POW camp and the parcels sent to, and received by Brocas, followed by a chapter of the associated letters from each camp as he criss-crossed Germany before finally being exchanged to Holland.

At most camps the German camp authorities tried to enforce strict discipline and conformity to orders however harsh or trivial. They did so often with unwarranted and unprovoked brutality. The attitude and atmosphere at each camp was dictated by individual camp commandants. The natural German psyche was completely opposite to that of the British and as a consequence they were never able to break the collective spirit of the British POWs. This sentiment was expressed most eloquently by Lieutenant Younger R.F.A. writing in his diary of 22 August 1917 at Clausthal POW camp. A sentiment that would be replicated in many post war reports.

> *The Germans have begun worrying and bothering us in petty ways again, this is very upsetting and set us all on edge. If they would only leave us in peace we should be perfectly easy to manage, but directly they start nagging and bothering us with all the orders, rules, forbidding of this and that, it gets our backs up, and instead of being quiet and tractable, we dig our toes in and give them trouble. But they cannot understand us and have no idea of how to deal with us: The new Hauptmann* [Captain] *said this evening to Lister "we treat you as gentleman", perhaps he honestly believes it. But that does not alter the fact that they never do and never have treated us as gentlemen, because they cannot understand and do not know how to do so. The system and customs of Prussian discipline are useless, when applied to Britishers. It merely produces the opposite effect intended! They cannot understand enforcement of discipline without harsh loud commands, unintelligent and unreasoning interpretation of orders, and iron-fisted tactless force. The discipline produced by quiet strength of character, firmness of purpose, tactful dealing, straightforwardness and intelligent understanding of human nature, is quite unknown to them, unluckily for them and happily for us. Their discipline will never stand the test of bad times and black days, ours has and will continue to do so.*

The POWs were indeed a band of brothers who shared with Brocas this unique challenge and struggle for survival. It is worth noting that only when he finally reached Holland did Brocas express any feelings of hatred and ill feeling towards his captors. In just three letters written in Germany and smuggled out was he able write freely. In his letters or cards home via the Prisoner Post, Brocas, like all POWs, was always mindful that any adverse comment would be either censored or simply not sent. The consequence being the loss of the vital, yet tenuous link to an anxious family back home, longing for news and the safe return of a loved one.

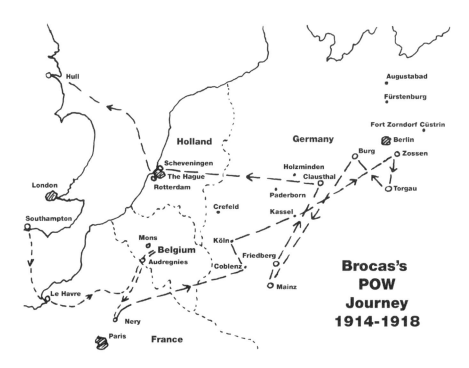

Sketch map of Brocas's journey as a prisoner of war

I

The First Days – Fighting – Capture – POW Journey

9 August 1914 – 14 September 1914

Montagu Brocas Burrows was 19 years old when he went to war. At the time he was living with his parents in Oxford where his grandfather had been the first Chichele Professor of Modern History. He had completed his schooling at Eton in 1913. On 10 August 1914 he set off from Aldershot with the 5th Dragoon Guards, part of the 1st Cavalry Brigade, to serve his country. 'Brocas', as a yet to be appointed second lieutenant, never did get to say a proper 'goodbye' to his family due to the speed with which he was whisked away to France. Within three weeks he would find himself a prisoner of war interned in a POW camp in Germany. On a misty morning on 1 September 1914 in the village of Néry in France, life for Brocas changed forever. Following his capture, he would spend three and a half years of his life incarcerated in six different camps.

In what was to become known as 'The Affair at Néry', he took part in an action which was a turning point for that part of the war, often referred to as the retreat from Mons. Néry, as the crow flies, is approximately 105 miles from Mons and only 30 miles from the centre of Paris. In just one week the 1st Cavalry Brigade would have travelled considerably further, fighting continual rear-guard actions along the way. From 23 to 28 August they averaged less than two hours sleep a night. Brocas's 'C' squadron, on the night of 31 August 1914, was billeted in the centre of the village. 'A' and 'B' squadrons were on the north edge of the village. The 2nd Dragoon Guards were to the south and the 11th Hussars on the south-east edge. Six 13-pound guns of 'L' Battery were limbered in a field a little further south as they prepared to continue the retreat which had been delayed by one hour until 5.50 am because of the mist. At first light, as the mist began to clear, the Germans, who had been camped on a plateau overlooking the village less than two miles to the east, commenced an attack without warning.

A battery of 10 or 12 guns of the German field artillery, at a range of only 800 yards, supported by a battery of machine-guns, pounded the British positions causing havoc and devastation. Only three guns of 'L' battery could be brought into action and despite heavy losses they fought gallantly until their ammunition was expended. For their bravery three men were awarded Victoria Crosses. When the guns fell silent the British 1st Cavalry Brigade was able to launch a counter attack which forced the German cavalry to retreat in disorder. Hailed by many as the turning point in the war against the Kaiser this was the first time the Allies had won the field of battle. It halted the German advance and the Allies never again conducted a significant withdrawal for the rest of the war.

Brocas would undoubtedly have been part of that counter-attack when, with the Bays, they saw off the German cavalry to the south of the village. As Sergeant Gough's account bears witness, it was only later that afternoon that Brocas was injured while asleep when a horse trod on the back of his head. The following day the Brigade continued its retirement leaving behind Brocas and about 20 wounded in the field hospital in Néry where he was taken prisoner as the Germans moved into the recently vacated village.

Brocas received many letters from his parents and sister during his internment. He kept them all but eventually had to destroy the majority before being exchanged to Holland in 1918. He retained only the most precious, being the first and most poignant he received. These tell lovingly of missing their planned 'goodbye', and how very quickly his parents dealt with the situation. How their pride took over as they came to terms with the reality of the challenges their son was facing. Despite the fact that the whole British Expeditionary Force was continually on the move in the days prior to his capture, one batch of letters caught up with him in the field in either Belgium or France. These were probably the ones he refers to in his letter of 17 November 1914 (*Letter 13*). He must have kept them throughout his internment as an enduring connection to his family and home. They continue to be carefully preserved in the family archives and are the first of this extraordinary folio. The many letters he wrote home, the basis of this book, were also carefully filed in date order, along with copies meticulously typed by his sister.

His story begins with the first letters from his father:

Letter 1

9 Norham Gardens, Oxford, 16 August 1914

My dear Boy.

Your letter came as rather a bomb among us this morning, for we had allowed ourselves to move along in a fools' paradise and so they have taken you! You have your hearts' desire and we are proud that you have been chosen and from our hearts congratulate you that Colonel Ansell has seen fit to confer this great honour upon you. You have fought bravely for it and entering off your own bat have got what hundreds of others failed to obtain. Captain Slessor was with us for some time this afternoon and could hardly believe that such luck was true and said you were the only one of your class who had succeeded so you are indeed to be congratulated. My darling boy we proudly give you for our King and Country knowing that you will give of your best glorious manhood in their just cause – Thank you over and over again for your dear letter, how we value it and shall prize it, and how we shall welcome you when you return with the Kaisers' head on a charger! What a glorious memory for us all your last Thursday will ever be, how grateful we are that it was allowed us. The dear home is full of happy memories of you and you so near to us, I can almost see you sitting on the stool in front of my dressing table chatting away of the many things. God bless and guide you ever dear one.

Just a line on to Mothers', dear old boy, to say how proud we are of you, and how certain we are you will play the man. Of course, there is no denying the news was a real shock when your letter came at 7 this morning, but we went straight off to Holy Communion, which is the one and only source of consolation, and from that time we have grieved no more, and only rejoiced in your good fortune. Slessor could hardly believe it, and said of course you did perfectly right. God bless and keep you, my only son. With a brave heart and a strong right arm and the soul of a Christian gentleman you will go far. Mother and Agnes behaved simply splendidly.

Your loving father
S.M Burrows.

Letter 2

9, Norham Gardens, Oxford. 19 August 1914

Daddy and Duchess are having a game of Billiards.

Our dear dear Boy,
We think of you day and night and try to possess our souls in patience for Kitchener holds all the channels of news in his iron grip, we know nothing except French's splendid reception at Boulogne and Paris and that our glorious navy has guarded you over the sea. Today's papers tell us that the German Crown Prince is wounded and is at Aix La Chapelle, is it wrong to hope that he is wounded unto death. They had a war meeting here last night Duchess and Ruth went with Mrs Allen and Jonny Rawnesly, there were over 1000 present and the enthusiasm was tremendous. The French national anthem, Russian English were sung with much verve. Mr Holdane and Naomi were wild with excitement. Many young men enlisted afterwards. Mr Price came this afternoon, Archie has joined the Motor Bicycle Corps for Coast Defence and awaits orders. As I write in the dear familiar library that is full of memories of you dear boy, Ruth Radcliffe, who you know is with us is reading aloud to me "How to be useful in war time". She is attending nursing lectures and is ready to bandage anyone that she can get hold of! We were taken over the Base Hospital here (in the Beamination? Schools) Dr Parker in full R.A medical Corp uniform. What a change, they have put in bathrooms, kitchens and about 500 beds, the names of the colleges that they have taken them from painted on the foot. Each bed is made ready for use. Mrs Halton writes today that her boy Edward has gone from "Dartmouth" on the Queen Mary, a battleship, went on the first so he was very probably one of those guarding the line when you dear boy and your brave companions passed over. Dear little Sandy seems to know that something is wrong, he is so devoted as if he could not leave us and lies on his back at our feet wagging his tail as his way of comforting us. I chat on darling as if I could not bear to stop, for while I write you seem near, and all the horrors of this present seem as a dream. You are always so near though so far. God bless and keep you is ever the prayer of your loving

Mother

Duchess is so brave and went today with Ruth to see Mrs Parry the Sergeant Major of O.T.C.'s wife, he has been promoted and is now an N.C.O.

Brocas's story continues, in his words. This is his own account of the start of his venture which would see him in incarcerated in a German prisoner of war camp within a month.

M B Burrows
5th Dragoon Guards

If found please return to Norham House, Oxford

Si on trouve ce livre je le prie de l'envoyee a: S.M Burrows a Norham House, Oxford Angleterre

Account probably initially started 9 August 1914 on the troop ship

Sunday Morning.

As soon as I decided to try to go to the front at the very beginning of this war, it struck me that it perhaps might interest some of my relatives & friends if I were to try and write an account of it and of my impression of what looks like being a war of wars. I meant to begin as soon as I joined my regiment at Aldershot but owing to the tremendous rush and bustle of getting ready and the awkwardness of a novice in the art of writing, I find myself on board the troopship sailing from Southampton to an unknown destination and my account not yet begun. For this reason, I will skip over the preparations quickly. Possibilities of war had been spoken of some days before I went on an Eton Rambler cricket tour to Kent and we only realised it on the Saturday when staying with Sir Marcus Samuel. We all returned to town that evening and after a very big night, I returned to Oxford next day to make arrangements. I was there told I was too young and I must go to Sandhurst for three months before being given a commission. However, I decided to make one last effort before this and went to Aldershot to see Colonel Ansell of the 5th D.G's to whom I had been attached in the spring. He said he would recommend me for a commission and advised me to go to town and to get kit.

I went and returned to Oxford that night. Next day I said my adieux and departed to Aldershot to start my new duties. My knowledge of cavalry drill was a mere suspicion and my knowledge of horses still less, but there was no time to put me through the ordinary course and so I had to get on as best I could. The first shock I had was when I was told I should have to wait at home in the reserve regiment as so many special reservists of much experience had joined. Imagine my horror – all my hustling wasted – however I decided that the wait was my best course and did so accordingly. I did various odd jobs throughout the week and on Sunday was inoculated against typhoid – this made me ill and all-day

Monday and, in the evening, I went up for my medical examination on the Tuesday morning. This was an awful business as I had not arranged a time and tho' I went at 10 am I was not examined until 7 pm. I dined with George, Alex and Leo Page and went back to Aldershot next day. The only train after an early one was the 5.40 which I caught. Wednesday and Thursday were ordinary days but on Friday 14th, father, mother and Duchess came down to see me and I spent the day with them at the Queens, Farnborough. We had an excellent day till 5 pm when I received a message from the Colonel to return at once. I did so and arrange for the family to come down again on Wednesday. Hence, I avoided the goodbyes! I returned to find a general bustle and the Colonel offered to take me out in the ranks and give me the first casualty vacancy. A fellow whom he was taking out had fallen and he had received orders to depart the next day. He gave me 10 minutes to decide so I went away and spun a coin and it came down heads so I went.

We were paraded at 4:30 next morning and it was now 6 pm and I had made no arrangements for anything. I wrote home and started to pack and managed to have things fairly well ready by next morning. We were the second squadron to depart and marched to Aldershot station where all the officers' wives said goodbye and also the reserve officers. We entrained wonderfully well and quickly and got to Southampton about midday, but the liner to take us across had not come in and so we were sent to a Rest Camp just outside the town. About now it began to pour and as there were hardly any tents at the rest camp we had an awful time and got wet through. Four of us went down to the town and had a very good lunch and returned at 2. At about four we left the camp and marched to our ship. Embarkation took a dreadful long time but was very interesting. The ship was the S.S. Cyprian of the Leyland Line and we and the 11th Hussars were on board with over 1000 horses and 1000 men and 50 nurses. We slept in the harbour for fear of mines and went out at about 5.30 on Sunday morning. They had no food on board and we had to feed the nurses who had none. We eventually arrived at Havre at about 3.30 and started to disembark into one of the store hangers there. This was a most trying operation and took a very long time. I was told to look after some wagons and did not get in till about 10.30. The hanger was vast and held us, the 11th, the Bays and two battalions of infantry. The noise was unbearable and we slept on corn sacks or rather tried to. Personally, I was very unsuccessful. We got up early and fussed about generally all the morning doing stables et cetera. We saw the Scottish Borderers going up towards the front and were told about lunchtime we could go out into the town of Havre. A

vast place of 400,000 inhabitants ranged along great rows of docks now full of transports. I went with two other officers and had tea at the Hotel Moderne where I had left my surplus baggage the day before. We then shopped a bit and I saw Mr Powell (Eton master) now a Motor Cyclist. At five we returned to the hanger and prepared to move up. We got our orders about 8.30 and marched by a fearfully circuitous route to the station where we embarked after finding our transport and got off about 1:30 am (Tuesday)
and so, ends!

Account continued at Burg POW camp 24 January 1915

The ease with which I find I forget things which seemed of vital importance at the time when they occurred has persuaded me to write down in black and white a few of the events which marked my captivity in Germany. Though they are not narrated at the exact moment of occurrence, I am going to try and express my sensations at that time to the best of my ability. At the end of this war we shall no doubt feel rather sorry for our late foes and the memory of their bravery and stubbornness in the struggle will probably out-weigh some of their acts which seemed so all important at the time. Hence a reference to these latter written more-or-less at the time may be useful.

I was taken prisoner on first of Sept. [1914] and must have been quite a pitiable sight with my clothes covered with blood, my face cut about and my head bashed in. The Jaegers took me out of hospital and their Colonel sent me back to headquarters in his car and treated me very well. All of them were quite nice, expressed sorrow at having to fight the English and said the English had fought magnificently. One of them accompanied me to headquarters and did all he could and even got a doctor to re-dress my wound, but he had to leave in the middle of this operation and then the fun began. I was put with 2 A.S.C. officers in a hovel near H. Q. where were about 20 German Reservists – the H. Q. guard – and as prisoners besides us a German deserter, four civilian French peasants whose sins I will narrate later, and the Mayor of the town as a hostage. The Jaeger subaltern said before leaving I should only be there for an hour or two. But he did not know his reservist officers. The Doctor knocked me about so that I fainted and eventually did me up so badly that I had to undo the bandage and get one of the A.S.C. officers to do it up. All the H.Q. guard came in at intervals to look at the 'Englander Schweinen' and to spit at the deserter who was lying bound hand and foot next

*to me. They were mostly bad shots. In the evening the smell was so
fearful and lying on the stone floor had become so painful that I
plucked up courage to ask the corporal of the Guard to go to the
Major and ask whether we were to sleep in this godforsaken hovel.
He eventually went though it cost 5 marks and later the 'Great Man'
came. He looked at us through his glasses and I tried to explain that
we were 3 officers and hoped for better quarters. He laughed and said to
the great amusement of all the listeners 'Gut genug fur ein Englander
schwein der wird morgen fruh geschossen!' * Then he went away. The
other 2 did not understand any German, so I never told them and I am
thankful to say they slept well – I didn't. We had no supper and when
we were moved out into the small garden behind next morning, I really
thought my last hour had come and funnily enough didn't much care.*

*We stayed in the hovel 3 days without seeing an officer and then
proceeded by cart to Compiegne, spending the night at Villers Cotterêts.
Of the insults suffered by the way I will not speak. Thank God I was
not alone. We stayed at Compiegne 2 days sleeping in the prison of the
French 5th Dragoons barracks and getting no food but bread and water
and being spat upon by all German soldiers. A very favourite form
of amusement with these men. From Compiegne we were marched to
Noyon – a process which proved extremely painful to me. Here we stayed
2 days in this awful place – the stable of the town hall and were moved
on to Chauny. At Noyon Lt Peskett (Lincs.) joined us. He had been
left in hospital there with dysentery and could hardly move. At Chauny
we had a glorious reception. I was kicked on the back by a German
sergeant because I sat down in the road being half dead with fatigue. We
waited for 5 hours in the dark in the worst seats in an ex-cinema theatre
and were then led to the station. Here we were searched and I had my
spurs taken away and was hit on my wound by a German unter-offizer
with his scabbard – it hurt a great deal. After this we were put into a
wagon which had come to the front with coal and had not been cleaned
out. Half of it was covered with straw and was reserved for the guard –
eleven in number and the other half was for us. We were now 40 in no.
Only about fifteen could sit together – so we took it in turns. We had no
food and so we journeyed having to open the carriage at every station
to be spat at and cursed by the Germans there. Just at this time the
Germans had spread that we had shot dum-dum bullets and this was
hurled at our teeth all the way.*

*So, we reached Coblentz in forty eight hours where I had a very joyful
experience. A very brutal looking officer came to the carriage to keep*

off a crowd of soldiers who were drunk and just off to the front. He asked if I knew Sir Edward Grey** or rather he said Mr. (Meester) Grey and I nodded. He then turned round to the others and said that there was an officer in the carriage who was friend of Sir E. Grey's. The ensuing hubbub was fearful and he then sent in 2 men who seized me and held me in the doorway for what seemed an eternity but was about ¼ hour. All kinds of articles were thrown at me most of which missed and went into the carriage where the men devoured all that was eatable. At Koln we had previously changed carriages and there was straw in this second one. I also had my wound dressed. Sixty hours after leaving Chauny we reached Cassel and here had our first food – a bowl of greasy soup and a chunk of black bread. On our way back, we had a bad time from the inhabitants and I was hit with a loaf of kriegsbrot *** a very effective weapon.

After this our journey was uneventful until we reached Zossen 96 ½ hours after leaving Chauny – absolutely exhausted and longing for anything to eat. We asked for something at the station and some of the Red X sisters amused themselves by bringing glasses of water and spilling them at our feet and holding out bread and then snatching it away. I couldn't have believed it of any women in the world. We were then marched to the encampment of the ex-garrison of Mauberge. – at least 10,000 of them and about 250 Russians. Here some of the French gave us some bread out of their little supply and I could easily have kissed them all. Here ended what I hope will be the worst journey I shall ever have to undergo. One of the A.S.C. had caught a chill on the way, and had fainted on the way to the hospital room at Köln station, and my head had never stopped aching, and I had caught a cold, as my overcoat had been taken away from me under the following circumstances. On the way to Chauny a wounded German officer had passed in a car, and, after having the car stopped and cursing and spitting at us, he asked my rank, and I told him I was an officer. Thereupon he said, "give me your overcoat, and I will take it to Chauny and give it to you there." I said I would rather keep it, as I did not like the look of him, but he said, "No it is a very hot day, and I promise you on my word of honour I will return it to you at Chauny." It was then taken from me forcibly. I was too weak to resist, and I have never seen it again. He was a regular officer. None of the men had coats or blankets, and had their braces, coat buttons and belts taken from them. We reached Zossen on the 14th, and I had not washed or shaved for a fortnight!

Zossen

This encampment was occupied at the time of my arrival by some 10,000 French territorials, 250 Russians, and about 200 Belgians. The only officers were a French artillery man, a Douanier, a Russian Hussar, and a dozen or so doctors. A large field had been enclosed by a high barbed-wire fence, and there were sentries every 50 yards, and 200 men always under arms in a small enclosure on a hill in the middle. The Railway ran along one side, and a main road along the other. All around the fence were ranged the latrines, of the most primitive and public sort, and three times a day there were excursions from Berlin to view the camp, and the crowd was always thickest round these loathsome objects.

Our food was: 5.30 am a bowl of coffee; midday, a bowl of soup; 6pm a bowl of soup. We could occasionally buy things at the canteen at fabulous prices, but the place was usually sold out. One day I was told we could have special suppers if we paid for them, but as they consisted of a raw egg, a sausage sandwich, a Bismark herring and a ham sandwich, and as this cost 2 marks, we had one and no more. There were tents for 5000 men, so the rest had to build themselves huts and live underground. Our numbers were augmented daily by the wounded French they sent back from Mons, and many died. Our men were so badly treated by the German doctor, that they said they would rather die than go there again. A French doctor kindly attended to them early in the morning, as this was really forbidden. We were sent in batches of about 50 to the barracks, 3 miles away, for our bath, and it was possible to get one about every 10 days. As officers we were allowed the corner of a tent in which at night there were about 500 people all told, packed like sardines. Sleep was impossible, but we slept by day. Here we spent a fortnight, and were then moved on to Torgau. Our journey was uneventful, as the officer in charge was nice to us, and we were allowed to buy a meal of hot meat and potatoes, jam tart and cheese, at Gütenbog. True, it cost us 5 marks a head, but still it was good! It was the first time I really felt full since I left England.

Torgau

We arrived here the evening of Sunday, September 28, in pouring rain, and, after a fairly stormy march to the fort, at last saw Englishmen again. The first who addressed me (Belfour) [probably Lt Belfour Royal Engineers] I mistook for a German! We were forthwith treated to tea (sausage and German coffee) and then told off to a shed to sleep. Here we slept on the floor on palliasses.

* 'Good enough for English swine who will be shot in the morning'
** Foreign Secretary – see attached encyclopaedia extract
*** war bread
**** bacon

A similar account by Sergeant Gough of the 5th Dragoon Guards also described the departure of the regiment to France and first few days of the War. It is worth quoting in full as it casts further light on the circumstances leading up to Brocas's capture and internment.

The Doings of the 5th Dragoon Guards from 14 August 1914 to 8 September 1914 (Taken down on 3 October 1914) when he visited Brocas's parents who presumably typed this account.

We left Aldershot 700 strong on the night of Aug. 14th, rested for three hours at Southampton and embarked for Havre. We stayed there that night and the following night, and at 9 a.m. marched through Havre to another station and entrained there. We were two days and two nights in the train, thoroughly well fed and looked after. The train seemed to be entirely in English hands; the guards the porters were all English, and the only Frenchman connected with it appeared to be the engine driver. We halted every 10 hours to feed and water our splendid horses (the best in the British army); and the kindness of the French people to us, both at these halts and the subsequent marches, was simply beyond words. They couldn't do enough for us. We passed through Amiens and Namur, and finally detrained at Ninove, a few miles west of Brussels, and a long way north of Mons. This was the extreme northern point that the British reached at all. Lieut. Burrows was in C. Squadron, (my squadron) riding as a Trooper, centre guide, till he could get his commission, which he got alright soon afterwards. Lieut. Hill, since badly wounded at the battle of Néry, did the same; and we greatly admired the pluck of these two boys in determining to come with us at all cost. From this time onwards when any French had to be talked, Lieut. Burrows did it all for us. We were told that we were sent up so far North to keep the Germans back by every means in our power, as the French could not possibly be ready for three weeks. Our Brigade consisted of ourselves, the Queen's Bays (2nd Dragoon Guards), the 11th Hussars, L. Battery R.H.A. We did not stay at Ninove; but marched south to Mons; and after three days hard fighting there the terrible retreat began. We had a desperate fight at Le Cateau, and again at Compiègne, where we were to have had 10 hours rest, but we were badly let in by the French, who failed to report to

*us that the enemy were close to us. The Germans surprised us with their
shells at 3 am. Our Battery R.H.A. had their horses simply blown to
pieces; but we captured enough Uhlan horses to man them. Our Colonel
(Col. Ansell) rode ahead of us to the top of a small eminence to survey
the position, and was shot through the right breast and lung. He rode
back to us and continued to give us orders; rode ahead of us again and
was shot through the left breast and lung. He gave us one more order,
got off his horse, walked to a tree, and was dead within twenty minutes.
He was the finest cavalry officer in the British Army, and died a great
death. On the afternoon after this battle we were resting under some trees
when a horse stepped back and injured Lieut. Burrows' head, at the
back. It was not a serious wound, but took a bit of flesh off and bled a
good deal. Captain Black bound him up, and I sent a Trooper with him
to the nearest Field Hospital. The Trooper returned and reported that he
had left him safely there. He had not re-joined when I was wounded on
September 7th. We lost 200 men at the battle of Néry; but up to and after
that battle, Lieut. Burrows had come through without a scratch until this
injury occurred, and was in splendid health.*

An extract from a further letter from Lieutenant Nettlefold, 5th Dragoon
Guards, Un-dated, elaborated further on the cause of his injury.

Letter 3

[No date or address]

To Burrows family

*Burrows was in C. Squadron. He left the Regiment September 1st the same day
as Maurice (Hill) was wounded. A horse stood on his head while he was asleep
on the ground and made a nasty little gash on the back of his neck. I believe it
cut a small artery and he went to look for one of the R.A.M.C to dress it for
him. He was chatting quite happily when he went off and did not look much
the worse.*

*This was near Compiègne during the retreat. I expect he went to some base
hospital. I am rather surprised his people have heard nothing, but the W.O are
very slow over these things and letters take a long time getting through from
the front. A letter I wrote my people on Sept.4th got through on Sept. 25th.*

I am sorry I can't tell you more.
Not signed

The Regimental War Diary of the 5th Dragoon Guards adds another layer of detail to the movements of the regiment at this time. Brocas is listed as a 2nd Lieutenant in 'C' Squadron along with Lieutenant E.J. Nettlefold. Lieutenant Hill, Special Reserve was in B Squadron along with Lieutenant J.H. Nettlefold Special Reserve. Presumably the Nettlefolds were brothers and it was most likely the former who wrote the above letter. The battalion had a total strength of 549 men of which seven officers and other ranks of Brocas's 'C' Squadron totalled 152. In addition, their number included 524 riding horses, 74 draught horses (for pulling the battalions' transport) and 6 pack horses, the latter being mainly used for carrying ammunition.

They saw action on several occasions between 23 and 31 August 1914. On 24th they were initially behind the infantry line at Audregnies where the 1st Battalion Cheshires, supported by 9th Lancers and 4th Dragoon Guards, were to fight a desperate battle later that day. On 26 August, with the whole BEF in retreat, and acting as flank guard, the 5th Dragoon Guards with the rest of the 1st Cavalry Brigade were fighting all day just south of Le Cateau. They were tired and exhausted having been continuously on the move for 10 days.

The Regimental War Diary entry of 27 August 1914 recorded:

'The night was cold and damp, but the difficulty lay, not in getting to sleep, but in keeping awake. For five nights the regiment had not averaged more than two hours' sleep each night.'

Only on the 30 August did they have a slight respite and during the day were able to wash and bathe in the River Aisne. By the night of 31 August/1 September the battalion found themselves bivouaced in Néry, a small village running North and South near Compiègne. The 5th Dragoon Guards had the north end, with their horses in the open, and the rest of the 1st Cavalry Brigade occupied other parts of the village with 11th Hussars and HQ in the centre, and the 'Bays' [2nd Dragoon Guards] and 'L' Battery RHA at the south end. Tuesday 1 September was a very thick misty morning and it transpired that the Germans, who consisted of about a cavalry division with 10 or 12 guns, had blundered into them in the fog.

The book *Mons – The Retreat to Victory*, John Terraine 1960, described the events:

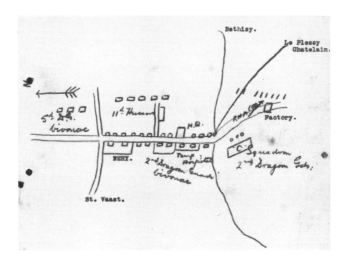

Sketch map of Néry 31 August 1914 showing location of bivouac, temporary hospital and Brigade HQ Source: 1st Cavalry Brigade HQ war diary in The National Archives

When the Germans had arrived at first light, from the heights above the village they were able to look down and see, in the misty valley below, the 1st Cavalry Brigade and L Battery, R.H.A., watering their horse and having breakfast. A patrol of the 11th Hussars dashed in with the news that German cavalry were about, and almost instantly a storm of fire from rifles, burst over the 1st Cavalry Brigade at a range of little more than 600 yards. It was a complete surprise. The horses of the Queen's Bays stampeded at once. L Battery was limbered up and standing in mass, presenting a wonderful target. Men and horse began to go down fast; the battery commander was hit. Captain Bradbury, the second in command, managed to get three guns unlimbered and turned round to answer the German fire. One of them was put out of action instantly by a direct hit, and almost immediately afterwards the second was silenced, the whole detachment being wiped out. The last available gun of L Battery then began its contest with the 12 German guns on the heights…

The Regimental War Diary continued:

'1st September – Partridge shoot begins! The ball opened with half-a-dozen shells bursting over the village. Immediately all was bustle. Everybody ran to the lines to saddle up under shell and rifle fire.'

Brocas's father wrote to his wife regarding this day after the war on 17 February 1918 (*Letter 176*), having spoken with Brocas while they were both in Holland. He clarified what happened:

> *He never was wounded in the groin at all as the War Office said. At the Battle of Néry he had two horses shot under him, and got a bad fall each time. He got hold of a third horse, but was almost done, on the top of 10 days terrific work, and his C.O. told him to go and lie down for an hour & get a little sleep if he could. He lay down, face downwards on his arms, and his orderly was told to hold his horse; but the orderly too was done and went to sleep, the horse was restive and trod on him and kicked the back of his head and inflicted a very nasty wound…*

It is hard to imagine the events of that day. His Commanding Officer Lieutenant Colonel Ansell was killed along with 10 men. 2nd Lieutenant Maurice Hill and about 20 men were either wounded or missing, half of them from 'C' Squadron; 60-80 horses were either killed or stampeded. 'C' Squadron had been despatched to the south end of the village to help out the 'Bays' who were anticipating a flank attack from their right. The maps of Néry taken from the Brigade war diary show the location of a field hospital in the middle of the village which is probably where Brocas was taken for treatment after his unfortunate incident.

His father's letter of 17 February 1918 (*Letter 176*) continued:

> *…He was practically unconscious until two days after he found a German peering over him in bed in the Field Hospital. He must have lost a lot of blood, as the first bandage was only partially successful, & he must have been bleeding for at least three hours until the doctor got at him…*

The Regimental War Diary of 19 September 1914, summarised the regiment's losses, and simply listed 2nd Lieutenant Burrows as 'sick', presumably as a way of distinguishing from being wounded.

This War Diary account tells graphically of the carnage, already alluded to, that 'L' Battery RHA experienced at the south end of the village where they were in a very exposed position, facing an enemy only about half a mile away:

*5th Dragoon Guards Regimental War Diary entry 19
September 1914. Source: The National Archives*

*L Battery suffered most heavily of all. All their officers and men who
were in the battery were killed or wounded except Major Sclater-
Booth, commanding, the Battery Sergeant Major, and their French
interpreter…. Captain Bradbury R.H.A. had a leg shot off and
continued doing his duty, until his other leg was carried away by a
shell, when his only request was that he might be carried to the rear,
in order that his men might not hear him groaning. All the gun team
horses were found shot and lying in their teams.*

The next day, Wednesday 2 September at 4.30 am, the Regiment
departed Néry and continued the retreat south, presumably leaving
behind Brocas in the hospital along with the other wounded. When
the Germans moved into the village they were taken prisoner and
Brocas's three and a half years internment began. On 3 September he
wrote a post card home to let his family know he was alive and well.
The celebrated post card, in German, was the first news the family
received either from or about Brocas. News from the War Office had
been sketchy and vague as the family tried desperately to find out what
had become of him. Unfortunately, the post card was not received
until 7 October 1914, by which time he had been a prisoner for nearly
five weeks. In his letter of 17 February 1918, *Letter 176*, from Holland
following his exchange, his father explained how Brocas managed to
send it:

*…The celebrated postcard in German was, as Byrne decided, written
entirely by him. On the way to Germany he temporarily fell into the*

hands of some decent officers, one of whom, a Dutchman, asked what he could do for him. Brocas had that old postcard in his pocket, scribbled it off & asked the Dutchman to post it which he evidently did...

```
Ich bin sauf und wohl aber prisonier und

beim Pferde verwundert.    Ich bin mit zwei

anderen officieren Englisch und nach Deutschland

gehe.    Mann tut uns gutes.

                    Brocas.
```

First post card home 3 September 1914 Source: Burrows family archive

At the joy of receiving the good news, to celebrate the event his father bought his mother a 'gold cross' which became a treasured possession of the family and continues to be passed down the family for safe keeping to this day. The above is a transcript of that message in the celebrated post card dated 3 September 1914.

After his hurried departure to France his parents and sister wrote to him every day for a month uncertain of whether or not he received them, and some he probably never did. Once news came through via his first card, they at least knew that he was alive and well, but they only learned of his whereabouts some days later. In response to this note his father wrote the following card on 16 October 1914, (*Letter 4*) which Brocas kept throughout his confinement together with one post marked 8 Nov (*Letter 5*) written several weeks later:

Letter 4

Oxford, 16 October 1914

Family in very good health in Oxford. Delighted to get your card and to hear you are so well. We got your card dated Sept 3 on Oct 7, but no other letters or cards. Since Oct 7 we have written to you twice a week and sent you two parcels of clothing. Let us know if they arrive, and what other clothing you want. Saw Agnes yesterday, she is very well and busy. George comes today. Alex is at Streatley. Sergt. Gough came and told us about you up to Sept 1. Can we send you money?

S. M. Burrows

Letter 5

9 Norham Gardens, Oxford, [no date part postmark Nov 8]

Dearest boy,
Your postcard reached us on Oct 6, and took five weeks to come. It was perfectly delightful to see your handwriting again and to know you were safe and well. I am very much afraid you have never got any of our letters, though we wrote to you every day from Aug 14 for a month, and then three times a week and sent you many parcels and papers. Sergt Gough spent some hours with us on Oct 3. And gave us full news of you up to Sept 1. I have also had nice letters from Martin and Nettlefold. We are all exceedingly well; Agnes is back at school, and in a position of great dignity and importance; she is second prefect and takes roll-call. She will be writing to you herself. We only heard yesterday that it was possible to write to you, and how we ought to address you. I am asking Cox & co. to send you money, and we hope to send you parcels of warm clothes, for you will have it very cold in the winter. Benning leaves England today and is very happy. We have in consequence laid up the car. George is at Crowborough, very happy and fit; Alex in London. Term began here today, and there are quite a lot of men up. We had a delightful fortnight at Folkestone, in the familiar lodgings of Mr Perkins. A dear letter from nurse rejoicing in the news of you. All friends have been so kind and sympathetic. Neither Dick nor George Rawstorne are up. Helen is at the Soulaly's? with Agnes and getting on so well. We met Mr Sendy? today full of enquiring for you. Mr Wickham-Legge? called to enquire and Lucy Butcher. There is never a minute in which we do not think of you and I love to think that the same moon and stars that we gaze on are also looking down on you,
Ever darling loving
Mother.

2

Zossen and Torgau (Fort Brückenkopf) POW Camps

14 September 1914 – 28 September 1914 Zossen
28 September 1914 – 26 November 1914 Torgau

Zossen Camp, described previously by Brocas in his account written at Burg on 24 January 1915, was a temporary camp about 20 miles south of Berlin and about 50 miles northwest of Torgau and where Brocas was to spend his first two weeks as a POW. Fort Brückenkopf, Torgau was one of two formidable Prussian fortresses built to defend the town in the Napoleonic era. It was situated on the outskirts of the town on the east bank of the River Elbe to guard the gateway and river crossing against attack from the east.

Fort Brückenkopf, Torgau c 1914. Source: http://unjouruneguerre.canalblog.com/
archives/2015/01/02/31008328

This was an officers' camp and many of the officers of allied forces captured at Mons and during the retreat were first sent to Torgau. Their number consisted of mainly British, French, Belgians and Russians. Most of them arrived tired and exhausted having endured a thoroughly miserable three-day rail journey of about 500 miles in appalling conditions. The grim exterior of the fortress was indeed one of the worst of its features. The formidable forbidding aspect laid emphasis on the "abandonment of hope" for any new weary, battle-stained, travel-worn new arrival. For most officers the experience of being made prisoner was almost the worst of any fate. Being removed from the conflict, and being at the mercy of their enemies for an indefinite period was a thoroughly demoralising state about which none had thought and few anticipated. The arrival in Torgau was made worse as they were marched through the town from the railway station, and were subjected to the abuse of the local population.

It was to here that Brocas was moved on 26 September 1914 with Lieutenant Peskett, Captain Bell, and Lieutenant Humphreys. Peskett in his statement (National Archives ref wo/161/96/93) wrote:

> *On arriving at the camp, Lieutenant Burrows and myself were each given a pallaise and two sheets and two blankets and had to sleep in one of the store sheds on the floor. We remained in the shed for about a fortnight, when we were transferred to a wooden shed (single ½ inch boarding) where we were given bedsteads.*

When Captain Knight-Bruce arrived on 11 October at 2 am, little had improved, as his statement (National Archives ref wo/161/95/42) testifies:

> *We were herded into a shed…it was too cold to undress or sleep so we sat huddled up on the straw until daylight. The shed was newly built and the snow drifted in through the cracks in the walls…It was so cold we had to sit in a circle round the stove all day.*

Sanitary arrangements were appalling. The latrine consisted of a plank with holes in it over a trough which was emptied from time to time. To use it at any time involved a long walk through the snow. It was made worse by the French and Russian habit of defecating on the seats.

Here in Torgau the routine and rigors of POW life were forged but it was also where Brocas began to develop new and lasting friendships and formulate strategies for rising above the adversity of their shared predicament. Slowly all the POWs were able to re-establish contact with families back home and gain the support essential to their physical and mental survival over the coming years. Initially, no contact with home was permitted but on 6 October 1914 all the POWs were allowed to write their first cards home (*Letter 7*) and before long a trickle of censored letters began to arrive. It was 22 October before Brocas received his first post card from his parents, and not until 4 November that he acknowledged receipt of his first parcel which had

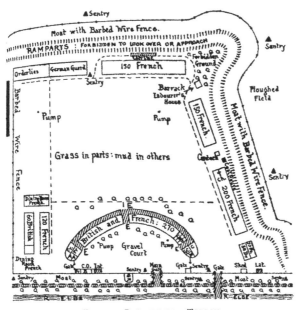

PLAN OF BRÜCKENKOPF, TORGAU

After a sketch by Lieut. J. E. T. Younger, R.F.A.

This plan is roughly to scale.
The black line on left edge of plan is the German shell store.
Dotted lines – – – – are paths.
In crescent-shaped building and sheds the letters are:

F—Quarters of French Generals.	Ch—St. Luke's Chapel.
Fr—Quarters allocated to French.	K—Kitchen.
B—Quarters allocated to British.	GC—German Commandant's Office.
C—Canteen.	E—Archway entrances.

On the line by Main Gate:

CO—British Senior Officers' Qrs.	GR—German Guard Room.
	QQ—Trees.

The fort is approached by a bridge over the Elbe, thus

c

Sketch Plan of Fort Brückenkopf Torgau POW Camp 1914 after sketch by Lt J. E. T. Younger. Source: In the Hands of the Enemy *by B G O'Rorke*

been posted on 10 October. During the two months he was in Torgau, Brocas wrote only seven letters home, and being cards they were short and concise as he acknowledged those he received and sought to reassure his parents as to his well-being.

Letters home rarely if ever contained complaint or damning criticism of the conditions or the prison authorities. To do so guaranteed the letter would be heavily censored, delayed or simply not sent. Brocas was probably typical of a young junior British officer but his letters clearly demonstrate he was an extraordinarily mature and talented individual, adept at coping positively with the mental aspects of deprivation and confinement. Traits that would stand him in good stead for the rest of life and see him rise rapidly up the ranks once the war was over.

Parcels from home

Throughout his captivity family and friends in England furnished Brocas with food and other necessities sent out in parcels. His mother kept a meticulous record of those sent by the family. The majority were numbered, the sent date recorded, the contents itemised, and she later recorded whether or not Brocas acknowledged receipt in his letters home. Quite often the contents were in response to his specific request. At other times they were simply items that the family thought he would need. As time went on the contents became more varied than basic necessities for survival such as food and warm clothing, and included items such as books, sports equipment etc. aimed more at helping with his physical and mental well-being. One of his most outrageous requests was for cricket matting and practice nets, although he cancelled this, probably on the grounds it was a step too far.

For officers such as Brocas, coming from a family of higher social status, the fare he received was varied, nutritious, and more than supplemented the meagre offerings provide by his captors. At one point he even declared that he was getting overweight. As the lists demonstrate most parcels reached their intended destination, albeit with the quality of the perishable contents sometimes compromised by the time they took to arrive. There were also rigorous checks for illicit items before the parcels were released to the prisoners, all of which took time. As time went on items such as maps, compasses and other essential escapers kit, were smuggled into the camps in hidden compartments, false bottoms, in cakes, jars of jam and the like. Often, they were requested by prisoners using simple code, and likewise advised and verified by the sender. There is considerable evidence from his letters that Brocas used code, and pencil notes on some of his letters indicate that the family understood the use of words or phrases to mean something else. For instance, 'Ellie,' referred to 'Russians,' and 'Govare,' to 'French.' These coded references are shown in **bold** text in the body of the letters.

The following is the full list of the twelve first parcels sent to Brocas during his stay at Torgau in October and November 1914. All were systematically recorded by his mother in a school exercise book. The items read like a social history of the time for the officer class and their families. Not all officers were as fortunate, and it is difficult to say how typical was the support Brocas received, especially with regard to food items, of which there were none during the first two months at Torgau. The items were exclusively clothing because the family in England, like so many, were coming to grips with what it was possible to send to their loved ones. As time went on the list contained a great variety of food stuffs, as well as other necessities, books and other items to help with mental and physical well-being. The food items listed as sent to later camps might easily convey a false impression of comfortable living. They mask the reality of the miserable caged existence of the prisoners, whereby the food they received in parcels was, in reality, essential to their very survival.

In the sections that follow, apart from at Burg, only 'sample' lists are included for each camp. They indicate the typical content and frequency of individual parcels. A full breakdown of all 2802 items sent in 629 parcels is included in Appendix I. It is worth noting that during the period of 1481 days when they were being sent, they averaged one parcel every 2.4 days, having reached a peak of one every 1.5 days while Brocas was at Friedberg. Some were sent direct from companies such as Twining, Tiptree and Harrods. However, the majority were from the family, whether from home or wherever they were staying on holiday or visiting.

List of Parcels sent to Lieutenant M Brocas Burrows at Torgau
10 October 1914 – 7 December 1914

OCTOBER

10th   *1 khaki shirt, 1 long drawers, 1 vest and Hdkfs*
        Acknowledged
14th   *1 Jaeger long sleeved vest, 1 belt, 1 ord. vest. 1 Woolly waistcoat, 1*
        Pair socks
        Acknowledged
20th   *1 khaki shirt, 3 Hdkfs, 1 Pr socks*
        Acknowledged
26th   *1 uniform breeches, 1 pr boots, 6 Hdkfs, 1 pr gaiters, 1 jkt, 1 pr*
        socks 1 pr boots
        Acknowledged

NOVEMBER

3rd   *1 Military overcoat, 3 Hdkfs, 1 pr Canadian gloves*
        Acknowledged
4th   *1 scarf (A's) 3 Hdkfs*
        Acknowledged
11th   *1 Pyjamas, 3 Hdkfs, 1 mittens, 1 white woollen gloves, 1 pr socks, 1*
        soft black & white under-woolly
        Acknowledged
16th   *3 Hdkfs, 1 warm vest, 1 warm drawer pants, 1 gloves, 1 pr braces*
        Acknowledged
22nd   *1 Khakis shirt & collar, 1 necktie, boot laces Hdkfs*
        Acknowledged

DECEMBER

2nd   *1 pr Socks, boot laces, Pyjamas, Hdkfs*
        Acknowledged
5th   *1 jaeger Blanket*
        Acknowledged
7th   *1 Plum pudding and other groceries F & Mason*
        Through Pape Gaston
        Acknowledged

3

Zossen and Torgau (Fort Brückenkopf) POW Camps

14 September 1914 – 25 September 1914 Zossen
26 September 1914 – 26 November 1914 Torgau

The Letters

Brocas wrote his first proper letter home on 18 September 1914 (*Letter 6*) from Zossen POW camp which he arrived at on 12 September 1914. Probably by smuggling out the letter via a French POW, he managed to send news home. There was no address but clearly, he was at Zossen.

Letter 6

[Zossen], *18th September*

My dearest Mother,
As to whether this will reach you I don't know but I hope it will, as I am afraid you must be rather anxious to know where I am.

Well I am a prisoner and through no fault of my own. I was hurt a little in a skirmish we had quite near Compiègne and sent to hospital where I was left and captured by the Germans next day. I write this from a prisoner's camp and am awaiting arrangements for my probable removal to a fortress. I will try to write to you again from there. It is very dreadful to have to keep still and wait when everybody else is up and doing, but, thank God, I am so far well and strong and am quite recovered. I am here with three other officers and we pass the time as best we can.
I do hope you are all well and that this war will soon be over and we shall all meet again in dear old England.

My best love to you, Mother dear and to Father and the Duchess.

Ever your loving son,
Brocas

On 26 September he was moved to Fort Brückenkopf, Torgau but it was not until 6 October 1914 that any of the POWs in Torgau were allowed to send post cards home; however, some men were already receiving letters. They had managed to get word out using a ruse whereby they wrote their address on the back of cheques making a small donation to the German Red Cross. Something they were loath to do because of the treatment they had received at the hands of the Red Cross ladies on the journey across Germany. Captain Dugmore, Commanding Officer 'C' Company Cheshire Regiment, also in Torgau, wrote in his diary on 2 October 1914:

> *First letters arrived from England today, and what excitement there was! Alas, none for me! Rumour that we will be allowed to write home soon.*

Brocas, like all the other officers, was in a rush to write his first letter or more correctly, a 'card', home on 6 October 1914 (*Letter 7*). The cards were censored both by a senior British officer and by the prison authorities.

Letter 7

Torgau (Brückenkopf), 6th October 1914

I am in very good health, prisoner of war. Taken September 2 in hospital. Reached Zossen September 12 and came here Sept 26. Write as soon as possible to tell me how you all are. Have you got any previous letters? Good bye.

Brocas

Censored B. L. Stapylton, Major, 6. X. XIV

Writing on 17 October 1914 (*Letter 8*) he had still not received any letter from home.

Letter 8

Torgau (Brückenkopf), 17th October 1914

Have not heard from you yet. Please send me out military overcoat, mine is in valise, which may be at Regimental base. My suitcase is in Havre (Hotel Moderne). If possible to get it please send me my jacket, breeches and also boots. Hope you are all well. All well here.

Brocas

Censored by N. W. Barlow, Major

In the very early days of internment, in an effort to get news home regarding the fact they were simply alive, or their condition, location, and predicament, the English initially had to adopt whatever subversive means available. Because other nationalities such as the French and Irish were treated more leniently, and had greater freedoms and privileges in the camps the British used friendships with these to send news. Brocas used a French soldier for this purpose but it wasn't until he had been at Torgau for nearly five weeks that the following telegraphic message was written and sent to his mother by the Uncle of a French POW from his office in Geneva (*Letter 9*). The prisoners and families back home also created a network, whereby one family would pass on news to another. In this case the Burrows family already knew that Brocas was safe and well in Torgau and he had received his first post card on 22 October 1914 but their first letter written 12 September 1914 did not arrive until 14 November 1914, a fact he refers to on 17 November 1914 (*Letter 13*).

Letter 9

J. Neyrac & Vars, Maritime Messaging Company, Travel Agents,
Genève 10 Grand Quai, 23rd October 1914

Madam Burrows, Norham House, At Oxford

It is with great pleasure, Madam, that I am able with these few lines, to give you news of your son, and, take from you the anxiety that you must be feeling about his fate.

Mr The Lieutenant Burrows is interned at Zossen near Berlin, a prisoner. It is my nephew, Paul Neyrac of St. Germaine en Laye (Seine et Oise) wounded and also taken prisoner by the Germans, who writes to us, who has begged me in the name of Mr your son to write you a few words to reassure you.

It would be very kind of you if, in return, you could tell the families of two other English officers who are at Zossen under the same conditions.

Here is their address:
1. *Captain J.A.D. Bell*
    14 Hardy Road
    Blackheath
    London S.E.

2. *Lieutenant L.G. Humphrey Esq.*
    Shournagh Lodge
    St Anne's Hill
    Co. Cork
    Ireland/England

As you cannot communicate directly with your son, I am at your entire disposition to send on your letter and those of the other two families.

Very sincerely,
Jean Vars

Marin Vars
Maison J Neyrac & Vars
10 Grand Quai
Geneva

Letter 10

Torgau, 1st November 1914
To: parents

So glad to hear that you are all well. I got your first P.C. October 22 and the 20 marks on October 24. Many thanks for them and also for your other P.C. which arrived 2 days ago and one parcel of clothing. I have not got any of your letters yet but hope to soon. For the present I have enough money to carry on with and will write if I want more. My letters will be short and one a week as we are not allowed to write more. Will you also please write short letters as the censorship is slow and the longer the letters the longer they take to get through. Have you any news of Jack or Mon and what is George doing now? Did you ever get the kit I sent off from Aldershot about August 18? If not, it is still there in our barracks. All are well here and the weather at present is grand. Our daily routine is, breakfast 7.45, parade 10.30, lunch 12.30 and dinner 8.30. Bed at 9. Has the Duchess gone back to school? Ask her to drop me a line. I suppose you are very busy doing Red Cross work etc. Please send me some cigarettes. We play rounders here and football at times!! Many thanks for birthday wishes.

Best love to all,

Brocas.

Letter 11

4th November 1914, Torgau (Brückenkopf)
To: parents

I am in very good health prisoner of war. Have received two parcels of clothing and also one package containing a pair of French drawers!! <u>Many thanks</u> for them. No letters arrived yet. Please send me a few magazines if possible as literature is scarce. Goodbye.
Best love,

Brocas

Letter 12

10th November 1914, Torgau (Brückenkopf)
To: parents

I hope this will be in time to wish you many happy returns of your birthday I got your letter of October 24 a few days ago, many thanks for it. So glad you are well. I hope to write to Duchess tomorrow. The clothes you sent are excellent. Please give all accounts, lists etc. for me on return. Both the officers as you mentioned in your letter are here. Goodbye.
Best love and wishes for birthday,

Brocas

Letter 13

17th November 1914, Torgau (Brückenkopf)
To: parents

All well, very cold here. Got your first letter undated but of about October 12 on November 14th, also one from Duchess. I got one lot of letters from you in the field but no others. How awful my letter not arriving till October 7. I wrote others on September 4 and three from Zossen and tried to send you news by means of a Frenchman who was writing to Switzerland.
Best love,

Brocas

Letter 14

24th November 1914, Torgau (Brückenkopf)
To: parents

Have enquired about Pte. Windram. He is probably at Sennelager, was shot through the hand and had to have it amputated. Please send me pyjamas. Am quite well. Very cold here, a little snow. Have received several letters from you and the £5 has arrived. All were most welcome.
Best love,

Brocas

4

Burg POW Camp

26 November 1914 – 19 May 1915

The officers camp was within the grounds of the artillery depot near the Niegripper Chaussee. It was a grim place especially in winter as shown in the picture below. All the English officers at Torgau were moved directly here on 26 November 1914 when it was at the time deemed a more suitable place for officers. The camp had been hastily formed by throwing a fence around a group of gun sheds and mobilisation store-rooms. It was about six hundred kilometres from the Swiss frontier and four hundred from Holland.

Burg POW Camp in January 1917 Source: Hunter-Blair family archive

The plan of the Camp at Burg in 1915 is taken from a diagram in the book *Within Four Walls* by Major M.C.C. Harrison and Captain H.A. Cartwright who escaped from here dressed as German officers in November 1915 having begun planning in early that year. They were recaptured at Rostock nine days later. They described the camp as follows:

The camp was bounded all round by a fence of solid boarding about eight feet high with six strands of overhung barbed wire on the top. Outside this was a twenty-strand barbed wire fence about 10 feet high – in all about thirty-one miles of wire were used for a perimeter of six hundred yards. There was one sentry – or more – at every angle outside, and sentries inside at every point where buildings stood close to the board fence. There were big arc lights dotted about all over the inside and small electric lamps at about twenty-yard intervals along the board fence.

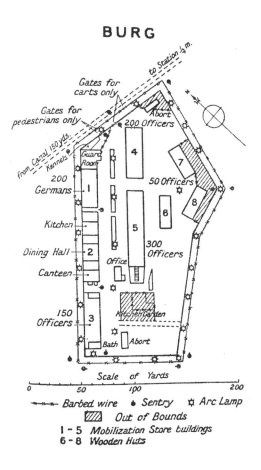

Burg POW camp 1915 Source: Within Four Walls *by M.C.C. Harrison and H.A. Cartwright*

Captain Dugmore, Cheshire Regiment, in his diary entry for 24 to 26 November 1914 also describes the preparations for the move from Torgau and the move itself of which Brocas would have been a part.

24th November. Ground thickly covered with snow. Told to be prepared to leave Torgau at short notice. Feeling very depressed, as I doubt if we will go to a better camp, and how I shall miss our nice little chapel, and also my French friends. Heard Shore had got the Legion of Honour.

25th November. Snowing most of the day. Packed up all my belongings in readiness to move. We were to move in two parties. I was in the second lot. The first lot about 130, all English left at 12.30pm. Never will I forget the strange sight of the departure of the party. British officers of all ranks; most of them dressed in extraordinary clothes, varying from khaki to corduroy trousers, linen socks, German infantry boots, and all sorts of head-dress. No transport was provided every officer having to carry his own belongings. They had parcels of all sizes tied in front and behind them and also carried them in their hands. They were kept waiting about an hour before they moved off, during which time they got thoroughly chilled and wet, and a large German escort on each side of them, who continually shouted at the wretched prisoners. I did not look forward to next day when my turn would come! I thought if only the move were to England!! Everybody very depressed.

26th November. The morning of our departure has come. Luckily it is fine. I spent the morning, making up my belongings into parcels which I could attach easily to myself; in cleaning out our room which we were ordered to leave in a clean and tidy condition; in saying goodbye to my numerous French friends; and I took a final farewell of our dear little chapel. We paraded at 12 noon, and were kept waiting an hour before we moved off. The Germans who have charge of prisoner arrangements seemed to have no idea of organisation, and their efforts in counting us are most painful. The escort takes its place on each side of us, we pick up our parcels and once again we are out on the public highway. The streets are crowded and its behaviour is just as it was on the last occasion, but we are used to this now. As we pass over the bridge we take a last look at our late prison and wonder if our new one will be better or worse? In any case we imagined it is the last we shall see of Torgau, and it is a landmark in our long and dreary captivity. Our escort is not of such fine material as the last one and their clothing and equipment is in a bad state. We imagine this is a sign of Germany being hard up for war material! On arriving at the

*station, we were halted outside, and remained there about an hour, the
crowd behaving in their usual brutal manner. At last we entrain; we
are put in third class carriages, about 5 officers in a compartment, and
2 sentries in each. The sentries would not allow us to have a window
open, and we had to keep the blinds down, so that we could not see the
country. We each carried some food, so were able to keep from feeling
hungry. We arrived at "Burg" at about 9pm. It was bitterly cold. I
shall never forget the march from the station to our new prison. It was
very cold and the roads were so slippery it was very hard to walk,
especially when carrying so many and such heavy packages. There
was a huge crowd, who were as insulting as ever towards us. If one
of us stopped for a second to change the position of the things we were
carrying, he was given a blow and sent flying. I saw Colonel Gordon
V.C. who was near me thrown from one side of the section of fours, to
the other, because he stopped to change a parcel from one hand to the
other. After we had gone a little way, some of us could not stick our
burdens any longer, and thus many parcels were dropped, to be picked
up eagerly by the crowd. It was about 10pm when we got inside the new
prison. As it was dark we could not see what things were like, but the
area seemed to be very small. When we were formed up, the German
commander, called out "All Irish and Catholics to the front." Many
carried out this order but I did not, which was unfortunate, as the
Irish were put in much the best room, and were treated better than the
rest of us. This was the beginning of the German campaign to get the
Irish to go over to them. Needless to state they did not succeed as far
as the Officers were concerned, though they did get a certain number
of N.C.O.'s and men to become traitors, as we heard afterwards. The
Germans imagined that the Irish would never fight alongside of the
English, and great was the Commandant's surprise when he heard
that Major Haig of the K.O.S.B's who was in command when that
small rising took place in Dublin shortly before the war, was one of our
present number, and was on good terms with the Irish Officers! We were
now told off to our rooms. My room was a big shed which had been
used for housing vehicles. There were very small windows, and the huge
room was warmed by only one stove. On our side of the room about
16 beds, in each of which was a Russian. On the other side and in the
middle of the room were some empty beds for about the same number of
English. The room smelled horribly and all windows were hermetically
sealed. At first the Russians did not take any notice of us. After a bit I
found one who spoke a little French. He told us that the Germans had
warned them that the English were coming, and that when they had
come their lives would be unendurable, owing to the brutal, savage,*

and immoral practices to which we were given!! However, we soon dispelled the poor Russians' fears and made friends at once. We were served with a sausage, bread and coffee, and then made for our beds. None of us thought we could get through the night in such a putrid atmosphere, so as my bed was next to the wall and window, I started to open the window just a tiny bit. Instantly one of the Russians jumped out of bed, and said I must shut it, or else we would all die. He said they never opened a window in a house in Russia during the whole winter. I replied that all the English would die equally, if the windows were kept shut. At last I shook him by the hand, and told him he had a window on his side of the room which he could keep shut, but the window on the English side, must be kept open. Thus, we were able to get through the night without dying of suffocation.

Captain Dugmore continued to described the Burg camp in his diary entry of 27 November 1914.

I remember that we all wished we were back at Torgau. The place consisted of an oblong bit of ground, which had once been a rubbish dumping ground, and so was not very sanitary. On each side of the oblong was several large sheds, which before the war were used for housing wagons and carts etc. Wooden partitions were put up, dividing each shed into several compartments, each of which accommodated about 30 prisoners, half English and half Russian, with very few French. Altogether we numbered about 700 as far as I can remember. We only had a small pathway about 100 yards long and 5 or 6 broad on which to take exercise, so we felt fearfully cramped. The feeding was worse than at Torgau, our food consisting chiefly of a horrible sausage and absolutely raw salt fish, which none of the English could eat though the Russians seemed to like them alright. We fed in our rooms. The canteen was quite good, and one could buy all sorts of things from travelling trunks to eatables and clothes, but the prices were rather high, so all I could afford was afternoon tea, which I thoroughly enjoyed. Many officers used to have their supper in the canteen and at first were able to have steaks and chops. Naturally these did not complain so much of the place as those who possessed less of the world's goods! The sanitary arrangements were simply terrible and the smell of the latrines enough to knock you down; there was only seating accommodation for about 8 or 10 so with so many hundreds of us, attending to nature's calls was a daily incident everyone dreaded! There were about 3 baths between us all, which were opened twice a week but you had to take your place in a long queue before you could get one.

Burg POW Camp probably newly built before it was occupied by POWs in 1914. Source: Hunter-Blair archive

In these relatively early days of their internment escaping was not high on the agenda as they clung on to the prospect of early exchange (*Letter 40*) or the less likely prospect that the war would soon end. Only one officer, Major Charles Yate, had attempted to escape from Torgau in September 1914, but was recaptured and died under dubious circumstances a few days later. Although Harrison and Cartwright were planning to escape from Burg [*Within Four Walls* by Major M.C.C. Harrison and Captain H.A. Cartwright] early 1915 there is no evidence that Brocas was part of this cohort before he was moved on in May. Indeed, he was probably far from well enough to participate. His father, writing from Holland on 26 February 1918 to his wife, said '*during half his time at Burg he was seldom free from headaches and neuralgia, and was much in bed.*'

Brocas, like most of the POWs, counted the days in captivity and noted 16 May 1915 (*Letter 44*) his '*175 days in the same yard*' at Burg. During this time, he wrote weekly letters to his parents and sister, and also one to his cousin Bene Cartwright and another to the Norwegian attaché who was attempting to find out more of his, Brocas's circumstances, on behalf of his parents. He also wrote to Liège, as he says, on the off chance of getting news of Gareth [Hamilton-Fletcher]. To keep track of the letters that he sent to, and received from, his parents they began numbering each letter. Writing on 18 April 1915 (*Letter 37*) he states the last letter he received was number 122 in captivity which was 228 days by that date. A remarkable number considering for about 21 days, at the start of his internment, no one knew where to write.

When they left Torgau for Burg in November 1914 their possessions were all they could physically carry. By the time it came to move to Mainz he acknowledged in his final letter from Burg 16 May 1915 (*Letter 44*) that, '*with all the accumulated baggage it will be "some" move.*' However, a more civilised process had been established and they were able to parcel or pack up larger bulky items, which they had purchased from the camp authorities or each other, and have them sent on by train. Even this process undoubtedly had its limits.

Parcels from home

While at Burg the food parcels, whether sent by his parents, friends or other relations, began to be numbered, and his mother made a note in her exercise book acknowledging that they had been received. By this means they were able to keep track of those that went missing, which in Brocas's case were relatively few. Due to delays with the mail it was not until 7 January 1915 that the first parcel was sent direct to Burg, although those sent throughout December had caught up with him and were acknowledged. The family were extremely generous in supporting other less fortunate internees known to Brocas. These included Private MacGregor his orderly, and Quarter-master Sergeant Wheeler and W. Bailey. When requested by Brocas, they also sent out items required by other officers and his Russian friends, with assurances that they would be refunded later or the cost was to be deducted from Brocas's account at home which he had authorised his father to administer on his behalf. Parcels were sent from Truro, Kinnersley, or whereever they were in England, and were quite often supplemented by a hamper or other goods or necessities from Harrods, Fortnum and Masons, or simply a box of jams from Tiptree.

Brocas was sent 68 parcels, plus three to other POWs, during the period of 139 days that the family knew he was at Burg. These included 200 food items as well as 102 clothing items, 42 necessities such as soap, tooth brushes etc., 11 social items such as tobacco, chess and domino sets, and eight books. At Burg there was no indication that Brocas was receiving items as a precursor to escape. The following list clearly demonstrates just how much the family had stepped up their effort to ensure that he not only survived captivity, but was as comfortable as possible. They were able to explore the limits of what it was possible to send, and as the following list demonstrates, establish a process by which they were acknowledged as successfully received.

List of Parcels sent to Lieutenant M Brocas Burrows at Burg
7 January 1915 – 25 May 1915

JANUARY

7th	*1 pr Trousers, 1 pr Socks, 1 toothbrush*
	Acknowledged
10th	*1 grey flannel belt, Hdkfs*
	Acknowledged
16th	*1 overcoat*
	Acknowledged
18th	*1 felt boot-slippers, 1 Puttees, Boot laces, 1 nail brush, 3 books*
	Acknowledged
27th No I	*1 pkt Bourneville chocolate, 3 tins tobacco, 1 pr socks*
	No 1 Acknowledged
30th No II	*Two books E.R.*

FEBRUARY

5th No III	*1 Khaki shirt, 1 socks, bootlaces, 3 Hdkfs*
	Acknowledged
8th No IV	*1 Tongue, Potted meat, shortbread, 12 pkts Bivonae Cocoa*
	Acknowledged
10th No V	*1 Book (Wisden's Almanack)*
15th No VI	*1 pkt Bournville nut chocolate alone*
15th No VII	*2 Tins Tobacco, 1 potted meat*
	Acknowledged
15th No VIII	*2 tins sardines, 1 potted meat*
16th No IX	*1 pr socks, 1 pr laces, 2 Hdkfs, 1 pants, 1 vest, 1 long sleeved vest*
	Acknowledged
23rd No X	*12 pkts Bivouac Cocoa*
	Acknowledged
23rd No XI	*1 Tongue*
	Acknowledged

23rd No XII	1 Tie, 1 Jaeger long sleeved vest, 1 pr socks, 2 French books
	Acknowledged
24th No XIII	1 box cigarettes
	Acknowledged
26th No XIV	2 tins Lob., 1 Jaffelas shirt. 1 collar, 2 pr boot laces
	Acknowledged
27th No XV	1 Tongue, 1 small tin Oxo
	Acknowledged
27th No XVI	1 box Raisons, 1 lb Almonds
	Acknowledged
27th No XVII	1 book
	Acknowledged

MARCH

3rd No XVIII	1 pr socks 3 pkts Peters Chocolate
	Acknowledged
3rd No XIX	1 Dundee cake, Bougard
	Acknowledged
8th No XX	2 pkts Turtle soup, 1 Bourneville Chocolate, 1 Tin Russian Toffee, 1 Prayer book, 1 Bible, 1 French book, <u>1 History of 5th D.G.s</u> 1 Tin chocolate
	Acknowledged
8th No XXI	2 large tins Sardines, 1 P & N Tongue, 1 Tin shortbread, 1 box Chivers soups (Cooper)
	(The above parcel was divided into two)
	Acknowledged
10th No XXII	1 cake Homemade, 1 Jerebone soap
	Acknowledged
13th No XXIII	2 lbs Potted meat <u>Pheasant</u>, 2 lbs Wheatmeal biscuits
	Acknowledged
	Parcel sent to W Bailey, Zerbst, Anhalt? Germany
	March 13th 1915 Socks, Scarf, soup, cocoa, tobacco
14th No XXIV	6 Hdkfs, 1 pr sock, 1pr laces, 1 packet chocolate
	Acknowledged
16th No XXV	2 tins marmalade, 1 tongue, 6 pkts Chivers soup
	Acknowledged
16th No XXVI	2 potted meat, 2 lbs Reford sausages, 2 large tins sardines, 2 lbs strawberry jam
	Acknowledged
19th No XXVII	2 tins biscuits, 5 pkts Bivouac cocoa
20th No XXVIII	1 half ham, 1 tin golden syrup
	Acknowledged
22nd No 29	1 cake, 6 lbs Tipperary biscuits, 1 cake soap in a Burrows tin
	Acknowledged

24th No 30	*1 pr socks, 6 Hdkfs, 1 pr boot laces, 1 pencil, 1 tin wheatmeal biscuits, 1 pkt Bromo*
	Acknowledged
25th No 31	*2 tins sardines, P & N tongue, 3 tins potted meat, 1 lb marmalade, 1 j. jam*
	Acknowledged
26th No 32	*2 tins tobacco, 4 books (Anna Karenine 2 vol), Russia History, Fletcher History, salt, pepper, sugar, lozenges, broth pies, pencil*
	Acknowledged
29th No 33	*1 Homemade cake*
	Acknowledged
30th	*Soup tablets, biscuits, sugar, hair oil, chocolate, Easter fish egg*
	Acknowledged
30th	*Tiptree has sent 6 lbs jam*
	Acknowledged
	Lady Sutherland parcel groceries and clothing – Ione sent a parcel
	Acknowledged
31st	*Kalie sent herrings & tomatoes*
	Acknowledged

APRIL

6th No 34	*6 Hdkfs, 1 tin macaroons, 1 pkt chocolate, 1 pencil, 1 bot laxeara tabloids, 1 nail cleaner*
7th No 35	*1 paté of chicken P & N, 1 tongue, 2 lbs Reford sausages, 2 tins sardines, 1 lb Cairns marmalade*
8th No 36	*2 pkts Harrods almonds and raisons, 1 pkt nut chocolate*
14th	<u>*Truro*</u> *– pepper, salt, sugar, mustard*
	Acknowledged
22nd	*1 tin dessert biscuits, 1 tongue, 1 cake soap, 1 tin lamb's tongue, 6 Hdkfs, 1 cake chocolate*
	Acknowledged
24th	*2 tins fruit salad, 1 pr laces (boots), 1 pencil, 1 tin digestive biscuits, 1 paint box*
25th	*2 tins bread, 1 tin (5lbs) cheese and assorted biscuits*
	Acknowledged
26th	*1 P & N tongue, 1 cake, 1 lb walnuts, 2 tins herrings, 1 keating, 1 Bivouac cocoa, 1 slab chocolate*
	Acknowledged
27th	*1 pr shoes Brogue, 1 pr laces, 1 pr stockings*
	Acknowledged
27th	*Two Russian books, 1 pr socks, boot laces*
29th	*1 tin rusks & 1 tin cheese assorted*
	Acknowledged

30th	*1 box dominoes, 1 box chess, 1 shoe laces*
	1 cake (Lizzies)

MAY

1st	2 tins bread
	Acknowledged
4th	*4 Taffelas shirts, 4 collars, 2 neckties, 1 pr socks, 6 cardboard*
	plates, 1 bone fork, 3 bone spoons
4th	*2 ½ lb potted pheasants, pepper and salt*
5th	*1 tin fruit, 1 shortbread, 1 chocolate, 6 pkts lazenbys soup*
	Acknowledged
5th	*2 tins bread*
	Acknowledged
8th	*1 tin dinner assorted biscuits, 2 tins sardines, 1 shortbread, 1*
	pkt chocolate, 6 bone spoons, 1 pr shoe laces, 1 pencil, 1 cap
	(Forage) 1 sun curtain for it
	Acknowledged
9th	*1 tin asparagus, 2 Dutch cheeses, 1 tin honey, 1 tongue*
	(Coopers)
	Acknowledged
10th	*2 loaves bread (brown & white) pepper & salt*
	Acknowledged
11th	*One (Lizzie) cake, 1 tongue (E Rawnsley), 3 plates*
	Acknowledged
11th	*To Quarter-master Sergeant Wheeler, 4 Dutch cheeses, 1 tin*
	sardines, 1 sausages, 1 milk biscuits
10th	*1 cigarettes, for orderlies, salmon, chocolate from Kinnersley*
	Acknowledged
13th	*1 box butter puffs, 1 sardines, 1 keating, 3 Hdkf, 1 socks, 3 old*
	thin vests, 2 prs old thin pants, 2 French books
	Acknowledged
14th	*2 loaves bread*
	Acknowledged
19th	*Almonds & raisins, laces, sardines, cake (Lizzie), stockings*
	Acknowledged
20th	*2 aertex pants, 2 aertex vests, 3 khaki silk hdkfs, 1 necktie, 1*
	sardines, 1 rusks, 2 paper plates, 1 pencil
	Acknowledged
20th	*Coopers 4 tins p. meat, 2 café au lait, 3 Bivounae cocoa, 1*
	tin herrings, 1 jam, 1 cream toast, 1 brawn
22nd	*1 Ticka kodak & films, 1 lb almonds & raisins, 2 hdkfs*
	Verboten
25th	*1 tin of bread (A & N stores), 2 tins sardines, 1 pkt*
	chocolate, 5 bone spoons, 1 hdkf, 1 necktie

5

Burg POW Camp

26 November 1914 – 19 May 1915

The Letters

Letter 15

My dearest father,
We were moved here three days ago from Torgau. The gaiters and the boots you sent me arrived just before we left. Many thanks for them. Both Escott [Estcourt] and Hunter-Blair are here and also a fellow called Butt who is a cousin of Molly Burrows. He is in the K.O.Y.L.I. there are some Russian officers here who are most delightful people. I am trying to make up my mind to learn their language and have got as far as buying a grammar, but it is a dreadful undertaking. I am afraid this will reach you long after Duchess's birthday but wish her many happy returns etc., this ought to be about the 17th, didn't it? Best luck to her. Your letters, cards etc. roll up at all times and are all <u>most</u> welcome. I've got your one of October 10th quite a short time ago and the one of October 24th came first. I am not sure I oughtn't to be wishing you a happy Xmas, but I hope to be able to write again before then. No need to say how much I shall long to be with you. Please send me out a plum pudding. I wonder whether you will be watching the Wall Game today. I hope the Oppidan's win and should like to know the result. I am afraid the illustrated papers will hardly have room for the usual full-page illustration!! Never mind; Floreat Etona! Had we remained at Torgau the 18 Etonians were going to play a wall game there, but we have no room here. Did I tell you we played a field game at Torgau! Great fun but we all felt very ill after it! Incidentally the football punctured in the middle! I wonder if you could send me some of the casualty lists, as we only hear enough here to make us hungry for the worst. Well, I must say goodbye.
Best love to you all,
Your affectionate son,

Brocas

Letter 16

9th December 1914, Burg

My dearest Mother,
A letter from Duchess and a P.C. from father arrived today and I got four parcels yesterday, so I am indeed lucky. What wonderfully useful things you sent me and the cigarettes were most welcome. I have just started to learn Russian here to pass the time and it is a fearful undertaking and especially so as my teacher talks only a little French, no English and a little German and the Russian alphabet has at least 36 letters. I don't know whether I like this place better than Torgau or not, the exercise ground is much smaller but the food is better. Part of us are going away tomorrow but I am staying here. So glad to hear you are all well and that Duchess "prizes" my letter so and has not yet "heard" if she is to be chapel girl yet. I hope she will be in spite of her spelling!!! Not too bad for a second prefect, eh?? I shall be thinking of her the day after tomorrow.

Just received yet another P.C. from you dated November 21st. Yes, Belfour is here and a very nice man. Had some wonderful adventures. Overcoat not yet arrived but I am alright with the wellies etc. And it is not yet cold—not even frost at present!

We tried to pass the time here by playing poker, bridge, vingt-et-un, and such like games and any indoor games you could send me out will be most useful, also any books, paper editions. I am afraid you will think me a dreadful beggar, but you can't think how time hangs when one thinks of what one ought to be up and doing. I shall never keep pets in a cage again!

Yet another post bringing a letter from Molly B. (please thank her very much from me as I have only my weekly letters), and also one from Duch. October 28. I hope she passed her cooking exam! I also have been trying my hand and having to eat what I cook. The first time we did potatoes we only did them for 15 mins. and did not sleep well afterwards. This ought to arrive about Xmas. Well, you know how I shall be thinking of you and wishing myself elsewhere, but – ! My head is practically alright now and quite healed up.
Goodbye and God bless you all,

Brocas
Have you any news of Jerry Freeman Thomas, or any 5th D.G.'s?
Please write me any casualties of officers in them.

Letter 17

14th December 1914, Burg

My dearest Father,
As my next chance of writing to you may not be till December 21 I am going to write to you my best Xmas and birthday wishes today. You may be sure I shall be thinking of you much on those two days and wishing you the best of luck and prosperity. That I shall be longing to be with you goes without saying. Anyhow let us look forward to our next Xmas together and hope it will be in 1915. The censors here have been getting through a lot of letters and so I have received many cards and letters of some time back and also several late ones. All are equally welcome and my chief pastime is looking forward to the next. Everything you have mentioned so far has arrived except the overcoat but I can get along without that. Never mind about my "flee bag" or valise – in fact I am rather glad you have not sent them. I have ample underclothing now thank you and my only requirement is a pair of "slacks" i.e. khaki trousers. The pyjamas have arrived and are excellent, also the cigarettes. Any sweets, toffee etc. are always welcome. The clothes you have sent are <u>excellent</u> and just what I wanted. Always glad to get news of any of the family especially Cousin Glenn's husband. Wise is here and very nice also a Davenport. Up to the present it has been quite warm here but I expect that will change soon! Duchess's letters are always most interesting and welcome. I expect she will be with you when this arrives. We get news here of officers on leave from the front! Lucky dogs! I suppose there is no talk of exchange ever. Hopes of it still keep us alive. I have been studying French very hard and shall be prepared to escort you anywhere there on return; my Russian also progresses and I read the German papers daily. Hence my studies are varied. I am getting as fat as a barrel from no exercise and you would hardly recognise me on return. I may even weigh more than Duchess!! Who knows? My spots are rather bad and some carbolic would be welcome, also some cascara. Goodbye.
Best love and wishes,
Your loving son,

Brocas

Letter 18

20th December 1914, Burg

My dearest Mother,
I hope this will reach you about the New Year and so send you my best wishes for it and hope that our next merry meeting will be during it!! This week I have received several letters – all <u>most</u> welcome – including another from Molly Burrows and one from Ruth R. Please thank them both immensely from me and say how delighted I always am to hear from them, but tell them I fear I cannot write them as my weekly letter <u>must</u> go to you. I am told to ask you to address all future letters to me here to <u>Burg direct</u> as that is the quickest way. My further requirement at present is a pair of puttees – preferably of a <u>light</u> khaki colour. <u>Fox's spiral.</u> The overcoat has not yet arrived but no doubt will and anyway I can get along without it as I am not out of doors much. So glad George is so well and with Geoffrey Jackson – send them both my love. What is Alex's commission in? So glad he has at last got it.

Sorry about my luggage from Havre but it contains nothing very valuable, my dress clothes and an old civil suit and a few spare odds and ends in case of a gay weekend at that fashionable resort during a rest! Will you please let me know the exact date of my commission and what pay I got <u>originally</u>, and I'm getting <u>now</u>, if any (?). Ansell was vague about this but said he would do his best for me. So sorry to be such a nuisance. Please send me a copy of Wisden's when it comes out, which I think is usually about now. Ruth tells me Douglas Radcliffe is just off to the fun. I wish him luck and envy him <u>fearfully</u>. I am afraid I shall not be able to do any skiing this year, but I suppose the snow can wait. If you should ever get my suitcase from Havre, please send me my <u>service jacket</u> but if not, it doesn't matter. So glad to hear Sandy failed to die of mange during the summer months. What are you doing about the shoot this year? Are you performing? Is there any chance of my getting my year's antidate date as a university candidate?!! I am afraid this letter is horribly disconnected but I am just recovering from a bad bilious attack and cold, and my thinking machine is still out of order!! Such things however help to pass the time!! The week's excitement was the advent of two American Kinematographists but it didn't last long thank goodness. Oh well, ca va à peu près, as our allies say. There are 12 of them in this room, also five Belgians and five Russians; and the Quadruple Entente continues happily, but I hope I don't snore as they do and wish I had not been brought up to so much open window!!!
Goodbye and my best love to you all,

Brocas
Ask Gareth to drop me a line if possible, and let me know where he is, please.

Letter 19

27th December 1914, Burg

My dearest Duchess,
I think it is about your turn for a letter and as you will probably all be at home together now I take this opportunity of writing. I had a great surprise today, to whit a letter from Bernard enclosed in one from Aunt Ione. How kind of them to remember me. Please thank them. My Xmas post includes letters from you all which are most welcome. None of the last lot of parcels have arrived yet, but no doubt will soon. I think it is quickest to send them straight here as you send the letters. Will you please write and thank Evelyn Hardcastle, (5 Eaton Square, S.W.) for her P.C. and tell her how delighted I was to hear from her and also from 'Chappy' and explain why I cannot write at present, but will as soon as I possibly can.

So glad to hear you are all well, including Benning. It has just started to be cold here but nothing very serious as yet. Poor old Jack, he has certainly selected the wrong time to be in Australia and I suppose they are hardly likely to let him come back. I wonder if you could possibly get me two of my regimental collar badges and send them out to me. Mine have been stolen. We received visits in the course of the last week from two representatives of the American Embassy who looked very nice and also at this place. My language learning goes on and I certainly get variety. French, Russian and a little German at times. Christmas went off as usual except that we had extra service and were allowed to buy "kuchens" (a special cake) in the canteen, as a treat. The Russians sing most beautifully and I spend much time listening to them, though they are not very fond of public performances. As I write this we are in the middle of an "appel" or roll call which means we have to go to our rooms and be counted by the "unter-officer" in charge of each shed. You can't imagine the trouble we have about open windows here with the French. Poor people, I thoroughly sympathise with them, but then health is more important than sympathy!!

Who won the Varsity Rugger this year? I hope jolly old Oxford. Also, who won the Wall match?
Well, I must end now. Best of luck for the New Year to you all,
Ever your affectionate brother,

Brocas

Letter 20

3rd January 1915, Burg

My dearest Mother,
So begins the New Year! Let's hope for a happier one next year. This week has only brought me one P.C. from Duchess dated December 14. So glad you took her to the hippodrome and that Harry Tate was as usual. No parcels have turned up yet, but I expect them daily and that helps to pass the time! My poor old tunic is at last giving out, so would you please ask Hawkes our regimental tailor to make me another. He has my measurements. I am not quite sure of his address but I think it is Piccadilly, anyhow they will know at the depot. Please ask him to make it rather long and of some fine stuff and smart. The underwear you sent me is excellent and wearing well. I very much look forward to the plum puddings, sweets etc. Always welcome. None can be got here.

The New Year festivities here were nothing exceptional but we managed an international lunch in our shed, 5 Belgians, 14 French, 6 Russians and 3 English. Quite amusing though the menu would not be considered very "chic"! The French made speeches after it and the whole performance lasted over three hours. It is very good of you to send me off the Russian books which will be most useful. It is a language! And when you have learnt to read and to write it you are no nearer to pronouncing it.

So glad George's letter is also excellent. He must be having a great time now. What do you mean by my letter of August 14 which "has just arrived"? Where did I write it from? Aldershot? And why has it taken so long to reach its destination?

News is somewhat scarce this week as our excitements here are few and far between and there is nothing much to relate in the ordinary everyday life of the place. We used to play a lot of bridge, vingt-et-un., but hardly ever play now. It is funny how soon one tires of these games.

Well I hope you are all in the best of health, spirits etc. I am very well, though hardly fit!!

Goodbye, best love to you all,

Your affectionate son,

Brocas

Letter 21

11th January 1915, Burg

My dearest Father,
This week I have been most fortunate as regards letters and I've also received two parcels, the overcoat at last and the wonderful khaki woolly of Duchess's manufacture. Many thanks to her for it, and also for the handkerchiefs that came with it. The P.C. of Oxford "à là guerre" most interesting and the Terriers marching down the High with fixed bayonets look rather smarter than realistic! I expect you'll be very sorry to lose your Belgian family, we like the officers here enormously which is lucky as we are thrown so much together. The list of my tutor's old boys is most interesting and cheers me up more than anything else I have seen or heard since September 1. What a wonderful percentage! And all about 15 civils before the war. Please congratulate him for me. I was told there was another parcel for me today but when I got to the office I found it was for my namesake. Great disappointment but it reminded me of old times!

So glad to hear Duchess is getting slighter, though I'm afraid I can't guess what the "100 up" is. However, if it is Tennis to lessen bulk I shall require a strenuous course on return – whenever that maybe. Ah me! It's weary work and the worst of it is one's brain becomes so clogged it is almost impossible to work for long at a time. We can no more get tobacco here of any sort, so will you please send me some occasionally – that stuff you smoke, please. Today is the weekly bath day which is a great treat and passes the time well. The overcoat is excellent and when the "slacks" arrive I shall be fully set up. I expect Duchess will be back at school when this arrives, taking roll call etc. I wish her luck. Fancy Capt. Balfour marrying. I had heard he was engaged. His first leave since the beginning of the war. He must have had a hard time of it. Who is now commanding the regiment? I am very sorry to see the death of Douglas Harvey ex Captain of my tutors and also that Lennox Harvey – my only fag master, is missing. We had some deep snow last week which gave way to slush and it is now freezing again slightly. I am very well, so not exactly fit!! A round of golf would do me a lot of good. Well I hope you are all well and fit and enjoying life.

My best of love to you all,
Ever your loving son,

Brocas

Would one of Lizzie's cakes as supplied to M.B.B. at Eton College keep long enough to get here? This, as you may guess is a hint.

A poor Russian soldier has just died here. Pray God we get out of this before summer and hot weather comes.

Letter 22

17th January 1915, Burg

My dearest Mother,
Yet another week passed!! I have received several letters from you all and an Xmas card from you and also one from nurse and a letter from Miss Rawnsley, who talks of having sent me off some books. How kind of her, please thank her immensely. She talks of the death of Reggie Fletcher. I am so sorry. Yet another Etonian. You asked me in a letter for any news of Colin Leechman, 3rd Hussars. No one knows anything of him here. Neither of the two officers mentioned by your Belgian friends are here. So sorry to hear about Hancock. He will indeed be missed.

Fancy nurse remembering to send me a card. Please thank her from me and explain why I cannot write myself. Was so glad to get mothers letter of January 1 and to see that you realise a bit what it's like here and don't think me an appalling beggar. I have just been given two more letters one from Duchess of January 3 and one from Molly Burrows. I hope you enjoyed your stay at Kinnersley and found them all well and fit. The Intercession Service certainly ought to have been very fine. If I am still permitted to make remarks about so great a lady, how wonderfully the Duchess's handwriting has improved. I wear the scarf she made all day and it is wonderfully warm. Please thank Molly B. from me for the letter and also in anticipation for the book and tell her I hope it's a proper one!! Please tell her also that my birthday this time last year was a put-up job for a "sportsman night". She'll understand it!! Many thanks for the pen which works excellently. I am plugging away at languages – six hours a day excluding conversation, but progress seems slow. So glad there are no recent casualties in my regiment. What regiment is George in now? And what is Benning actually doing? It certainly is an opportunity for him. I still keep well though my headaches are still frequent, though lessening. I think I am beginning to agree with the headmaster of Dulwich re the war, though I fear our objectives are widely different! We had a very excellent service today, in one of the rooms here. Very suitable – absent friends and comrades – God protect you all.

So long.

Brocas
Food of all sorts welcome!

Letter 23

24th January 1915, Burg, bei Magdeburg

My dearest Father,
Many thanks for your letter of January 6th, 14 (!) from the Athenaeum and also to Mother for her card of January 15th which has just arrived. Sorry to hear the parcel was refused but it doesn't matter as I can get on without. I can't think what can have happened to the other parcels you have sent me as none have turned up lately, but I still live in hopes. So glad to hear Gerry Freeman Thomas is all right, we thought here that he was dead. You ask me what Belfort belongs to? Who is this? Do you mean Belfour? If so he is an engineer. Col. Gordon is still here with the remaining Subalterns of his regiment, but Col. Neish has been sent elsewhere. Hope you enjoyed your stay at Kinnersley. Did you shoot? So, Duchess is now back at school and I hope enjoying herself. When is she going to come out under present circumstances? Are there many men up at Oxford this term and have you any news of Gareth Fletcher or Con Benson? Cousin Ted's position sounds most important and I hope he likes it. Flea Bag has not yet arrived. We are about 60 English Officers here. So glad you have ordered the tunic. My only wants at the present moment are a khaki tie not silk and one that spreads out, and a khaki sweater low necked and of a kind of wool, silk, probably advertised for officers at the front. An officer here got one sent via Page Gaston on October 28, so perhaps they are beginning to come through at last. I am still plugging away at Russian though it is very difficult to concentrate thoughts in the combined noise and atmosphere of our sitting-dressing-bedroom. Things go on as usual and time passes quicker than one would expect, but the end being so horribly indefinite is what makes it seem so long. I am afraid my letters are appallingly dull but of news of the outside world we have nothing and the events within these 4 walls are rarely worthy of note. We hear today that coffee is to be stopped – a great blow to us.

Could you please send me a packet or two of cocoa as we can make that as long as we have fires. An O.E. here has just received a list of O.E.s in the war. Most interesting but 150 killed in action is a fearful toll to pay. I know so many of them. It was weird to see on another page the teams for the Wall Match. I suppose all is much as usual chez vous. Some officers here even talk of dances, they have heard of. Well, well!
Best love and wishes to you all,

Your loving son,

Brocas

Letter 24

31st January 1915, Burg

My dearest Mother,
This week has brought me 2 parcels and a letter from my tutor. How kind of him
to write to me. Please thank him enormously – tell him I got the list of his old
Boys and their doings and thought it wonderful. It seems that the 2 Burrows's
are about the only two not doing their duty at the present moment. Say I should
be only too delighted if he would drop me a line occasionally in German. If you
could send me an occasional Chronicle it would be most welcome. The 2 parcels
were of January 19 and January 21. The first containing a wonderful pair of
slippers – beauties – puttees, nail brush, and 3 books. Most useful, and the second
parcel contained cigarettes – now a most precious article as we cannot buy even
the local product here.

Fifteen officers of mixed nationalities, including Colonel Gordon and 3 other
Englishmen or rather Highlanders were to have left us today for Blankenberg
but didn't go at the last minute. Yesterday I had my first serious Russian
conversation – a wonderful show! What a language it is. I really quite despair
at times of ever learning it, when it comes to having to use a different verb
when I knock you once instead of twice!! So glad you have ordered my coat
from Hawkes. Please also send me a pair of short pants.

I can't think what can have happened to the parcels you sent me between
the middle of November and the 19th of January. None of them have turned
up and now they seem to be coming regularly. Could you please send me a
tongue!! An odd request but it would be most welcome. In future I shall write
to you on a letter card as I can get just as much news on it and am allowed
two cards instead of one letter. So glad you sent me that Russian campaign of
Napoleon in French. Just exactly what I wanted to read. How you would laugh
if you could hear us trying to prophesy the end of the war and the wonderful
arguments we use why it should only last a very short time. They really do
*seem quite convincing at times, but somehow, they don't come off. Is **Jack J***
[allies] *still going strong and is he still contented? The news my "**cousins***
germains" [probably a reference to German newspapers] *send me is so*
*conflicting as regards him. How many **daughters** [allies] has he got? I am*
now taking to violent exercise every morning and evening and am reducing
the superfluous immensely. Won't this make Duchess jealous!! I am also
taking lessons in Highland dancing from the Scotsmen here [probably David
Hunter-Blair]. *The worst of all this exercise is that though it clears the brain*
it wastes an immense amount of time. However, I find I can't exist without it.

Please ask Cox to send me another £5, as I have run out of cash, and I wonder whether you could send me a copy of my regimental history to study? As to how you can get it, I don't know. But I suppose I shall be expected to know something about it on my return – whenever that may be. Have you ever heard anything about my kit? or the Havre suitcase?

(Deletion by Censor).

Hence forth I shall number my letters so that you can let me know if they arrive. Up to date I have written to you weekly from about mid-October. Please number yours in return.

Well, so long, good luck and best love to you all,

Your affectionate son,

Brocas

Please send me a large box of almonds and raisins.

Letter 25

7th February 1915, Burg

My dearest Father,
This week I have had the good fortune to receive three parcels, one containing Tobacco, sweets and chocolate, one containing Lizzie's cake – excellent and much appreciated, and one containing Jack's gloves, pyjamas and handkerchiefs. Many thanks for all three. Lizzie's cake quite reminded me of old days at Eton, but here it disappeared even more quickly than it used to there and the remarks of the devourers were if possible more unanimous in its praise. The gloves will be most useful. I also got two letters, one of January 8th from Kinnersley. So glad to hear you have been sending some things to 5th D.G.'s. How very kind of you. Doubtless it must be fearfully cold at the front now. So glad Duchess enjoyed her first week end all by herself. What a woman of the world!! Apparently sending letters straight here is not as quick as by the G.P.O. The other letter, received yesterday was from Mother on the 22nd January. So glad to get the picture of Gerry F.T. and to hear he is all right. So glad to hear the prayer hour is still at 8.30 and not earlier. Here we have had a heavy snowfall all last night and it is still going on. It ought to be a good year for the few who are in jolly old Switzerland, doing the winter sports. Here it seems so sad that so much snow

should be wasted. Col. Gordon and three other Englishmen left us a few days ago for another camp. We are all very sorry he has gone, but he certainly looked appallingly ill. Though I am not actually doing the 100 up, I am taking part in a course of violent Swedish drill every morning and this with a two-hours walk every evening and a brief spell of 'Reel' dancing is reducing my size and lessening my headaches wonderfully. Please tell Duchess that the one souvenir of my brief campaign that I have managed to retain is the little wristwatch she lent me, which in spite of everything still keeps excellent time and has only suffered from two glass breaks since repaired. Sorry to hear George is not very fit. I hope it is not the result of your plum pudding, if so, it is perhaps as well mine never arrived!! **Page Gaston appeared today but we weren't allowed to get at him.** [Probably a suggestion they were getting news via the French POWs] *Please send nurse my best wishes for her birthday which I think is March 5. All luck to her. I hear there is to be no Varsity Boat Race this year. How sad. Fancy postponing such an event for mere trifles like European complications! I am afraid the "slacks" have never turned up but they don't matter much. Otherwise my clothing is excellent and the only requisite is food. Solid stuff such as potted meat etc. are always welcome as also cakes etc. We can get none here. What news of Jack in Australia? Is there no chance of him getting home? Well I must end, owing to lack of news. Is there no talk of exchange? I suppose it is wrong to grumble but it seems very hard.*

Best love to you all,

Your affectionate son,

Brocas

Letter 26

15th February 1915, Burg

My dearest Mother,
On Thursday I had a tremendous surprise. Twelve of the long-lost parcels turned up together from Page Gaston. I received a message to go and get parcels and went into the room where they were and there saw a pile of twelve. I don't think any heap of Xmas presents when small caused me half the pleasure and it was a real difficulty to decide which to open first and I eventually decided on the biggest!! We had to sort them in a hurry so I couldn't make out a list, but there was food from Fuller's and Fortnum and Mason, cigarettes, many clothes, including the "slacks", books etc. etc. Many many thanks to you all. There were two Xmas puddings in one of the parcels and one of these is already among the casualties. Next day I got two more parcels, one from

Mother containing cholera belts etc. and a book from Molly. Many thanks to you and her please. I am now quite set up in clothes for some time to come.

I have also received two letters in the course of the week, so I cannot grumble – one from Father of January 13 received February 10 re-my pay etc. Most interesting and many thanks for finding out for me and would you please also enquire if there is not a chance of my being gazetted to the regiment above those fellows who got their commissions about August 15 and were not taken out. It seems rather hard that I should be below them. The other letter was from Mother of December 15 received yesterday!! Many thanks. Still no news of Leechman. No, I have not got my Prayer Book and its history does not bear writing. But it shall be told – anon. If you could send me one with hymns A. and M. and also a small bible. I should be most grateful. You all seem in excellent spirits which is very good. Here we seem to be finishing with winter though is it still cold. (New pencil). Personally, I am much as usual and life rather exists and does not change much. We still have our hopes etc. which will all doubtless be thwarted in due course, to give way to others! Please send 'Nurse' my best wishes for her birthday, long life, happiness and all such.

Best love etc. to you all and may we meet as soon as possible.
Ever your affectionate son,

Brocas.

Just off to do my morning Gym.

Letter 27

[No date], *Burg*

My dearest Father,
I have no doubt you must be very busy and I'm afraid I shall be giving you no little trouble by this request. But nevertheless, I feel in duty-bound to ask it. There is a Belgian officer here, Lieutenant Gilet whose wife and two children aged 7 and 9, are in England. They have apparently received inadequate attention from the Commission which deals with refugees, and Mons. Gilet is very worried. They were first sent to a place called Prospect House, Charlton Kilmersdon, near Radstock, and then were moved to 97 Peckham Road, London and they fear yet another move, and have not been comfortable or very well looked after. I wonder whether you could write to the Commissioner or responsible person and try and get these poor folks settled somewhere as comfortably as possible? Mons. Gilet quite understands the difficulty of dealing

with such large numbers, but surely an officer's wife deserves special attention. The ladies correct name is Madame Leon Gilet, Dame d'officer Belge. I should be so obliged if you could manage to see to this for me, though I am exceedingly sorry to trouble you. I forgot to number my last letter which should have been 111 [probably should have been XXX or 30].

All here much as usual and if it were not for my Russian I don't know how I should exist at all. It passes the time wonderfully. Today is a quite perfect day, sunny and crisp. It makes one dream of golf clubs et cetera. Afraid I shall need at least a stroke a hole at our next contest. The Russian books you sent are exceedingly good and exactly what I wanted and could not get here. With them and a book by Lanson on French literature I am fully occupied.
Well goodbye to you all and best love and wishes for Easter (almost time I suppose!!)

Your affectionate son,

Brocas

Letter 28

24th February 1915, Burg

My dearest Mother,
The commandant has just read me a letter transmitted by a certain Herr Bulow in which he says you are worrying about my health and headaches. He has asked me to write and reassure you. They are much better and fast disappearing and there is certainly <u>no</u> cause for <u>any alarm</u>. Everything is healed up and <u>perfectly well</u>, and to make doubly sure the Commandant asks me to get the English doctor here, Major Thompson, our R.A.M.C. to certify to this effect. <u>All is perfectly well</u> – as I hope you all are. I've just received three parcels from you which I will acknowledge in weekly letter. Among them the tongue most welcome.

So long and for <u>goodness sake don't worry.</u>

Your affectionate son,

Brocas

M.B. Burrows is in quite good health and need occasion you no anxiety.
(Signed) A.G. Thompson
Major, R.A.M.C.

Letter 29

27th February, 1915, Magdeburg, Buckan
From: Dr Sug. Kurt Sorg.
Translation

Dear Herr Bulow,

I have received your letter of the 7th instant, and have made enquiries about Lieut. Burrows from the commandant of the Camp for Officer prisoners at Burg bei Magdeburg.

The Commandant writes to me very kindly today in the following words:-

"Lieut. Burrows is in sound health, and has written a letter to his Mother which can be sent on. The English doctor has also attached a certificate to this letter to the effect that the Lieut. Burrows is in the sound health".

I am forwarding to you this information, I send at the same time the enclosed letter from Lieutenant Burrows to his mother, which perhaps you will kindly forward.

I think I did what you would have wished me to do in expressing the sincere thanks of Lieut. Burrows' relations to the Commandant of the Officer prisoners' camp for his kindness in dealing with this matter.

Letter 30

1st March 1915, Burg

My dearest Mother,
This week no less than four letters from Duchess. Many thanks to her. If she only knew the pleasure they give. Also letters from Gareth and Aunt Io and a card from Father January 27. Also parcels from Aunt Io, Lady Sutherland and Miss Queenie. How very kind of them. Please thank them for me and explain my inability to write. Also note from Cox and co. Please tell them I got money from October 28, 1914. Cutting from paper re me was torn out by English Censor, so I still remain in doubt. Fancy hearing from Gareth – a letter from "THE FRONT". How distant it seems. All as usual here, 3 hours Russian conversation per day. Please send me small History of Russia in <u>Russian</u>; and also, nice little history of England as a present for my Russian teacher **Fundiran reorundobura Muropadobura!!** [a coded message – no details]

Afraid I may miss acknowledging parcels but most seem to turn up. Tongue was excellent. Also received the Baccy and more underclothes and potted meat. All excellent. Please send me good hamper for Easter. What a beggar I am. Fancy Duchess first prefect. What a "knut". I hope hair won't be up before I return. Please send me family photographs. I have no doubt it is time you were all done again. Father not in the cap please.

Best love,

Brocas

Letter 31

13th March 1915, [no address and to either parent]

This week brought me another parcel containing books, ties and woolly waistcoat. Excellent! Also letter from Mother with most descriptive account of drawing room. February 28. I can quite imagine you all at this moment there!! Also two letters from Duchess of February 28 and March 7. Both grand and I shall be thinking of her "Old Girls" match next Thursday. Fancy George being with you. I hope he was fit and well and not seriously suffering from the swollen feet Duchess suggests. I also received an excellent letter from m'tutor in German however I managed to decipher by means of dictionary. How interesting about the Belgian boys at Eton. Have you any news of Gareth? I also received a card from Mrs Hardcastle – please thank her. We have had snow here during the week but the weather has now broken and tonight it is very warm which is a great blessing. I expect J.S.B. is in England by now, give him my love. So glad about J.J. [the allies] That's grand!! Where are you going for Easter? Perhaps Folkestone as per usual. I am afraid I shall not be able to accompany you this year, as I am busy! I don't think!! I hope you have a good vac. Has Duchess got her hair up yet? If not, when does this occur?

Here all as usual except that I have joined the choir. We had snatches of news about the Palaces [POW camps for Germans] erected for our "fellow sufferers" in England and I must say I am glad the old country is showing how such things should be done. It doesn't affect us.

Best love,

Brocas

Balliol list just arrived – many thanks

Letter 32

22nd March 1915, [no address or name]

This week 6 parcels containing tongue, almonds and raisins, 2 French books, Buzzard's cake, Russian grammar (very good) and shirt and tobacco. Please send me two more shirts like that for summer (from Woodward). Also received tongue from Kinnersley, please thank. Many welcome letters. From M. of March 14 and also of March 4, from F. of 11th and Duchess of 14th, also 6 P.C.'s of Oxford and 5 D.G. and a letter from Norwegian Embassy making enquiries through Mrs. Max Muller. Many thanks to all of you for everything. Please try and get me Regimental Forage cap (green and red), shaped like R.F.C. caps. My poor old Flea Bag has never turned up and I don't expect ever will now, but it doesn't matter.

I have enquired about all the missing you mention but nothing is known here. Poor Gareth, God grant he is alright somewhere. So sorry about Neville Talbot, though I expect he is rather too big for trenches. M. Gillet here sends heartfelt thanks for your kindness and indeed it is very good of you. I feel I have put you to great trouble re Reg. History – apologies. The new Russian Grammar is excellent, though involved. The wristwatch, this is Duchess's I have here, and I don't think you ever gave me one!! Intentions good perhaps, I will hold you to them on return. Slacks have arrived and I have two overcoats. Boots not required but a pair of brogues and stockings would be useful. Food all excellent and I much look forward to the potted pheasant. I hope no funny person makes me an April fool this year.

You enquire about songbirds here. Well a certain ally has ideas about his voice but – otherwise they do not exist. I am well, very well, cheerful, short tempered, optimistic and bored.

*All news of **cousins*** [allies or British officers] *most welcome. Please express to Mrs. Fletcher my deep sympathy about Gareth and tell her I will do my best here, alas so very little. I expect he will turn up.*

Best love to you all and best wishes for Easter,

Brocas

Letter 33

28th March 1915, Burg, bei Magdeburg,
To: the Norwegian attaché

Dear Sir,
It is very kind of you and of Mrs. Max Muller to make enquiries about me
for my Mother who I am afraid is rather apt to worry. Please tell her that I
am now in the best possible health under the circumstances, that my wound
has healed long ago and any indisposition is entirely due to lack of exercise
and change. It is of course extremely difficult to get enough of the former in the
strictly limited space at our disposal here, and to anyone who is accustomed to
as much exercise as I am this is of course a drawback.

Time on the whole passes extraordinarily quickly and things generally show a
slight tendency to improve.

Please forward my respects and best thanks to Mrs. Max Muller and tell her I
much look forward to the time when I shall have the honour of partnering her
in a game of tennis again.

Please accept my cordial thanks for the trouble you have taken and believe me,
Yours very truly,
M. Brocas Burrows,
Lt. 5th Dragoon Guards.

Letter 34

[No date, address or name but must be to Mother]

This week I have received five parcels from you dated March 3rd, 9th, 9th and
15th, and another containing potted pheasant, etc. Regimental History most
interesting and all foodstuffs most welcome. The new diet is making me feel a
better man already. Also, a magnificent parcel from Lady Sutherland. How
awfully kind of her. I am writing to thank her myself. A letter from F. of March
18th complaining of having received no letters for three weeks from me. I am
very sorry but I suppose that must occur. So glad he got a letter from Martin
and to hear all well. They seem in grand form and no wonder!! George seems in
luck too. Fancy being at Nice! To say how nice would I suppose be commonplace.
I shall think of Duchess joining you in three days. So glad to get the prayer
book (marked) and Bible. What a kind thought. Please send me some fruit for
a compote and also 2 more of those shirts from Woodward with collars and 2 silk

ties and let me know cost of these as they are for 2 Russian friends who think them excellent.

Sorry to hear about Alex's knee but I suppose it is better to get it over now, isn't it? We hear there are to be more parcels today but alas few letters. The excitement and expectation is quite thrilling. Lady S.'s parcel was most useful. She sent me some Keatings!! I wonder who has been telling her about this place? I suppose no news of Gareth yet? Please send me one of the flaps worn on the back of caps as sun protectors.

Here all are well as can be and the weather today is glorious – frosty and sunny. Yesterday we had snow and during the week thunder.

So long and good luck to you,

Your affectionate son,

Brocas

Letter 35

4th April 1915, [no address]

My dearest Mother, Father and Duchess,
This week brought 4 letters, Mother's of 21st, Duchess's of 21st, Father's of 24th and Molly Burrows' of 24th March. Many thanks for them all. Fancy Duchess with her hair up next term. I wonder if she was photographed thus for the picture I expect soon. Also 4 parcels – one containing handkerchiefs, chocolate and laces, the "flea bag" at last and also two old December parcels from Fortnum&Mason, containing plum pudding. Easter passed here as most days, we had an excellent service in the morning and a very full attendance. This is the greatest fête in the year in Russia and they did their best to enliven matters yesterday. So sorry to hear of deaths of Ld. Teignmouth and Professor Bullock. Have you any news of Gareth? George seems to have had a grand time. Will you please send me out a box of 'stump balls' like we used at Eton, i.e. solid India rubber and also a brace of stump bats. I may have one at home or if not get one of my older bats cut down. We hope to find space here to play. Please also get me a good box of Windsor and Newton's best paints, water colours, and let me know the price. It is for a Russian friend who paints here and he cannot get these from Russia. He will pay me and I will keep the money for you. Please also send me a loaf of white bread occasionally as we can get none here.

(Deletion by Censor)

Biscuits are also most welcome. News of Jack J. seems grand. There is no news to tell you as all is just as usual. Weather rather muggy and slack, but no more cold. We are all well and fairly fit. Lady Sutherland sent me some Keatings Powder. I wonder who had been telling her about this!!
Well, goodbye and good luck to you all,
Your affectionate son,
Brocas.

For heaven's sake put no more of my letters in the papers! [presumably a reference to letters being published in a newspaper — no details]

Letter 36

12th April 1915, [no address and probably to Father]

This week excellent letters from mother, Duchess and Bernard. Most welcome. You all seem very flourishing. Also, seven parcels, the first 4 dated March 10th, 20th, 22nd and 24th. Then one containing histories, salt, tobacco etc. another ctg. book and also No.31. Thanks. My Russian friend says words fail him to express his thanks for the history and I certainly must compliment you on your choice. Fancy Duchess learning Italian. Several officers learn it here and it certainly sounds delightful. Fancy you investing in a "run about" – grand! Duchess must teach me to drive same on return. All car experts here praise your choice. I see you now have maid servants in the Athenaeum! Well I'm – !! Professor Vinogradoff is quite right about my Russian friend and he is a most interesting man to talk to about all subjects. Please send me out some recent Quarterly Reviews and XXth centuries and also occasionally some woodbine cigarettes for the poor orderlies here. George appears to have had a grand time at Nice and he is now "at it again" no doubt. Any news of Gareth yet? Sorry to hear of Benning's illness, and hope he is now well again. Please write and thank Bernard for his letter and congratulate Aunt Io on his remarkable manipulation of the pen. If he is keen on soldiers as I was, please send him a box of 5 D.G.'s which can be bought at Hamley's and charge it to me. Please keep a list of all the things you are getting for me and my Russian friends here and I will pay you on return. I am daily looking forward to the arrival of the family portraits and hope they will be better than the last effort, Mother, Duchess and I!!! Send me out any interesting little Kodak snaps you take, in your letters. So glad to hear you have taken over the county "boy scouts", though I suppose it will mean all the more work. I hear there will be no Lords or varsity match this year. How sickening for those who get their XI.

Re-health, etc. I am much better now that I am living almost entirely on food
from home and Lizzies cakes have never been more welcome.
Goodbye, good luck to you,
Love,
Brocas.

Letter 37

My dearest Mother,
Yet another week gone. A letter from you of April 2nd saying you have had
no news of me since March 1st. I can't understand it as I have written every
week one of these P.C.'s. So glad to get your other news. What a fool the "head"
must be. I'm sure Duchess will greatly enjoy the car and hope she doesn't
smash it up before I return. Is she going to take it back to school? Also, a letter
from father of April 7th, for both many thanks. Spring seems to be beginning
in earnest here and we watch the trees etc. **(Deletion by Censor)** *very enviously.*
Though young I fear our fancies will do but little this year in turning to various
thoughts. If you have not yet sent off stump cricket bats, please do not but if
you have no matter. I received two parcels this week, one from Miss Queenie
containing fish etc. (potted) and one from you containing chocolate, fish soup
etc. Many thanks to you both. Poor old Alex. How sickening about his knee,
but he will be in at the kill yet I suppose. Any news of Gareth? This last letter
I received was my 122nd in captivity, not bad going. I am trying to get some
bets on the grand total! I expect you are at Truro about now or else Yewhurst,
at either of which places it ought to be very nice about now. Of news from here
there is none, everything as usual. I am well and so are we all, wonderful to
relate, we are all hopeful and patient and that seems to pass the time somehow.
Good bye,
Your affectionate son,
Brocas.

Letter 38

To Father

This week 5 letters from you, yours of March 31st, April 15th, and 18th, M.'s of
April 10th and Duchess of April 12th. Most welcome. So glad to hear there is
a rumour about Gareth, that is at any rate something. The commandant here
kindly gave me leave to write to Liège on the off chance of finding him and

getting news and I have done so and hope for the best. But it is true it sounds curious that he hasn't written himself. Fancy, Duchess's hair being up! Please send me a photo of this phenomena. I heartily congratulate her on being such a "swell" at school, and only hope her duties will not deter her from writing to me!! So glad you were down at Truro and Yewhurst and that Bernard is in such form. I can't understand the gap in my letters but hope they are coming more frequently now. It is not for want of writing! I received 5 parcels this week. One from Lewes which I presume is due to the kindness of Aunt Io, and four from home containing underclothes, cake, 1 Tiptree parcel and biscuits. <u>Many thanks.</u> My only wants appear to be now a few thin underclothes real thin and please silky, as it can be hot here in the summer and will doubtless fry. I shall have enough thick to last me through next winter. The Russian goes on slowly and is certainly a good exercise. I think I ought to be fairly proficient in another three months. I am beginning to wonder what would be my best course to adopt after this show but suppose it would be best to "wait-and-see". News as usual does not exist here.
(Deletion by Censor).

All your news is most interesting and reminds one that there is something outside.
(Deletion by Censor).

The news of the little car is most interesting. I am afraid there must always be a sameness in my letters but please excuse it. I am becoming quite vegetable. Health – good – now much skipping.
Best love to you all,
Your affectionate son,
Brocas.

Letter 39

10th May 1915, Burg

My dearest Duchess,
Many thanks for yours of April 25th, so cheery etc. Also, of May 2nd from school, where you seem very busy, which is the best cure for most things. How I should like to see you with your hair up! Though I suppose it would be "strengstens verboten" to laugh at it. Never mind; I shall yet. What news have you of the **sick man?** [possibly a reference to the Russians but more likely the Germans] *When is his death expected? If you don't know, ask Miss Soulsby. They say the garden has been very carefully planted, and that you expect the sweet peas in July this year. I hope this is true! I shall think of you on June 10th and wish you luck. I wrote a letter to George last week, which I hope will arrive some time. It*

seems pretty difficult to find Gareth, but I hope still. Send my love to Sid and Ruth if you write ever. I hope you saw a good play the night you were in town. News from here is as usual: nothing doing; and I am getting really quite used to writing it. Much looking forward to getting your photos and hope they are good. Well, best love,
Your affectionate brother,
Brocas.

Letter 40

10th May 1915, [no address]

My dearest Father,
Great joy, 5 letters this week. One from M. of April 28th with news of George's birthday. Can get no more news of Windram (G.H.) except that he was shot in the hand at very close quarters and as far as is known was left in hospital. I will however try again.
(Deletion by Censor).

Photo of car most interesting. So sorry no more news of Gareth. Letter from D. of April 25th with news of all my cards arriving together. So glad they have turned up at last. So looking forward to getting her photos. Also, one from you of April 23rd. I am afraid my requests must keep you horribly busy. My Russian friends thank you enormously for your kindness and it is indeed good of you. Eleanor Butler very kindly wrote to me. Please thank her immensely, she seems most cheery and tell her I quite sympathise with her qualms during the motor ride she mentions! Also, a wonderful letter from Duch. of May 2nd. So busy and cheery. That is excellent. I suppose she is not allowed the car at school? I await the photos anxiously!! And thoroughly sympathise about the hair. No parcels this week but with all the correspondence I have little to grumble about. Please let me know exactly when Douglas Radcliffe leaves. Have you ever read 'Napoleon the Gaoler' by Edward Fraser? If not, you should. How we envy them! News here is as usual. Is there any chance of an exchange? Please let me know.

Well. I must close with apologies for an extra dull card.

Best love to you all,
Your affectionate son,
Brocas.

Letter 41

13th May 1915, Burg. (Postmark) Copy
[Brocas to George]

Dear Bene,
Have been meaning to write for some time, but facilities are not of the best. I hear frequent news of you from home and envy you accordingly. Fancy a fortnight at Nice! But of course one always gets a drink in the middle of a long knock. As to what wicket you are batting on now I have no idea, but hope it is a good one. My knock was a short one, though I was outed unluckily and have a grievance. However I survived some very good deliveries early on, and ought, I suppose, to be thankful for a mere "retired hurt" instead of a final decision. It is quite bad enough though. [Brocas describing his fighting, wounding and capture rather than being killed and he goes on to ask how the war is progressing in cricketing analogy] *They tell me the county championships will be very keen this summer, though there is no doubt the old firm will pull through in-spite of all the matches being "out matches". Of course we know least of all about this out here, and I should like your opinion expressed as concisely as circumstances will permit. How soon is the sick man likely to expire? He seems rather up against it, though of course one knows little about his guts.* [This suggests the 'sick man' is probably Germany] *Baby has been writing to me quite frequently, and sent me a photo! I pass my time studying the Russian tongue, and a magnificent pass-time too! Perhaps we shall be able to travel there anon. Of news from here there is nothing. Boredom intense and stiff as hell. So glad Camac is joining the posse and leaving the muck tram. Well, Bene, I will close, there being no more to talk about.*

So long; good luck. Keep it low and go hard in the loose, and an extra slick for me occasionally.

Yours till they cease,
(Deletion by Censor).
Brocas.

I was very nearly dealt a final decision after retiring. [killed]

Letter 42

[No date or address but almost certainly to parents]

Two letters from you this week and the photos! What a look of martyrdom! Never mind I feared as much, knowing how you hate the operation. The first letter was from Kinnersley of April 17th and the second containing photos from Oxford of the 22nd. Many thanks. So glad to get your news and that all is so excellent. So glad about Alex, though what a nuisance his knee is. Also about George. Warm weather here at last and it will be really hot in summer. No shade. Please tell Hawkes to make and send me a pair of drill riding breeches, thin summer material, light grey to white colour and latest cut. Also a pair of thin puttees, spiral and a pair of puttee-stockings. Please stop sending cigarettes and tobacco because I have given up smoking altogether and also the percentage of arrivals is quickly diminishing. Curiously enough (!) I find my health much improved without tobacco and drink! Two parcels arrived last week one containing salt, sugar, etc. and the other containing some little book, I think an O.E. list, but I was not allowed to see it as it had to be censored and I am told I shall probably not see it at all. A pity but I suppose it can't be helped. How many Burrows's on active service has Cousin Eustace discovered? Please send me a photo of Duchess with "sails flying"! Also one of those small 'Ticka cameras' and some films. Where are you going for the summer holidays this year or haven't you decided yet? Is there still no news of Gareth. I wrote to Liège on the off chance but have as yet had no reply. News here none, health good, also spirits. Goodbye.

Best love to you all,
Brocas.

Letter 43

[No date but probably sometime well before
20th May, no address]

My dearest Duchess,
My last card was so dull it is up to me to try again. No peace for the wicked. We have got to move to Mainz on Thursday – a fearful performance with all the luggage etc. now accumulated. But such a change is always something, and on the whole it is a bit nearer to Tipperary. Will you please get me a collection of P.C.'s of my regiment, other Cav. regiments, and Foot Guards, and send them to me as I want to show them to my Russian friends. I hope you are enjoying your Summer term and becoming proficient at Tennis. Here all as usual but there will be no mean bustle the next few days. Well good bye,

Best love,
Your affectionate brother,
Brocas.

Write me any news of Gareth please.

Letter 44

16th May 1915

My dearest Father,
A card from Mother of May 3rd and a letter from you of May 5th composed my bag this week. So glad you are both in good health. How interesting about Naomi's father. Please tell me more. So glad to hear of the increase in **Cousin Jack's family** [Admiral Jellicoe]. Someone told me they had been quarrelling among themselves recently and had hurt each other but I hope this is quite untrue. Please let me know. Yes I got a Wisden Almanack all right and apologies for omitting to acknowledge it. No peace for the wicked. We leave for Mayence (Mainz) on Thursday and with all the accumulated baggage it will be "some" move. It is a fearful nuisance but all the same these things pass the time quickly. A change is always welcome after passing 175 days in the same yard. This week I got 6 parcels, shoes, 2 loaves, tongue, rusks, cheese biscuits, fish, Russian books and a couple of sacred books from Mowbrays. Many thanks for them all.

The bread arrived all right and was excellent, though I believe it would come better in grease paper and then in a tin. I have not got the Russian books yet as they are being censored but have no doubt they are excellent. So glad to hear George, Alex, and Mon all right. Please thank Benning from me for the box. How very kind of him. Health here good, weather warm and news – nothing. Please send fruit and also some P.C.'s of my regiment.

Good bye, Best love,
Your affectionate son.

Brocas

6

Mainz POW Camp

20 May 1915 – 15 June 1916

The POW Camp at Mainz was in a former Prussian fortress about 200 yards from the west bank of the River Rhine and a similar distance from the southern railway station. The railway itself ran in a tunnel under the eastern bastion of the citadelle entering through a tunnel portal close to the main perimeter wall. Mainz was an officers' camp of mixed nationalities. In all there were about 100 British officers, 200 French and 200 Russians and a few Belgians, most of whom like Brocas, had been captured in the early days of the war. Brocas and his fellow officers arrived at Mainz as Brocas said, '*dog-tired*' after an uneventful nineteen-hour 250-mile train journey overnight from Burg.

Mainz citadelle was a formidable star shaped structure on the edge of the old town. The accommodation was grim and basic. Captain Ian Henderson who arrived 18 August 1915, in his debrief statement, described his room as follows:

> *It had thick stone walls like a casement with curved ceiling facing north, and about 38 feet long by 18 feet wide and about 11-12 feet high at the apex of the arch sloping to about 5 feet at the sides. There was one window at the north end and a door at the south, near the door a stove. The rooms were draughty and damp and naturally got no sun. In these were 11 officers and to get any reasonable amount of room (as we had to live, sleep, and eat our own meals, not German meals as these were scarcely touched, in the room) we had to place three beds on top of others.*

All the officers slept on straw filled sacks on boards. It would be Captain Henderson who was on the first exchange to Switzerland on 29 May 1916 and who shared Brocas's room, with among others Captain Pelham-Burn, who brought out with him messages from Brocas and details of the proposed code to be used in letters. In his debrief statement, Captain Henderson, in commenting on the effects of imprisonment on officers, paid tribute to the efforts of Brocas and others:

My impression as to the effect of the long imprisonment upon the officers is that, except in a few cases, they have borne it amazingly well. I put this down largely to the games (outdoor) organised and carried out systematically. In my own camp Captain Usher, Gordons; Lieutenant Sampson, Royal Fusiliers; Lieutenant Burrows, 5th Dragoon Guards; Captain Humphreys, Army Service Corps, were largely responsible for the success of the games and sports under great difficulties.

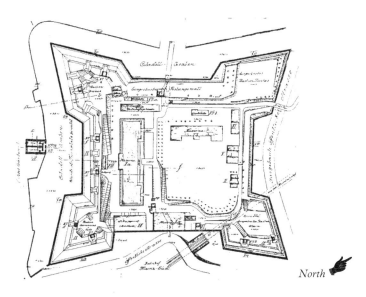

North

Mainz Citadelle in 1921 Source: http://www.festung-mainz.de/zitadelle

Stone battlements about fifty feet high surrounded the buildings. A sentry was stationed at any point where it would be possible to jump down, and between these battlements and the buildings were two distinct rows of tangled barbed wire that were continually patrolled by a whole company of infantry which was changed every 24 hours. The whole place was littered with sentries posted outside the wire fences and each one was over-looked by his neighbour. The daily relief made it impossible to bribe the sentries, as was often possible at other camps. It laid emphasis on captivity. No one ever managed to escape from Mainz though numerous escape attempts were planned and some even executed, but some prisoners suggested that even if the war had lasted for another twenty years it would have retained its impregnability. The German camp authorities were particularly on the alert because most of these original prisoners of war, being regular officers, were considered valuable prizes as potential instructors of the new armies. Also, Mainz being only 130 miles as the crow flies from the front line at Verdun, and with the wind in the right direction, the sound of the guns kept the reality of the war firmly fixed in the minds of their captors. The slightest slackness on their part was punished by immediate dispatch to the front – a punishment which they dreaded as much as the death sentence.

The commandant's building, Mainz POW Camp c 1900. Source: http:// www.festung-mainz.de/zitadelle

Brocas was one of a group of six British officers who undertook an audacious tunnel escape which came within days of succeeding when on 16 June 1916 all the British were given 48 hours' notice to leave for another camp. There was some excitement at the final roll call owing to the absence of the three British officers who were concealed in the half-finished tunnel which they had hoped to finish and escape by within a few hours. In all probability it would have been several days. Unfortunately, they were quickly discovered, but not before the rest of the prisoners had already departed by train.

The group included an officer of Cheshire Regiment, 2nd Lieutenant Ian Fairweather captured, unwounded at Audregnies on 24 August 1914. Captain Eric Walker R.F.C., captured Douai 7 July 1915, Lieutenant 'Willie' Loder-Symonds of the Wiltshire regiment, who was a bull of a man, taken at Le Cateau when shot through the leg. The other two members, adding further energy and enthusiasm, were probably Lt Frederick Sampson from the Royal Fusiliers and captured at Bertrix early September 1914 and Captain John Edward 'Talbot' Younger, R.F.A. also captured at Le Cateau on 26 August 1914. With the exception of Walker, they had a common bond of being captured in the first few days of the fighting and had been together throughout their internment, first in Torgau and then Burg POW camps.

The story of this failed escape was published twice. First as 'An attempt that Failed' initialled 'B' for 'Brocas', written and first published in *Royal Military College Magazine & Record* of Christmas 1924, and later in *Journal of the United Service Institution of India* VOL LVIII NO 252: JUL1928 Pages 501-512 and titled 'An Attempt that Failed – An Incident in the Life of a Prisoner of War in Germany by "KG"' [KG being an abbreviation for 'Kriegsgefangener', the German for Prisoner of War].

By deduction, "F" = Fairweather, "L" = Loder-Symonds. "W" probably = Captain Eric Walker RFC who occupied the bottom bunk below Brocas but could have been Captain Douglas Wise, Royal Fusiliers. "S" almost certainly refers to Sampson who was a close friend of Brocas throughout and shared the same room. "T" probably refers to John 'Talbot' Younger, Royal Field Artillery, who shared a room with Brocas, but could have been Tahourdin, Toogood or Tailyour who were also listed at Mainz. The writer, Brocas, in the both versions only refers to himself as "I" but he initialled the article with a "B" in the Royal Military College publication.

In his letters there are many coded references to how the war was progressing and several obvious hints at escape and the items he required to support an escape attempt. He requests a ping pong set as early as 23 August 1915 (*Letter 59*) and a reference in his parents' list of parcels sent confirm a first ping pong set was sent out on 8 September 1915. A further 24 ping pong balls were sent on 18 March 1916, which suggests that at this point the tunnel was well under way although his parents probably did not know why he required them. The article clarifies why ping pong was an important part of the distraction process. The following is the complete article as originally published, excepting the participants referred to by letters have the most likely names substituted by the editor.

An Attempt that Failed – An Incident in the Life of a Prisoner of War in Germany. "KG"

In early 1916 many of us had begun to despair of ever effecting an escape. By this time the efforts of the neutral embassies in Berlin, to cause a slight improvement in the treatment of prisoners of war, began to take effect on the camp authorities and they decided to extend their area of the camp and include within its bounds a gun shed as a recreation room, which would be open to us by day, though closed after evening rollcall at 5:30.

We had continually explored all buildings and perimeter boundaries for possible weaknesses, without success and were toying with the idea of escaping dressed as German officers. The plan was maturing when the possibilities of the newly opened gun shed and the grandstand revealed themselves. On the outside of the gun shed was a road leading to camp headquarters, then a barbwire fence, and outside that, about 15 feet of wasteland, where a sentry was posted, and finally a cliff. On a visit to the doctor in the town Fairweather had noticed as he returned that this cliff was about 20 feet high and the ground below was used as a chicken farm. In an ancient guidebook to Mainz citadel which we had procured, we read that there used to be a tunnel leading from about this part of the citadel down to the river, which was a few hundred yards away. After a council of war, we decided to dig a tunnel from under the grandstand, at a depth of about 10 feet and aim for the chicken run, hoping to strike the ancient tunnel en route. We were obviously aware that the noise that the arrival of six human beings into the hen-roost by night would create quite a commotion, but decided that the risk was worth taking, especially as there was a good chance of striking the old tunnel. We worked out that under the grandstand they would have room for about 440 cubic feet of earth. As the tunnel would only be about 35 feet long, 3 feet high and 1 foot wide at the top, increasing to 3 feet wide at the bottom, we would have plenty of room to spare.

The tunnel entrance was in the billiard room which was established in part of a former gun-shed when the camp was extended to provide more recreation facilities. The gun-shed was divided into two rooms by a wooden wall. One third was reserved as a silence room and the remainder as the billiard room. There was a bar in one corner at which a trusted German NCO sold extremely pernicious white wine at prohibitive prices. As the billiard tables were dominated by the French and Russians the principal amusement of the younger British officers was a race game called 'They're Off', in which you selected and backed a horse and it advanced by throw of dice over a steeplechase course, being penalised or disqualified for landing on or underneath any of the obstacles. We simulated the race course atmosphere as much as possible with book-makers, tipsters and of course the rowdy crowd. This was to the great amusement of the camp authorities who were only too delighted to see their captives being entertained by this harmless pastime. Eventually, we persuaded the German camp authorities to allow a portion of the billiard saloon to be partitioned off at the end furthest from the bar and reserved exclusively for this game. The partition was three-quarters the height of the shed, and in order to increase the reality of the race atmosphere, the prisoners were permitted to have a wooden grandstand erected against the silence room wall. The grandstand consisted of four wooden steps each about 2 feet high, 18 inches wide and 15 feet long. Festooned with bunting and flags it was an impressive structure. On this we would sit, watch the race, place bets and cheer loudly doing our best to simulate the atmosphere back at Home. On special occasions, such as the Grand National or Gold Cup days there was a great atmosphere and large crowds, as prisoners of all nationalities took part. The excitement was intense, the heat terrific, and noise so tremendous that the silence room was rendered unusable for its intended purpose.

Having formulated our plan, we wasted no time in getting started, but difficulties presented themselves at every turn. To begin with, secrecy was essential. In every camp a large portion of the prisoners had no occupation whatsoever, and so busied themselves with the affairs of others. As a result, it was extremely difficult to carry out without interference, all the minute preparations necessary for an escape. Once the weak spot in the defences was selected, one had to have a very close look at it. If one prisoner surmised what was happening and told another, it was inevitable that the next day everyone in the camp glanced at the spot as he passed it wearing an inevitable conspirator's look. By the evening, the ever-watchful Germans would place a sentry at the point of interest and the possible exit was blocked! Caution and secrecy were the key to success but a task involving several weeks' work made this especially challenging.

To get underneath the grandstand meant making the top of the wooden steps removable. This had to be achieved when no one else was present, and to avoid arising the suspicion of the German barman who happened to be a most alert and suspicious person. From the top of the grandstand this man was just visible as he sat in his bar and sold liquor so we decided that there should always be someone in that position, reading, watching the race game, to accustom the bar man to someone's presence there. We made several attempts to move the step but to no avail and as the barman was disturbed by the least noise and came to see what was happening. Eventually the problem was solved when I received from home the gift of a **ping-pong set.** [Sent 18 March 1916 by parents] *This was set up in the race game room and we began to play during meals when no one else was in the recreation shed. After a day or two the bar man found the game really absorbing, and watched incessantly and became frantically excited when there were long rallies and good strokes. To further keep his attention those not playing bought drinks off him, and everyone made it a rule to make as much noise as possible. Before long, his interest waned and one day during the lunch hour two of them played as noisily as possible, two others cheered lustily from the top of the grandstand while Fairweather and Loder-Symonds succeeded in getting out the long nails from the step, taking it up and substituting short nails. We were then able to lift the top on and off noiselessly and rapidly. As soon as this was done Loder-Symonds, with a bit of shoving was got under the stand to investigate what confronted us. After a few minutes he was extracted without difficulty and our first objective was achieved. It was time for another council of war.*

The investigation showed that the whole floor was of cement and it was impossible to judge how thick it was. The first task was to cut through this but we only had minimal tools, a hammer and various old pairs of scissors. The other main difficulty was to get in and out of the grandstand before anyone else was in the room. This could only be achieved immediately after 9 am rollcall, or during the lunch interval, or immediately before evening rollcall when everyone left the shed and the barman was busy putting away his bottles. Nevertheless, we decided to start work the next day and began by going under the stand one at a time with a relief at midday. To communicate with the diggers, we arranged a series of alarm signals. One loud knock on the grandstand meant make less noise. Two knocks meant, carry on, all clear. Three knocks equalled great danger. Don't move! A continued rubbing on the top board with hand or boot meant, I want to talk to you through the boards.

We drew lots for duties and Loder-Symonds had the honour of going 'down the mine' first and starting the work. He would be relieved at midday by Fairweather. Two of our number constituted the 'noise party' as required. The other two would form the 'Cave' party taking turns to work under the grandstand dealing with the excavated material. That night, after final roll call, by candlelight in their room, we opened a bottle of wine to the success of our enterprise happy in the knowledge that things were at last moving forward. We slept well that night lulled by the wine and the prospect of a 'Great Escape'.

We woke early the next day and everything was in our favour as we rushed to the hall immediately after roll-call, and began a violent ping-pong match. Loder-Symonds was again pushed under the grandstand with difficulty due to his large frame and the relatively small aperture. By the time he got his bearings and was ready to start operations the race-game crowd arrived. The 'noise party', Talbot and myself got into position, one on top of the grandstand and the other stood around trying to look as innocent as possible, talking with the two relief workers. To those expecting it, when Loder-Symonds got to work the clink, clink of the hammer hitting the scissors seemed to echo round the hall, but the gamblers, intent on the progress of their 'horse', did not notice it. The barman, who by now was just setting up for the day, carried on in equally blissful ignorance. After an hour or so I had sudden misgivings about the noise in the adjacent 'silence' room and went to investigate. To my horror it was as though Loder-Symonds was working with no partition between him and the occupying senior officers who were stoically doing their utmost to ignore the noise. Every blow of hammer on scissors seemed to make the whole room vibrate. One reader even enquired what on earth was going on outside. As hastily as possible the order went out! 'One knock!' In order to continue monitoring the noise levels, I remained in the room pretending to read.

There were no further dramas that morning. At lunchtime the 'Gamblers' departed necessitating another rowdy ping-pong match so that Loder-Symonds could be extracted and replaced with Fairweather, complete with another pair of scissors and an improvised pad to deaden the sound of the blows. Loder-Symonds was so filthy from his mornings work that we decided to send some old pyjamas down to Fairweather to use as working overalls. He was extracted and cleaned up in time for evening roll call, where he took precaution to conceal his badly blistered hands. That night, at our council of war we decided, to have someone permanently on duty in the 'Silence' room and to work in overalls all the time. Despite eight hours work, the cement was so hard that that we had made only a slight impression on the concrete, while rendering two pairs of scissors utterly ruined. On the third day when I went in to take my first turn. It took me sometime to even find the site of 16 hours work even though I knew the location of the 'hole' was three feet from the outside wall. German officers made regular untimely visits to the 'race game' resulting in frequent stoppages, and worse still the volume of noise emanating from the room was decreasing as enthusiasm for the game was waning. On several occasions the clink, clink, was noticed by the barman and the work stopped until his attention was distracted elsewhere usually by one of the conspirators buying him a drink. After a week of minimal progress, and increasing despondency our luck changed. A German workman was sent into the camp to effect minor repairs and although he was carefully guarded by an armed soldier, we managed to steal two superb chisels and his hammer. Although the concrete was thicker than anticipated these new tools increased progress but despite the pads, the noise level increased. The players of the race game decreased steadily to such an extent that one morning nobody turned up. Those on the outside, began to tire of trying to make more covering noise than the actual worker under the stand.

One evening while considering how best to proceed I had a brainwave that worked perfectly. Ping pong would again be our salvation. Two of us would play continuously with the aim of making rallies as long as possible and the worker would clink in time with sound of ball on bat. The server would announce "Are you ready? One, two, three!" and then the clinking would proceed in unison with the first blow until someone took his eye off the ball, missed, and a solitary clink reverberated through the hall. It took us a fortnight to get through the five-inch thick concrete, but there-after we worked with renewed vigour to widen the hole so that a man could squeeze himself down and dig. The challenge this presented cannot be overstated, as anyone trying to work in a confined space would bear witness. It was quite dark under the grand stand so we acquired, or rather stole a night sentries' lantern which was not being used during the day. To help the process of transporting excavated material from the hole to the opposite end of the grand stand and stacking it, we sewed bags made from any old discarded clothing we could acquire. For digging we also stole a couple of shovels and a fork, which all needed the handles shortening to allow them to be used in the confined space. After a month of digging we had sunk a ten-foot-deep shaft and made it wide enough to squat at the bottom and dig.

With less noise at the bottom of the shaft we were able to dispense with the man in the 'Silence' room and work with two under the stand at the same time. We would alternate duties as the man digging tired, to be replaced by the crawler and stacker. Whenever possible we relieved the pair with a double change at mid-day although sometimes this was not possible and the unfortunate pair were left down the mine all day. The trickiest, but essential extraction was always in the evening before rollcall and nerves would be on tenterhooks waiting for barman to leave. Sometimes this manoeuvre would be very last minute with barely time to clean up although by acquiring further work clothes and felt slippers which were kept under the stand, we came out fairly clean. Somehow, our luck held but not without the occasional hairy moment. One day the alarm went off in the middle of the mid-day switch but fortunately at the very moment the relieved couple got out and before the other two had got in. As the German officer of the day walked in they were nonchalantly sitting on the board having got it back just in time. On another occasion a particularly fussy general and his staff came to inspect the camp on a pre-arranged visit. We avoided working on inspection days as they usually involved sudden roll-calls. On this occasion, with not a care, we were taking a break from ping pong and were sitting, playing cards on the scene of their operations. He took great interest in the ping pong bats and poked his nose into every corner. To our horror he even noticed the loose board and proceeded to curse all and sundry with customary Teutonic violence for not having it put in order for his visit. The grovelling camp commandant promised the camp carpenter would put it right before being despatched to the front. Fortunately, the matter was quickly forgotten.

There was further drama another day, when I was sitting guard on the top of the grandstand a German civilian arrived carrying a bucket of water and scrubbing material and accompanied by the inevitable armed sentry. He had been instructed to scrub the grandstand, of which task I immediately volunteered to assist, saying I had nothing to do. The sentry, no doubt expecting some form of bribery, declined the help proffered and warned me that the civilian would lose his job and I would be taken to solitary, as speaking to a civilian was "Streng verboton". This conversation so frightened the civilian that he started work as far away as he could from where I was seated. At this point with '3 knocks' I sounded the alarm repeating it at intervals, but unfortunately the civilian had started rubbing the boards which was the signal for conversation. I could hear Loder-Symonds who was on stacking duty below whispering, "Yes, what is it?" I continued

knocking and yelled to Fairweather and his friends in the billiard
room that they were scrubbing the grandstand. This brought a crowd
to watch and the sentry, growing nervous began a loud conversation
with the civilian. At which point Loder-Symonds gathered something
was up, kept quiet and half an hour later the scrubbing operation was
complete but not before both Loder-Symonds and Fairweather were
thoroughly drenched. The water also played havoc with the paper
recently put along the inside of the grandstand to prevent the earth
from leaking out of the cracks. It was a sorry looking muddy pair who
were extracted that evening.

A week later we had progressed some six feet towards our destination
averaging about a foot a day. The digging was getting easier and all was
going well until one day, when I was digging a large slap of the tunnel
roof fell in. It did me no damage but the prospect of being buried alive
did not sit well with us. As we were now under heavily used road into the
camp it was obvious that some supports were needed. Ping pong again
came to our aid. There were several tables in the camp, one of which
belonged to me. We stole a saw and cut it up into six-inch-wide planks. To
get them to the tunnel they had to be carried tied around the waist under
an overcoat. The ruse was never noticed despite the fast approaching
heat of summer which this year was exceptional. Everything was going
so well that attention also turned to the escape and we dared to think
and plan our journey across country to freedom. As always this was as
challenging as the actual escape and many attempts failed prematurely
at the journey stage. Then one day, when Fairweather was working in
the tunnel he crawled back to the shaft and whispered up excitedly to
me, as I was bag man, that the wall in front of him had fallen in and he
thought he had struck the old tunnel leading to the river. He went back
in to investigate further but couldn't work out what exactly was going
on, and so we swapped places. On moving some more stones there was
an entrance about 2 feet 6inches square but with no apparent exit. The
atmosphere was so awful that the lantern went out, and after trying
in vain to strike some matches and re-light it, I crawled in feeling my
way round. I ran my fingers along two stone slabs on either side and on
crawling further bumped my head against a wall at the end which was
also composed of large stone slabs. On digging down in the soft earth I
immediately unearthed a skull! We had struck yet another tomb. Feeling
already nauseous, I thought due to lack of oxygen, in consultation with
Fairweather we decided to strike off at an angle and use the tomb for
storing earth. The mid-day relief could not come soon enough. Loder-
Symonds and Talbot went in having been appraised of the recent turn

of events. It was 5.30 when they too emerged having filled the tomb and made good progress, but they were looking grey and drained, by which time Fairweather and I were also feeling really ill. The atmosphere down the tunnel was bad and had begun to pervade the recreation room as well. The next morning all four of us who had been down were all ill and with the most painful sore throats could hardly speak. We were laid up for three days and in consequence all work ceased.

By the end of six weeks we reckoned we were about halfway to freedom, advancing as much as 3 feet on some days. Continuing at this pace we thought they would be ready in about 10 days which would get us out about mid-June. Most of our escaping kit, including a stolen electric torch, a forbidden fruit in all POW camps, was already safely stored under the grandstand. As time went on we had to admit several other prisoners to our secret because we thought they had guessed it. These proved a great help with noise and distraction. Because of their loyalty it was arranged that they too could, if the escape route went undetected, close the tunnel after the initial escape and re-use it 24 hours later. A week later a bombshell! The bugle went for a spontaneous roll-call at 4pm. The couple on duty in the tunnel were extracted just in time to be cleaned up and got on parade. To their collective horror the interpreter read out that all British Officers were to be on parade at 10.30 a.m. the next morning and ready, with all belongings packed, to leave the camp at 11.

To say we were dumfounded would be putting it mildly. We held a meeting and decided there were only two courses of action; either hand over the tunnel, lock, stock and barrel to either the French or Russians; or go down it ourselves the next morning, be nailed in and dig our way out the final 10 feet, hoping that our estimate of the distance was correct. Views on these strategies differed primarily because of the uncertainty as to the point of exit. After much discussion myself, Walker, Sampson decided to go to the new camp with possibility of escaping en route. Fairweather, Loder-Symonds and Talbot decided to go down the tunnel and dig for freedom. That evening the whole place was a hive of activity with Germans and British rushing about all over the place. We took the opportunity of removing from under the grandstand the kits of the three of us who would take our chances en route, just before our arranging an impromptu concert in the recreation hall to bid our 'remaining' allies farewell. It was late when we finally turned in having packed our most personal possessions and keepsakes that we treasured most.

At 8am the following morning there was an unexpected roll-call and fortunately we were all present having decided to delay the escape until after the escapers had fortified themselves with as much breakfast as possible. As soon as it was over we put Fairweather, Loder-Symonds and Talbot under the grandstand. Unfortunately, they decided not to have the loose board nailed down reasoning that they would benefit from coming up and stretching their legs that night when the room was closed and empty as it could be a day or two before they made the final exit. This decision was to be their undoing.

At 10.30 the fateful rollcall took place and the three escapees were found to be missing. The Germans were furious and there was much yelling, huffing and puffing and marching up and down, counting and recounting. They knew that they had been on parade at 8 am and could not have escaped in the intervening period. However, in the middle of all the confusion the officer and escort arrived to take the British to their unknown destination and for once, without further delay we were duly march off to the station and put on a train for Frankfurt. As soon as we had been marched out, pandemonium broke loose in the camp. All the remaining prisoners were sent to their rooms and a special company of soldiers was borrowed from the town garrison, marched to the camp, and told to search it until the missing officers were found. The sentries around the camp were doubled and teams with dogs began scouring the surrounding area.

The search in the camp lasted fully two hours, and the recreation hall was visited and re-visited but no one suspected the grandstand. Boots hammered up and down and the grandstand rattle as frustration grew. Just as they were thinking they had got away with it, when the hubbub in the hall had died down, a solitary fed up soldier came in mumbling and grousing to himself. Unfortunately, he sat down plumb on top of the loose board, and noticed that it moved, lifted it up and the Mainz tunnel was discovered. Fairweather, surrendered the group almost immediately but the startled soldier started yelling and screaming and threatened to shoot them. The commotion brought officers and men rushing in from all directions and in the unheard-of chaos and shouting, under a battery of revolvers and bayonets, the poor would be escapees were permitted to crawl out. Von Tecklenberg, was in melt down which turned to a frenzy and he threatened to shoot them on the spot when he discovered that not only had they been hiding, but that there was a nearly complete tunnel.

It would be an understatement to say that the use of a room given to the prisoners by the beneficence of the authorities greatly irritated the Commandant, Von Tecklenberg. The three British officers were treated like criminals. Fairweather was deemed to be the ringleader of the attempt, and so for the trouble he caused, he was stripped naked and searched before they were all unceremoniously bundled on to the next train. Two hours later a jeering crowd hustled along the platform at Frankfurt and in the middle of it were some German soldiers escorting Fairweather, Loder-Symonds and Talbot dressed only in the tattered pyjamas they had been digging in. To much cheering by the British they were bundled into a 3rd class carriage to join the rest of the contingent on their train and without further delay, continued their journey in captivity.

We learned later that the Germans had become increasingly suspicious that something was brewing in Mainz. Various articles of theft such as torches, chisels etc, which almost always related to escape, had frequently gone missing. Also, prisoners were sometimes 'missing' when the censor had been looking for them and on one occasion Loder-Symonds and I were only just got out in time for the resultant roll-call. In truth there were other times when we could not help but look plain guilty and it was something of a miracle that the tunnel had not been discovered earlier.

The upshot of this escape episode was that the three escapees each got six days of arrest and a further 14 days solitary confinement in a civilian jail at their destination. They were also then separated and sent to different camps, although Fairweather stayed in Friedberg where he would remain with the main body of prisoners transferred from Mainz. On account of the heightened level of alertness we three fellow conspirators never did manage to escape from the train.

Curiously, when he arrived at Mainz, Brocas says there were four parcels waiting for him, (*Letter 46*) but it is not obvious which or when they were sent, but it is assumed they were sent on by the German authorities at Burg. His undated letter to his sister (*Letter 43*) and to his father of 16 May 1915, states he would be moving at short notice from Burg *'on Thursday'* and this was presumably the first the family knew of the move. His mother recorded that the first parcel was only sent to Mainz on 28 May 1915. He acknowledges (*Letter 47*) dated 30 May 1915, 'tongue' (from by Miss R) which was sent on 11 May 1915 which confirms parcels were taking about three weeks to arrive.

Writing on 8 June 1915 (*Letter 48*) he references his father's letter of 19 May enclosing 'army form' re lost kit, which astonishingly suggests that even as POWs the army were pursuing the men for equipment lost at the time of their capture. Wisely, Brocas decided to delay his response until after any Court of Inquiry Proceedings after the war. The consensus of opinion was that the circumstance surrounding the lost equipment could not be properly explained while cooped up in a German POW camp.

On 23 July 1915 he wrote to his mother (*Letter 55*) '*Fancy there being a chance of my returning for my twenty firster! Wonderful! Even though it is a slight one.*' His twenty first birthday would be 31 October 1915. The rumour never became a reality as the war dragged on. With his second Christmas passed in captivity by 24 January 1916 (*Letter 77*), and 501 days a prisoner, Brocas had received 300 letters and he had kept them all. His friendship with Russian POWs was clearly apparent and his close friendship with Lieutenant Nicolai Miloradovitch is evident from a letter from him dated 8 June 1915 (*Letter 49*). This was the first of several his parents received from the Russian. Even by that early date Brocas was well on with mastering the Russian language and by 24 January 1916 (*Letter 77*) he had moved on to Hindu and Italian as well as continuing with French.

The letters from Mainz ended abruptly with the last undated (*Letter 95*) presumably written early June 1916 because Brocas and all the British officers were moved from Mainz on 15 June 1916 following the failed escape attempt and discovery of the nearly complete tunnel in which Brocas had partaken, although at the time he was not incriminated. The letters from Mainz offered few clues to the escaping attempt he was involved in. Ping pong balls were requested and acknowledged but there is no indication that his parents were aware that they were to be used as part of a ruse to cover up the noise from the tunnelling operation. There is a request for solid methylated spirit (*Letters 87* and *93*) regarded as an essential part of escape kit. Three letters express a degree of annoyance that Tiptree jams had not arrived for some time but it is not certain that his parents were concealing escape items within jams at this time. None were noted in the record of sent parcels. Regarding the clothing items it is almost certain that some of the requested items were required for adaptation to their escaper's outfits. One phrase 11 April 1916 (*Letter 87*), '*Perhaps "try first you don't succeed", answers the question!*' is an oblique reference to an escape attempt in progress.

In an effort to circumvent and deceive the censors the letters indicate the use of basic code words. For example, Brocas refers many times to *'Ellie'* – Russia and *'Govare'* – The French, and the progress or their status as the war was progressing. Generally, he speaks fondly of the plight of the Russians and is more sceptical of the efforts of the French Army, probably because of the perception they had been let down by the French at Mons. *'Cousin Jack'* (*Letter 51*) 22 June 1915, is a reference to Admiral Jellicoe, a distant cousin of Brocas who was in command of the Grand Fleet. The meaning of the phrase *'Fabius seems to have been revoked!'* (*Letter 65*) to which he refers again (*Letter 69*) *'Sorry Fabius stumped you but we were deceived here'* probably refers to the strategy used by Fabius to defeat Hannibal in the second Punic War by using a cautious strategy of *'delay, and avoidance of direct encounter'*. Clearly this was an attempt to deceive the censors.

They left Mainz for Friedberg at very short notice on the morning of 15 June 1916 and embarked on a relatively short rail journey of 35 miles via Frankfurt. Friedberg would be the fifth POW camp for Brocas and many of his fellow British officers who were captured in the first few days of the war.

Parcels from home

His family and friends sent 220 parcels to Brocas, and a further ten to his orderly, Private McGregor during the period of 398 days that Brocas was at Mainz. These included over 700 food items as well as 86 clothing items, 40 necessities, 83 social items, and 49 books (see Appendix I for full details). His mother did not record any hidden escape items in her lists sent to Mainz but it is likely that some things that Brocas specifically requested such as solid methylated spirit, chocolate bars, biscuits etc. were to be part of his 'escapers kit' as were 'Iron rations', but they could be sent openly in normal parcels.

The amount of, and variety of food stuffs sent out increased dramatically during his time at Mainz. He received over 120 different food products in varying quantities of which the most numerous were 39 tins or jars of potted meat, 51 tins of sardines, 47 cakes, and 48 loaves of veda bread. Butter in 1/2lb tins was sent twice weekly, and tinned fruit of all kinds were a significant addition to his diet. Dry non-perishable products such as biscuits, nuts and chocolate, arrived in various forms as did other tins of meat including tongue, brawn,

S.M.B. addressing a parcel to Brocas, 1916.

Stephen Montagu Burrows (Brocas's father) addressing a parcel to Mainz in 1916
Source: Burrows family archive

sausages and even a boar's head. He received 19 dozen eggs in dozen lots, of which only a few were broken, the boxes with false bottoms were later used to conceal newspaper items and other disallowed printed matter and notes.

In addition to her own parcels, his mother also made arrangement for a variety of foodstuffs to be sent in parcels directly by Harrods and others such as Twining, and Tiptree. By the time he left Mainz the considerable number and type of books in Brocas's 'library' is a testimony to his character, intellect and thirst for knowledge. It contained several books on historical conflicts as well as volumes in French, Italian, Russian and Hindustani to further his language skills. Although not devoutly religious, early on, he had received a prayer book and bible. The following is a sample record his mother kept of all the parcels that were sent, and as at Burg, the majority were safely received.

Parcels sent to Lieutenant M Brocas Burrows at Mainz
(Sample list only)
1 December 1915 – 3 January 1916

DECEMBER 1915
TO MAINZ

1st	*Cake, pheasant*
	Acknowledged
2nd	*Plum pudding, chocolate*
	Acknowledged
4th	*1 case Tiptree jam, 1 ham, 1 doz. apples, 1 pkt. quaker oats*
	Acknowledged
5th	*4 twill sheets*
	Acknowledged
	4 grey army blankets
	Acknowledged
	4 twelve mince pies
	Acknowledged
7th	*1 cake, shortbread*
	Acknowledged
9th	*3 doz. apples from George*
	Acknowledged
11th	*1 Hussif (leather folding fitted case) Selfridge*
	Acknowledged
	1 galantine turkey, 1 cocoa essence, 1 petit beurre,
	1 dessert biscuits

15th	*1 cake (Lizzie), 12 apples, 3 tins soup*
	Acknowledged
18th	*2 tins biscuits, 1 bath olivers, 1 3lb jar marmalade*
	Acknowledged
22nd	*1 cake (Lizzie), 2 pots honey*
	Acknowledged
24th	*1 ham and chicken, 1 bacon, 1 biscuits*
	Acknowledged
28th	*Cake (Lizzies), 2lb butter, 1 tin beans*
	1 P & N large tongues, 2 tins sardines, 2 cocoa and milk

JANUARY 1916

1st	*Butter, biscuits, ginger, ham and tongue (potted), herrings and tomato, milk, parsnips*
	Acknowledged
	1 scarf (Agnes), music
	Acknowledged
3rd	*1 box jam (Wilkins)*
	Acknowledged

7

Mainz POW Camp

20 May 1915 – 15 June 1916

The Letters

Letter 45

Note address.

In good health.
Offizier gefangenenlager,
Mainz.

Brocas.

Letter 46

22nd May, 1915, La Citadelle, Mayence

My dearest Father,
*Here we are arrived in our new prison and not sorry to be out of the last one. We left Burg at about 3 p.m. on Wednesday and arrived here about 10.30 am on Thursday, dog tired, which shows what sort of condition one is in. The journey was comparatively uneventful. I received 4 parcels on arrival containing bread, shirts etc. and cigarettes. Many thanks. The bread is a little mouldy outside but otherwise a delightful change. I have received no less than seven letters this week – wonderful. One from the Duchess, one from Mother, 2 from you, one from the American Embassy, one from Miss Canning and a most remarkable one from Aunt Em, which of course I am answering. The photos are most interesting please continue them. So sorry about George but still I am not so sure he is not really most fortunate! Tell him from me that **I hope he will continue his knock later with all success.** [meaning return to the fight in France] So glad the cousins flourish. [Allied armies] Please send my stump cricket things after all. Sorry for the trouble. Re food, please send now only fruits (plenty please), biscuits, jams, butter and cream and some cigarettes again! Heavy food not needed at present! My Russian friends thank*

you immensely for the shirts. Today it is very hot but I am casting no "clouts" yet. Well, good bye, best love to all,
Your affectionate son,

Brocas.

My namesake was here before us, but is now departed.
Please send me my field service pattern hat which should have been in my kit sent home, if not please order from <u>*Cator.*</u>

Letter 47

30th May 1915, [No Address]

A letter and P.C. from you this week. Most welcome also innumerable parcels of which I have lost count as others got them for me, but contents were roughly, forage cap, <u>*much*</u> *bread,* (<u>*please send no more*</u>)*, 2 parcels from Montreux, Switz. (are these from Aunt Em?), tongue (from Miss R.), fruits, sardines, cake and biscuits. So glad to hear George is all right again, but no news of Gareth is serious. I have had no answer. Health good but have not quite got over the change yet, weather glorious though hot. Rooms here are better than at Burg, and on the whole less noise – a great blessing.*
Best love to all,
Your affectionate son,

Brocas.

Letter 48

8th June 1915, Mayence, La Citadelle

My dearest Father,
You must please excuse my scant correspondence of the last few weeks since arrival here, but I have had a slight attack of fever with severe neuralgia, from which however I have now totally recovered. But the result has been total chaos amongst my parcels, of which I am receiving a quantity. As far as I can remember I have received the following – one from Switzerland, one from Paris containing rusks, the camera which was verboten!! Handkerchiefs, bread in tins, rusks, sardines, fruits, a parcel from Kinnersley and Miss Rawnsley, 2 French books, underclothes, cigarettes etc. Many thanks to you all, but henceforward I require as regards food only (?) fruits, chocolate, butter in tins, cream, biscuits (Butter Puffs were very good), jam, cigarettes and tobacco. Please send me

*also music, as we have a piano in our room here and a musician. Old Musical Comedy scores and any of my old songs please, and also some of the modern stuff. Did you ever get my letter asking for current magazines and reviews? You can't imagine what the heat is here? It is immense and at present we are not accustomed to it, hence all work is very hard. Re letters. First from M. of May 9th. So sorry about Wilfred T. and also Gibson. So glad George has recovered and will be on duty at home for a month. Also a letter from you of May 19th, enclosing Army Form re lost kit. About this I have made enquiries and find the consensus of opinion is that it is advisable to wait till return and after Court of Inquiry proceedings. Also the exact circumstances would probably not all get through and I think it will be better to wait. But if there is any special reason why I should not I will keep the paper and await your reply. A card from you of 21st. Never mind puttee-stockings. Also one from M. of same date. One from Duch. of 23rd with good news of George. Did he play at Eton on the 4th? We played the Boating Song here. Is it possible to get E. Ramblers year book for last summer? Or perhaps there wasn't one? A letter from you of 23rd. Poor old regiment! Though I suppose it is the same everywhere. It is the second time Joe Nettlefold has been wounded, poor chap. The bread has arrived good but please don't send any more, biscuits are better and please send me some powders etc. to make lemonade squash and any other drink. An excellent letter from M. of May 27th with news of **Naomi's relations and sick man** * [a reference to Allies or specific country probably Italy and Germans] *and garden. Please send me more as soon as possible. Many thanks for all your kindness about Lt. Chardome. My Belgium friend sends you all sorts of messages and is immensely pleased at the first full news he has got of his friend since his wound. Everything goes on much as usual. My few days in bed have reduced my superfluous flesh to almost normal. The Russian continues so so and I am thinking of starting Italian, as owing to the noise and nervous state one is in here, it is quite impossible to get beyond a certain point in a language and I think it would be very useful to be able to converse in Italian and apparently I shall have time to learn. We are 8 in a room here 4 English and 4 French and can see the Rhine and some houses. They tell me the famous village of Hochheimer is within coo-ee of here but that is all. There are some trees. Well we hang on the valuable thread and try to imagine we are not vegetables.*

We hope it will finish quickly and cleanly. 10 wickets or an innings. I hear an opposing bowler should have been no-balled but is now master and scored off. [Referring to a quick end to war and questionable activity of Germans] *Well good bye and good luck to you all. Your affectionate son,*

Brocas.

Letter 49

8th June 1915, Mainz
To: S. M. Burrows Esq., Norham House, Oxford, England

Dear Mr Burrows,
I find it difficult to thank you for your kindness in sending me the box of paints. To receive such a present from one, who does not know me affects me very deeply especially in my present condition, as a prisoner of war. I must congratulate you on your son. I am quite astonished how quickly he has learned Russian. He speaks very well now. With again many thanks.
Yours very sincerely

Nicolai Miloradovitch (Leutenant)
Abt. 1 Iin 33

Letter 50

15th June 1915, Mainz

My dearest Father,
Quite a number of letters and I will leave them to answer in my fortnightly letter. Please thank Eleanor Butler for hers. It is so kind of her to write. We were all moved here from Burg and were joined here by some new Russians from another camp. An English officer came in who was made prisoner in December and says his people have no news of him yet. Still a chance for Gareth. Please tell his mother he was at Lille. I am well and am slowly acclimatising. Looking forward to arrival of Stump cricket.
Best love,
Your affectionate son,

Brocas.

Letter 51

22nd June 1915, Mainz

My dearest Father,
Too many letters this week to answer them all separately, so I will just reply to the general news. You can't think how welcome they all are and how I look forward to the distributions. Please thank Molly for an excellent letter. She seems wonderfully well, as indeed you all do from your letters. We all came here together

*from Burg and have been joined since by several others of all nationalities who have cheered us up considerably. Everything looks so much blacker than it is from a cage and even gold looks tarnished!! The event of the week was the arrival of Duchess's photo. I like it – nothing exceptional but pleasing and I think you will remember that this is about as far as I ever commit myself in such affairs! Everyone here says they could have picked her out as my sister among any crowd. "Quelle resemblance", and other less intelligible remarks. Whether as banalities or not I do not know!! So sorry to hear about Lord Jersey. Also that you still have no news of Gareth. I suppose his mother has tried to get news through Geneva Red Cross. An officer here who was 5 months at Lille says they can get anywhere and if they cannot find him – there is but little hope. This however strictly between ourselves. There is of course still hope and after my experiences I can quite imagine the possibility of her getting no news! Is it known how or where he was wounded? I have no answers from Liège. Please send Mrs Fletcher my respects and tell her how deeply I feel for her. **What a pity the sick man is dying so slowly, though I suppose it is better so.** [Sick man almost certainly refers to Germans] Duchess's letters are most interesting and I hope she had a good leave, and is keeping smiling. So glad George got my P.C. and is answering it. News of **Cousin Jack** [Admiral Jellicoe] most gratifying and also of **Naomi's relations** [probably a reference to Allies or a specific* country, Italy who declared war on Austria-Hungary 23 May 1915]. *Most important, no doubt. So glad **Ellie's people** [Russians] are really all right. I heard they had a bad collapse and were not likely to recover. Of course, I did not believe it, but such things may happen in time of war. I will of course remember Aunt Em's birthday and write her a special letter. **What chance is there of celebrating my twenty firster "chez vous"?** [reference to the war ending* by 31 October 1915, Brocas's twenty first birthday] *Please tell me plainly. Do you remember the preparations we used to talk about! You say you like to hear all about us here. Well there is but little of interest. Pro. tem. I have given up exercise as, though <u>very well</u>, I am still a bit weak and can work better without. We rise about 8 a.m. dress and breakfast and then have an appel at 9. At 10 I start work. Russian till 12 then lunch and work 1-3 with another Russian and then walk 3-4 with a 3rd. Then tea and appel at 5. After appel an hour's French. Supper at 7 or 8 and then a walk till 9.15 and so in and to bed. Lights out 10.15. So I keep rolling and time passes somehow. The languages learnt here are marvellous and include to my knowledge Russian, French, Italian, Spanish, English, Breton, Gaelic and Esperanto. Shorthand and telegraphy are also practised and so what with reading the occasional French reports in the German papers we are fully occupied. Today my breeches arrived from Hawkes and also cigarettes. I have not entirely given up smoking, though I shall at the end of this. Here it helps to pass the time. Fruit also arrived and also lemonade. Bread not necessary but biscuits always welcome. So glad Aunt Io, and Bernard flourish and also Mrs.*

Weir. **Do you remember where when still very young I lodged the custard on father's head?** [coded reference to a place – no details] *I expect they are pretty busy there now? Leech [CJF] and Wise both flourish. The other English in my room are a Captain Younger, R.F.A., Lt. Sampson, Royal Fusiliers and Lt Pelham-Burn, Gordons and also 4 French. We no longer sleep alternately.*

Well must end. Good luck to you and may we all meet again soon,
Your affectionate son,

Brocas.

Please send me some rolls of fly-papers also 4 proper regimental badges (collar).

Letter 52

30th June 1915, Mainz

My dearest Father,
Since my last letter from Mother of June 16th and cutting re 4th June. So glad George got runs. Also card of June 18th. Letter from you of 20th and from Duchess of 16th. So glad to get them all. So sorry to hear Wynwood and Blackburne are wounded. Please tell me all casualties. The cricket things have arrived, many thanks. Please send more balls. Fruit is also coming well. No more bread required. Please send me some Gramophone records. Gramophone Co. Type-Modern ones. Only 15 lines allowed!
Best love,

Brocas.

All well!

Letter 53

9th July 1915, Mainz

My dearest Mother,
Excellent letters from you of 23rd and 27th June, also from F. of 25th, Duchess of 27th and Jack, Aunt W. and Bernard. To answer various questions. Tell Duchess I think the young gentleman of Eton would in all probability be "severely dealt with" if he wrote on "Pop" paper without belonging to that great society. The

other three Englishmen with me here are Capt. Younger R.F.A.; Lt F.A. Sampson, Royal fusiliers and Lt H.P. Burn, Gordon Highlanders. So glad you got the P.C. from my Russian friend. The Italian books and music, as also the Eton and University lists arrived today and are at present in the hands of the censor but are doubtless exactly suitable. Many thanks as also for shirts, handkerchiefs and biscuits and also cake, cream and fruit. All most excellent. **Surely it is pathetic for the sick man to linger on so long? Is anything known about his will?** [a reference to how the Germans were progressing in the war] *Jack's letter was of April 29th. Please thank him duly. So glad Bernard liked the soldiers. I hope they will persuade him to the right profession. Please thank Aunt W. for her letter. I hope Duchess's play comes off and she plays her part to perfection. The post cards of George are excellent, but had I been allowed to keep my haversack I'd have backed it against his coat.!! The Stump Cricket is a great success and we play here every Wednesday and Saturday at 1.30 and though the space is very limited we get lots of exercise. The reason we selected these days is because they are the bath days. Please send me some more balls if possible. Please ask Meyer and Mortimer, a well-known hosier in London, whose address I forget, to send me patterns of shirts, khaki and civil, underwear etc. and also please send me a Burberry's catalogue. Also please a "firm" pair of sock suspenders, not to go round the calf but to attach to the vest! Also some piccalillies, chutney and sauces. Sweets etc. always desired. Tobacco is for me, some arrived today and suits exactly, also cigarettes though I prefer Navrati No.3 to No. 2. Please also send me another pair of "slacks" (trousers) as I have nearly sat through these! Weren't there a pair in my box at Aldershot? So glad to hear Wynwood and Blackburne were in Despatches. Please let me know all about them and others. Please send me an occasional military history book.*

Have you still no news of Gareth? A <u>list of "missing officers"</u> arrived here lately and Gerry Freeman Thomas was on it. But surely he has been found? No news from here – all as usual. We are all tired of being prisoners of war!! By the way what about my money at Cox's? Is it best to leave it there or what can be done? I hear I should write a chit to you so that you can inspect my account. Please let me know exactly how it stands. The Woodbine cigarettes are much appreciated by the orderlies. Jack appears to have done pretty well with his car in Australia. I can quite imagine how bored he is.

Can you possibly gather any information on the standard required for an interpretership in Russian, French or German? If it is difficult, never mind, as it is only for a matter of interest. It is very hard to work in this hot weather and under these circumstances but one simply must, to kill time, which though a poor is a very strong incentive. I am very well now and feel I should be playing cricket better this year!! Well, I must close.

Best love to you all and apologies for a dreadfully disconnected and rambling letter,
Your affectionate son,

Brocas.

Messrs. Cox & Co.
16 Charing Cross, S.W.

Please permit my father, S. M. Burrows, Norham House, Oxford to inspect my account.
Brocas Burrows, 2Lt. 5th Dragoon Guards.

Letter 54

16th July 1915, Mainz

Dear Father,
3 letters since my last, yours of 30th, M. of 4th and D. of 4th. Also, one from Miss Owen – how kind of her – please thank her for both letter and list. The photos of the car and chauffeur (!) taking lady for joy ride are excellent!! You say you have sent magazines. <u>None have ever arrived.</u> Cakes, biscuits, fruit, cream and butter have arrived – very good. Also music and Italian books. Hope George gets his staff appointment. Health good – weather coldish and rainy. We exist and hope. Please send me my old score of Princess Clementine. Good bye.
Your affectionate son,

Brocas.

Letter 55

23rd July 1915, Mainz

My dearest Mother,
3 letters since I last wrote, 1 from you of 11th, Duchess of July 11th and Father of July 14th. An excellent account of your health, Mother, from Duchess caused me great joy. Gaining weight too! Or is this only jealousy on Duchess's part? So glad about George, my congratulations to him and tell him to write to me please! The officer who came here from Lille is Lt. Dennys, of the Somerset L.I. [He was on first prisoner exchange and first train to Switzerland 29 May 1916 along with Captain Henderson]. *Nothing*

known of Anstruther here. My respects to O'Rorke if you see him which I hope you will do. So glad he got home. Father's letter of July 14th was full of news and was only a week on the way. Fancy there being a chance of my returning for my twenty firster! Wonderful! Even though it is a slight one. Can make nothing of J.S.B.'s movements. But never mind if he has finished out there, so much the better. Good luck to him elsewhere. **News of Ellie's people most reassuring.** [a reference to Russians] *I heard a very different account from another source. I shall think of you all at Yewhurst in August and wish myself with you.*

For goodness sake don't worry about my health here. I am coming through this if only to get some of my own back. This I should think could be explained by O'Rorke. It is difficult however to strike a happy medium as too much exercise means I don't feel inclined to work and too little means I work but get unfit. I suppose however I shall learn by practice. I had the honour last Monday of being chosen to represent the officers here at the funeral of a French officer of the Dragoons, who died in captivity. The saddest of all deaths! You can't think how strange it feels to get outside the bars again, even only for an hour! And also to wear belt and spurs again.! I had to borrow them as mine were taken from me. Another parcel of music arrived here recently but that is all this week. Will you please send me some packets of Whiteley's Vanilla chocolate in slabs and also from time to time some gramophone records as we have invested in a gramophone between us. A selection of decent songs and waltzes. And please keep the bill for me, as this is of course entirely my affair. The music you sent is a great success and much appreciated by the select and international audiences who attend our séances. Lately I have found it very hard to work here but it has not been hot yet. The dog-days perhaps. I am sticking hard at Russian and French at present till the end of this month and shall then decide what changes to make. If we are here in the winter I shall learn a bit of Hindustani, as it is bound to come in useful.

So glad to hear the good news of my regiment especially about Blackburne. Please always keep me informed. I wrote a cheque on Cox & Co. today for £10 and have since remembered you have invested my money there, but I suppose it will be alright. I don't think I have answered your query re-my teeth. They were dealt with forcibly by a Mr. Bünger at Burg who lived up to his name and I have decided to put off any further offensive movements till my return home, if possible. Many thanks to Duchess for the photo, she seems to be having a strenuous time at school. So glad she played tennis at Fulham. Have you come to any decisions as to what she is to do re-school after the summer? Cigarettes and Baccy just arrived – many thanks. Well I must close, of news there is none I fear and this letter is even duller than most. Goodbye.

Your affectionate son,

Brocas.

Please send me no more handkerchiefs, underclothes, socks till I write.

Letter 56

30th July 1915, Mainz

My dearest Father,
3 letters since my last one from Mother of the 18th, Duchess of the 18th, you of 21st. So glad to get all the news. Hat arrived today. So glad you are in correspondence with Perry. He knows. **News of Ellie's people good.** *[a reference to Russians] Had heard very different. Please keep me informed. Gramophone a great joy. A Lt. Noel in K.O.Y.L.I. was at Torgau – know of no other. So glad to hear such good news of Duchess. So glad she studies languages. So glad to hear you have been cricketing again. Finding it difficult to work just now. We were told officially that G. officers in England are now treated better!*
Best love to all,

Brocas.

Letter 57

9th August 1915, Mainz

My dearest Mother,
Since my last I have got excellent letters from Queenie Brocklehurst – to whom many thanks for her news about your health and Father's, always most welcome from an outside source. Also from Mr Radcliffe to whom many thanks. Father's letter of 24th most welcome. Parcels arrived mostly intact, though some biscuit boxes have been rifled and many cigarettes have not turned up. Balls arrived this week, many thanks for them as also for butter, fruit and cream, which is now coming regularly. A book arrived yesterday, but it is still in the hands of the Censors. Please send me no more Eton or University lists as it is no good. The last three have been confiscated. Anxious as I am about the fate of so many friends, I must however wait in patience. There are seven orderlies here but they are getting things from home alright and arrangements have been made for them by officers here. Nevertheless, cigarettes and biscuits

are always welcomed by them. How appallingly sad about Gerry F.T. [kia 14 September 1914] *I had thought him safe. So glad to get Duchess's letter of July 21st. How pleased she must be to get home after her strenuous term. I suppose you are now all together at Yewhurst. Mothers letter of July 27 arrived yesterday. It is quite awful to look back on this time last year and how we shall pass our respective days of fighting and captivity of a year back, I don't know. The books father has sent are just what I want. Many thanks. One can't spend all one's time learning languages and I shall stop for a bit and read them. So glad to hear Mrs R. is quite wrong, but that doesn't help **Ellie** and Co.* [the Russians] *much does it? They tell me O'Rorke has been holding forth, is it impossible to stop him? He was severely spoken to about this before. It is most annoying. George certainly is most fortunate. The Eton Chronicle was most interesting. So glad they beat Winchester.*

The days are beginning to get noticeably shorter here, which shows summer is passing. I should have got enough clothes to go through the winter, so please send me no more as they are a nuisance if we have to move. Everything here is as usual which you are perhaps tired of hearing, and we are all very thankful that so far we have had cool weather. My personal health is excellent, no more neuralgia but spots still bad which is a nuisance. Lemonade has been arriving and works excellently. I hope to be able to send you a small photo of self in a few days as I am allowed the use of the Ticka to take pictures of friends with, but my knowledge of photography is so small, I fear a good many failures will result. Please however send me some more films. The 14th was the day you spent with me at Aldershot last year at the Queens. Do you remember? Ask Duchess if she still remembers the Flying Corps detachment! Thank God the year has gone quickly but even so it seems an eternity since I was free! What is Duchess going to do next term? Back to Miss S.s or this place at Malvern? Fancy her being 18 in December! Recently I have taken to getting up early in the mornings and going for a walk – at about seven, grossly energetic! What with this and cricket I get enough exercise to keep me from becoming a vegetable and that is all I want at present. I feel this letter is even duller than most and duly apologise. Send me any little snapshots you take.
Goodbye and best love,
Your affectionate son,

Brocas.

Letter 58

16th August 1915, [No address]

My dearest Father,
A letter from you of August 1, M. of August 4th and Eleanor Butler of August
2nd. Many thanks to you all. So glad the trip to Yewhurst was a success
and that M. saw O'Rorke. Many parcels have arrived this week including
"slacks", fruit, cream, butter, books, Swiss parcel, socks, cigarettes and tobacco.
Many thanks. Also gramophone records – excellent. It is a great joy. This day
last year we arrived in France!! I thought of you all a great deal on the 14th
our day at Aldershot. I fear I knew more than I pretended to about my going,
but it was for the best. May we meet before the next anniversary.
Your affectionate son,

Brocas.

Letter 59

23rd August 1915, Mainz

My dear Duchess,
Four letters from home since my last card. One from Cousin Leonard. Many
thanks to him and it may tickle His Grace's sense of humour to know that
the local Censor wrote "besser schreiben" on it! Yours of August 7th, Mother's
of 12th and Father's of 9th have also turned up. Many thanks. I'm dreadfully
sorry about Douglas Radcliffe. Please express to them my deepest sympathy
for their loss. But one must be prepared for such things nowadays. So glad to
hear of King Albert's nomination to be C.in C of the regiment. Georges news
*seems wonderfully good. Some people seem to have all the luck! So glad **Ellie***
[Russia] is better. I hope she will soon be entirely out of danger. Please keep
me informed, as I had no other news about her. It is certainly time J.S.B. had
a little fun and I wish him luck. are Hedley and Righton both soldiers? If so,
what in? Several parcels this week including the Stump bat, sauces etc. butter,
lemonade and fruit. All very excellent. The gramophone records you sent are
excellent and George Grosmith's song very amusing. So glad you are enjoying
Yewhurst. I only hope you are having better weather than here. We have so far,
except for a few weeks in June, had cold and wet weather and have escaped
the hot summer we feared. As regards the winter which it seems probable that
we shall pass here, I need no clothes at all, except two pairs of pyjamas – very
thin please and a pair of Newmarket boots for the winter wet. Maxwell the
well-known bootmaker in town whose address I forget, has my measurements.
Please tell him to make them on the small side. Please also send me in future

occasional tongues, potted meat and jams as before. The histories you sent are *excellent. Please repeat from time to time. News from here is rare – almost* *non-existent. I am well and have started to do gym again every morning* *at 7 o'clock, and a cold shower afterwards. With this and the cricket I keep* *comparatively fit; time passes quickly and I am always busy. Two roll calls a* *day occupy a good deal of time.* **I hear Naomi's father has been very** **successful.** [this probably refers indirectly to an offensive by Italy] *This* *day last year (22nd) was my first day under fire and really does not seem long* *ago. It is really rather amusing to remember one's sensations and how little I* *thought I should be where I am now!! Let's hope for better luck on the next* *anniversary! I'm writing my next letter to* **Aunt Em,** *so you will only get a* *card. I hope she is well and not suffering from nerves, as regards to getting her* *last few runs!!* [a reference to her approaching 100th birthday]
Please send me a **ping-pong set** [used to mask the sound of tunnel excavations] *as we can play here when we are snow-bound.* **I hope Cousin** **J.J. is going strong.** [the Commonwealth allied forces] *Well I must end* *an even duller letter than usual. Your letters are always most welcome and you* *do not write too much.*
Best love to all,
Your affectionate son,

Brocas.

Letter 60

My dearest Father,
Letters this week – M.'s of 18th, D. of 15th, F. of 15th, M of 19th (card) and D. *of 21st. Quite a tapaul. So glad to get them all. You can't think what pleasure* *they give. I can get clothes washed. MacPherson was here and had tea with* *us. Many thanks for photos. Please send some of yourselves and Duchess. All* *well here as usual.*
(Deletion by Censor).
Please send me works of Byron, Browning and Tennyson. Weather changeable. *Next letter goes to Aunt Em. I shall think of you all there. Please send food* *and cigars for October 31!!*
Best love to all,
Your affectionate son,

Brocas.

Letter 61

9th September 1915, [No address]

My dearest Mother,
No space to answer letters separately as mine goes to Aunt Em. But the usual
tapaul has arrived – may it never decrease. Your news has cheered us up
greatly, so it takes a lot to make the old "gaol-birds" downhearted nowadays!
We are all very glad that a time of sad memories is over and hope
to spend its next anniversary more gaily. [looking forward to the
war being over within a year] *Cricket balls, tobac, and butter arrived. My*
congratulations to George R. Poor Dick. A roommate is learning the violin.
This we hope is not catching or incipient madness. We are all merry and bright.
So glad you had good times at Yewhurst and Kinnersley.
Goodbye,
Your affectionate son,

Brocas.

Letter 62

9th September 1915, Mainz
To: Miss Gardiner on her 100th birthday

My dear Aunt Em,
Though the fortune of war prevents me from personally offering you my
congratulations on your hundredth birthday, I am sure you will know that they
are none the less sincere, though inadequately expressed on paper. May you
survive it to see many more birthdays, and long enjoy health and happiness.
I shall be thinking of you much on the 30th and wishing myself with you. I
often hear of you from Father and Mother in their letters, and they say they
hope to be with you for your birthday, so I should be able to think of you all
together. I am afraid that news from here is scarce, as of course our existence
is somewhat monotonous, but we are kept cheerful by our excellent news from
home, and we have now been prisoners so long that it takes a great deal to alter
our mode of life. Personally I am in excellent health, I manage to get enough
exercise somehow, and pass the time in working at languages which I hope
will be useful to me afterwards. Needless to say, our one thought is how soon
this dreadful war will be over, and how soon we shall get home again, and it is
at times very difficult to wait inactive while everyone else is doing so much. I
have learnt the truth of the proverb that "Patience is a virtue". A good lesson,
no doubt. I very nearly paid you a visit that day I left England last August,

as we spent several hours at Southampton, but I did not quite dare to, as our plans were very uncertain, and we did not know when we were going to leave.

My kind regards to Miss Canning, who I hope enjoys the best of health; and with again my congratulations and best wishes to you,
Believe me,
Your affectionate great nephew,

Brocas Burrows.

Letter 63

16th September 1915, [No address]

My dearest Father,
Many thanks for yours of 6th, D.'s 4th and M.'s of 9th. Also Exam. papers, Eton and Balliol lists, music and Lizzie's cake. All received and welcome. I knew Barker slightly at Torgau. So glad he is home. Please ask Cox if all my allowances have been paid in up-to-date. Please send me (1) Tobacco, 2lbs. called "Quiet Moments" from the Army and Navy stores and ask them *to send it straight from bond. Please let me know price, as it is for a Russian Colonel here. (2) razor blades (safety), several packets and also let me know the price. (3) a ham! (4) Some plays for a few characters and (5) a box of good cigars for the 31st! Please continue Oman series. Exam. papers most alarming! Still working at Russian – some language. Very well. Best love.*
Your affectionate son,

Brocas

Letter 64

24th September 1915, Mainz

My dearest Mother,
Only one letter from you since my last – Duchess's of September 11th, but I hope this is due to the irregularities of the post and not to any diminution of your letters to me.
(Deletion by Censor).
Re-parcels, I receive butter regularly and have received fruit, gramophone records, a cake (Lizzie) and also one from Harrod's and chocolate biscuits, chocolate and tobacco etc. Many thanks for all. As you will see the chocolate biscuits rolled up alright. I fear my cheques on Barclay have been a nuisance

but I had only their cheque-book. I will use it no more. So glad to hear Dick R. is well, though I don't expect he is very happy. Our existence here has been saddened by the death of Capt. Stiven, Royal Scots Fusiliers. He was wounded at Mons but entirely recovered, got ill at Burg and after so long in captivity hadn't the strength to pull round. Only Col. Jackson and two other British officers were allowed to attend his funeral, and a Russian, a French and a Belgian went. It is dreadfully sad – after a whole year. Otherwise all here is as usual. We have substituted hockey – played with a kind of walking stick on sandy gravel – for cricket and had our first game yesterday. Much exercise and dust. It has been quite cold here recently though warmer today. Miss Rice Wiggin very kindly wrote to me. Please thank her for her most welcome news, and tell her her letter escaped the fate of the Bishop's. I shall be wishing you all the best of luck on the 30th and hope you have decent weather for the great event, and that the old lady is in her best form. You seem to be making excellent use of the little car and it must certainly be a great joy for you all. What is the old Renault doing? Longing to hear what happens to J.S.B. You say Hedley was the first to inform you I was missing – what date was that? So glad he and Righton are both going on strong. What is Alex's new job. I hope he is as lucky as George. Will you please send me a translation of Pickwick in Russian if it is obtainable. Otherwise my wants this week are zero. Health is excellent as usual but I have contracted a slight cold, which is already passing off.

Duchess is of course back at school again by now and I suppose you will be mostly at Oxford this 'term' – if such a thing still exists. How many men are up? Excuse a very dull letter. We are all cheerful and more confident than ever which says a lot.

Best love,

Your affectionate son,

Brocas.

Letter 65

30th September 1915, [no address]

My dearest Father,

Received yours of 13th and 20th, M. 15th and 22, D. 18th and one from Aunt Em. Many thanks. Aunt Em is wonderful. I feel the books have caused trouble, but will be excellent. How sad about Mon. Duch mentions tennis at home, where does this take place? So glad you had an extra week of her. **So glad Ellie is better, we were sure she would recover.** [Ellie being the

Russian army] *Have got ping-pong also fruit, cakes, butter etc. for which many thanks. Please send me a ham and 8 big and 8 small 5 D.G. buttons. I shall be thinking of you much tomorrow (30th). Weather here cold and rainy – health and spirits excellent.* **Fabius seems to have been revoked!** [a reference to Fabius who defeated Hannibal in the second Punic War by a cautious strategy of delay and avoidance of direct encounter] **Capt. Stott 5 D.G. aviator** [Brocas's best man] *was here recently for a short time but went on to another camp.*
Best love to you all,
Your affectionate son,

Brocas

Letter 66

9th October 1915, Mainz

My dearest Mother,
Your letter of the 28th just arrived and most welcome. I do hope the weather held out for the Moss Leigh celebrations. So glad my letter arrived in time. I have no doubt Mr. Gibbon was in good form and I am very pleased it cheered you all up. Fancy you having a river picnic on September 27th. The weather here was very different; so much so that I got a cold and passed a couple of days in bed. However, I am now completely recovered and in excellent health and spirits. Many thanks to Duch for her letter of the 25th, also the photos. Uncle Edward B. looks in great form and I was so glad to get a photo of Kinnersley. How excellent about Tom. He must have done very well. The photo of you two and Gladys Mayne is also excellent. Father especially looks very spry! Alas! My first lot of Ticka films were a failure but I am trying again and hope for better luck. The weather is not favourable at present. Many thanks to Eleanor Butler and Miss Owen for their kindness in writing to me, which I immensely appreciate. So glad Miss O's school still flourishes. Miss B. also seems very busy. Chaos reigns in my room here, as one of my friends has received a jigsaw puzzle of no less than 800 pieces and a difficult one at that! It was sent him from a "puzzle club"!! **The ping-pong which has arrived is a great success and will no doubt pass much time agreeably.** [reference to the ping pong being used to mask the tunnelling operation] *Other parcels arrived including biscuits, butter and butter puffs, cigarette, cakes, two parcels of books and music. Many thanks. So glad you have sent off Scotch buns – I know them of old and they are excellent. Pyjamas also arrived. Re-orderlies, you would be doing a great kindness if you would send off occasional parcels to private MacGregor, Kings Own Royal Lancaster Regiment. He has been my servant all the time, Zossen,*

Torgau, Burg, and here. Cigarettes and biscuits are what he most requires and of course any extras are always most welcome. So glad the books have arrived and I shall get down to them as soon as the Censor has finished with them. One needs some other form of literary recreation (!) Besides languages. These progress though I am only studying Russian and French just now, and have not started Italian yet. Better to learn two very decently than to fiddle with several, I think. What is Duchess going to do about school? When does she close down? Or is this not yet decided? The Belgian officer here – Lt. Houssa – to whose friend you so kindly wrote, came and told me yesterday that he had had a letter from his friend full of thanks to you and saying how much he appreciated your kindness in writing to him. I fear he has got to undergo another operation before he will be alright again, how serious I do not know. Well news fails me, so I must end. All are well here and very confident and cheerful. Hope you are likewise. Best love. Your affectionate son,

Brocas.

Father's delightful letter of September 30th just arrived. So glad all went off so well. What a kind thought to write actually on the day. I hope Barker is now better. I did not know him well, but we ate sausage together for some time!! Hope you enjoy your time up north.
M.B.B

Letter 67

19th October 1915, Mainz

My dearest Mother,
Have received Duchess's of October 5th yours of 3rd and Father's of 5th. Many thanks. So sorry about Righton also letters from George Rawstorne, to whom heartiest congratulations and thanks. Ruth Radcliffe, George C. and Jack S.B. please thank all for me and tell G.C. his arrived intact and was much appreciated, Jack's was less fortunate. I will write Molly a card. Parcels received include tongue, sausages, cigarettes, boots (excellent), butter and a book from Mrs Huntingford to whom many thanks. All much as usual here. Please send me out 12 more big and 12 little buttons (regimental) as we have been stopped wearing leather buttons here!!! Hope you enjoy Harrogate. Best love and thanks to all Your affectionate son,

Brocas.

Merry and bright!

Letter 68

23rd October 1915, Mainz

My dearest Mother,
I should have liked to have written to you actually on 31st, but owing to the
vagaries of the post, this must be your birthday letter, I think it will be better to
keep to this, the official day of writing, and send you all the best possible wishes
for the 15th and hope that as fate has separated us for two of your birthdays
successively, it will be more kind to us for the third. Your letter of 10th has just
arrived from Harrogate. All I remember about our stay there was that we
disliked it and thought the place too fashionable! No doubt our opinion would
be very different now. I remember however that the air was excellent and I
hope it will do you all the good in the world. I remember there were some very
good gardens there and a band that emitted sounds musical and otherwise.
Poor George. I hope he enjoys his pewter. I am indeed sorry for the Bishop and
Cousin Anna and Molly. I am writing a card to them. Duchess's of the 10th
has also arrived. Many thanks to her, but tell her from me not to learn too
much "Xtian Year" and too little "Harry Graham"!! I hope she is studying
French as much as possible. Father's birthday letter of 12th has also arrived.
Many thanks. I much appreciate the kind thoughts. This week I received so
few letters there must have been some blockage somewhere, as nearly everyone
was in the same condition, and ordinarily they come through quite regularly,
and you can't think what a difference they make, even to 'old stagers' like us.
I have just been looking up my old letters and see that I got my first news from
you on November 1st last year. We have no news here of either Rawson, Gethen
or Blake. Rawson was my fag at Eton. I hope he is alright. Many thanks to
Messrs. Radcliffe Gibbon and MacMillan for their kind thoughts and to the
latter, in anticipation for the books. Aunt Katie has with her usual exactitude
remembered my birthday. Many thanks to her for her kind thought and my
best love to all at K.M. She also announces the sending off of a Kinnersley
cake. I know these of old and am much looking forward to it, as also to Lizzie's
which are always devoured voraciously. The highest compliment we can pay
to them. A copy of Tennyson arrived during the week which I see was a gift to
you from Aunt Dolly and will treasure accordingly. Also cigarettes for orderlies
whose thanks are quite over-powering. I think one of them is going to write
and thank you himself. So glad you have sent off some old classics for me to
read. I am trying as much as possible to complete my education in this line
and make up for wasted time. A long job! I am at present doing a course of
Kipling. No news about my 2nd roll of films yet, but I hope they will come out
all right. I obeyed all the rules very strictly. Your news re all relations is always
most welcome and certainly so far we have been lucky. How is Sid getting on,
is she still at the flat? My respects to her and Uncle Will. All here is much as

usual. "No change". We play our hockey twice a week and do Gym at 7 every morning, followed by a cold bath (shower). Hence our exercise is assured. I have just bought a little writing table of my own and so I have at last got a spot where I can be as untidy as I like without annoying the others. We remembered Nelson in due form last night and another anniversary enabled us to follow the example of Aunt Em, or was it Aunt Bee, many years ago. I believe they are going to put all the English in rooms together here. We have all got so used to living mixed up that we protested against the change, but all to no purpose! I often think of the experiences of "Brown, Jones and Robertson", and the author certainly drew a remarkably clever picture. It is quite dreadful to think what a lot I shall have to tell you on return, and I fear I shall forget a lot of things, as I have never kept a diary. Some of the remarks coming under the heading of "English as she is spoken" are certainly mirth inspiring! Well, I must close this rigmarole, by again wishing you all luck and happiness and health, till I come home and repeat these wishes verbally. Best love to you all. Your affectionate son,

Brocas.

Letter 69

30th October 1915, Mainz

My dearest Father,
Received letters from you, Duch, Sid, George, Miss Canning and Miss Owen. My best thanks to all. I will answer them more in detail in my next letter. We have now been put in rooms by nationalities and I am with Capt. Le Hunte (Hampshire's), Capt. Peskett (Lincoln's), Capt. Usher (Gordon H.), and Lt. Fairweather (Cheshire's), Lt. Walker (R.F.C.), and as before Younger and Sampson. More noise than before. **(2 lines deleted by Censor).** *All well and best of spirits. Georges letter intact and much appreciated.* ***Sorry Fabius stumped you but we were deceived here.*** [a reference to conflicting reports of the progress of the war] *My best love to you all, and thanks for your good wishes.*
Your affectionate son,

Brocas.

Letter 70

11th November 1915, Mainz

My dearest Father,
Such a glorious crowd of letters and parcels since my last that it is difficult to know where to begin to answer! I got your letters of the 20th and 27th, Duchess of 17th and 24th, and Mothers of 23rd and 31st. All most welcome and arrived exactly at the right time. Also letters from Miss Canning, and Aunt W, Miss Rawnsley. Miss Owen and school, and Sydney, not to mention George and all the ladies of the late Gstaad party. I have sent a card to these latter and to George but would you please thank the others for me. Another wonderful letter from Aunt Em. has just arrived for which many thanks. To answer some of your news; so glad you are continuing Oman but please don't send Pitt. He can keep but Russian can't! Of course he must be read again on return. Wise seems in excellent health, also Le Hunte who sends his respects to the Fitzgeralds. He and I are in the same room and have much in common as we have learned Russian all along. No sign of Alistair McDonald. Captain Loder-Symonds is well and cheerful. I hope Duch floored her examiners with success on the 6th. Tell her to keep the paper if possible for me to look at. Has she read any of Ian Hay's books, if not give her the set of five for her birthday from me and let me know the price. My late servant <u>*MacGregor*</u> *has been sent away to Darmstadt. Very annoying as he looked after me ever since I was completely hors be combat at Compiegne, and heaven knows what I should have done without him. If you address his parcels to Private MacGregor, the Kings Own Regiment, Engländer Kriegsgefangener, Darmstadt, Germany C/o G.P.O. etc. (!) it should reach. He did me very well. The Chronicle you sent me arrived yesterday, but the obituary to Gareth has been cut out!* **(Deletion by Censor)** *Do send me some more occasionally.* **(Deletion by Censor).** *I have received in parcels, Lizzie's cake magnificent, also a cake from Kinnersley, the nuts and pheasant, the ham – excellent, please repeat at intervals, apples, also very good. Books including one from Mr MacMillan, chocolate, tongues etc., tobacco. Letters come quick but unfortunately parcels come slow. Please send me 2 pairs of gloves, one shammy and one brown – unlined for smart wear! Also some Quaker Oats and Eno's Fruit Salt. So sorry you have had so much trouble to get me Pickwick. I think it would be advisable not to mark on the parcels what they contain. Please let me know what my combined pay and allowances will have reached by the end of this year, and deal with the money as you think best reinvesting. Duchess's letter of 31st just arrived. No doubt about my staying young! So tell her not to worry about that. Please send me a copy of O'Rorke's book.* [*In the Hands of the Enemy*, describing the early days of POW life in Germany] *So glad she is sure we shall meet soon – more than I am. I start Italian on January 1st as it is quite impossible to sit down*

and learn technical words in Russian here, especially as I shall forget them if I don't use the language for some time after I return home. It is easy enough to learn a language enough to get on well, understand and explain oneself, but when it comes to trying to learn one really well it is a fearful matter in a place like this. Perhaps I am wrong but I have thought much about it and can explain reasons better verbally when we meet. All goes well here and have just finished a great game of hockey and I am duly tired. The weather today is perfect, and the sunsets here are very fine (how artistic!) The sunrises I fear I am usually too sleepy to consider in that light, though we are still keeping up our Gym. at 7 a.m. followed by a cold shower. No mean performance at this time of the year. On the 30th a Capt. George whose birthday was on the 29th and I gave a little dinner. So the great day didn't go quite uncelebrated. We were eleven in all. We eight, Capt. George, Suffolk Regiment, Major Nutt, R.F.A., and Capt. Graham Toler, Middlesex Reg. Owing to the vagaries of the post his parcels as well as some of mine arrived late, but that didn't matter in the least, as one of our number, Walker, is a very expert chef, and the dinner, though amateur, quite came up to the name on the menu, which valuable card was prepared by our local artists, (I did not assist!) and duly signed by all the participators afterwards, to the best of their ability!! We are all very cheerful and time goes quicker than I should have imagined possible. I hope my letter to Mother arrives in time for her birthday. It is very difficult to judge the distance! So glad to get all your news of **Ellie and Cousin Jack** [Russia and Admiral Jellicoe] *and to hear of great improvements in the condition of the former. It has been a hard time for her no doubt, but from what little I know of her I would back her for any money! I fear this is an appalling ramble but curiously enough I am really quite busy in little ways. My best love to you all and cheer oh! My next letter will be my Xmas one!!*
Your affectionate son,

Brocas.

Please send me 4 blankets and 4 sheets, and let me know price of former as 2 are for a friend.

Letter 71

30th November 1915, Mainz

My dearest Mother,
This must be my preliminary Xmas wishes in case my next arrives too late.
May you have all luck etc. etc. I have quite forgotten the correct phraseology
but I mean well!! The same to Father for his birthday and may he have many
more of them. A long way to go yet if he is to compete with Aunt Em! 3 letters
from you this time all most cheery, many thanks. In parcels, I have got butter
1000 cigs. for orderlies, tobacco (please let me know cost) and sausages, biscuits,
choc, etc. Many thanks. Very cold here, snow and ice. Health excellent. Gym
at 7 am very difficult! Please send me out 3 pairs of <u>long</u> silk socks, reaching
to just below the knee. Best love to you all and may we be together next Xmas.
Your affectionate son,

Brocas.

Letter 72

7th December 1915, Mainz

My dearest Father,
This letter must contain my feeble attempt to send you my best wishes for your
birthday and my Xmas wishes to you all. Let us hope next year will see us
united. Since my last letter I have received from you Duchess's of November
21. So glad you are going to see a play on the 8th. Very good for you all, I am
sure! Hope you will see some more in the Xmas holidays. What an excellent
idea to have Aunt Ione and Bernard with you for Xmas. My best wishes to
them. Perhaps it will be a hard winter for a change. We have had it very cold
here but today it is quite warm and all the snow has melted again. The boots
are a great success, and keep out everything. Mother's letter of November 20th
has also arrived. So glad you are seeing many Australians. How interesting
it must be. I hope Ruth manages to visit you. Father's of November 24th has
also arrived. So glad you have got the Pickwick at last but I fear it has caused
too much trouble. How excellent about Alex. Best news I've had for a long
time. The best of luck to him. I'm going to have the Duchess's photo copied in
charcoals by a Russian here who does it very well. I shall wait till you send me
the new one and see which is best – <u>in my opinion!</u> and this I think is usually
at variance with the opinion of the rest of the family. I start my own Xmas
holidays on Saturday, till the New Year. I shall try and finish all the books you
have sent me. Parcels have been coming through badly. But I have received
up to date all the plays, the dispatch box (which is just what I wanted); what

a kind thought of Mother's to send it off on her birthday, all three books in the dispatch box, butter and cigarettes for orderlies. All most welcome. For the moment we have run out of food here, only owing to the delay of the post, but we all think it would be advisable to lay in a substantial store in case of "lean times". What we want chiefly is butter, tongues, potted meat, condensed milk, tins of coffee and milk and sardines. Other forms of tinned meat and fish are always welcome as also tinned vegetables. In future I will keep an exact list of all parcels. I started Hindustani a few days ago but I'm not going to spend much time over it till after Christmas. Not much news from here. Hockey continues as usual and keeps us going well. Out of about 70 British nearly 50 play. Not a bad average. Today we started practicing our carols for Christmas. Though not exactly high-class perhaps, the singing will be full of verve. O'Rorke has kindly sent us out a lot of copies. What news have you of J.S.B.? I have not heard of him for a long time. George I presume is still looking after Kent. Another parcel has arrived containing a cake and apples, which arrived at the most opportune moment. Poor Dick Rawstorne, do you mean he is only allowed to write very few cards or what? From what I hear he is likely to be better off than his brothers in adversity elsewhere. Needless to say our allies in trying to master the English tongue are apt to make slight errors, which I fear cause much inappropriate mirth, for instance a Russian officer recently informed us that his friend had been "drunk how a pork", and when order was again restored he turned to a senior Major and told him he "had not the sign of old man". Another on being shown a sketch-book said, "I much admire to see your draws"!! "There are moses in the mattress" was another officer's attempt to form a new plural from "mouse"! And a French officer's definition of ferreting was "Chase at the burrow or hole"! And so the good work goes on! Again my best love and wishes.
Your affectionate son,

Brocas.

Letter 73

13th December 1915, Mainz

My dearest Father,
Since my last I have received from you D's letter of N. 28 and yours of 31. So glad you are doing Russian. **Tiptree jams arrived but I have not had any for some time.** [a possible early reference to lack of escape materials] *Hope Duch did her oral well and Miss S's temper is better. I received 3 tins of butter this week most opportune. Quite warm here though rainy. M's*

letter of D. 4 and Duch's of D. 5 just arrived. Many thanks. The Xmas parcels sound magnificent. How kind of you. Please send me the following books: – "When the Red Gods Call", B. Grimshaw, and "Wellington's Army", Oman. Also some "Veda" Bread once a fortnight and eggs, an egg substitute, ping pong balls. Do send me Mrs. H. F's letter in E.C.C. and also my respects and New Year wishes to her. The same to you all most sincerely. Keep young and smiling and may this year bring better luck.
Your affectionate son,

Brocas.

So glad about the Oppidans.

Letter 74

My dearest Mother,
Since my last card I have got Father's letter of December 7 and am glad to hear he finds the Russian alphabet a "puzzler", but tell him to wait till he comes to the verbs. I am writing this after playing in 3 games of hockey in succession, all 8 aside and so am a little more than comfortably tired. On **(deletion by Censor)** *today we were told that we could inform our relations that the "pink slips" put into our letters by the German authorities some months back were not to be taken any notice of. This merely means that the limit put on the correspondence we receive is now less restricted. Yesterday a lady of the Swiss Red Cross came and looked at us, so we have been quite seeing the world. I just received a very kind letter from Miss Owen and am going to write her a P.C. to thank her great kindness in writing her good wishes to me and also the boys at her school. The Xmas parcels you have sent me sound most magnificent. Since my last I have received (1) a vast box of almonds and raisins, (2) a cake and some shortbread, (3) Pickwick in Russian, (4) 200 cigarettes, (5) butter and (6) miscellaneous parcel, ctg. dates, sausages, etc., (7) Reg. buttons, (8) cheese. Many thanks for all. My requirements this week amount only to 2 other copies of Pickwick in Russian for two other fellow countrymen who are grappling with the language, (and address one of them to Capt. Boger R. E Royal Flying Corps, Mainz). I only venture to ask for this as I think in having succeeded in getting it once, you will not have the same difficulty again. Please send me the price of this as the officers insist on paying. Also I would like 2 very nice books to give to 2 Russian friends here, one a well bound copy of Lambs Essays or something like that, and the other illustrated book of travel or adventure in the style of the books you have in the drawing room at home. Please keep the bill*

of these for me when I return home. Are the Cappers still in Oxford, if so please give Miss Mabel Capper the best wishes of Capt. Usher, Gordon Highlanders. I am at present engaged in reading Darwin's Voyages in H.M.S. Beagle and am much enjoying a momentary rest from language learning. **What do you think of the fate of my Gstaad friend's namesake?** [No clues to who this might be] **I have excellent news of Ellie from a new prisoner who saw her a little before his capture and whose praise of her recovery is even higher than yours. She certainly is wonderful.** [Good news of the Russian army successes] *We heard recently of rumours of an exchange but I fear this is only like the others. Everything here is as usual, the weather is balmy and very pleasant, and I spend a great part of the day out of doors. In fact my health has never been better, thanks to the supplies of food from home and the fact that 3 members of my room are fresh air and exercise maniacs and no excuses on my part are taken for absence off Gym. in the morning. To be pulled out of bed is far the easiest way of getting up! I fear I am still rather fat, however that is warming!! We are practicing Xmas carols with great gusto and a Russian music expert is coaching us and I do the interpreting which is good practice for me. We are singing good old "Wenceslas, Noel and The Manger Throne". We are looking forward to a small concert to be given in the chapel here next week by a German who is so pleased with the treatment his son has received as a prisoner of war in the Isle of Man, that he offered to give us a small musical entertainment. This however was only permitted on condition that it was religious! This has made us think a bit and thank God we are Britishers! I fear this letter is of more than habitual dullness and apologise accordingly. I must close as they are coming round to collect the letters. Good bye. Best love to you all and best luck for the New Year. Your affectionate son,*

Brocas.

Letter 75

24th December 1915, Mainz

My dearest Mother,
Duchess's and your photos have just arrived and I like 2 very much. The one of you 2 together very nice and natural, and also the head and shoulders excellent. The full length "what-a-good-girl-am-I" and the "Juliet on the balcony" are not quite so good. I am getting one copied in charcoal and enlarged, and will send it home to you. All well here. Much slush after snow and thaw. Since my last, musical instruments in this room have increased by 4, 2 penny whistles and a Japanese violin! Ugh! Thanks so much for these parcels – (1) ham,

(2) gloves and books, (3) cig., (4) apples (George), (5) plum pudding and butter, (6) **jam Tiptree.**[There is no indication from the parcels list that escape materials were included] *(7) choc. and plum pudding, (8) cake and pheasant, (9) butter. Best love to all.*
Your affectionate son,

Brocas.

Letter 76

My dearest Mother,
My first letter of the New Year goes of course do you three at home and you may be sure I have thought of you a great deal during the Christmas season. Things are supposed to have a habit of going in threes and as I have now been three Xmases away from home, perhaps No. 4 will see us together again. The post seems to have been rather delayed but parcels have come along alright. So glad you had George, Ruth, Aunt Io, and Bernard with you for Xmas. Quite a party and I have no doubt Bernard regaled himself to the best of his ability. I closed my holidays last week and I've started work again, though serious lessons don't start till Monday as yesterday was the Russians Christmas and they refuse to work on their feast days, and quite naturally too. It was a great day, much handshaking and good wishes. They get much more excited about these things than we do and certainly made the most of present conditions. I hear Miss Corbet is very ill. So sorry and hope she will pull through alright. We have just had a table built for the ping-pong and now have great games here and it certainly is the best of indoor games. Please send some more balls and also some of those covered ones if attainable. I got the following parcels since my last (1) sheets, (2) mend-all, (3) tobacco, (4) biscuits, (5) butter, (6) ham from Aunt Katie, and (7) biscuits etc. (whether from you or her I don't know), (8) blankets, (9) 2 books, (10) apples and soup. Many *thanks and also to Aunt Katie. My love to her and all at Kinnersley. Please thank my tutor for his card and send him my best wishes and to Mrs Byrne. Please also thank Miss Rice Wiggin for her kind letter and send her my best wishes as also to Mrs R. W. Eleanor Butler who has also kindly written to me again. She is very kind. F's letter of 22, D's of 26, M's of 25 and F's of 28 have arrived, many thanks. Cigarettes for orderlies no longer necessary. Many thanks for those you have sent. Please send me out a pair of brogues, brown, and also a pair of tennis shoes. I think I ought to have a pair amongst my things. Also two silk khaki ties, 2 pairs of stockings, 2 of my cricket shirts and a fairly thick sweater, without binding. Many thanks for the two Xmas cards. Lt. Walker R.F.C. who*

is in my room here has met Father at Oxford when he came down with Baden Powell about Boy Scouts, and sends you his regards. We are all well here and of course cheerful. The weather is extraordinarily mild and today we actually have some sun! Tell Aunt Em. I am making a collection of Russian proverbs which I should be able to add on to her French and Italian ones. I hope she is fit and well. By the time you get this I suppose you will have decided whether Duchess is to return to school or not, I should be most interested to hear. I see the name of Rawson on the list of missing posted up here. He was my fag at Eton. Alistair MacDonald is also included, so I fear he must be done in too. You can't imagine how I look forward to being in a room alone again in comparative quiet. Here of course "the more the merrier", is perhaps as well, but never having a single moment to one's self tells in the long run. Never mind, that will come, as the fatalists say! Aunt Io sent me a capital picture of Bernard in his kilt, he certainly looks magnificent, and I'm sure get you all going at Xmas. Well I must close down by sending you my best love, wishes etc. Your affectionate son,

Brocas.

Lizzie's plum pudding was voted far and away the best of the many received here and was annihilated almost immediately. The mince pies were also a great success and arrived almost intact. M.B.B.

Mother's letter of Jan. 2 just arrived. Many thanks. We should much like some Veda bread.

Letter 77

24th January 1916, Mainz

My dearest Father,

*Since my last I have got the following letters from you. Duchess's of Jan. 7, M's of 8, F's of 5 combined letters of 12, and M's of 16. I fear a snapshot is impossible. So glad to hear Alex is fixed up at last. He ought to be just about right for **the final drive!*** [Optimistic final offensive] *Capt. Usher would like to be remembered to Porteous who hopes he is flourishing. Yes, I saw J. Wren – a good show. All luck to her. Your last letter brought me my net total of 300. I have got them all and also the few I received from you while still at the front. The Eton C.C. also arrived today. Many thanks. I hope the paper gets home alright that you sent me from Radcliffe. I got permission to send it off immediately. The financial experts here tell me I should invest the money now. But no doubt you will make the best possible arrangements for me. I fear I have lost my list of parcels received, very* *careless, but as far as I can remember they were, 2 tins of butter and also 2lbs not in tins, a scarf, a cake, 2 parcels of potted stuffs, 2 books, the blankets and sheets and some songs and cigarettes. Many thanks. Not much chance of catching cold in the scarf. Sheets and blankets excellent. I think the eggs ought to be all right as others get them here. So glad Neville Talbot has got the M.C. I am very busy here just at present as I am starting Hindu and Italian, rather have done so. I think they both ought to be fairly easy to get a grounding in. How is the Russian going? Everything here is as usual. We play hockey 3 times a week and do our Gym etc. The winter has so far been very warm and not over-rainy. Aunt Em. is truly wonderful and I wish I could have heard her read prayers. So you have decided to send Duchess back to school for another term. I suppose she will be the devil of a knut there. Duchess's picture has just been copied by a Russian friend of mine. I have not yet decided whether I think it is good or not. Will you please send me out some packs of cards and some bridge markers. Also some more of those red stump cricket balls if procurable. What are Henderson and Ballayne doing now? If you are in communication with them please send them the respects of Lt. Walker, R.F.C. So sorry to hear of poor Miss Corbet's death. I am afraid mother will miss her a great deal.* **Ellie certainly seems to have done wonders. Modern science seems capable of curing everything.** [the progress of the Russian Army] *What news of J.S.B. Thank you so much for being so kind to MacGregor. I hope he is alright. You must have had a most exciting Xmas with all these parties. Excellent for Bernard. That book on Russia you sent me is very good and just what I wanted. Will you please tell Hawkes to send me two yellow bound khaki epaulettes for my overcoat and also send me a decent* **book for autographs.** [this is not in the Burrows family archive] *I feel this letter is appallingly dull but there is nothing to tell you. We are now allowed to walk in the yard till 5.30 p.m. but otherwise the regime is as usual. Loder Symonds seems well as also Wise and Price. My best love to you all. Your affectionate son,*

Brocas.

Letter 78

31st January 1916, Mainz

My dearest Father,
Many thanks for yours of 19th. Strange about Gibbon. Few parcels lately, 2 books, socks, butter and a cake. Many thanks. All well here. I've just been teaching the French to play Hockey and I'm now teaching the Russians. Both are good! Charcoal picture of D. leaves immediately. I am not very pleased with it myself. I fear you will get no photo of me as yet. V. interesting about your interview with Secretary of State. Daily expecting a promised letter from Aunt Io with full account of you all. So glad about Alex. Goodbye. Best love to Mother and you.
Your affectionate son,

Brocas.

Letter 79

31st January 1916, Mainz

My dearest Duchess,
Many thanks for yours of 17th I hope you're enjoying your last term at school and being a good girl. So glad Ian Hay's books please you. No, I have not read his last. A Russian friend here has just finished a copy of your photo which I will send home. I am not frightfully pleased with it. So glad to hear you have done well in French, most important. My Italian is not going very well at present, as I am doing so many other things as well, but I expect there will be plenty of time.
Best love,
Your affectionate brother,

Brocas.

Letter 80

9th February 1916, Mainz

My dearest mother,
So glad you have been having a "breather" at Folkestone for a few days and I hope it did both you and Father a lot of good. I'm sure a week there would soon set me up. Glad to hear Ruth Brinkley is married, I don't know the fortunate

man but some here do. Several letters to hand viz. M's of 22 and one from Folkstone undated, F's of 26, D's of 23 and 30 and a capital one from Aunt Io. Your Fijian must indeed have some interesting stories to tell. I shouldn't mind following his example for a few months! Fancy Mon being a captain already. Is he still engaged? Send him my congratulations if you write as also my love to Cousins Ted and Claudine. Your accounts of Bernard are most entertaining, he must be "some" boy as Yanks would say. What is Mary going to do about Smalls? Compete again or give it up? The whole affair was her own idea was it not? Duchess writes that one of her friends is the relation of Major Blackburne of mine, ask her to send him my best wishes and congratulations on his Majority. I had not gathered that this Miss Abbott was an importation from some other school. I thought she was one of the other mistresses. It must indeed be a great experience for Duchess. The eggs you send are a great success and much appreciated. We had almost forgotten what they tasted like. The Veda bread has arrived twice and is very good. I have also received butter, and a cake. Can you send me oranges occasionally? Please also send me a pair of boots – brown of course and very light so that I can walk or ride in them. Mine are at last dead! Maxwell would, I think make them best, as the Newmarket boots fit me very well. So you have sold the old car at last. Well it has done noble service – 8 years isn't it? No particular news from here. Both the Russians and the French have now mastered the rudiments of the game of hockey and play it with much verve and even a certain amount of accuracy. I have just recovered from a slight cold – my first this winter – and start my violent exercises again tomorrow. It is surprising how weak one becomes the moment one relaxes at all. We have had one or two real spring days but today is winter again. On the whole though we have escaped both heat and cold very lightly. The monthly consignment of cigarettes has just arrived. Many thanks. The jars are most useful and serve as sugar basins etc. Tobacco has also arrived but I may have acknowledged it in my last. Can you possibly send me the page in the army list which my regiment is on, I think it will get through all right. I have just bought a small alarm clock to assist me to rise in the morning. The late risers in the room want to raise objections but these have not been allowed! Please send me out some silk khaki ties and two more of those thin summer shirts and collars. So glad Hartley has got the M.C. What is he up to now? I do hope J.S.B. gets home to have some fun. So I gather he had a certain amount of excitement "en passant". George is I suppose still in Kent. Well goodbye. Best love.

Your affectionate son,

Brocas

Letter 81

25th February 1916, Mainz

My dearest Father,
I am afraid I have been very lazy about writing lately, it shall not occur again.
Many thanks for letters – 4 in number – M's of 12, yours of 1 and 15 and D's
of 12. Your two scraps of local gossip are true. I was not affected. How very kind
of Mrs Eccles to send me the bread – always a highly appreciated article here.
Please thank her. The eggs are voted a great success and out of three lots only
two eggs have been broken. Fancy Benning making a war marriage! Don't
bother about the P.P. balls. So sorry to hear they have given the Rugby colour at
Eton. I do hope it won't affect the Field game. Our latest adventure here consists
of walks in the country round and along the banks of the local river. They were
started recently and last about an hour and a half. We go out by nationalities –
a German officer leads the way, we follow and another German officer brings
up the rear. He is followed by an armed guard of about 10 men at a convenient
distance and military police on bicycles circle around us. Anyhow it makes a
very nice change and one gets out about once a week at 8.15 or 10 a.m. Many
thanks to Mother for the two P.C.'s. No 2. got severely censor-mauled. Jack
dropped me a line recently. My last to him took five months to arrive. In parcels
I have received shirts, and a sweater, 2 from Folkestone, 2 cakes, butter, eggs and
2 other parcels of tinned veg etc. Please send me the "Confessions of a Thug"
and also the pipe Jack gave me if you can find it. I have decided to complete
my khaki wardrobe in order to be ready for all eventualities immediately on
return. So please order and send to me here the following (1) a Sam Brown
belt – not a brand new one but a dark coloured one. (2) at Maxwell's a pair of
spurs with chains, (3) at Hawkes a pair of riding breeches – regimental pattern
and cloth buttoning on the inside of knee, (4) at Hawkes an officer's pattern
overcoat. Major Blackburne must have my <u>*British warm*</u> *as my old overcoat*
had a different fate. Please keep that for me. Tell Hawkes to make the overcoat
as smart as possible and of course of regimental pattern. Have you read Baden
Powell's new book "Indian Memories"? If not, do so, I have just read it here.
You know he was Colonel of my regiment. At present we have snow here but it
is not very cold. Price's brother was certainly lucky. He, Loder-Symonds and
Wise are all well. At present I am studying Hindustani hard and it is not very
difficult and great fun writing it. My professor is Younger, R.F.A. who was there
before the war. I am also reading a lot of military history and so I'm quite busy.
Don't send me any more books at present as I am full up, so to speak. George
is now quite a regular correspondent and seems in great form. I hear Jack's
chauffeur, Harrison, is dead. Ellie [Russia] *sounds alright again, all luck*
to her. Please halve the tobacco ration as I don't smoke as much as you send.
Hockey continues here as usual though we are getting a bit tired of it. Please

send me also another pair of puttees Indian khaki colour.Well, I must close. Best
love to you three.
Your affectionate son,

Brocas.

Please send Nurse my best wishes for her birthday. Better late than never.
Many thanks to Miss Owen for writing to me.

Letter 82

[No date], *Mainz*

Dear Aunt Io,
It was so kind of you to write me such an excellent letter with exactly the news
I wanted. It cheered me up not a little. So glad to hear Bernard has decided to
be a soldier. He certainly looks strong and lusty from his photo. Our carols at
Xmas were quite moderately successful, all things considered! though I fear we
were not a very talented choir. It is dreadful being shut in this spring weather,
but one hopes it is not for much longer. Best love to you and Bernard.
Your affectionate nephew,

Brocas Burrows.

Letter 83

28th February 1916, Mainz

My dearest Mother,
Since my last I have got a letter from you (Feb.19) and 5 parcels, including
Miss G's bread – most excellent, many thanks to her – eggs, books, ties, hockey
balls, cards, chocolate, sweets and biscuits. Many thanks. Lovely weather here,
snow finished. This is about the most difficult time here. One longs to be up
and about even more than usual. I hope Jack is really coming west. Eton
*Chronicle just arrived.Very sorry about MacCulloch's death. **The old place***
seems going on much as usual, little affected by the controversy as
to who is or was "Joby". [reference unclear] *I shall be interested to hear*
Geoffrey Madan's further movements. All well and cheerful here.
Best love.
Your affectionate son,

Brocas

Letter 84

7th March 1916, Mainz

My dearest Father,
Have received yours of Feb.23 and M's of 26. Many thanks for Rugby
*account. So glad about **Ellie** [Russia]. **Govare** [French Army] is no doubt*
all right. So sorry about Hedley. No parcels of late but we live in plenty as we
have been able to put aside a reserve. I have lots of clothes and warm ones too
so don't worry about that. Spring weather here, very nice. Fancy deep snow
so late. I can imagine it quite puzzled the Australians. In future I hope to
write to you every Sunday as I did at Eton. So I hope you will get them more
regularly. I am just going to start a course of dentist here, a brief one I hope.
*Nothing serious but as well to get it over even though there is no **Buxton***
***Ryle**. [Anaesthetic] Best love.*
Your affectionate son,

Brocas.

Well and cheerful.

Letter 85

13th March 1916, Mainz

My dearest Mother,
I write this in the midst of a tornado! Our local musicians are inspired, and
hell let loose would have no chance against them. The pianist is quite good. The
scraper of the Japanese violin is very mediocre and doesn't practice. Our flutist
when he does get a note won't let the poor thing go, our bagpiper can't get in
tune with piano (this however does not affect him), our ordinary violinist (quite
extraordinary in reality) is quite out of form today. Another comrade in adversity
has got a piccolo which can be turned into a flute and he is quite unable to decide
which form of torture suits him best (thank goodness he can't play both at once).
Then we have a most offensive champion of the penny whistle, for which he
occasionally substitutes the mouth organ, and a friend from another building
has obliged somebody (we don't know who, luckily for the person) by adding his
voice to the "ensemble". He is usurping my post of big drummer i.e. one of your
tins inverted met forcibly by a hockey stick, and I should be acting as director
of the whole caboodle and also, when my lungs permit, wielder of the good old
"comb and paper"! A repertoire for such an orchestra would I am sure puzzle
Sir Henry Wood, but we excel at "Rule Britannia", and on Sunday evenings kill

several hymns. Perhaps it is the Spring time, perhaps incipient lunacy – we can't tell, but still hope, nay even am quite confident that it will pass. Since my last I received letters from Father of Feb. 29th, and from Duchess of F. 27th. Today is quite glorious, but we have also had much snow in the course of the week. This however has affected me but little as I started my bout with the dentist here last Monday and his excavations prove more serious than I expected with the result that I have spent the last few days cursing everything and confined to my room with severe aches! This however has now subsided and I am now chewing with my accustomed force, though I rather dread my next visit. If Maxwells have not got my boot measure I should think Gane had better make my boots. Howey is here and well. **How interesting about Cousin Jack. We live in hopes.** [Admiral Jellicoe] **Is it true that Ellie may visit Gstaad?** [a reference to rumours of Exchange of British POWs to Switzerland] **Govare** [The French] *sounds busy just at present. I hope he won't get over-worked. From what little I know of him I should think that was always a possibility. I bet Dick R. is excited about now. Duchess seems very flourishing. Sorry about those suede shoes! I have got no less than seven parcels, namely (1) eggs and shoulder straps etc., (2) cake, bacon and coffee, (3) milk biscuits, (4) book and ping-pong balls – a great success, (5) shoes and book, (6) cigarettes and (7) eggs and butter. Many thanks. The shoes fit like a glove. I forget whether I acknowledged the Autograph book and bridge cards and markers or not. They have arrived and are exactly what I wanted. I see you send me shoulder straps with two stars on, does this mean I have been promoted? If so, when? Could you also find out for me more or less the state of my finances with Cox & co. or rather what they will be at say about April 1st? Please send me no more books for the moment except to finish the Dutch Republic series, as I have still a lot on hand and reading is always difficult here. An Eton chronicle has just arrived. So glad to get it. They are always most interesting. I see Phillips has been killed – a great friend of mine. Very nearly time you send me some more snapshots of yourselves. They are always most welcome, and form a very good souvenir. The hockey continues and today there was a very good match between the best French team and 8 English. The later won but the French played very well and are extraordinarily keen. The Russians also continue lustily. We are beginning to get a wee bit stale and I wondering what we should play in the summer, as we are too many for cricket. However, we live in hopes of better things than that. What is Duch going to do after this term? Is Malik still at Oxford? Isn't he going to fight a bit? Wise, Loder-Symonds and Price are all well. Howey is I think a friend of Eustace Burrows and also an O.E. Well I must close. Best love to you all.*
Your affectionate son,

Brocas

Letter 86

22nd March 1916, Mainz

My dearest Father,
Several letters since my last, yours of Mar. 9, M's 4th, D's of 12th and M's of 12th. So glad the picture pleased you. Fear one of me is impossible. The artist only copies photos. The shirts sent are excellent. Particulars of artist in next letter. So sorry about Nigel Madan. Many thanks for the photos of Rupert G.S. Poor chap. What a horrible idea this intensive poultry keeping sounds. But I don't exactly know what it means. However hope my old room will not be required for incubating or any such monstrosity. Our room orchestra has just started practising the Burglars Dream. Hence comparative chaos reigns. The weather has been perfect this last week. Trees out all over the place etc. We have even been able to spend nearly every day out of doors reading in the yard. Several parcels have arrived, shirts, cigarettes, 2 bread, choc. and a cake and books. Many thanks. So glad to hear you are going north for the summer. What about Strathpeffer again? Please send me some lemonade powder and some more 'fly papers'. Best of luck to you all.
Your affectionate son,

Brocas.

Letter 87

11th April 1916, Mainz

My dearest Mother,
*I fear I have again allowed more than a week to pass since my last card and feel duly ashamed of myself for having done so. I am indeed sorry to hear of the **Master's** [J.L.S. Davidson] death. I shall always regret that in my brief sojourn at Balliol I did not come across him more, as all who knew him had such a profound respect for him in every way and it was evident even to the most unpractised eye how much he deserved it. I can fully understand what an irreparable loss he will be both to the college and his friends. I think it is today Duch returns home from school isn't it? All luck to her at home! We have all been hearing about the bad weather at home and have been very lucky to escape it here, where the weather has been excellent. There was a Knight Bruce at Torgau with us in the distant past but he was left there when the rest of us got shifted. Doubtless both Molly's are in their element these days. So glad Hedley is better. Glad to hear news of **Cousin Jack**. [Admiral Jellicoe] First I had heard here at all! There is a Lt Howey here of the Bedfordshire Yeomanry, who*

is a friend of Cousin Eustace. Since my last I have received 6 letters, yours, F's of March 21 and 28, D's of 26 and April 2 and yours of 25 and April 1. Many thanks. The parcel mails are most irregular but today five turned up, 2 doz. eggs, 2 cakes, Veda bread, butter, overcoat and breeches and belt. I have also received spurs, Choc., bread and some tinned food. Many thanks. George sounds in luck's way, that is if he is already where he wants to be. Will you please send me a decent sized air-cushion preferably of this shape. 'Two circles' the lines representing a circle and also two dozen tennis balls. You will be surprised to hear we have invested in a parrot! He is quite a magnificent bird, has bitten one of us once and our French orderley twice, says "Jacko" (his name), adieu and one or two other German expressions and is at present trying to master a little elementary English. An exceedingly difficult operation, as most of our well-meaning friends are determined he should swear and do their best to teach him whenever we are absent. At present they have had no success. The orderly is equally determined the poor bird should learn French. It may sound strange that we should keep anything captive but we excuse ourselves by thinking that he has never known anything else! Esperous – le. **What news of Jenny?** [Probably a reference to the Gallipoli campaign in Turkey] ***Will you please send me some solid methylated spirit.*** [useful as a fuel source during an escape attempt] *The 'Eggo' powder you sent is excellent. What news of Aunt Em? My respects to George for his birthday. Glad Dick R. is moved. I thought he might be. Your combined letters have entirely filled that little despatch case you sent me and it is certainly very nice to be able to re-read them. The walks here are a great boon, as new sights and sounds mean a great deal in this confined space. I have not been out the last twice but hope to go on Thursday. Fancy Easter again in a few days, certainly time does pass quickly when one begins to "vegetate". The only annoying part of it all is that this time last year our hopes were just the same as now.* **Perhaps "try first you don't succeed", answers the question!** [this is probably a coded answer to a question about how the escape attempts were progressing] *Well my best love to you all.*
Ever your affectionate son,

Brocas.

Letter 88

17th April 1916, Mainz

My dearest Father,
No letters or parcels have turned up this week, so I have nothing to reply to.
All well as usual here and we have real spring weather. Please thank Mrs
Owen for her kindness in writing to me and give her my best wishes, as also
to her boys. I hope they won the old boys match. I hear you were playing!
Excellent! That ought to keep you fit for tennis on return. Will you please send
me a monthly ration of sugar, lump and castor, and also mustard. We can buy
no more here, also another dozen tennis balls and let me know cost per dozen,
also some best brown boot polish. "Wrens" I believe is best and also some brass
polish. My best love to you all.
Your affectionate son,

Brocas.

Letter 89

26th April 1916, Mainz

My dearest Father,
I have delayed my letter till today because I had had no news from you since
the 9th and felt sure a letter must arrive any minute. Yours of the 5th arrived
yesterday and right glad I was to get it. Also the account of the Sports at Eton.
You have indeed had an exceptional year as regards floods and storms. We
have all heard about them. I am very sorry to hear nearly all the old trees on
Upper Club and Poets Walk at Eton have been blown down, and am equally
glad to hear of the resignation of the Head. Who is going to succeed him? I do
hope they will choose some man of action of the **Warre** *type.* [a reference to
a previous Eton head Edmond Warre 1884-1905] *So glad to hear Alex is*
off at last and is in a nice battalion. I also got a letter from Aunt Em and one
from Miss Canning yesterday. So sorry to hear the old lady has got so much
weaker lately and hope she will entirely recover in the warmer weather. I am
writing her a card. Parcels and letters have been badly held up of late, but old
stagers like us are but little affected, though it is annoying getting no news.
However, we oughtn't to grumble, as there were times when we got none at all!
Well, we have killed another Easter here, rendered quite fairly amusing by the
Russians. It is their greatest feast and they say a mystic word to each other
and embrace on meeting! I avoided this by skulking about like a condemned
criminal for some time but was caught at last and had to undergo the ordeal!
An amusing though embarrassing custom. A new arrangement has been come

to about the walks here. We now sign a paper stating we will make no attempt to or preparations for escape during the walk, and so the guard of soldiers is dispensed with, though we are still to be escorted by 2 German officers, presumably to protect us from the populace. Colonel Jackson has advised us to sign this and has written for further instructions. I think it will be an improvement. I have just read a most interesting book on the Panama Canal by J. S. Mills. If you have not read it, you should do so. Please send me out Ian Hamilton's "A Staff officer's Scrap book" and also some book on each of the Americo-Spanish and Turko-Italian wars. Also two more thin shirts of yellow khaki colour like the last, and some tea. We had a most amusing incident here the other day. A Russian Colonel came to tea with us. As you no doubt know the Russians drink a great deal of tea and are, or at least consider themselves, tea experts. This old gentleman congratulated us on our tea, praised its excellence and said how glad he was it wasn't Ceylon tea, as Ceylon tea, had so much tannin in it. He further stated that he could recognise Ceylon tea a mile off or words to that effect. He then asked if the tea he was drinking was Indian tea; no one seem to know and so he said he was sure it must be, and we agreed. I however had made the tea and knew that it was not only Ceylon tea but out of one of those dreadfully sandy boxes with soldiers etc. on the outside! However, "ignorance is bliss"! Please tell Maxwell the spur-chains he sent are too short and tell him to send me another pair 9.75 inches long. **I hear Ellie has gone travelling and has visited Jenny.** [probably a reference to the Russian offensive in Caucasus] *Have you any more news of Dick R.? or J. S. B? Well I must close, my best love to you all and do send me some snapshots as soon as possible. I appoint Duchess my photographic correspondent.*
Your affectionate son,

Brocas.

Please send occasional Quaker Oats.

Letter 90

30th April 1916, Mainz

My dearest Mother,
Since my last I have received yours of April 9 with news of long gap between my letters. This may be partly my fault I fear, but not entirely, as the posts are most irregular and here I am sure a lot of your letters to me are missing, and also some parcels. What changes at Eton? I hope Alington is chosen head and not the other you mentioned. So sorry Austin Leigh is dead. A great loss. Many thanks for the mustard and cress you have sent off. I'm sure it will be a

*great success and it's just what we want. One parcel has arrived since my last containing Veda bread, tongue, chocolate and coffee and milk. Many thanks. Please send me some soap preferably Pears, as we can only get one piece per month here! Also some shaving soap. Please also send me out the other Field Service Dress Jacket you have got for me and order me a Field Service Cap from Cater. One of the new sort, i.e. soft (not absolutely flabby) and with a khaki waterproof cover. Wiggett has not turned up here as yet, but I expect has gone to another camp. I hope Father's chill is nothing serious. At any rate you ought to have some warm weather soon to help put him right. Here we have real spring and it is quite glorious. We are losing all the French officers here who are being sent away to another camp – why, when and wither we don't know, but soon. This is a great nuisance as it precludes further study in French and it is annoying to be separated from people one has been with so long. Two more parcels have just come of April 1 and 5 respectively, containing 1 doz. eggs, Veda bread, chocs. cake and shortbread. Many thanks. The parrot has learnt his first English word "come on". Why we don't know, as we had not tried to teach him it. Please send me out a standard work on the Russo-Turkish war. We had our third and unfortunately our last concert yesterday as of course the departure of the French who formed the chief part of the orchestra, ends them. Our orchestra, however, will continue though we have not decided to give public concerts as yet! They might not go down well. **How are Cousin Jack's affairs?** [Admiral Jellicoe and the navy] I have heard some adverse criticism about them, but presume it is incorrect. Here all is as usual, perfect weather, bugs everywhere, etc. We played tennis today as it is now too hot and dusty for hockey, hence I am horribly stiff and aching all over! However it is quite nice to have such aches again!! Sorry to hear Geoffrey Madan is wounded. Will you please send the sum of £5. 4. 0. (five pounds four shillings) to the following address. M. Louis Bohin, 19 Avenue d'Orleans, Paris. I may want you to do this for me again, so would it not be best to get Cox to take it off my account? So glad to hear that Duchess is off to Torquay. Sea air ought to do her good, though I fear it will be too early for the bathing. Well I must close this dull letter. Best love to you all.*
Your affectionate son,

Brocas.

I expect the Keans are having a lively time. Glad that fish was caught.

Letter 91

8th May 1916, Mainz

My dearest Father,
Since my last have received yours of April 12, Mothers of April 16 and a card from Duch of April 16. Many thanks. **Tiptree jams have not arrived for a long time.** [a further reference to concealed escape items] *So glad you have Duchess at home. Hope she gets on well with her allowance! Poor Aunt Em, I quite appreciate her annoyance at her Dr. being called up. Several parcels since my last including oranges, 2 doz. eggs, Veda bread, mustard and cress, handkerchiefs, dripping and biscuits. Our wooden stools in the room have been now replaced by wooden chairs! Glorious weather here. All the French officers have been sent away to other camps, including the one I worked with, a nuisance. I think it would be better to send "Eggo" powder instead of eggs during the summer, as the latter won't keep, especially as parcels are taking longer than heretofore. Please send some more red stump cricket balls. Cricket season starts tomorrow! Too dusty for hockey. All well and cheery here. My best love to you all. Your affectionate son,*

Brocas.

Letter 92

15th May 1916, Mainz

My dearest Mother,
Since my last I have received yours of Easter Sunday and Duchess's of April 24. Many thanks. I should be most interested to hear who is to be the new master of Balliol. Many thanks to Father for investing my money for me. My rheumatism etc. is entirely at an end and I could hardly be in a better state of health. Final visit to the local dentist on Wednesday I hope. Have told Estcourt you had seen his wife. He is very well. We had a service on Easter Sunday. Col. Jackson always takes them and the choir still goes on, if not tunefully at least heartily. There is a Russian priest here – a most delightful man with whom I frequently have talks. You ask me if I sing much. The answer is strictly in the negative. We have a superfluity of would-be music as it is in this room without any efforts on my part. A piano always collects kindred spirits, at any rate in this camp, and so I feel it up to me not to air my vocal chords unduly. You ask me also to give you a specimen of a day here, well I rise at 7 (this is an <u>ideal</u> day) shave, and do Gym outside at 7.30-8. Then cold douche, dress and buy any necessaries in the canteen, breakfast at 9 o'clock. "<u>Absence</u>" 9.30. **Then work on and**

off till lunch at 12, this counts as another "absence" or "appel". [probably a reference to work on the escape tunnel] *After lunch I read the paper or arrange sides for hockey on Mon. Wed. and Fri. Hockey is played at 1.30-2.30 and then I read or work till tea at 4, and after tea till "appel" at 6. I then usually walk till about 7 when there is a supper and after that I walk with a Russian till 9.15 when we are shut in the barracks and there is another "appel" at 9.30 and lights out at 10.30. So you see one might be back at school again. Our great meals are tea and breakfast when we eat food from home only. We get letters at 3 p.m. and our parcels usually in the morning. A list of these latter is put up and we go and stand in a "queue"! Church is on Sunday at 10.15 and we have a choir practice on Saturday at 11.15. A German parson takes the service about once a month, but I don't attend. At present I am working at Italian nearly the whole time and the days pass quite quickly. We are still in the same room 8 of us and I sleep on a double decker with Walker R.F.C. I on top! So there is our daily programme in a nutshell. I have received 4 parcels. Tobacco, cigarettes, books, choc. and food. Many thanks. Duchess seems very cheerful and I hope she enjoys her stay in Devonshire. Please send me the following: 2 khaki socks, some of the red stump balls if obtainable, 2 lbs of rice per month, some curry powder, mustard and pepper and macaroni. Now that we may no longer benefit by the exchange here I intend to spend as little money as possible in the canteen. So you will understand why I write to you for so much. Please also send me out by American Ex. Co. a large case of tinned meats, milk, vegetables and butter and jam to act as a general reserve in case of a rainy day. The weather has looked very threatening lately. Well I must close to catch post. My best love to you all. Your affectionate son,*

Brocas.

The parrot is still alive and has said "shut up" and "how are you".

Letter 93

22nd May 1916, Mainz

My dearest Father,
3 letters since my last, yours of April 9th and 26th, and Mother's of 30th from Malvern. Walker most interested in your Boy Scouts. They seem flourishing. Hope Duchess is enjoying her visits. Have only got 2 cheeses in all. Many thanks for the snapshots, always most welcome. Glad to see that there is not much change in the old place. Beautiful weather here and one can sit out of doors almost all day. Received 2 parcels with eggs, bread, shortbread, etc. many thanks. **Please send me some solid methylated spirits.** [required for

the escape attempt which is getting close] *All your news most interesting. I did not know Mother was secretary of the Schools. No doubt very interesting. So glad to hear about Aunt Em and* **Cousin Jack senior** [Admiral Jellicoe's father]. *I fear I shall not be able to send you a photo unless the Ticka condescends to perform, but you would notice very little difference except perhaps for slight moustache (subject of much sarcasm) and general fatness. Best love to you all.*

Brocas.

Letter 94

31st May 1916, Mainz

My dearest Father,
Since my last I have received yours of May 3rd. Health of course is excellent and I have now finally got into the summer regime which I believe means I really get up at 5 o'clock, reckoning by Greenwich. Never mind, one soon gets accustomed. The parrot is very well and the only objection to him is that he is an even earlier riser. At times he laughs in the most amusing way, but up to the present his English is very limited. Parcels are coming much better now. The Malvern parcel has arrived and the methylated is excellent. Please continue sending tea occasionally. I have also received, salt, sugar, etc., eggs, cake, eggo and tins and today Field Service Jacket, tobacco, Ian Hamilton's book, eggs and cake, eggo, shirts and small despatch case. Many thanks. Very glad to hear A. L. Smith was elected master and also that F. R. B. (F R Benson) has been knighted. I am sure he deserves it. **The marmalade does not arrive nor do Tiptree's jams.** [possibly intercepted by the camp authorities] *Sorry to hear about Keene. We all know who caused it. All the British officers going to Switzerland – or rather hoping to go – are coming in here and so we are very busy.* [the first exchange to Switzerland of wounded or sick took place on 29 May 1916] *Chaos supreme. But it is most interesting to hear their news. Most of them are comparatively new boys compared to us! Colonel Neish has come amongst others and seems very cheerful. I went and re-introduced myself and had quite a long chat with him. He is looking far from well. So glad to hear you have been having a fairly quiet time at Malvern. Please thank Eleanor Butler from me for her letter. It is most kind of her to write. Tell her I have got a slight moustache, which it is the correct thing for all "funny people" not to notice. However I have hopes of arriving at the heavy cavalry standard some-day. We have just started playing Rounders here, as it is getting too hot for hockey. Did I thank you for the tennis balls? They are excellent. Please send more from time to time. Since my last we have celebrated our full year in this*

camp! What a thought! Seven of the Britishers here left about a week ago for Switzerland and, we hear, are now there. Lucky devils. Really there are quite a number of advantages in being ill. They are going to Chateau d'Oex just near Gstaad. A most delightful place which of course I know quite well. Well, I must close to catch post. Best love to you all,
Your affectionate son,

Brocas.

Letter 95

[No date], Mainz

My dearest Father,
Many letters since my last. M's of May 6th, parrot is in cage. So glad to hear you contemplate a visit to Gareth's home. My respects to his people. Yours of 16th. Gower is here and I have passed on message. **So glad about Ellie.**
[Good news about the Russian army's progress] *Duch of 20th and photos. M's of 20th and yours of 4th all most welcome and interesting. So glad to get the photos esp. those of home. How well they are taken. I have also got a letter from George who seems flourishing. All well here. Please send more ping pong balls. The candidates for Switzerland are still here and it is most interesting to see some new faces again. Several of them are cavalry and we played a hockey match yesterday cavalry and gunners v. the "Skagerracks". We won, this time. Several parcels arrived including songs, books, Ian H's, cigs. m. and cress, bread, cake, eggs, eggo, tea, etc. Many thanks. So glad you enjoyed your time at Malvern. Very cold weather here. But this apparently is to be expected in June. The songs you sent me meet with great approval. Love to all.*
Your affectionate son,

Brocas.

8

Friedberg POW Camp

15 June 1916 – 23 March 1917

With failure of the escape at Mainz and the removal of the British officers to Friedberg a new chapter in Brocas's internment began. In his book *An Escaper's Log*, Duncan Grinnell-Milne described the camp as follows:

> *Friedberg proved to be close to the once-famous Bad-Nauheim and about twenty-five miles north of Frankfurt. The camp lay outside the village in open countryside. It was roughly square, bounded by double fences, barbed wire and a wooden palisade, and guarded by two rows of sentries. It contained two large three-storied buildings and a gymnasium, all of which had been created just before the war and were to have been used as infantry barracks. In the centre of the camp there was a large parade ground about eighty yards square, and on one side of this lay a piece of ground 100 yards long by 20 yards wide where prisoners were allowed to make themselves small gardens, which ran down to within a few feet of the wire fence surrounding the camp.*

Initially the camp housed about 600 prisoners of whom 12 were British, but this number was boosted by some 150 British when Brocas and the other officers arrived from Mainz.

Friedberg was not an easy camp from which to escape due to the lack of cover afforded by the surrounding countryside, and the fact that several abortive attempts by French and Russians had made the Germans very wary. When the new arrivals from Mainz arrived, Duncan Grinnell-Milne teamed up for a tunnel escape, initially with his brother, Douglas, also of R.F.C. captured near Lille, Lieutenant W.G.R. Elliot, Cheshire Regiment captured at Audregnies 24 August 1914, and Captain W.M. Campbell, Suffolk Regiment, captured at Le Cateau. The tunnel was planned to start from a kind of summer house erected on one of the 15-foot square garden plots about 20 feet from the boundary fence. Later Lieutenant I. Fairweather and Captain E.G.S. Walker were brought into the scheme which ultimately failed when the Germans got wind that something was a foot and the tunnel was discovered. Campbell later escaped on 20 March 1917 with Lieutenant P. Godsal by jumping from the train when about 80 of their number, including Brocas, were being moved to Clausthal because Friedberg camp was being abandoned as a POW camp for British officers. The two escapees made it to Holland twelve days later.

The same group had a 'Rope scheme' in place, but they abandoned this in favour of departing the camp dressed as German officers, by which means the two Grinnell-Milne brothers and Fairweather escaped successfully on 25 September 1916. They were eventually re-captured after several days of freedom. Brocas, soon after his arrival also described a garden. 30 June 1916 (*Letter 100*) '*Four of us also got a patch (3 yards square) of earth under cultivation. At least we intend to build a hut to sit in in summer and plant veg. round it.*' He wrote, 11 July 1916, (*Letter 101*) '*We have planted the m. and c.* [mustard and cress] *and erected a tent of sorts.*' However, there is no evidence that this 'tent of sorts,' was an early reference to the same plot and escape plan described by Grinnell-Milne in his book *An Escaper's Log*.

Due to the fact that since 29 May 1916, long-term wounded POWs were now being exchanged to Switzerland, it had become possible to pass on direct messages to families without any censorship. By this means, through the exchange of Captain Ian Henderson, who was in the first group of 32 officers to be exchanged, Brocas was able to establish a more specific code for items he required for an escape attempt, and how they were to be concealed. The names listed in the following note, Loder-Symonds, Burrows, Pelham-Burn and Massy, are probably the families to whom the code was to be passed by Captain Henderson.

By his own admission, in a letter date 17 February 1918 (*Letter 176*) from Holland, his father to his mother wrote, '*He* [Brocas] *clean forgot about that code (Begin-end), & never noticed any of our messages, or used it himself*'.

From Brocas's letters, and particularly Mrs Pelham-Burn's letters (*Numbers 105 and 106 of 1 and 7 August 1916 respectively*) to Brocas's parents, it is obvious that he had some escape scheme of his own or was acting as facilitator for these other attempts. In February 1917 (*Letter 136*) to Bene Cartwright, smuggled out with a French POW, he says '*Two attempts to re-join you failed unfortunately*'. One of these would have undoubtedly been the

1) Code in letter to commence with the word 'begin' in some form or other & to continue with every <u>seventh</u> word, finishing with some form of the word 'end'.

2) Small compass   15/-   } in jam

3) Small parcels of blue dye.   <u>Tiptree</u>

4) Small map, now procurable of Friedberg district (near Mainz) sent in empty gelatine soup case inside Tiptree jam-pot.

5) Small bottle of whisky to be packed in tin of home-made beef, well surrounded with lard, so that ends do not touch tin.

Captains Loder-Symonds, Burrows Pelham Burn, & Massy.

Note regarding code for concealed escape items. Source: Burrows family archive

attempt from Mainz. Also, in his letter of 17 February 1918 (*Letter 176*) from Holland, writing to his wife, his father described the means by which uncensored letters were concealed. '*The uncensored letters were sent inside the woodwork of carved frames by the French, a most ingenious contrivance too lengthy to describe. They all got in, but there were not many of them, so ours are precious.*'

Despite Mrs Pelham-Burn's plea for restraint, for fear of her son being implicated, and indeed caught receiving 'Contraband' escape items, Brocas's parents were sending out virtually all the items the coded message, brought out by Captain Henderson, suggested he required. Then six months later they sent items listed in the letter to Bene Cartwright.

The following is a list of illicit escape items, taken from his mother's record of parcels, that were included in the items sent out to Brocas while at Friedberg:

Parcel no 31	*1 August 1916*	'Compass' in jam
Parcel no 33	*3 August 1916*	'Maps' in Consommé Ack 20 August 1916 (Letter 109)
Parcel no 34	*5 August 1916*	'Maps' in Consommé Ack 16 Sept 1916 (Letter 112)
Parcel no 35	*7 August 1916*	'Dyes' in jam
Parcel no 36	*9 August 1916*	'Whisky' in potted meat
Parcel no 38	*9 August 1916*	Primus cooker. Ack 16 Sept 1916 (Letter 112)
Parcel no 151	*27 February 1917*	Maps, Flash lights refills Ack 30 April 1917
Parcel no 152	*27 February 1917*	Luminous watch, Army rations Ack 15 April 1917 from Clausthal
Parcel no 156	*7 March 1917*	'Compass' in jam, Rations Ack 13 May 1917
Parcel no 160	*14 March 1917*	'Wire cutters' in potted beef steak Ack 13 May 1917 from Clausthal

These parcels, which Brocas acknowledged receiving in part only, (*Letters 109 and 112*) suggest that the compass, dyes and whiskey which were not acknowledged, were probably intercepted by the camp authorities when they vetted the parcels. He describes (*Letter 109*) with emphasis, these as '*All most welcome*'. It is possible Brocas was at this time providing logistical support to the Grinnell-Milne tunnel which had failed in late August. The arrival of contraband items suggests Brocas was aware that his parents had received his requests from Captain Henderson but curiously (*Letter 137*) undated but probably March 1917, he was asking if they had heard from Henderson.

At Friedberg, Brocas was almost consumed with organising, taking part in amateur theatricals and preparing the accounts. The first production, a 'Vaudeville' entertainment as Brocas described it, were evening performances at 6.55 p.m. on July 26, 27, 28, 29 plus a matinée at 1.15 p.m. on July 29. The audiences were generally mixed nationalities excepting the matinée which was almost entirely French

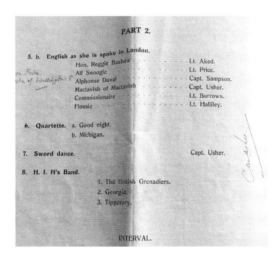

Part of the Vaudeville Programme at Friedberg July 1916
Source: Burrows family archive

and Russian with two English men assisting with translation. Six German officers and two Russian generals also attended. Part of the signed programme below, was elaborated by Brocas. (*Letter 103*)

> *It went off very well indeed and the audience was most appreciative though about 75% can't have understood a word. We had a vaudeville entertainment.* The items being a conjuror [Lt Berry], *a soloist* [Captain Moseley], *a quartet* [Captain Jervis, Captain Moseley, Captain Younger, Captain Sampson], *a comic orchestra which made a horrible noise, a scotch dance* [Sword Dance by Captain Usher], *2 plays* ['L'Anglais à Paris come on l'imagine' and 'English as she is spoke in London'] *written by officers here and a "potted" play a la Pelissier. The play we potted was one acted by the Russians about a month ago.* [Burlesque 'Le High Life' founded on the comedy of M. Chekoff] *I acted in this* [Lord Albert Flower] *I also played the part of a commissionaire who had to try not to laugh.*

The Orchestra, *'which made a horrible noise'*, conducted by Captain Bertie Massy, comprised Lieutenant Cecil Graves Royal Scots, Lieutenant Reginald Peskett, Lieutenant William Brown RFC, Lieutenant William Mortimer-Phelan RFC, Lieutenant Cecil West Royal Dublin Fusiliers, Lieutenant John Younger RFA and Captain Herbert Pelham-Burn Gordon Highlanders and one other. After the last performance there was a supper in room 46, building II, where the programmes were probably all signed by the participants.

Throughout the winter of 1916/17 the performance of 'The Importance of Being Earnest' was postponed several times before eventually being performed in March 1917, shortly before they left this camp.

There was a performance of 'Friedberg Follies' on 3 October 1916 in the gymnasium, and an Xmas 1916 pantomime production of Cinderella in which Brocas, who played the part of Prince Aboukir of Badoura, twice had to kiss Cinderella (Captain Moseley) on the lips to the immense amusement of all. (*Letter 127*)

His numerous sporting activities included tennis, for which he won £3, badminton, golf and cricket, although the following detailed request of 31 January 1917 (*Letter 131*) for nets/matting and ancillaries was soon disallowed as mentioned 9 February 1915 (*Letter 132*).

What we want is (1) <u>64</u> (sixty-four) yards of netting <u>10</u> (ten) feet high
(i.e.2 sides of 30 yards and 4 yards width). A top cover 25 (twenty-five)
yards long by 14 (fourteen) feet wide and a <u>stop net</u> to go at the back 15
(fifteen) feet high and 18 (eighteen) feet long. Also all the rope stays to
fix this up. We can get wood here, and also the tent pegs. Please also send
a strip of coconut matting <u>22 yards</u> long by <u>4 yards</u> wide with all the
apparatus to fix it down. I leave it to you as to the best way to get the
netting. Please let it be <u>tarred</u> netting as the other kind tears so easily and
please have the <u>stop net</u> of a fine enough mesh to stop a golf ball as we
hope to practice driving into it. Perhaps a net like this could be got second-
hand somewhere, also coconut matting.

To complement this apparatus, and thinking well ahead, as early as
31 January 1917 (*Letter 131*) in the same letter he requested his entire
cricket wardrobe and also his golf clubs.

Please send me my Cricket bag (leather) with my bats, 2 pair pads,
batting gloves, 2 pair boots, golf driver and brassey 6 (six) cricket balls
and some old golf balls, also wicket keeping gloves if I have got any.

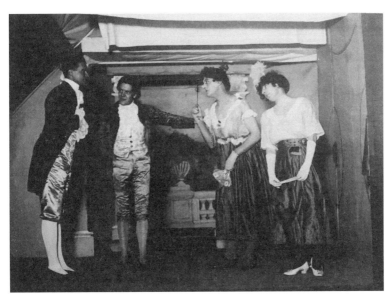

Brocas as Prince Aboukir of Badoura on left in Act II of Cinderella at Friedberg. Source:
Burrows family archive

These were more extreme examples of the extraordinary lengths the prisoners went to satisfy their needs, comforts and maintain links with a life back home before the war. Football and hockey were not possible. In the winter they tried without success to convert the tennis court to a skating rink, (*Letter 126*) but later managed to make two small rinks which were very crowded. Brocas's reading and language studies also helped fill his daily schedule, so much so, it would appear from his letters that he had little time for planning or taking part in further escapes, although undoubtedly the thought of freedom was never far from his mind. After the escape of Fairweather and the Grinnell-Milne brothers, security at the camp was probably tightened. It was not until March 1917 that further escape items, a compass and wire cutters, were sent out by his mother, probably in response to one of his two letters to Bene Cartwright.

In the second of these letters, *en cachette*, (*Letter 137*) approximately March 1917, he asks for a repeat of the items sent in August as well as a luminous compass and wire cutters, these being the items duly sent in parcels 156 and 160, of 7 and 14 March respectively. This letter is undoubtedly the most revealing regarding his escape plans. He elaborates further on how messages and various others items could get through to facilitate a successful escape:

> …*but if ever you want to get any message through to me, they never search the bottom of the parcels sent, and we can always take away the boxes. Hence a false bottom could conceal Weekly Times, monthly magazines and illustrateds, and these are always most welcome. Please repeat the etcetera's you sent me last summer for the purpose of me joining you, and please send maps of the country round here in all possible directions, and if you can get news of any unguarded places on Dutch or Swiss frontiers, please mark them on maps. Please send also (1) a compass, (2) a* <u>luminous</u> *wrist watch (3) an electric torch, (4) a pair of wire cutters, and any kind of food that will be useful for trekking. No. 2 can be sent openly and also the food, and the others had better be hidden in Jam. Please send luminous compass. Chances of success are small, but still they do exist. Did you ever hear from Capt. Henderson, or get private letter I wrote Sept. 14…?*

In the first of his letters to Bene Cartwright from Friedberg, (*Letter 136*) approximate date February 1917, Brocas describes for the first time the true circumstances of his internment particularly in the first year, and how they relied on food parcels. He also mentions two failed escape attempts.

> *...I don't think you can have any idea of what we went through at the beginning. The first year was absolute hell, and I personally suffered horribly from my head. But this is now passed and as our captors begin to see that all is not as good as they could hope and that we are the cause of all the trouble, they have begun to treat us very differently. As regards food there is practically none here, and we live entirely on what you send out...*

Lieutenant Nicolai Miloradovitch, Brocas's Russian 'Professor', who became his best friend, kept in touch at Friedberg by writing to Brocas's parents (*Letters 104, 122 and 128*). This followed Brocas's request of 30 June 1916 (*Letter 100*) for his parents to write to Miloradovitch. His parents even sent Miloradovitch a cake. (*Letter 128*) As a gift before they left Mainz, Miloradovitch had given Brocas, as he said '*...a most glorious copy of Tolstoy's War and Peace...*', a treasured priceless illustrated First Edition, in two substantial volumes inscribed with the message '*To my friend and first English teacher Brocas Burrows who I expect will not forget Nicholas Miloradovitch, Mayence 19 May 1916*'. Somehow, Brocas managed to keep them in perfect condition throughout the remainder of his internment. They remain in the family. An interesting conundrum is how, in the first place, a Russian lieutenant POW had managed to have them in his possession. There is a suggestion that Miloradovitch was related in some way to a Russian noble family. By contrast his orderly, a humble 'Tommy' Private A. MacGregor 8035, The Kings Own R J Regt. also wrote to his Brocas's parents expressing thanks for parcels (*Letters 98 and 110*).

With only two days notice, on 20 March 1917 Brocas sent his heavy luggage down to the station in Friedberg knowing only that the following day he would be separated from many friends and depart to a hitherto unknown destination. His parents had no way of knowing that his nine months stay at Friedberg was about to end. By the time the escape items sent in March were acknowledged (*Letter 146*) on 13 May 1917, he was safely ensconced in his sixth camp, Clausthal in the Harz mountains. He wrote at the time. (*Letter 141*) '*My little all consists of one vast wooden case ctg. Pots, pans, crockery, theatrical outfit and odds and ends, one large basket containing clothes, one case with books and eatables, 2 suit cases, my polo sticks and a table!*' He signed off that letter hoping that his sojourn in the next camp would be a short one and his last. Unfortunately, it would be another ten months before he tasted freedom.

Parcels from home

From the way his parents supported him with food parcels throughout his internment it is clear they were unstinting in catering for all his needs, whether by their own volition or in response to his requests. Brocas was never in danger of dying from starvation, or suffering from a bad diet that lacked the necessary vitamins. At one point he even describes putting on weight and getting fat, and how he needed to exercise to lose weight. No doubt this was all part of his constant effort to reassure his parents that he was in good health.

During his nine months (267 days) stay at Friedberg, Brocas received 176 parcels the frequency and content of which can been seen in the sample list. The majority directly from his parents, although they also funded one sent from Harrods and twenty from Twining which from December 1916 was a regular monthly grocery parcel. Bread, butter, cake, biscuits, milk, potted meat, tongue and sausages were staple items but were supplemented with tinned fruit, nuts and raisins and many other items. The variety was slightly less than at Mainz. Social items he requested were increasingly exotic, for example, the cricket nets etc. referred to previously. If they were sent, they were usually in response to a request from Brocas. While at Friedberg his substantial library was only augmented by six books.

It is interesting to note the background to which these parcels were being sent and that in England at this time, food rationing was in force. A newspaper article of 6 February 1917 in England clarified the rations at home. The meat ration was two and half pounds per head per week to include bone and fat. The bread ration was four pounds or three pounds of flour for bread making per head per week and was expected to include that used for cakes and puddings. The sugar ration was three quarters of a pound per head per week. The parcel lists of food items sent to Brocas, if typical, suggest the 'upper' class families of officers were better resourced than those of the general rank and file, although even these were being support by the government with parcels of prescribed content.

Parcels sent to Lieutenant M Brocas Burrows at Friedberg
(Sample list only)
1 August 1916 – 30 August 1916

AUGUST 1916
TO FRIEDBERG

(concealed escape items in brown X indicated the item)

1st	No 31	1 Peas 1 Jam X *(compass)* 1 apricots, 1 milk, 1 sardines,
2nd	No 32	(Twining) tea, cocoa, raisins, jam, rice, castor sugar,
		lump sugar, café au lait, soap
		Acknowledged
3rd	No 33	Eggo, veda bread, consommé X *(maps)*, swiss milk, peas, soap
		Acknowledged
5th	No 34	Cake, consommé X *(maps)* apple pudding, eggo, sardines
		Acknowledged
7th	No 35	Biscuits, milk, honey, pineapple jam X *(dyes)*
9th	No 36	Potted meat X *(whisky)* bread
	No 37	(Twining) soap, sugar, rice, jam, raisin, cocoa, tea
	No 38	Cooker, primus
		Acknowledged
12th	No 39	Cake, chocolate, lemon squash, marmalade, butter
		Acknowledged
15th		From *Pittlochry*, biscuits and groceries
		Acknowledged
15th		To *McGregor*, socks, heather, and groceries
		Acknowledged
16th	No 40	(Twining), café au lait, soap, jam, tea, castor sugar, lump,
		cocoa
		Acknowledged
	No 41	Lemon squash, butter, veda bread, milk, potted meat, petit
		beurre biscuits
		Acknowledged
19th	No 42	Mutton chops, milk, soap, cake
		Acknowledged
23rd	No 43	(Twining) soap, café au lait, sugar, rice, jam, raisins, cocoa, tea
		Acknowledged
	No 44	Bread, butter, honey, milk, lemon squash, mutton chops
		Acknowledged
	No 45	Cake, apple puddings, peas, milk, soap
		Acknowledged
		From Pittlochry, biscuits and heather
29th		3 vests, 3 pants
30th	No 46	Veda bread, butter, tin corn, French beans, peas, soap
		Acknowledged

9

Friedberg POW Camp

15 June 1916 – 23 March 1917

The Letters

Letter 96

15th June 1916, Offizer-Kriegsgefangenen-Lager,
Friedberg in Hessen

Health: Good!

Brocas

Letter 97

19th June 1916, Friedberg

My dearest Mother,
Here we are after our fourth move in this country, trying to arrange ourselves
and get things straight. This time only the English left Mainz and were sent
on here and it really was a great wrench leaving our Russian friends after
no less than nineteen months together. Here we have joined 70 other English
and they are a completely new lot of French and Russian officers. I have not
been here long enough to compare the two camps and so will leave that till
later, this is, however, certainly better than Burg. We are still the same party
in our room and have managed to bring the parrot and the gramophone
along with us. There is a new tennis court here which we hope will turn out
well, but have our fears as it is rather like the small loaves and 2 fishes! I was
fortunate enough to get 4 letters from you before leaving. A card of May 29th,
letter Mother May 27th, Duch May 28th, and one from Miss Owen of May
28th. Most welcome all. So glad to get news of 5th D.G.'s. What is Curran
going to transfer to? **Ellie's complete recovery is surprising me a lot**
and of course makes excellent reading. [a further reference to the*
Russian campaign] *Col. Neish came to Mainz just before he left to go before a*
Commission to try and pass for Switzerland. He was full of messages to father
and asked if F. remembers MacNeal who accompanied N. when he came to

Annarad Japoorah (?)!! (if that is how it is spelt!) The Colonel has aged a lot since I saw him last (in Nov. 14) and was not looking very well, but if he can only get to Switz. he ought to be alright. Please continue food supplies here as before, and also send some brown boot polish, two pairs grey flannel trousers, one pair white tennis shoes, and one pair stirrup guards from Maxwell, just like the last pair. I will write to you more fully in a few days when we have settled down. At present it is a complete pandemonium everywhere and I have lost everything. No more tobacco please, but cig. as usual. I have almost chucked smoking. Health good. Best love to you all.
Your affectionate son,

Brocas.

Letter 98

26th June 1916, Soltau, (Hanover) POW camp
To: Mrs Isobel Burrows, 9 Norham Gardens, Oxford

This is in reply to your letter of April 27th and your card of May 23rd. Your parcel containing biscuits and the "V.V.s" [Veda bread] arrived yesterday. I thank you very much for the latter articles. Your informants were right – they are <u>needed</u>. I am taking the risk of incurring your displeasure by writing this, but I beg to be allowed to send you a card now and then – I prefer to meet my obligations personally and direct. I have written to my mother fully explaining the circumstances, and I'm sure she will agree with me in this matter. Please inform me if I make any mistake in the address. Glad you like my photograph and mothers.
Yours Gratefully,

Pte A McGregor.

Letter 99

27th June 1916, Friedberg

My dearest Father,
Will you please send me 2 Badminton nets 8 rackets, and 6 dozen shuttlecocks. Please send the rackets in a Press and also let me know the cost. All well.
Your affectionate son,

Brocas

Arrived July 11th. [an indication that letters were taking about a fortnight to arrive]

Letter 100

30th June 1916, Friedberg

My dearest Mother,
Several letters from you since my last and all most welcome. You certainly seem very busy and I hope are in correspondingly good health. Your report of **Cousin Jack** [Admiral Jellicoe] *is most revealing, though I never was in any real doubt. Even so it's better to be certain. The photos are a great source of pleasure. You all look so well and cheerful esp. Cousin Ted. Iced Easter cake arrived and was duly consumed! I will in future keep much more exact list of parcels and apologise humbly for trouble caused. So glad to hear Summer Fields is as usual and Mr. Alington still bowling. That Father is still playing tennis hard is also good news and I shall hope for a match with him in the near future. I should be so pleased to hear an account of your visit to Sherborne. Two members of Gareth battalion rather the one he was with on Jan. 31, '15, are here. Capt. Hutchinson and Major Morrison Bell. But I fear they know nothing of what happened to him. Please give my love to Mrs Hamilton Fletcher. Have you had any news lately from B.P.? Please let me know. I am writing this at 6.45 a.m. in order to catch the post, so please excuse any bad writing etc. We are gradually beginning to settle down here and I think we will eventually prefer it to Mayence, but it is early to judge yet. We are much more in the country here and there are fields all round. It is however much colder and the soil is very sticky clay. There is one tennis court and we are engaged in building another.* **Four of us also got a patch (3 yards square) of earth under cultivation. At least we intend to build a hut to sit in in summer and plant veg. round it.** [Duncan Grinnell-Milne used such a hut to cover up an escape tunnel as reported in *An Escaper's Log*, but there is no reference to Brocas being part of this or using a similar method] *Still very cold here and no summer yet at all. But of course we still hope. We propose getting up some theatricals of sorts and I am to be stage manager, so I am very busy. "Voice trials" etc. are almost hourly occurrences and I think we ought to get up something quite funny before the end! My late* **Russian professor** [Lt Nickolai Miloradovitch] *has given me a most glorious copy of* **Tolstoy's War and Peace** [1st Edition of two volumes in superb condition now in Burrows family archive] *which I am reading at present. Would you please send him a letter to say I am well and send him my best love as also do all the old numbers of 'Stübe 75'. Ask him to pass it on to all our old friends there and tell him we hope he still continues the hockey. His*

address is Lt. N. Miloradovitch, Russian Prisoner of War, Offizier-gefangenen-lager, Maintz, Germany. In parcels I have received one lot of Swiss bread, Tripoli book, lives of Scott and Beaconsfield, enough books for the present thanks, new cap and cover, chocolate, eggo, tinned fish, etc., stump cricket balls, parcel of salt, sugar, etc. All most welcome. So glad to hear the tins are on the way. We are all in a room together here as before including the parrot. So glad you have seen Ward and Champion. I knew the former, please remember me to him. I hope Col. Gordon is well. Please ask Cox & Co. to transfer £10 (ten pounds to Sterling) from my account to the account of L. G. Humphreys at Sir C. McGregor Bart & co. 39 Panton Street, Haymarket, London, S. W. Well I must close. Best love to you all.
Your affectionate son,

Brocas.

Letter 101

11th July 1916, Friedberg

My dearest Father,
*Well we are at last beginning to settle in and I think we shall prefer this to Mayence. The worst of it is that the soil is clay which greatly precludes exercise on wet days. We are at present engaged in erecting a tennis court ourselves and find digging excellent for health and bending muscles. We are also getting up some theatricals and so the time is passing quickly. This latter is great fun and as I am supposed to be manager my time is very full up. Any new songs duets etc. of the comic or quasi comic order as also any small plays mostly for men, will be most welcome. Have received several letters and parcels from you since my last, yours of June 14th. So glad to get news of **Ellie and Govare** [Russians and French]– Col Gordon. I will write him a card. Very glad to hear he is better. Duchess's of June 18. You certainly seem fully occupied and Mother's of June 17. As I told you in my last Graves is here and is a prominent member of the orchestra. He plays the trombone. I wish you could hear this remarkable band. I doubt if there has ever been another like it. Of course our daily programme here is rather different and may interest you. I have for the moment given up early morning Gym. and don't get up till 8. The cold douche and breakfast at 9. Roll call at 9.30 and from 10.30-11.30 help dig the tennis court. 12-1 Russian lesson. Lunch at 1. After lunch I shall ordinarily learn Italian but at present we have rehearsals and I am very busy till about 4, when we have tea and then exercise till 6. Bath and supper 6.30 and then conversations with foreigners passes the time profitably till 9.30 when we have another roll call and go in. Lights out at 11. Till this theatrical show is over*

I am not going to make final arrangements for work. We walk twice a week in the country round which is quite pleasant and of course the life in general is very open air and so what with this and a practically total absence of the **"little drops that mystify"**, [probably "whisky"] *Health is excellent. Most of us have little patches of garden here, of course quite minute. We have planted the m. and c. and erected a tent of sorts.* **The "Iron ration" has arrived and is just what I wanted.** [Reference to a case of groceries and other parcels sent 6 June] *Never starve now. Other parcels received are cake, soap, clothes, parsnips and eggo, choc. tongue, veda bread, and butter, Tripoli book and 2 condiment parcels. Many thanks. I have now got enough mustard for an Army Corps. Any news of the Winchester Cricket pro. would interest me much. Please send me a "double cooker – 4 pints size" – our culinary expert tells me you will know what this means. So I wish you luck! Walker (R.F.C.) and I have arranged for ourselves quite a nice corner of the room here, divided it off with curtains and made it very snug. I am sure the great Warden would call it a "nosy cook". I hope Alex was* **in time for the fun.** [deployment in front line] **How is Uncle Will?** [could be a reference to another nationality e.g. Americans] *4 more parcels have just arrived including 6 red stump cricket balls, bread, butter and fish, cake and biscuits and 1 tin biscuits. Ever so many thanks. You really are wonderful at sending me what I want and you don't know how grateful I am. The parrot is still going strong though I fear he has not learned to talk much yet, and whistles too much for my liking. We put him out in the garden one day but the poor fellow nearly died of fright and has not properly recovered yet! Surely it is about time you sent me some more photos of yourselves. Well, I have no more news for you just yet, so will close. My best love to you all.*
Your affectionate son,

Brocas.

Letter 102

21st July 1916, Friedberg

My dearest Mother,
Since my last I have received parcels number 1, 5, 7, 8 and 9 for which many thanks, also letters M. of 24th. Holy poker cut out. **Air cushion arrived.** [not obvious why he requested this specifically] *F. of 22nd, F. of 28th, with exc. photos of news of money. D. July 2 and M. July 1.* **All true, re – Gerard.** [Gerard Freeman-Thomas missing 9 July 1915] *An excellent and most legible letter from B.P. of Sheffield. Many thanks to him. All flourishing here and I am really busy. Our theatricals are most occupying. We are potting a play just acted by the Russians. I am the hero!! And in another play a commissionaire*

who gets a drink. What news on my regiment. I am on tenterhooks. So glad you have heard of Capt. Odiaux. He was in the next room to me at Mayence. We are building a tennis court here and I have taken to violent skipping and I'm keeping v. fit. So glad to get such exc. news of you. Best love. Your affectionate son,

Brocas.

Letter 103

31st July 1916, Friedberg

My dearest Father,
I fear it looks as if some of my letters have gone astray lately. I am very sorry but fear the material lost is but slight! 3 parcels since my last. Nos. IX, X and XI. Many thanks. Also letters from Duchess of July 9 and you of 4th. Many thanks. I returned the Document duly signed and witnessed by Captain Sturt a German officer here. It sounds most satisfactory about my money though I fear it must be giving you much trouble. Your news is certainly most reassuring, if that is necessary, and I sincerely hope you are right. [probably a reference to the progress of the war] *I've also received M. letter of July 15 and Duchess of July 16. Many thanks. The case of groceries arrived and I acknowledged it duly, with many thanks. Did you ever get my letter asking for 3 new vests and 3 pair pants, thinnest possible material? If not please send them. I fear this is even worse written than usual, but the truth is I am very tired. We have just finished our theatrical show, and it ran for four nights and one matinée and the whole thing has been rather a strain. It went off very well indeed and the audience was most appreciative though about 75% can't have understood a word. We had a vaudeville entertainment. The items being a conjuror* [Lt Berry], *a soloist* [Captain Moseley], *a quartet* [Captain Jervis, Captain Moseley, Captain Younger, Captain Sampson], *a comic orchestra which made a horrible noise, a scotch dance* [Sword Dance by Captain Usher]*, 2 plays* ['L'Anglais à Paris come on l'imagine' and 'English as she is spoke in London'] *written by officers here and a "potted" play a la Pelissier. The play we potted was one acted by the Russians about a month ago.* [Burlesque 'Le High Life' founded on the comedy of M. Chekoff] *I acted in this* [Lord Albert Flower] *I also played the part of a commissionaire who had to try not to laugh! The Russians kindly lent us the room they had rigged up as a theatre for a whole week, and so we have practically lived there. In a way I am very sorry it is over, as I'm sure it is very good for one to learn to run a show like that, and it certainly passes the time, but it is a great relief to get it off one's chest. Most of the scenery fell down on the last night but otherwise*

*all went well. I will send you programmes etc. later if I can. We hope soon to get a place of our own and arrange it ourselves. We have been having the most glorious weather here the last few days, quite warm. It is surely about time too. You must have had a most exciting time with all the servants away. Four more of the old stagers left us for Switzerland a few days ago, **but we don't envy them.*** [tongue in cheek comment to reassure parents] *What must it be like to be in Switzerland now? Well, well, my best love to you all. Your affectionate son,*

Brocas.

Letter 104

30th July 1916, Room 99 Mainz
To: S. M. Burrows, Oxford, England forwarded to Atholl Palace Hotel, Pitlochry, Perthshire, Scotland

My dear Sir,
I had today the greatest pleasure to get your letter with news about your dear son and his friends from the room 75. I am very happy to know them all in good health. I ask you that very kind messages from me and Pavel Meyer may be passed on to all the members of the room 75. It was very dull when the English friends departed from Mayence. Now many of Brocas' Russian friends have been sent away in another camp, for example Basilie, Tam-Tam, Long Tam, Peter and little colonel. I am very happy that your son likes and reads the book, which I gave him. My dearest idea is to meet my English friends especially your dear son, who were all so kind to me in Germany. Yours Sincerely

Nicolas Miloradovitch

Letter 105

1st August 1916, Sandy, Limpefield
[Probably to Mr Burrows]

Dear Sir,
Mr Beruer? came to see me yesterday. He told me he had delivered to you a similar message to the one he bought me via Capt. Henderson in Switzerland – from your son about his escape from Germany. My son has often spoken of him and I think your son talks German and my son does not – and he has

translated... for him. May I ask what line you are taking about supplying the things your son asks for, to help escape. Risk of severe punishment for my boy and those who are innocent of trying to escape seems so acute. Please forgive me for troubling you. I've already lost a boy in the war and am so very anxious this one return safely.

Yours

M Pelham Burn

Letter 106

7th August 1916, 34 Islington Gardens, Eastbourne

Dear Mrs Burrows,
I am much interested to hear you have sent those contraband things to your son. With the code message. I am much perplexed still, and have done nothing definite. I feel so afraid that if several have these things sent the plan for escape is sure to leak out. My son used to be reckless. I fear what he may do. I am a chronic invalid with R. Arthritis. For 11 years I have not being able to stand or walk. I am grateful for your suggestion that I should see you – I will write again if I may – my second son in Black Watch is on light duty at Kinross (was wounded and had a fall as Icarus?) He also was begged to send these things but thinks risk too great as the war's signs now are better as regards the end than they were.

Yours Sincerely

M. Pelham Burn

Letter 107

[No date], *Friedberg*

My dearest Father,
*Since my last I have received parcels number 13, 15, 17 and 19 and also Badminton things. Please tell Ayres to keep bill for me. Also received letter from mother of July 22 full of news. So glad you have met Leggat and Green. Here all is as usual and I am getting down to work again. Photos of **theats.** [theatricals] not a great success, but I will send if poss. I hope you will mind the ladies, esp. their dresses which were almost entirely home-made. Please send me out a new pair of "slacks" and also write to Messrs. Thomas Duncan*

and Co., 55 Princes's Street, Edinburgh, and tell him to make me a pair of boots precisely similar to those he made for Capt. Younger, R.F.A., and send them to me here. The last pair you sent, were I fear, a failure. Never mind. All flourishing here but longing for home. Best of luck to you all.
Your affectionate son,

Brocas.

Letter 108

[No date], *Friedberg*

My dearest Father,
*Only one letter from you since my last but that one most welcome. Fancy Ramsay nearly being chosen head. Surely that is somewhat curious. Green very kindly wrote to me. Many thanks to him. I hope he is getting on alright. My love to Leggat also please. It is indeed unfortunate for him to have sprained his ankle playing football at this period! Four parcels from you since my last, No's 23, 20, 21, and 19. Also the Badminton things which are excellent. We are forming a small badminton club here and pooling the nets and shuttlecocks. Will you please pay for what I order and let me pay you on return, or please do whatever you find best. Also order me 6 doz. more shuttlecocks and 3 Ayre's "F.H.A." double strand rackets. Please also send me a supply of gut and an instrument to restring rackets (including a drill). My friends here are inquisitive as to whether the tennis racket you sent me was meant for tennis or self-defence!! I enclose a copy of the programme of our performance here and also photos taken of us after the show. These latter are I feel bad as we had just finished a matinee and had a horrible rush to get the theatre ready for the evening performance. The midshipman really made an exceptionally pretty girl and none of us looked quite as blackguardly as we do in the photos, except perhaps the band. My costume – pyjamas – is due to the fact that the author of the play considered it necessary that Lord Albert Flower whom I impersonated should appear in this costume among many others. The whole play "Le High Life" was a "Pot" of a play acted by the Russians here with a few additions for the benefit of the French. We are now getting up a Pierrrot troup and so the good work goes on! Tonight I am going to a theatrical performance given by the Russian orderlies which I hear is most amusing. Hence as you see we keep alive in spite of everything. Letter from Mother of July 29th has just arrived. So sorry to hear about Boswell and Henderson. Capt. Boger has gone to another camp. I don't know where. But if you send his copy to Mayence it will find him. Please send another copy here. I fear it has given you much trouble. Case of food arrived and I acknowledged it. **We have***

been most busy emulating Winston here, but have failed. [Probably a reference to Winston Churchill and trying to escape] *Glad to hear the Anzacs are at it again. Please send me a supply of modern songs of the Revue type and also ask Cox and Co. to forward me ten pounds (£10) through their Rotterdam agents or rather the equivalent of that sum. What news have you of my regiment? Please also send me some books on horses, stable management (I believe Ansell wrote one) etc. One of the new Naval Officers here has many relations in the Ceylon. His name is Halliley. He himself has been there and knows Newara Elaya. You can't think what a pleasure your snapshots etc. give. They are all so good too. Those of you 3 Leggat and Green are excellent. What news have you of nurse Pugh? Give her my love when you write. I am at present studying "Scouting for Boys" – a wonderful book. All as usual here, but we are if anything gayer than usual I think. My best love to you all. Your affectionate son,*

Brocas.

Letter 109

[No date], *Friedberg*

My dearest Mother,
Letters scarce but parcels good. Have received Nos. 26, 27, 29, 30, 28, 32, 33, [33 contained concealed maps] *also D's letter of Aug. 6, M's of Aug. 5th, F's of Aug. 2nd and also a letter from Aunt W. All most welcome. I do hope you will enjoy your stay at Pitlochry. I remember passing through it on our way down from Scotland. The Badminton is going strong here and is a great boon, as football and hockey are not possible. Please send me two dozen more shuttlecocks and three more rackets like the first lot and also a press to hold six rackets and let me know exact cost of each item and keep bill for me.* **Ellie seems grand** *as also Govare.* [Russians and French] *All luck to them. We are now forming a Pierrot troup here. Lucky for you that you can't hear us practising. I am at present trying to avoid singing a Rag Time solo. Well I hope to goodness you are correct when you say you think we should be together for my 22nd! It's a long long way! Best love,*

Brocas.

Letter 110

27th August 1916, Soltau, (Hanover) PoW camp
To: Mrs I C Burrows, 9 Norham Gardens, Oxford

I am writing this in answer to your last two cards. I am glad to say I have received your 3rd of July parcel, I will drop you a card when the last-mentioned parcel arrives. Was very glad to hear that your son's new home? is more healthy than the old. Please tell him how sorry I am to hear of his separation from his Russian friends, two of them he will miss very much. Dear madam this is perhaps my last chance of writing you in time – please enclose in your letter to him – my good wishes and many happy returns of his birthday. I thank you very much for parcels, and also for sending on my letters to mother I am naturally very much upset over my dear brother's death, and deeply appreciate your sympathy.
Yours truly,
A McGregor

Private A McGregor 8035
The Kings Own R J Regt.

Letter 111

31st August 1916, Friedberg

My dearest Mother,
Very glad to get yours of the 12th and also Duchess's of the 13th. You seem to be having an excellent time at Pitlochry. I remember passing through it on a motor journey down from Scotland and thinking what a nice place it looked. How excellent that Duchess is getting such good tennis. I hope she will soon be an equal to Mlle Lenglen! Since my last I have received the monthly supply of cigarettes and tobacco (please stop the latter) also a parcel with No. obliterated containing a box of Crawford's biscuits and Chinese figs (most exc.) ***Also No. XXX with Lizzie's extra special brand of home-made potted meat.*** [Probably a reference to parcel No. 31 sent 3 August 1916 which contained concealed whisky] *Indeed a luxury which we all appreciated immensely! I have been spending all day putting the cement surface on our new tennis court which we are finishing here. Most arduous work but I think we shall have an excellent court when it is finished. We are also rehearsing a Pierrot troupe which is most amusing. We have two experts here in this kind of entertainment, one an actor by profession and the other a sailor so it really ought not to be a bad show. I have unfortunately got to sing a solo – a topical*

song to the tune of "I've got a motto"! Dreadful, isn't it? I am also a Pierrette at intervals! This in spite of my 13 stone. So glad to hear such continued good news of **Ellie and Govare**. [Russians and French] What news of my regiment? Please thank Aunt Io for the parcel she so kindly sent me and wish her the best of luck as also Bernard. At present we are having it very cold here and autumn seems to be closing in already. We are now shut in our barracks at 8 o'clock. Will you please send me a parcel containing the following articles: 30 tins Nestles condensed milk, 25 lb tins of butter, 25lb of sugar, 25lb of biscuits (a mixture of Captain, Petite Beurre, Albert and that type) and 2 tins of Scotch Shortbread, also 5 khaki shirts and 10 collars size 16 round neck, 2 khaki shirts and two collars 15 ½ round neck, and twelve white pocket handkerchiefs and 4 khaki ties. Please also send me here the bills for each of these articles and either pay them at home and keep a chit for me on return, or else keep them unpaid, which ever suits you best. Many apologies for giving you all this trouble. Please also send me a dozen Japanese lanterns. These are for our theatre which we are constructing here. It is being decorated "a la Japanaise", also a side of bacon! And please start eggs again. Are you going to do any visiting this autumn, or do you intend a busy time at Oxford? I expect you will be very occupied at the examination schools. One of our jailers, here, is an old Etonian! A curious coincidence. There are 7 O.E.'s among the British P's of W here and we had an O.E. lunch a few days ago with Major Morrison Bell M.P. (Scots Guards), and chatted about the old place for hours. All seem pleased about Alington's appointment. Mon has certainly been most fortunate up to now. A nervous time for Cousin Claudine I fear with both him and Charlie at it. Well, I must close. Best love to you all.

Your affectionate son,

Brocas

Letter 112

16th September 1916, Friedberg

My dearest Mother,

Since my last I have received Father's letter of Aug. 16th yours of 27th, D's of 27th and F's of 29th. All most welcome. I was so pleased to get the snap of Duchess. <u>Some</u> costume! As they say across the pond! So glad your time at Pitlochry was such a success and that you got tennis etc. in such profusion. Tell Duchess she will have to take care or she will be the heaviest member of the family as I am now only 12.6! **Very glad to hear of Ellie's new acquisition.** [A reference to Romania joining the Allies] Here we have *been having a most exhilarating time with a tennis tournament and a Pierrot performance. The former was a handicap and my partner – a French captain – and I got knocked out quite early on, but afterwards I issued a challenge to the winners and beat them. So, we are quite satisfied! The Pierrot show was a great success. There is a large Drill Hall here in the camp and we gave it there before all the officers. I suppose about 400. Most of them have never seen such a show before and much appreciated the novelty. I sung a topical solo to the tune of "I've got a motter", with a verse in French(!) which if it could not be repeated in the drawing room went down extraordinarily well! In another song I sang a Russian verse! A dreadful undertaking! We had some photos taken which are not very good. I will send in next letter.* At last I have got a snap of myself for you doing touch judge during a tie of the tennis tournament here. I am not really as fat as I look. I have just sent off a card to Aunt Em. to congratulate her on her magnificent performance. It really is wonderful. Sorry one of my letters has gone astray as it must mean a gap in my correspondence. I have received parcels No. 34,* [contained concealed maps in consommé soup] *39, 40, 41, and 42, also Swiss bread, which comes in good condition. The veda bread varies but is usually alright.* **The Harrods jam was excellent and also the soup.** [Jam contained concealed compass and dyes, soup contained concealed maps] *Anything in that line most welcome. The double cooker is a great success. The Italian is going along "lentamente ma sicuramente" (if that is correct)! I get excellent practice in French and Russian in my capacity of manager of a theatre. I have chucked Hindustani at the moment as I don't think it would be any use trying to learn a vocabulary as I should only forget it and I think I could pick it up again on the voyage if I go East after this. It is dreadful how one language makes you forget another. I have met several French officers here who know Compiégne well and I have had some most interesting conversations with them. I have just been inoculated against enteric and I'm feeling a bit stiff in the arm. I wish I had kept count of how many times I have been done since July 14. I still get most cheerful letters from most of our late Gstaad party who all seem very "merry and bright". Did you hear the little story of the Yank who on reading of some big battle in this war said, "Some fight!" to which an Englishmen replied, "Some don't". Not bad eh?*

Well I must close. All as usual here. My best love to you all.

Your affectionate son,

Brocas.

★I enclose this and hope it reaches.

Letter 113

[No date (probably late September)], *Friedberg*

My dearest Mother,
Since my last four parcels No.s 43, 44, 45 and 1 Scotch. [concealed in potted meat in parcel 36] *Many thanks.* **Please send me more meat stuffs i.e. some steak and kidney pies and MacConachie rations.** [Probably a coded requested for more escape items] *Also some special food for birthday dinner. Five letters have arrived. M. of Sept 2nd and 10th, F. of 7th and D. of 3rd and 10th. All most welcome as also the photos. So glad the theatre photos arrived and you liked them. I will send 2 more next letter. Please write at once to Miss Olave Soames, Gray Rigg, Lilliput, Dorset and tell her not to take any notice of the message of June 9. All as usual here, rather cold. Please send me a really warm sweater and also a really warm woolly waistcoat with sleeves, and also 3 khaki shirts of thinnest poss. material and 2 silk ties to match, size of collar 15 ½, also some self-raising flour. Sorry to hear of Nurse's change. I hope it is a good place. Best love to you all.*
Your affectionate son,

Brocas

Letter 114

30th September 1916, Friedberg

My dearest Mother,
Three letters from you since my last, yours of September 17th, Duchess's of Sept. 3rd and Father's of Sept. 14th. Very many thanks. I have also had letters from Aunt W., Miss Rice Wiggin, and Leggatt, the latter of July 21st. Please pass on my thanks to them. So glad Aunt W. and Bernard have been with you and that they recovered from their colds quickly. Please tell Aunt W. I got the parcels she so kindly sent me some time back and am sure I wrote and thanked her for them. They were most welcome. So glad the theatre photos pleased. The ladies were really much more charming to look upon than they appear in the photos and in fact caused quite a "fureur"! I enclose two photos of the Pierrot troupe which I fear are not very good but they were also taken by flash light. The costumes are again home-made. We are now rehearsing the "Importance of Being Earnest" which we hope to produce at the end of next month. I am taking one of the girl's parts – Miss Fairfax. Don't laugh! I fear my measurements don't quite compare with those of the Venus de Milo but my "swain" is correspondingly bigger than Adonis! Fortunately among

*our number here is a professional actor who knows all about it and has acted this before. All is much as usual here though we are now starting the winter season. We have "appels" at 9.30 a.m., 4.30 p.m. and 10.p.m. this last one in our rooms. We are shut in doors at 7.30 p.m. A French doctor has now been put into our room temporarily, in place of **Walker who attempted to leave this one without permission of his hosts.*** [a reference to an escape attempt by Captain Eric Walker RFC – no details] *So glad to get news of **Cousin Jack, Ellie and Govare.*** [Admiral Jellicoe, Russians and French] *I have received the following parcels 46 (a & b) 47, 48, 49, 50 and 52. Many thanks. I don't know what I should do without the stuff you send. My only requirement this week is 2 pairs of gloves for parade wear – preferably those that pull on without buttons or clasps. It is wonderful to think that Aunt Em is 101 tomorrow. May she live to have many more birthdays. The photo of her taken on her 100th birthday still adorns my little corner here. So glad the aviary goes well. Bingham is here and we are all very pleased he has got the V.C. There are several gunners here who knew Mont in Ireland and all express their grief at his death. It is really very sad after going through so much. I hear Lionel Tennyson has also been killed. I have passed on your message to Graves whose people seem very pleased with the photos. Cox writes to say he has sent off the money but it has not arrived yet. It always takes some time. Reports I received from outside the home circle marvel at the enormous amount of work you and father are getting through. I hope this does not mean you are doing too much. Looking after the Anzacs in Oxford sounds no mean job. So glad to hear Port Meadow is occupied again and proving itself useful. Please send me a book each on the Russo-Turkish, Balkan and Americo-Spanish wars and a standard life of Napoleon III. My best love to you all.*
Your affectionate son,

Brocas.

Sorry to hear of Nurses change. The last snapshot of the Duchess is excellent. Many thanks. More please!!

Letter 115

6th October 1916, Friedberg

My dearest Father,
3 letters since my last – yours of September 21, M's of September 23 and D's of 20th, most welcome, also parcel No 52, a magnificent cake from Aunt Katie, to whom many thanks please, and the Badminton things are excellent. All as usual here – much rain. Please send me out the scores – music and words of the

"Marriage Market" and the "Sunshine Girl", also 2 khaki silk ties. So sorry to hear about Rex Benson's death. 40 of our Russian friends are going away tomorrow and we don't know who is to take their place. So glad Port Meadow is in use again. Quite a new form of interest for you. I hope you will try a ride yourselves. I mean to as soon as possible on return.
Best love to all,

Brocas.

Letter 116

My dearest Mother,
I have received F's letters of 28 &5th and M's of 30th, also Aunt Em's and Miss Cannings, very many thanks. So glad your visit to Moss Leigh was a success. Aunt Em seems wonderful, and I am much looking forward to meeting her again after a few more years of this! Parcels 54, 55 & 56 have also turned up and also the Badminton racquets. All excellent, many thanks. Please pay all bills out of my money at Cox's and see I always have about £20 balance there if this is possible. All as usual here, we are playing a Football match v. the French tomorrow. We are hoping to get up a Pantomime for Xmas so if you have anything that would be useful please send it out. Please send tinsel and crackers. Best love.

Brocas.

Letter 117

My dearest Mother,
Once again I write I wish you all luck and happiness on your birthday and to express my regret that fate prevents my spending it with you. Well – they say misfortunes come in threes and this is your third birthday since Aug. 14, so let us hope it is a good omen – for a union before your next. Your birthday letters to me are all arriving and give immense pleasure. Never doubt for one moment that I shall last this out. As time goes on one tends to get hardened to it and does not notice the monotony anymore and this make things much easier. And then we have excellent occupations here which help enormously. This theatre is wonderfully useful in that way and I am sure the time passed in it is far from wasted. It does one good to see the pleasure that even the most simple little entertainment gives. I

have also started to learn to play the Balalaika! With a Russian friend. It is not difficult and helps to keep my Russian going. Three parcels have arrived since my last, one was the songs and the other contained a ginger cake etc. A friend got them for me and forgot to bring the Nos. the music is excellent. Father's letter of Oct. 12 has arrived, as also Duchess's of Oct. 16 and yours of Oct. 14 all full of news – many thanks for them. My only need at present is a decent Italian conversation book and also some light novel in that tongue. The photos of Aunt Em and co. are wonderful; everyone here to whom I show them is amazed. I have got them one on each side of the photo taken of her last year on her birthday. Bernard has certainly grown and looks very well. Our old room (75 at Mayence and 25 here) has at last been split up, in that one of us has been sent to another camp **on account of an unfortunate illicit exit. (I refer to Fairweather)** [referring to a successful escape attempt by Lt Ian Fairweather with the Grinnell-Milne brothers described in the book *An Escaper's Log* by Duncan Grinnell-Milne – all were eventually recaptured] *and another Peskett has been taken very ill and is in the hospital room. I hope he will get to Switzerland with the next lot, hence we are at present only 6. Walker's brother, a recently captured aviator may come to fill up. I enclose 2 photos of our Pierrot troupe taken at our second performance. I think they are better than the first which were taken by flashlight. So glad you like the little snapshot. The 2 officers in the distance are as a matter of fact French and the building is the barrack in which we live. The court, was built by the officers before we English arrived. It is really very good. I played a single on it today; not bad for Oct. 27. We have lately been afflicted by fleas, so will you please despatch some most violent kind of exterminator. We have Keating's concoction, but the objects of his hate seem to flourish on it. Please send me two pairs of suspenders – the kind that attach onto the shirt and not go round the calf. The Swiss bread arrives regularly from Berne and is usually excellent. Well I must close. I shall be thinking of you much on the 16th. Best love to all.
Your affectionate son,*

Brocas.

Letter 118

3rd November 1916, Friedberg

My dearest Father,
Great excitement, the ½ pig has arrived and is excellent! I could hardly carry it! The butter parcels have also arrived and also Nos. 67 and 65. The birthday cake is an absolute chef d'ouvre and all here (room 25) send their heartiest congratulations to Mrs Griffiths on it. It is worthwhile having a birthday even

here for such a cake! No letters this week. Please send me out 4 stars for sleeves and 4 for overcoat. Gut has arrived for rackets. We have just built a **Polo pit** [a place in which a polo learner sits on a wooden horse while practicing hitting a ball] *here so please send out some sticks and balls. Best love to you all, Your affectionate son,*

Brocas.

Letter 119

10th November 1916, Friedberg

My dearest Father,
A letter from each of the three of you since my last and also one from Miss Canning who is always most kind in writing to me, and also the description of a game she and Aunt Em have sent me have arrived. Have received parcels Nos. 71, 73, 75, 79 and 80 also one from Fortnum and Mason, including puddings, a priceless ginger bread from Aunt Em. Many thanks to you for all! Life here as usual. A new aviator has just come into our room, so we are now full up again. The Japanese lanterns are a great success. Please send some more candles for them. We have just started rehearsing pantomime. 'Earnest' temporarily postponed. All well.
Love,

Brocas.

Letter 120

17th November 1916, Friedberg

My dearest Mother,
I wished you the best of luck yesterday and hoped most sincerely that I should be able to assist you to celebrate your next birthday. Only one letter since my last, Father's of November 1, most welcome. The bills look very large on paper. Badminton saves our life now. We play in a large drill hall here and so can be sure of exercise wet or fine. 10 degrees of frost last night! A good beginning. All well. Parcels 87, 81, and 142 from F. & M. contg. puddings have arrived. Many thanks. Please send me 20 dozen shuttlecocks – quality need not be so good. I am told A. and N. Stores supply cheaper ones. Best of luck to you all. Your affectionate son,

Brocas.

Letter 121

[No date], *Friedberg*

My dearest Mother,
Just received yours of Nov. 4. Many thanks, also Duchesses of Nov. 5, both
most welcome. George certainly looks well! Received also two parcels but have
stupidly lost numbers. They contained (1) apples (v.good) and (2) cake and
Mak. Ration. Many thanks. All much as usual here. Grossly busy, what with
Italian, pantomime and Balalaika – the latter great fun and of course helps
my Russian considerably. I am learning several musical terms in R. which I
don't know in my own tongue. In the pantomime I am to be the "Prince" and
have to sing a love duet (frequently) to the tune of the "Eternal Waltz" and
also a song called "Come round London with me" – most unprincely. I hope
Duchess knows these tunes. My "fairy" Princess is alarmingly large and so
you can imagine our "love scenes" cause much amusement to the rest of the
caste – it is an awful affair. We are not allowed to be comic. We have now a
new addition in our room – Sub. Lt. Newman R.N.A.S. Goodbye. My best
love to you all.
Your affectionate son,

Brocas.

Letter 122

28th November 1916, Mainz
To: Mr Burrows

My dear Sir,
I wish you a happy and bright Xmas and also to your dear son and to all
my friends from the old Stube *75, to whom I send my best love. It is really sad*
to pass this day without them. The friendships embellished our mournful and
sad life of prisoner of war. I hope that your son is in good health, and you too.
Yours very sincerely

Nicolai Miloradovitch

Letter 123

30th November 1916, Friedberg

My dearest Father,
St Andrew's day once more and it is time for me to write once again to wish
you many happy returns of your birthday I do wish you <u>all three</u> the happiest
possible of Xmases. Would that I could spend it with you! It seems quite a short
time only since we spent this day together at Eton. The time now is 12.45. so
they are no doubt playing the Wall game. I wonder if the Oppidans will win for
a change! Here the local Scotch officers are going to give a dancing exhibition
with the help of some Russians who will also dance etc. I think it ought to be
quite amusing, then this evening they are having their St Andrew's day dinner
in our room! Much to the annoyance of the non-Scotch members. Luckily
there is a birthday party in another room which most of us are attending – so
I expect in the end we shall do down the "braw Highlanders!"

Three letters from home since my last Duchess's of Nov. 12 which looks as if it
had had some enclosure taken out of it, as it arrived with a clip attached to it
and nothing else! How amusing the St Giles' Boy Scouts. I am sure however
Ethel Burney will be an excellent scout mistress. Mother's of Nov. 11. full
of news. I am sorry for Leo Page's brother-in-law. I was very nearly outed
too! Poor old Jack. He seems fated to be kept out of the show! I can bet he is
*cursing his luck! So sorry to hear about **Ellie's youngest child** [Romania]*
but I do hope it is only a temporary indisposition. Father's of Nov. 8 has just
*arrived. So glad to hear about **Govare**, [The French] I am indeed surprised,*
long may he thrive. Please send me out a copy of "In the days of Chivalry"
if you can get one. Russell's book has arrived and is of course excellent. Today
I received parcel No. 89 and also a box of ginger nuts, I think from Aunt
Katie but I'm not sure, many thanks to her. I hope soon to be able to send
you another snapshot of self if it is good. 6 p.m. – the Scotch show went off
quite well especially the Russian dances which are most curious – you need to
be an acrobat to do them successfully. We have just hired a sewing machine
and are going to begin to make our dresses for the pantomime to save expense.
We are I suppose most ambitious, and the ladies are to wear Empire dresses.
Of course we are hiring the men's costumes to match and the Fairy Queen's.
Half a dozen gnomes and a private detective are difficult! I am writing under
difficulties, as the preparations for the Scotch dinner are under way and they
can't decide who to borrow the different necessities from! Highly typical, what?
I am just reading War and Peace – Tolstoy – a present from my late Russian
instructor Miloradovitch – a priceless illustrated copy! Well I must close down
again, my dearest father. My very best birthday wishes. I shall think of you all
doing your Xmas poetry reading, and on the 26th morning. Au revoir,

Ever your affectionate son,

Brocas.

Letter 124

9th December 1916, Friedberg

My dearest Father,
I am indeed sorry to hear my letters have been arriving badly, and especially the one for Mother's birthday, but I fear is it almost impossible to judge the time accurately. Two letters from you, yours of November 15 and Duchess's of November 19. So glad Duch. enjoyed her Gondoliers. We are full of rehearsals for our pantomime here and so very busy at present and in a few days I am going to indulge in an Xmas holiday! Parcels 93 and 94 have also rolled up – many thanks – the cheese is grand. All as usual here, wet and not very cold. I have just met a Frenchman here who knows some 'de Brocas' in France and have had some long chat with him. Please send me some more of **Mrs Griffith's famous potted meat** *soon.* [Probably a request for concealed Whisky] *Well my best love to you all and I do hope my Xmas letters have arrived.*

Your affectionate son,

Brocas.

Letter 125

17th December 1916, Friedberg

My dearest Mother,
I don't know how to tell you three how sorry I am my letters have failed to turn up, especially so at the time of your birthdays. I most sincerely hope they are beginning to come better by now. It is certainly not my fault as I have never missed a week yet, though I don't always write on the same day. All is of course well here and at present we are in the throes of final rehearsals for the Xmas pantomime and so are very busy. I have just been translating the Dramatis Personae and a short Precis of the Piece. A most laborious task, as I had to make many copies of each in both French and Russian. Your letters to me have been coming through well, and I have got Mother's card of November 30, Father's letter of November 28, Duchess's of 26, Mother's of

25 and Father's of 22 all most welcome. The Chronicles never arrived. Don't worry about Balalaika music, I get lots here. The boots have arrived from Edinburgh and I am breaking them in, I think they will be excellent. The Jaeger vest has arrived and is most welcome though it is not really cold here yet. It is very wet and muddy and this unfortunately makes exercise difficult. I have received the following parcels Nos. 97, 96, 100, 1 Buzzard parcel 92 98, 99, cigarettes, 2 parcels of books, one with a notice inside from "Mudies Select Library" "A gift from Miss Kingsbury" (indeed kind of her) also a cake from Kinnersley, and 102, 103, 104 <u>*many thanks*</u>*. This will see us through the Xmas 10 days beautifully. Re-details, the beef is excellent the first I have eaten for 29 months. Please repeat. Cheese also very good, and crackers and plum pudding is just as desired, as also apples. You are really wonderful at sending exactly what I want. Please send me 7 lb Civil Service Tin box of flour, and if possible some pheasants (i.e. if Father is still shooting). Some arrived here in excellent condition today. So glad you are pleased at* **Cousin Jack's** *change.* [Admiral Jellicoe] *The songs you sent me arrived a few days ago and are excellent. Just what we want. I think you will find among my books at home Henderson's "Stonewall Jackson", if so please send it. An occasional book of that sort is always welcome. I am attending a course of motor lectures here, and they are certainly most interesting. At present I think I have learnt about most possible mishaps and really wonder why a car ever goes at all! I am much looking forward to receiving Duchess's new photo. I hope it is a success. I am always meaning to face the man here but he only performs on Sunday mornings early and the last few Sundays have been horrible days, and (to tell you the truth) I fear I may not look my best at such an early hour. Sunday here is a* **"Europe morning"** [meaning a lie in – a term also used by Ian Fairweather as a title for his painting of Lieutenant J.E.T. Younger (Sam) enjoying his 'Europe Morning', see back cover]. *(Later) I have just been inspecting some of the home-made pantomime dresses. How I wish you could see them. They are priceless, especially those of the comic sisters and the old Countess. Halliley is our chief seamster and he's really quite a professor. I was talking to Graves here about Blickling* [Norfolk] *a few days ago. He knows it very well and acted in the pageant there that we went to see. Well goodbye and best love to you all.*
Your affectionate son,

Brocas.

I hope this gets through quickly.

Letter 126

[No date], *Friedberg*

My dearest Mother,
Three delightful letters from home, F's of Jan. 3, yours of 6 and D's of 7, have arrived since my last. So glad you have heard from Peskett. How is he? Could you not manage to send me the photo of Col. Neish and his charges? I fear I have several requests, (1) Lux, a small monthly supply, (2) candles 1 doz. per month, (3) 8 large and 6 small leather buttons <u>with price</u>, (4) a decent tennis racket. I have just received £3 for prices won at Tennis here last summer. I am keeping money here so will you please deduct £3 from my Cox's account and buy me a decent hunting crop up to that sum. Please also send me out two tablecloths for a table 4ft by 3 ft. Molly Burrows has also written me a letter full of apologies for not writing for such a long time. I owe her the same though perhaps my excuse is acceptable. I will write to her. She seems "some" busy! We are just back from a walk in the snow. I very seldom go but it was good fun today. I am working at Italian like "..." now, 5 hours a day and hope to master it soon. Not v. difficult. I have also just finished the theatre accounts up-to-date. No small undertaking and so I am feeling very virtuous. We are trying to make a skating rink on our tennis court here, but up to the present have had no success. Lots of snow and a real good frost. Snowball fights every day, otherwise "no change" as they say in the official reports.
Love,
from,

Brocas.

Letter 127

31st December 1916, Friedberg

To Mother, Father and Duchess,
My final wish of the old year naturally goes to you three at the old home and is of course for all good luck and happiness during the coming year and amongst other things (perhaps I ought not to include this under good luck) the return of a most undutiful son. I have received several letters since my last to you, one from Miss Owen, one from Miss Rice Wiggin and one from Eleanor Butler, (please thank them for me) and Mother's of Dec. 3. F's of Dec. 6 and Duch. of Dec. 3. Many thanks to you all. Groceries and half pig arrived, also three parcels Nos. 105, 106, 107, and two parcels of books and music. Also a parcel from Aunt Em. Many thanks to her. We are now fully in the middle of our pantomime and having a great success. There is such a lot of movement and variety in it that seems to appeal even to foreigners who don't understand a

word. I enclose a Russian program as for the moment the English and French ones have run out. I will send you photos etc. next week. All things considered we had quite a cheerful Xmas here, and I expect I shall stay up to see the New Year in and curse the old one as it peters out! How you would love to see me acting (?) in this pantomime! As you will see from the programme, I am the wretched Prince [Prince Aboukir of Badoura] *who comes on in early Empire costume and sings "Come round London" with an admiring chorus of courtiers and females, then meets Cinderella, falls violently in love with her and adopts the love-sick swain attitude. The poor fellow kisses Cinderella (a Captain in the Munster Fusiliers who is nearly as big as the Prince)* [Captain Moseley] *twice on the lips to the immense amusement of all, and also waltzes with her on the stage in all kinds of fantastic attitudes. Poor, poor fellow!!! Well, this is the third New Year I am starting in this country and pray God it will be the last. Who knows? An English clergyman Mr Williams, came here on Friday to hold a service. You all seem wonderfully busy at home and I have no doubt you find your work most interesting, only I hope you aren't overdoing it.* **So glad you approve of Cousin Jack's change. I don't quite understand it at present.** [a reference to Admiral Jellicoe's recent appointment as First Sea Lord] *You have sent me no news of* **Ellie** [Russians] *lately, I hope she is well. Peskett who was with me is now in Switzerland and I hope will write to you re-me. If not, write to him. I hope he will soon get better. Well I must close. My best love to you all.*

Your affectionate son,

Brocas.

Letter 128

[Date approx. January 1917?], *Mainz*

Dear Mrs Burrows,
Thank you very much for your good wishes for the New Year and for the beautiful cake which I received the 9 – 1 – 1917. I ate it with my Russian friends who knew your dear son and as I, remember him always with great pleasure. It is indeed too kind of you to think about me. I am very glad that your son speaks well Russian. It was only a pleasure for me to learn with your son and I am very sad to be separated with him and he was a good friend. My best love to your son and my best wishes to you and to your husband.

Your very sincerely

Nicolai Miloradovitch

Letter 129

12th January 1917, Friedberg

My dearest Father,
Congratulatory letters are not in my line. I find them even more difficult
than speeches, but Duchess's epistle has just arrived telling me of your C.I.E.
[Companion of Indian Empire] *and I feel it up to me to try and express to*
you a little of the pride and pleasure that this has caused me. Honestly nothing
has pleased me so much since I last saw you. I rushed up and seized the first
Whittaker [Presumably a source describing New Year Honours] *I could*
find and got all available particulars, so now I am quite "au courant" with the
honour conferred upon you and can add with conviction "c'est bien merité".
Knowing what I do (alas! but little) of your great work firstly in Ceylon and
then at home, I can fully understand that it is but the "honour to whom honour
is due", and were honours conferred on fathers for what they do for undutiful
sons I fear a K.G. would far from suffice in your case. Anyhow, though it is
difficult for a son to write an adequate letter of congratulations to his father,
I hope you will gather from this how really pleased I am. Your letter of Dec. 27
and Mother's of December 30 have also turned up and were as usual more than
welcome. The boots from Edinburgh arrived and I acknowledge them, also the
ham which was excellent. This week I have received parcels Nos. 102, 109, 110,
111, 112, and 113. All most excellent. The tinsel and stuff will be most useful and
the pillow and p. cases will enable me to have a clean head-rest weekly, indeed
a boon. I have just recovered from a wretched cold and I'm quite alright again,
but would you please send me out some quinine tabloids and also some aspirin
in case (unlikely) of recurrences! I got it out snowballing! I enclose in this letter
17 postcards of our pantomime. Unfortunately they are not very good and the
ladies all come out very badly indeed. I hope, however they will get through
alright. I hope Duchess's theatricals went off well. I wish you could have seen
the bouquets that were presented to Cinderella and the ladies of our chorus!!
We are going to produce "Earnest" about the end of this month. My dress is
nearly finished. "Some buxom wench"! Next letter I am going to write home
and ask you to make some arrangements for a cricket net and coconut matting
which we hope you have here next summer. We are forming a small cricket club.
This afternoon I attended a play given by the Russian orderlies. A most curious
performance. I certainly hope I should be able to go to Russia soon after my
return. The home-made bread arrived today and is excellent, the best I have
tasted in captivity. Will you please double my ration of cigarettes? A few days ago
I attended the Xmas tree festivities given by the Russian officers to their soldiers
here, a most interesting proceeding, during which they danced national dances
and sang their songs, some of which are very pretty especially the "Volga" one,
which Duchess ought to learn to play on the piano. Please send Jack my heartiest

congratulations on his engagement, I don't know Kathleen Osborne of course, but have heard a lot about her. I am writing him a line. It is indeed sad about Conrad Jenkins. Com. Bingham here knew him at Dartmouth and says what an excellent fellow he was. "Whom the Gods love …"

Well I must close to catch the post. My best love to you all, and again, my dear father, my heartiest congratulations to you.

Ever your affectionate son,

Brocas.

Letter 130

16th January 1917, Friedberg

My dearest Father,

*Several letters from you since my last. Duch. of December 17, you of 20, M. of 23. and Duch. of 24. Many thanks to you all. Also, three parcels 104, 105 and 108. v. excellent. Well, our pantomime is all over and had a "grand success". The flowers presented to our ladies on the last night quite reminded me of the Gaiety. Today is Russian Xmas Eve! A most dangerous evening. I am dining with some of their senior officers. The last night of the pantomime I had to make a speech from the stage in Russian!! We have had our first snow of the season here today, all is quite white. My Xmas holidays end very soon and I shall find it quite difficult to get down to work again. The Italian books have arrived and are just what I wanted; also a Capt. Montgomery (7th D. G.'s) has come, who speaks Italian, and so we are going to work together. He was at Torgau and Burg with me. Have you read **Hamiltons "First Seven Divisions"?** [The First Seven Divisions by Ernest W. Hamilton (Late 11th Hussars) published 1916] A curious account of Nery! Please send me a dressing gown, v. chic, one of those bath-towel ones, of some light colour. Also a pair of bedroom slippers, not those high ones. Best love.*

Your affectionate son,

Brocas.

Letter 131

31st January 1917, Friedberg

My dearest Mother,
Only one letter since my last to you, Father's of January 20. Many thanks. So
glad you have made him be painted or should I say "crayoned". I suppose it
would be impossible to send me a photo of it? We are having it really cold here
and skating is the order of the day. We have built two small rinks ourselves, and
the only pity is that we are dreadfully crowded all day. We have about 10°Cent of
frost every night and our best has been 15°. I am at present leading a very retired
life owing to my studies, and so the cold affects me but little. I retire to the reading
room here every day at about 10.30. and stay there till 2 p.m. when I lunch,
and then have an hour's exercise and then more work till 7 when we dine. After
this there is usually a rehearsal for "Earnest" which we hope to stage in about
3 weeks. It is going much better and I hope I am becoming more lady-like! My
throat has been a bit sore lately which has caused the sweet Gwendolen's Voice to
be somewhat of a "voix de coches". My costume is quite "ravissante", and my
corsets of the latest cut! I have received the following parcels Nos. 102, 121, 122,
123, 118, 117 and today the monthly American Express one. Many thanks you
are quite wonderful at sending me my requirements. I hear Col. Jackson has got
to Chateau d'Oex. Please send me news of Peskett's health. I hope he is better
by now. Can you get me a book on India before the Mutiny, on military lines if
possible? Will you please also make the following arrangements for me. We intend
to have a <u>cricket net</u> here next summer. We have collected about 20 people all
told and I'm going of course to share all expenditure. What we want is (1) <u>64</u>
(sixty-four) yards of netting <u>10</u> (ten) feet high (i.e.2 sides of 30 yards and 4
yards width). A top cover 25 (twenty-five) yards long by 14 (fourteen) feet wide
and a <u>stop net</u> to go at the back 15 (fifteen) feet high and 18 (eighteen) feet long.
Also all the rope stays to fix this up. We can get wood here, and also the tent pegs.
Please also send a strip of coconut matting <u>22 yards</u> long by <u>4 yards</u> wide with all
the apparatus to fix it down. I leave it to you as to the best way to get the netting.
Please let it be <u>tarred</u> netting as the other kind tears so easily and please have the
<u>stop net</u> of a fine enough mesh to stop a golf ball as we hope to practice driving
into it. Perhaps a net like this could be got second-hand somewhere, also coconut
matting. Several people here suggest the stores (A. and N.) but you of course can
judge best. I apologise for giving you all this trouble. Please send me my Cricket
bag (leather) with my bats, 2 pair pads, batting gloves, 2 pair boots, golf driver
and brassey 6 (six) cricket balls and some old golf balls, also wicket keeping gloves
if I have got any. Your letters have been rather held up lately which is a great
nuisance but they will no doubt roll up in time. I have not been able to pluck up
courage to face the photographer here yet, it has been too cold, but I will do so as
soon as the weather gets warmer. I hope the Pantomime photos have arrived by

now. I wish they had been better. Well I must close. My best love to you all and I hope you have managed some skating on Port Meadow or elsewhere.
Ever your affectionate son,

Brocas.

Letter 132

My dearest Father, Please <u>counterorder</u> the Cricket net and <u>all appurtenances</u>, including the coconut matting. Please send me 3 cricket balls. It has been decided here not to allow us to have a Cricket net. Hope I have not caused trouble. All well here.
Best love,

Brocas.

Letter 133

My dearest Mother,
Several letters since my last to you – yours of January 13, D's of January 21 and 24, F's of January 19 and 24. Duchess seems thoroughly busy and I have no doubt enjoys it, it must be most interesting but 7.15. is v. early. Fancy my kit rolling up. I fear I cannot remember if anything is missing but I don't think so. I hope you got my card cancelling the cricket net, most unfortunate. The frost still continues here and skating is rife. I have had a slight touch of flu but I'm now quite recovered and in the best of health. Three parcels have arrived Nos. 123, 126, and 129. They are coming through badly just now. Please send me some more flour. Can you send me a life of Lord Kitchener and also a book on the Austro-German war of '66? I hope the photos have reached you by now. So glad to hear of Molly B's engagement. Please send her my heartiest congratulations. "Earnest" is being held up a bit by illness but we shall persevere. Best love to you all.
Your affectionate son,

Brocas.

Letter 134

3rd February 1917, Friedberg

My dear Duchess,
Snow and ice everywhere and really cold. Would that I was somewhere where I could make use of this. I wonder whether you are having the same. No news of you for some time which is annoying, but I'm sure this means you are alright. Bad news travels fast enough! We are still fully engaged in rehearsing "Earnest" and unfortunately several of the caste are laid up with colds. However we seem to progress a bit. Please send me half a dozen pairs of thin long socks and 3 white cricket shirts, not flannel. One parcel has arrived containing the tights. I think 116 but I'm afraid I am not quite certain. All letters and parcels seem to have been much held up of late. All as usual, health excellent.
Best love to you all,

Brocas.

Letter 135

21st February 1917. Friedberg

My dearest Father,
I was going to write this three days ago but I've delayed it till after a funeral, which I was selected to attend as representative of us here. Such an event – sad though it is – counts as an entertainment here, as it gives one something to write about. It was a funeral of a French and a Russian orderly who died in hospital in the town here. Hence we had the two services conducted by a French and a Russian priest. Most interesting to see the different rituals. It was unfortunately very cold. We are all keeping very quiet here at present as two officers have got pneumonia rather badly. Hence our poor old "Earnest" has been put off again. I am beginning to despair about ever getting it on! The frost has at last broken and we are preparing for "some" thaw. Most of our exercise ground has been used as a skating rink, so there is a large quantity of water to disappear. Several parcels since my last including Nos. 124, 125, and 128 also a parcel of books and several of Swiss bread. All most welcome. Cheese and flour excellent. An excellent letter from Sydney has just arrived. Please thank her from me and tell her I much appreciate hearing from her and will write to her as soon as possible. From you I have Mother's letters of Jan. 20 and 28, Duchess's of 31 and yours of 31. Many thanks. So glad to hear good news of Peskett. The home-made bread is excellent. My best compliments to the maker. It is really time I also mention the good old home-made cakes again. All the inmates and privileged guests to tea or lunch in this room admit they have never tasted anything so good and

personally I must say I like each one better than the last. **My best thanks are due to Mrs Griffiths and I hope I shall be able to tender them to her personally before long.** [Possibly a reference to an impending escape attempt as several escape items were recently concealed in potted meat] *I remember the Y.M.C.A. in George Street and I'm sorry it is burnt down. So sorry to hear of Ruth R's German measles, hope she'll soon be better. Leach and I have many laughs over what we called the "Prisoner of War's Relations Co. Ltd."! He is very well and cheerful as also are Wise and Graves. The latter is quite indefatigable as our theatre property man, no sinecure! The stuff you sent me in my parcels is really most excellent. The only thing we ever seem to lack is tinned meat, of course the more fresh stuff we get the better, and hams, bacon and beef are most welcome. Would it be possible to arrange for fresh vegetables from Denmark or Holland? We really rely entirely on what we get from you. The polo sticks and shuttlecocks have arrived per Am. Ex. Co. and are excellent. Please send me three dozen tennis balls and also some prints for pictures in the theatre. I issued a cheque on Barclay recently here. Will you please invest some of my money in war stamps, just a few sets, I have bought some here, they will probably be a good investment. Duchesses photo has just arrived and I really don't think I shall recognise her on return. I like it immensely, and all who have seen it here are very complimentary. I am sure the hair must take a very long time to do. The Italian is still going along in spite of interruptions, and is certainly a delightful language. Well I must close. My best love to you all, Your affectionate son,*

Brocas.

Letter 136

[Approximate date, February 1917.], *Friedberg*
[Copy of uncensored letter from Brocas to George conveyed in some unknown way through a French agency.]
To: Lt G.H. M. G. Cartwright, The Conservative Club, St James Street. London. W.

Dear Bene,
You will be surprised to get this from me, and I am writing it as if this should gets caught it will be more difficult to discover me. Please send it on to Father. Well, I can't tell you much about myself that you don't already know. I am well, we all are; abominably fat and fearfully busy about nothing in particular. Hence time passes, and we hope for the best. I don't think you can have any idea of what we went through at the beginning. The first year was absolute hell, and I personally suffered horribly from my head. But this is now passed and

as our captors begin to see that all is not as good as they could hope and that we are the cause of all the trouble, they have begun to treat us very differently. As regards food there is practically none here, and we live entirely on what you send out. I fear, one way and another, I get through quite a lot of money here, but it is not wasted, and if some expenditure is not quite necessary, I think there is some excuse after so much privation.

Re-languages, I have quite a good knowledge of Russian and French, and a working knowledge of Italian and German, and a bit of Hindustani. I intend to learn a certain amount of several languages instead of really getting down to one, as in this way I have more strings to my bow, and once the ground work of a language is mastered, a few months in the country are more use than years of book-working. I have also done some history work here and picked up a certain amount of pretty varied experience. Two attempts to re-join you failed unfortunately. [Referring to two failed escape attempts presumably while at Friedberg but one of these could have been the attempt at Mainz] *What do you think I should do in the future? I of course know nothing of affairs at home, especially as regards money. I should have much liked to continue in the army, but perhaps not in this branch, as I am no great horseman. This of course could easily be learned. Should I have enough money to go into the Guards? (I am no spendthrift nowadays, and I think pretty carefully about money). Of course I would prefer to leave this till after the war. When one gets a bit unwell here it is too awful, as one seems to think of what might have been, etc. Never mind; it can't be helped. You certainly won't recognise me when I return. Even here all tell me I have completely changed since we first met for better or for worse I don't know. I hope to repeat this at a later date and will then have more time to think about an epistle. This is done in a great hurry. So glad to hear of Jack's engagement. I have met K.O.* [Kathleen Osborne] *and she seems very nice. Well, I wish things would get a move on. I long to get back to you all and see you all again. I shall appreciate home as I never did before. Well, goodbye. I am well and in good spirits, so for goodness sake never worry about me. I hope you are all well. Don't work too hard.*
Love to you all.

BENE. [Brocas signed as BENE and did not use his name in case the letter was discovered]

Letter 137

[No date]
(Second uncensored letter)
Lt. G. H. M. Cartwright,
The Conservative Club, St James' Street, London, W. England.

Dear Bene,
This is the second chance are writing to you en cachette, and please forward this
also to the Governor. Nothing much really to relate, **but if ever you want**
to get any message through to me, they never search the bottom of
the parcels sent, and we can always take away the boxes. Hence a
false bottom could conceal Weekly Times, monthly magazines and
illustrateds, and these are always most welcome. Please repeat the
etcetera's you sent me last summer for the purpose of me joining
you, and please send maps of the country round here in all possible
directions, and if you can get news of any unguarded places on
Dutch or Swiss frontiers, please mark them on maps. Please send
also (1) a compass, (2) a luminous wrist watch (3) an electric torch,
(4) a pair of wire cutters, and any kind of food that will be useful
for trekking. No. 2 can be sent openly and also the food, and the
others had better be hidden in Jam. Please send luminous compass.
Chances of success are small, but still they do exist. [An important
request for escape materials] ***Did you ever hear from Capt. Henderson,***
[Probably keen to know if his note regarding code for concealed escape
items had been passed on by Captain Henderson] ***or get private letter***
I wrote Sept. 14? [A reference to Letter No 6 sent from Zossen 18
September 1914] *Nowadays we are comparatively comfortable here and are*
treated more or less as officers. But I don't think any of the old stagers will ever
forget what it was like at the beginning. I don't intend to write it all down in
black-and-white, but we all are determined to make known on return exactly
what we saw and felt, especially the wounded. When one is brought up not to hit
a man when he is down, it makes one feel ill to see the worst wounded selected
for the biggest kicks, and this frequently by women. It is all like a nightmare.
You can imagine how we pray that the fight will allow us to play an active part
again before the curtain falls. I am well and so are we all here, and personally I
have never been so busy in my life. Your letters are a real tonic, they are always so
cheerful, and seem quite to make one forget temporarily where one is. Food here
is very scarce, and the rations supplied us almost uneatable. We pay 1.60 a day,
and the accounts (kept by our hosts) are not to be seen! Scandalous! So long.

Bene.

Letter 138

28th February 1917, Friedberg

My dearest Mother,
I fear I have forgotten to write and ask you to convey to nurse my best wishes for her birthday, but better late than never, so please do so now and send her my best love. No news from you since my last letter. Your letters are temporarily held up but parcels have begun to come through well again and I have received Nos. 126, 130, 131, 136, 137 and a case of tea. All most excellent. The bread (home-made) is quite delicious and the apples arrived in prime condition. I can't remember if I ever thanked you for the polo sticks and Badminton things. If not I apologise and add my thanks for this matter to that for the other parcels (v. complicated). Please send me a big box of sulphur ointment and a monthly supply of suet. I am learning to cook! and can now make pastry of a sort, rock cakes, and Welsh rare-bits (apt to be leathery). An unfortunate Russian colonel came to a meal with us a short time ago and I built him a curry. He was very polite and ate all he was given – but they say he has hardly been able to speak since. It certainly was a bit "East of Aden". The frost is at last breaking up and I personally am very thankful. Skating is still continuing on what remains of the rink and we are fearing a very muddy fortnight when the thaw finally sets in. We have finally decided to do "Earnest" tomorrow week (March 8) and shall be very glad to get it off our chests. Our two invalids are much better and I hear quite out of danger. It was a near thing. I am really beginning to enjoy my Italian now, but the difficulty is to find a professor, as mine cannot speak the language though he knows the grammar and reads well. Please send me out some elementary Spanish books as I hope to make a start on this too in the summer. I hope you aren't under the impression that I speak all these languages perfectly; far from it; what I hoped to have before the end is a working knowledge of each as it is difficult to know which will be most useful after the war. The more I look at Duchess's photo, the more I like it. Is it possible to send me a larger copy? I sent off to Cox yesterday cheques to the sum of £60-10-0. To be paid into my account. Please tell him that this is money subscribed to our theatre here and I intend to have it sent out in drafts as necessity arises. Please ask him to send me £30 of it on receipt of this. Please send me also two pairs of tennis shoes, one with rope soles, and one with India rubber soles. I think Gane at Eton would make them best. The last pair you sent me were a bit too big, I don't think my foot has grown at all. If the Duchess is not too busy ask her from me to write to Peskett in Switz. and find out if it amuses him to receive letters. If so she might send him some of the news from here and pass on to me any of his. Of course, this is only if she has time, I know he has very few relations and I think he might be only too glad to hear from someone. I expect she will curse me like anything for this!! Well, I seem to

have written a lot of selfish rot re self but really I have nothing to answer from you and I am most anxious for news. Bad news always comes fast enough so I know all is well with you. We are starting another musical play in a few days which we hope to bring on towards the end of April. Qui sait? Can you send me out an account of colours and significations of the Burrows coat of arms? I regret my ignorance on this subject. Best love to you all.
Your affectionate son,

Brocas.

Letter 139

18th March 1917, Friedberg

My dearest Father,
But a very hurried line in the midst of indescribable chaos. We are going to another camp, but we do not know where and you can't imagine what packing up means to us now. We travel like the tortoise with our homes on our back. Never mind, I think it must be an improvement. Will write more fully on arrival. "Earnest" was a great success though but few became enamoured of the fair Gwendolen! I will send the pictures. Have received parcels No. 146, 144, 145, 143. Many thanks. Also Am. Exp. Co. parcel and several letters which I will answer as soon as poss. We are being split up into two parties and so lose some of our oldest friends. You can't think how difficult this is to us poor K.G.'s but I suppose a change is good for one. I hear you have met Capt. Sampson's people.
Love,

Brocas.

Letter 140

[Approximately 20th March 1917
Copy of uncensored letter from
Brocas to George Cartwright (nephew of mother)
It was forwarded from Limours on April 25 to Madame Loffage,
and followed the nephew to the French front where he was with 4th
Guards Machine Gun Coy, and so back to parents in May.]
To: H.M. Cartwright Esq. Coldstream Guards
Conservative Club, St James St. London

Dear Bene,
Yet another chance of dropping you a line en cachette. Please send on to the
family as before. Nothing much to relate except that we have got to change
plans, which is a horrible nuisance. I hear our characters are getting it in the
neck in France! Great! It will be interesting to see how they take it. I shall
watch with interest during the journey. Everything here is topsy-turvy. So
glad my last got through. Please arrange for me to have a balance about £150
with Cox on my return. We are now allowed to have wine sent out here, so
please send an occasional half bottle of sherry. ***Please also send me some***
brandy in a bottle labelled cough mixture, [Possibly for an escape]
as this camp is getting worse and worse. It is always the way in this country.
The Germans here really seem despondent at last, and if only we can hit them
hard now, I believe it might do them in. Of course we are not optimistic after so
long, but really Baghdad and this new show have cheered us up. ***Do send me***
out papers in the bottom of cigarette jars and also in the bottom
of the egg boxes. [This ruse was used quite a lot until it was discovered]
Well I must close. Best love to you all.

Brocas.

Letter 141

20th March 1917, Friedberg

My dearest Father,
Just time for another hurried line before parting from this our dwelling place
of the last nine months. I don't know at what hour we are off tomorrow nor
whither we are going but I suppose uncertainty should add to the interest.
Needless to say everybody thinks they know and the whole camp is rife with
"tuyaux". I don't think I ever told you that both our serious invalids have
quite recovered. One comes with us tomorrow and the other, Col. Wallace, goes
to hospital here entirely to recuperate. Thank goodness we got the "Importance
of being Earnest" off our chests before this move. We only finished our last
performance on the 14th. It was a great success though previously we had
feared that we were being too ambitious. Of course very few of the foreigners
could understand any of the dialogue, but they seemed to follow the plot and
enjoy the situations. I will send you photos as soon as possible. It is indeed
a blow to have to give up our theatre here, as we had just finished it, which
meant that the dirty work of our entertaining programme was over and the
easy part just beginning. However I think in many ways it is for the best as I
personally was getting a bit tired of theatricals and they certainly take up a
terrible amount of time. Both Leech [CJF] and Wise are separated from the

*main body, so I fear you will get less news of me from other sources! Graves
comes on and so does Sampson. A parcel of books has just arrived from
Blackwood ctg "Dantes's Inferno". Many thanks. I don't know what to do
about Italian, as of course my professor here is staying on and Italian speakers
are somewhat rare birds. However I hope for the best.* **I hear Ellie has made
a wonderful recovery.** [Good progress of Russian campaign] *I am so
glad and it is pleasant to think how much we had to do with it. I hope her child*
[Romania] *will get on as well. The photos of Duch as a nurse and the garden
under snow have arrived and given great pleasure. It has indeed been a hard
winter and I hope this means it will be a good warm summer. I expect George
will be off very soon now, won't he? I wrote to him to congratulate but fear it
was very late. He has written to me once or twice but his letters invariably take
months to arrive. I don't know whether I ever explained to you exactly my
transactions at Cox. I have sent home the sum of £60. 10s to be paid into my
account. This is the sum subscribed by cheques to our theatre, so please instruct
Cox to keep this in my account as I intend to draw upon it as necessity arises.
We have decided to give whatever remains over at the end to some charity, and
if possible to give entertainments at our next camp on this balance. I have had
a very busy few days settling up our theatre and badminton accounts, but all
is settled now and balance sheets published! I shall be quite an accomplished
accountant on return and Graves and I hope to take special lessons from an
expert* [Major Barnardiston] *who is with us at the next camp. No letters
from you for some days, but I still have some to answer; unfortunately I had
to pack them in the heavy luggage and that has all gone down to the station
today. My 'little all' consists of one vast wooden case ctg. Pots, pans, crockery,
theatrical outfit and odds and ends, one large basket containing clothes, one
case with books and eatables, 2 suit cases, my polo sticks and a table! So you
can imagine the mobilisation necessary for a successful start. Fortunately here
the train awaits for one and tho' one pays for heavy luggage it is comparatively
little nuisance to one during the journey. Please send me out a good life of
Napoleon and some history of his campaigns in Italy. Well, I must close this
my last letter to you from Friedberg, hoping that our next camp will be our last
and our sojourn there will be a short one. Best love to all.
Your affectionate son,*

Brocas.

10

Clausthal POW Camp

24 March 1917 – 6 February 1918

Brocas and his cohort set off on 21 March 1917 for Clausthal. They eventually arrived tired and exhausted after a 26-hour train journey which they thought would be only 12 hours. Captain John le Hunte 1st Hampshire Regiment, described their arrival in his debrief statement (17 December 1917 Chateau D'Oex, Switzerland, National Archive ref 161/96/66).

> *We arrived on a bitterly cold night, and there were no arrangements made for wounded officers or for bringing hand baggage up to the camp from the station; it was freezing hard, and as the way lay up a steep hill it was a pitiable sight to see officers who had wounds and senior officers staggering up the hill endeavouring to carry some kit. When we arrived at the camp it was between 10 and 11 pm and there was no meal of any description provided by the Germans; officially by the Germans we had only been given a cup of coffee between Friedberg and Clausthal, and the journey lasted between 24 and 36 hours.*

The records show they arrived on 24 March 1917. From a note in Brocas's mother's record of parcels, she sent her final one to Friedberg on the 11 April 1917, implying she still was not aware he had moved camps. It would be his last POW camp in Germany. In his second letter home from Clausthal dated 2 April 1917 (*Letter 143*) he wrote: '*I am much frightened at being reminded that my letters are being bound and kept.*'

The conserved letters are the basis of this book and the very reason it has been possible to produce such an informative record of Brocas's POW experience. The following image, original of *Letter 167*, demonstrates the method of censorship, undertaken at Osnabrück, a process which delayed both letters and parcels, sometimes for weeks and even months.

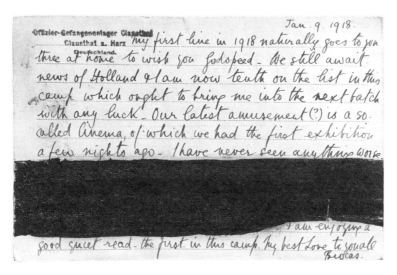

Offizier-Gefangenenlager Clausthal
Clausthal a. Harz
Deutschland.

Jan. 9. 1918.

my first line in 1918 naturally goes to you three at home to wish you godspeed. We still await news of Holland & I am now tenth on the list in this camp which ought to bring me into the next batch with any luck. Our latest amusement (?) is a so-called cinema, of which we had the first exhibition a few nights ago. I have never seen anything worse

good sweet read. the first in this camp. My best love to you all *I am enjoying a*

Brokas.

Original censored letter 167 sent to parents 9 January 1918 from Clausthal POW camp
Source: Burrows family archive

Dr. Carl Ohnessorg, a surgeon of the United States Navy carried out an inspection visit of the camp, and filed the following report from Berlin published in a British newspaper (no date or source):

> …*The building used for interning these officer prisoners is a wooden building on stone foundations, placed on a highway on the outskirts of the town …the building was modern, eight years old, and in peace time was used as a hotel…The camp is screened off from the roadway by a high board fence, topped with the usual barbed wire. A moderate sized yard, approximately a hundred yards long by ninety yards broad, in the rear of the building served as a recreation ground for the officers. The space in front of the building was laid out with walks on which were placed benches and steamer chairs.*
>
> *In pleasant weather the roll call was held in the space in front of the building. At one side of the main building was being erected a small building which I was informed was to be used as a squash racquet court by the English officers. I found several of the English officers amusing themselves in the yard with golf balls and sticks. An open-air bowling alley had been erected and a tennis court was in the process of construction …The house was heated by hot water system. The open*

porches on the various floors, the Commandant informed me, were to
be enclosed with glass for the winter.

Captain George Cecil Graves was among the group of British officers
who came on from Friedberg. He shared a room with Brocas at
Clausthal and wrote the following letter, also on 2 April 1917, which
was later partly copied on to the Burrows' family headed note paper. It
describes the camp and their activities in considerable detail.

Clausthal, 2 April 1917
[On 9 Norham Gardens headed note paper]

…We are now quite settled in, and installed in our rooms. Our room is
on top floor facing east. It is cold here, and there is snow everywhere,
but it seems as if a thaw were coming.

One has to somewhat reorganise one's scheme of work owing to the
absence of Russians and French. However, I am working at both
languages by myself, and Skaife and Burrows and myself give Russian
classes every morning. The people who are learning do two hours every
morning, and we divide the twelve hours in the week amongst the 3 of us.
It is quite a novelty teaching Russian, and no easy matter, but by trying
to teach other people one learns a great deal oneself. Burrows and I have
also arranged a French class, which meets for an hour every afternoon
and we each take three days. Other occupations are my mathematics
which I shall continue with Major Tailyour, and Major Barnardiston is
going to instruct me in book keeping which he has learnt here.

It is not so easy to take exercise here, but I walk around for a couple
of hours every day, and there is a squash court built by the original
inhabitants in which I have managed to get a couple of games. I
cannot however look upon this latter as a regular form of exercise as
the number of members is very naturally limited, and limited of course
to those who paid for the court. When the snow goes and the weather
is warmer we shall probably be able to start a physical training class
in the morning.

The original inhabitants gave an entertainment a few days after our
arrival, comprising a short concert of three items, and a three act play
by John Galsworthy, called "The Pigeon". Major Tweedie was the
leading part in the play and performed his role with much success,
especially as it was his maiden performance.

The dining room here has a stage at one end of it all ready-made. The camp is an hotel, and the dining hall so built as to be able to be used as a concert hall or theatre…

We have services here on Sundays in the dining hall which are taken by officers who were in training for the church before the war. We have formed a choir of quite a number of performers, and have a cheerful musical service…

There is a veranda off our room – not an open one, in which we perform our ablutions and in the morning I do my Muller's exercises there…

The air here is quite nice and invigorating; the hotel is surrounded by woods and hills, and from our window we can see what is I believe the highest of the Hartz mountains.

Our balalaika Orchestra was of course broken up owing to our departure, but there is an orchestra of mandolins here which is incorporating such balalaikas as we have brought with us.

We do not feed in our rooms, as in Friedberg, but take all in the dining room – the five of us in our room have formed a mess together, we each take a day on which to prepare the food.

We are all well and fit.

Another of his fellow officers at Clausthal, Lieutenant W.H.S. Chance, described the camp as follows:

…The camp at Clausthal was a converted hotel in the Harz Mountains about a mile uphill from the railway station. The Kurhaus zu Pfauenteichen, (The Peacock Lake Hotel), was a wooden building converted into a Lager and surrounded by a high wire fence and with wooden barrack huts built at the rear of the hotel. The Kurhaus stood above a lake – the Pfauenteich or Peacock Lake – surrounded by plantations of fir trees, and in the distance, one could see the Brockenberg – the mountain famous in German myths and allegories. Some of our officers were housed in the hotel, and some in three hutments adjoining the hotel. The huts had rooms each holding six officers and were so small that beds were arranged in pairs – one above the other according to German barrack practice. There was only room for a few chairs and two small tables, and no space for our belongings. Each room had a

Officers' POW Camp at Clausthal, in Harz Mountains.
Source: article by Sir William Hugh Stobart Chance courtesy
of Louis Scully http://www.worcestershireregiment.com

stove and during the winter months they could generally buy logs. But
the un-insulated huts were icy, so overcoats and sweaters were essential.

In the summer they were allowed to construct a tennis court and to have
a squash court built by a local contractor at our expense. They were
able to take exercise in the area in which the courts were located. In the
winter of 1917-1918, the tennis court was flooded and used for skating.
There was also a small golf putting course which we laid out. A favourite
sport, particularly among the senior officers, was "bee ferreting" as there
were lots of field mice on the golf course. A captured bumble-bee was
introduced into a hole and persuaded to act as a ferret by a stream
of smoke blown from a pipe. It was amusing to see ancient colonels
competing with each other on bended knees and puffing away into the
holes, having laid bets on who would first cause a mouse to bolt!

The Camp was surrounded by a high wire fence, inside of which was
a barbed-wire fence – crossed at the peril of one's life from the trigger-
happy guards who patrolled round the perimeter. Outside the Camp
was the Guard Room, Kommandantur and the block of cells which
had to be enlarged owing to the number of officers who fell foul of the
commandant. "'Drei Tage Stubenarrest" was the penalty for incurring
his displeasure. The Germans had little sense of humour and were
unmercifully ragged. "Mad Harry's" flow of invectives was met with
laughter, making his complexion even more purple than usual. "You
go right 'avay' – forty meters ago. I send you to little arrest 'ouse". A
sentry was summoned and the offender marched off to the cells. In

April I wrote to my sister to say that there was plenty of snow – "We get a fall nearly every night". Keeping warm had been a problem and with a diet lacking in vitamins, small cuts turned septic. Most of us went about with bandaged fingers. There was a stage in the Dining Room and officers interested in acting ran a very successful Dramatic Society, putting on several plays. Parcels followed us from their previous camp, but because it was discovered that some tins contained compasses and other escaping kit, all tins were opened in the Tin Room and their contents tipped out…

Chance went on to describe a dinner attended my nine Old Etonians including Brocas:

On the Fourth of June, 1917, the Old Etonian officers celebrated the occasion with a dinner to which nine of us sat down and drank the toast "Floreat Etona". The menu consisted of turtle soup, salmon mayonnaise, curry and rice, cold tongue, fruit salad and coffee.

During the summer they were allowed a number of walks on parole in the surrounding countryside, but after an incident these were discontinued. Leisure activities were numerous and included tennis, squash, golf, boxing and indoor baseball with a set acquired by some Canadians. (*Letter 146*) Brocas described how they also fashioned a 'Polo Pit' for a pastime of indeterminate nature. (*Letter 147*)

…We have at last got the Polo pit in action after a new lot of alterations. You can't imagine the difficulties of getting the slopes and angles right. We have to make the flooring out of stamped earth which is continually getting rubbed up and then the slopes have to be such as to make the ball come back the right distance away from the horse. All most complicated!…

By July they were having great fun on a miniature golf course they had constructed. (*Letter 152*)

Golf balls have arrived and as we have at last been able to construct a small mashie and putting course, they are in great demand. I would love you to see us playing "ye olde and ancient game". The course consists of 6 holes, all of which cross and re-cross completely regardless of danger or anything else. The whole thing is on the slope of a small hill on which the camp is situated and is about the size of the school

yard at Eton. However the fun is fast and furious and up to the present
casualties have been rare.

The course was laid out by Captain Cecil Hutchinson, 1st Coldstream
Guards, and assisted almost entirely by 2nd Lieutenant William
'Tommy' Martin-Tomson, according to Gerald Crutchley [letter of
6 March 1918, Grand Hotel Scheveningen to Mrs Martin-Thomson
source: Crutchley archives] who says it was 40 yards square. It was
further described as 'a most wonderful golf links' in an anonymous
letter home published in an undated newspaper article held in the
Burrows archive. The article went on:

> *The six cunningly made holes with little bunkers were in an area*
> *thirty yards by thirty-five yards. We get any amount of fun out of them*
> *and they are always crowded. We had a tournament the other day –*
> *eighteen holes (three-time round), which was excellent. It was most*
> *amusing to see all the old colonels and majors playing as seriously*
> *as if it was the final of the world's championship. It must be Captain*
> *C. K. Hutchinson, the old Eton Athlete, cricketer, and footballer, and*
> *"runner-up" for the Amateur Golf Championship in 1909, who is the*
> *ingenious designer of this extraordinary course.*

For less physical activity they were gambling, drinking, acting, studying
and planning to escape. According to Chance:

> *…The real big escape plot was the making of a tunnel. The floors of*
> *the huts were some feet off the ground and the space below them was*
> *boarded off. A hole was made in the floor and using bed boards to rivet*
> *its sides, a shaft was dug which went down several feet. Digging took*
> *place during daylight hours and at the end of the day's work, a cover*
> *was placed over the shaft and covered with earth. From the bottom of*
> *the shaft, a tunnel was dug in the direction of the perimeter fence. This*
> *was lined with bed boards and air for the diggers was provided by a*
> *bellows with attached tubing. The earth removed had to be disposed*
> *of and this was done by filling small sacks hung inside trousers which*
> *could be opened up and the contents spread on the ground under the*
> *other huts. Work on the tunnel had progressed to the point where it was*
> *under the wire fence before it was discovered…*

There is however, no firm evidence that Brocas was involved with
this particular escape attempt but he hints several times at escaping,

although the reference of 31 August 1917 (*Letter 157*) may have been to positive news regarding exchanges to Holland or Switzerland.

> *19th June 1917 (Letter 149)*
> *send me a cap to wear with blue with a khaki cover, not a forage cap*
> *like he sent me before. It is rather difficult to explain.*

> *30th July 1917 (Letter 152)*
> *may we meet soon in Holland or elsewhere.*

> *31st August 1917 (Letter 157)*
> *All concerned are deeply indebted to you for the good luck!* [Referring to extracts from newspapers sent in egg boxes with false bottoms.] *Well au revoir and by Jove, it looks more like a meeting now!*

This was more likely a reference to parcel no 213, 14 July 1917, the contents of which his mother listed as follows: *'Cake herrings, cocoa, chocolate (Enclosure and Good luck)'* the implication being that the enclosure was in either the chocolate or cake and that something i.e. an escape was pending.

Clearly something was afoot but exactly what, remains a mystery. It would seem the egg box ruse had been discovered as writing on 8 October 1917, (*Letter 159*) he asked for them to be discontinued, although this would not have reached his parents before the last two concealed letters were sent on 3 and 10 of October 1917. As these were not acknowledged by Brocas it is reasonable to assume that they never reached him and were withheld by the authorities.

The following is a list of illicit escape items or concealed letters sent to Brocas while at Clausthal, taken from his mother's record of parcels. The 'Rations', whether described as 'Army' or 'Iron' rations were sent openly but were probably the best way of sending 'dry' food stuffs that would not deteriorate and would be useful to any prisoner making his escape across country:

Parcel no 175	*16 April 1917*	*Rations*
Parcel no 183	*5 May 1917*	*Rations Ack 30 May 1917*
Parcel no 184	*9 May 1917*	*Rations*
Parcel no 187	*16 May 1917*	*Egg box – with cuttings and letter*
Parcel no 188	*22 May 1917*	*Egg box – FB cuttings and Chronicle Ack 30 June 1917*

Parcel no 196	*5 June 1917*	*Egg box – with letter*
Parcel no 197	*9 June 1917*	*Rations*
Parcel no 202	*20 June 1917*	*Egg box – with letter Ack 30 July 1917*
Parcel no 206	*30 June 1917*	*Army Rations – Cake with false bottom*
		'Good Luck Cake' Ack 17 August 1917
Parcel no 209	*7 July 1917*	*Rations*
Parcel no 212	*11 July 1917*	*Egg box – Chronicle & letter re change in*
		sending parcels
		Ack 19 August 1917
Parcel no 213	*14 July 1917*	*Chocolate (Enclosure & Good Luck)*
		Ack 19 August 1917
Parcel no 219	*1 Aug 1917*	*Egg box – Bee's letter + Times Ack 19*
		Aug 1917
Parcel no 240	*3 Oct 1917*	*Egg box – letter*
Parcel no 242	*10 Oct 1917*	*Egg box – with cutting and letter*

At Clausthal Brocas continued to participate in camp entertainments and was an active member of the theatricals group. His first involvement was probably a 'Vaudeville' concert on 16 April 1917 which was repeated with variations on 7 May, 11 June and 11 July. In the May and June performances, he starred as 'Jack Annerly' in a farce in one act entitled 'Q'. The July performance included string orchestra, a farcical comedy in one act, entitled 'A Little Fowl Play' and after the interval a first performance of 'The Clausthal Curios' about which the programme stated: *'The recent heatwave is responsible for this deplorable outburst'.* Brocas's contribution was described as: *'entertaining himself at our expense'.* The Clausthal Curios was repeated in November. In the August 1917 performance of 'The Naked Truth', Brocas played the role of Mrs Hayter, whose husband Mr Hayter was played by Major Bryan Chetwynd-Stapylton of the 1st Battalion Cheshire Regiment. Although, as he says, he became increasingly bored with the theatricals, in October 1917 Brocas was nevertheless, heavily involved in a very successful, stopgap performance of 'The Importance of Being Earnest' after only a week of rehearsals. He featured as 'Hon. Gwendolen Fairfax' the role he had played at Friedberg with most of the cast also being the same as from Friedberg production. (*Letter 161*)

'Tantalising Tommy' was produced on 16 December after '*…a lightning spell of rehearsing of 3 weeks duration…*' (*Letter 165*) with Brocas playing the role of 'Harry Killick'. This was followed closely by a Christmas pantomime performance of 'Cinder-Ella' in which he is not listed as a member of the cast although he describes J.B Lawton's

Brocas (seated left) as Hon. Gwendolen Fairfax and left to right Lt O Price, Capt. J Younger, Lt. M Chidson, Lt Davidson, Lt. G Crutchley, Capt. F Sampson in 'The Importance of Being Earnest' probably Act III at Clausthal POW Camp 10 October 1917 Source: Burrows family archive

Brocas (right) as Hon. Gwendolen Fairfax with Lt Crutchley as Cecily in 'The Importance of Being Earnest' at Clausthal POW Camp 10 October 1917 Source: Burrows family archive

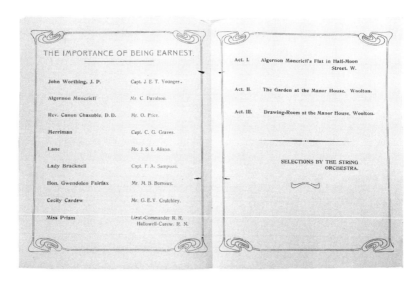

The Programme for 'The Importance of Being Earnest' at Clausthal POW Camp 10 October 1917. Source: Burrows family archive

performance as Prince Aboukir of Badoura as *'the new prince being most excellent in spite of my assistance'*. (*Letter 166*) He also took no part in an April performance of 'Charley's Aunt', nor the 'The Little Damozel' on 28 June 1917, and a September 1917 performance of 'Dale Sahib of Dustypore'. The impressive series of entertainments all organised by the British Entertainments Committee whose secretary throughout was Major G S Tweedie, of the Royal Scots was as follow:

> The Pigeon – 19 March 1917
> Vaudeville Concert – 16 April 1917 Music and song and
> Burlesque…The Village Concert
> Charley's Aunt – 23 April 1917
> Vaudeville Concert – 7 May 1917 and 11 June 1917 Mikado Act 1,
> songs / music, Farce 'Q'
> The Little Damozel – 28 June 1917
> Vaudeville Concert – 10 July 1917 A Little Fowl Play and The
> Clausthal Curios
> The Naked Truth – August 1917
> Vaudeville Concert – 13 August 1917
> Dale Sahib of Dustypore – Sept 1917
> The Importance of Being Earnest – 10 October 1917
> The Clausthal Curios – November 1917
> St Andrews Day Entertainment

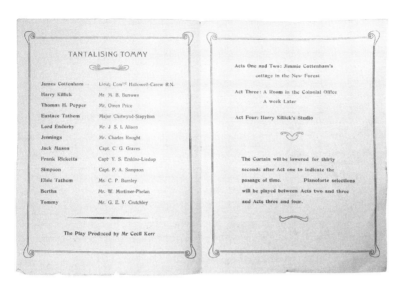

Programme for 'Tantalising Tommy' at Clausthal December 1917 Source: Graves family archive

Tantalising Tommy – December 1917
Cinder-Ella – December 1917 delayed to January 1918

The performances were as much about keeping sane and active, keeping up morale, having fun, as they were about entertaining others. The men were never afraid to make fools of themselves for the enjoyment of others, often, as in Brocas's case, by necessity as a member of the opposite sex.

By August there was increased talk of prisoner exchange to Holland but Brocas was not alone in finding the rumours and uncertainty most challenging. (*Letter 155*) '*...These possibilities of going to Holland are most nerve trying, and I fear one is rather apt to stake all on it coming off...*' As the year progressed the references to exchange to Holland became more frequent and more optimistic. Finally, on 31 December 1917 (*Letter 166*) Brocas wrote that the first party had gone and the second would be leaving the following day. Although on 9 January 1918 he was tenth on the list at Clausthal by 31 January 1917 (*Letter 169*) he still had no firm date despite being packed and ready for a month. The uncertainty of the last month was probably the toughest, mentally as he saw his friends leaving in small groups. Finally, on Sunday 3

February 1918 at 4 in the morning Brocas departed Clausthal for
Aachen, and three days later he was one of the 96 officers in the fourth
party to arrive in Holland.

Parcels from home

Parcels to Brocas, including monthly ones sent from Holland,
continued to arrive in great number (123) although apparently with
increased irregularity and were only being sent at a rate of one every
2.6 days compared with one every 1.5 days at Friedberg. Back in 1914,
when parcels were first permitted, Brocas was only sent one every
seven days whilst in Torgau, but at Burg they were leaving England at
a rate of one every two days. A phenomenal effort but it is possible his
mother was either tiring or more likely, the prospect of exchange was
reducing the apparent need and incentive.

Gerald Crutchley who was also at Clausthal, wrote on 6 March
1918 from the Grand Hotel Scheveningen, Holland to the mother of
William Martin-Tomson still interned in that camp:

> *I do not know what I can tell you about Clausthal save that parcels
> are an absolute necessity. The food provided by the Germans is almost
> non-existent. Breakfast: Nil. Lunch: Potatoes and mangel-wurzels
> mixed into soup and very nastily served, and an inferior type of meat
> served twice a week. Dinner: Soup – and further more when tinned
> food is sent out it is advisable to send large tins, as opposed to half size
> tins, since the difficulty of drawing out one's tins from the tin-room is
> very great (one gets in twice every five days and then only 6 tins per
> head may be drawn) – were it not for this limit officers would only get
> in once every five days.* [Source: Crutchley family archives]

Food, consisting mainly of staples such as bread, cakes, milk, butter, sugar
and eggs continued to be the most important content of the parcels. Fewer
other necessities such as toiletries were sent than at previous camps. Eggs
were the most frequently sent item. This was probably because of the
family's effort to communicate in secret with Brocas and support any
escape attempt that was pending. The ruse, having been rumbled by the
camp authorities, was discontinued. Social items comprised primarily
materials for theatricals or sport. Clothing including a raincoat tended to
reflect the harsher climate of the Harz mountains although it would seem
that Brocas's wardrobe was already well stocked during this period.

As the rumours of an exchange to Holland intensified the drive to escape must have inevitably subsided and the POWs settled down to a period of survival through the winter. Escape on foot in the winter was never a sound proposition. The last parcel, comprising bread, butter, eggs, sardines, and soap was sent to Clausthal on 27 December 1917. Brocas never acknowledge its receipt nor two others of the last sent. Almost certainly their contents were consumed by others, and even more likely, by a hungry German. It would be another five weeks before he left for Holland and only on 30 January 1918 did he write to acknowledge three parcels sent as far back as 14 and 19 December 1917. Time must have dragged as the days passed and they waited patiently for their turn in the queue and for 'exchange' to finally materialise.

Parcels sent to Lieutenant M Brocas Burrows at Clausthal
(Sample list only)
1 May 1917 – 31 May 1917

MAY 1917

Concealed items in brown

1st	*No 181*	*Box of Groceries Twining*
		Acknowledged
2nd	*No 182*	*Bread, butter, eggs, milk sample*
		Acknowledged
5th	*No 183*	*1lb cocoa, cake, rations*
		Acknowledged
7th		*Books from Blackwell Life of Napoleon*
9th	*No 184*	*Bread, butter, eggs, socks, rations*
12th		*Squash racquet bats*
12th	*No 185*	*Shirt, hdkf, air cushion, magazine, 2 sticks shaving soap*
		Acknowledged
12th	*No 186*	*Cake, candles, lux, peas, mustard and cress seed, cocoa and milk, café au lait, corned beef*
		Acknowledged
12th		*Cake (George)*
16th	*No 187*	*Eggs (with cuttings and letter), bread, butter, razor blades, brandy*
17th		*Jacket and cap sent from Hawkes (cap far too big)*
		Acknowledged
18th		*By American Express Co. Small deal case (Twining), bottle of brandy, 1 bottle chutney, 1 bottle lime juice*

19th	*No 188*	*Cake, herrings and tomato, chocolate, rations (F.B. cuttings and chronicle)*
		Acknowledged
19th		*Cake George*
21st	*No 189*	*Enlarged photo of A.N.B.*
22nd	*No 190*	*Apples*
		Acknowledged
22nd	*No 191*	*Eggs (letter and cuttings) bread, butter, potted chicken, soups*
		Acknowledged
26th	*No 192*	*Lampite, cake, cocoa and milk, peas, rations, herrings and tomatoes*
		Acknowledged
26th		*Cake George*
30th	*No 193*	*2 prs tennis shoes (1 pr returned rubber soles)*
		Acknowledged
30th	*No 194*	*eggs. Butter, bread, jam, milk, lux*
		Acknowledged

11

Clausthal POW Camp

24 March 1917 – 6 February 1918

The Letters

Letter 142

26th March 1917, Clausthal

My dearest Father,
We arrived here two days ago after a 26-hour journey. **(deletion by Censor)** *this is an all English camp of about 250 officers. Hence no languages which is a great nuisance. However I think we shall be able to arrange French, Russian and Italian classes. Our heavy luggage is arriving today. Mother's letter of February 17 with excellent photo of you just arrived. Many thanks for both. So glad you've got some good skating. Please ask Mrs Leach to tell her son that I reckon the expense at 10721*.* [1 July 1921] *Please send me all news of him you can you pass on mine.* **(deletion by Censor).**
Best love,

Brocas

**A guess at the date when the war would end.* [this note added by one of Brocas's parents]

Letter 143

2nd April 1917, Clausthal

Enclosed 1 check (£17)

My dearest Mother,
At last we are more or less settled in here and things are beginning to look something like ship-shape. I am now in a room with Capt. Sampson (Royal Fusiliers), Capt. Graves (Royal Scots), Capt. Skaife (R.W.F.) and Capt. Rose-Troup (The Queen's). We have not got at all a bad room really and we shall certainly be more quiet than at Friedberg. This place was a hotel, I believe, before

*the war, and is very high up. I don't know exactly how high. We have snow here everywhere and it is very cold, especially as the only heating is done by hot water pipes these are turned off except on the ground floor. Our sitting room is a vast hall which apparently served as dining room to the hotel formally, and here we spend most of our time. We are about 250 all told and the tower of Babel is completely put to shame. Our hours are much the same as at Friedberg, morning appel 9. o'clock, lunch 1. p.m. evening appel 6. p.m. and supper 7. p.m. lights are turned out at 9. p.m. Quite like old days. I fear I shall be unable to write to George – a pity – we had a very long journey here 26 hours and arrived here very tired as we had only expected about 12 hours. We travelled third class and got coffee at Cassel en route. As regards exercise here it is not promising. There is not very much space as it is mostly on a slope. There is one tennis court and one squash racket court, but as you can imagine this is not much among some 250 British officers. We hope eventually to get leave to build some more. Of course posts are for the time being completely deranged; however I have some letters to answer which arrived at Friedberg before we left. Duchess's of Feb 12 with photos taken by you – and most excellent too – it is indeed a long time since I have seen the garden looking like that, Father's of Feb 21. mentioning proposed dinner to Russians – this unfortunately is now off for obvious reasons – **so glad to hear of Cousin Jack's success.** [Admiral Jellicoe] – Duchess's of Feb 24 with news of Aunt Em's wonderful recovery from her cold for which I am very glad. Please send her my best love – so sorry Duch is getting a bit fat – never mind I am sure she can't compare with me! – Mother's of Feb. 24 with account of allotment – most amusing – please thank Aunt Io for her excellent letter of Feb. 14 and tell her I intend to answer Bernard's wonderful French epistle as soon as possible, but am rather shy of embarking on a reply to such exquisite French, Mother's of Feb 17 arrived just before leaving Friedberg and gave much pleasure, especially the picture of father and his N.O. friend – he certainly could not look better or younger – I fear I should be taken for "pater familias" on return and he for the "young hopeful" – I told Capt. Leech [CJF] you said he looked "well nourished" in his photo and he has had his leg pulled unmercifully ever since!! We all miss him very much, he is one of the best. **I am much frightened at being reminded that my letters are being bound and kept.** [Without these this book would not have been possible] I think I shall in future have recourse to a dictionary and complicated phrase book!! I fear I have been rather remiss in writing lately and in answering letters but the move has knocked me "all of a heap". I will describe to you my luggage in a later effort. I am sending separately some photos of "Ernest" which I hope will amuse! What about my waist now? I expect it will make the Duchess jealous, 28 ins! Please also have the enclosed check paid to my account (£17).*

Best love to you all.

Brocas.

Letter 144

15th April 1917, Clausthal

My dearest mother,
Several letters to answer I am glad to say and also three parcels (Nos. 147,
155, and 158) and an American Express Co. case, all most welcome, **the**
wristwatch which arrived just before [a luminous watch sent in
parcel number 152 dated 27 February 1917] *is exactly what I wanted,*
many thanks to you for it. Of course I have still got the Duchess's safe and
sound, but it is not luminous. A parcel of cigarettes has also arrived, the ham
arrived in excellent condition and also the bread, butter and eggs. Graves tells
me his mother has got the recipe for the bread, it certainly is most excellent.
Please stop flour till further notice and other baking accessories. Today the
weather is rather better and the snow is I think starting to melt. I hope this
continues as we have had quite enough winter and we hope soon to start
building something to play tennis on. You can't think how I miss the French
and Russians, it is very difficult to keep up one's studies, however I have found
an Italian professor and am giving lessons in Russian and French. I am also
starting book-keeping which I think will be useful to know and at any rate
it makes me add and subtract, a thing which I fear I was almost forgetting,
I am also Treasurer of our Entertainment Committee, so I am quite busy.
We hope to have another Pierrot show sometime in May and also to act the
"Magistrate" by Pinero sometime later, but all this is very much on the Knees
of the Gods and it is all very very different. I have met several old friends here
of Torgau days and also Gerald Crutchley who sends his love to George, you
may remember him as the Harrow bowler of about 1910. We are about 250
here; there is 1 squash racket court and 1 lawn tennis court, we hope to build
more but it is tedious work. **Poor Baba** [probably a reference to the navy]
is, as you no doubt know, in a very bad way, we are all very sorry about it
I hope something can be done to better his lot. He certainly has been most
unfortunate but of course will pull through. What news of George, I fear I shall
not be able to write to him anymore. Had I known what was going to happen
to **Baba and Co.** *I would have made arrangements with him, but it is no*
good crying over spilt milk. Your letter of March 11 has been most interesting,
it is almost impossible to find fault with what you sent me, it is all excellent,
I really mean this. Very rarely things have arrived in bad condition and this
is always due to the lateness of the parcels. Occasionally the sugar bag in the
Am. Ex. Co. parcels gets broken, but that doesn't matter much. Duchess's letter
of M. 14 also most welcome. I consider Phyllis Thompson most fortunate, still
some brave men left! Hope you saw Mrs. Hamilton Fletcher; Crutchley here
has told me a lot about Gareth; I fear there is no doubt. * Father's of M. 28
gave me great pleasure. Please keep the £3 as you suggest. So sorry to hear

Mrs. Griffiths has been unwell, I hope it is merely a temporary indisposition and that she will be about again by the time this arrives. My respects to her. So glad her school flourishes so, all luck to them. I am in the best of health and really working quite hard. **Mr Muller's system** [J P Müller's (1866-1938 Danish gymnastics educator) 15-minute full body workout and exercises] *is I hope helping to reduce my figure. Best love to you all. Your affectionate son,*

Brocas.

***i.e. of his death** [a note added by one of Brocas's parents]

Letter 145

30th April 1917, Clausthal

My dearest Mother,
Several letters and parcels since my last the latter included Nos. 148, 155, 157, 170, 159 and two more got by a friend who forgot to notify Nos. they included eggs, cake, bread and butter. All most excellent. Many thanks. Will answer letters in my next. Sorry to hear **Baba** [probably the navy] *is still very poorly off. Please send me a pair of fawn coloured trousers for summer weather. Stimson might make them. Buckles at side. Fairly wide in leg and pleated in front.* Also some old golf balls *and my niblick, mashie, iron and cleek. Books and music just arrived. Just what I wanted. Am acting in a small sketch called "Q". Do you know it? Amusing. I play Jack Annersly. You all seem well. Letter from Mrs. Chitty. My best thanks to her and respect to Mr. Chitty. Best love to you all.*

Brocas

Still cold.

Letter 146

13th May 1917, Clausthal

My dearest Father,
I fear I have allowed rather more than a week to elapse since my last letter to you. My apologies are profound and sincere. I have much to thank you for, firstly solids including parcels No. 161, 172, and 174. Or as good as ever. The

*cakes and bread could not be improved upon and put Buzzard to shame. **Mrs. Griffiths home-made potted-meat and Jam were a real treat and arrived excellently, and leave nothing to be desired.*** [a reference to escape items Parcel no 156 sent 7 March 1917 included a compass in Jam and Parcel no 160 sent 14 March 1917 included wire cutters in potted beef steak] ***How kind of George to send me a little present.*** [a reference to a cleverly written letter by George Burrows] *Letters have been arriving well, or rather altogether and I have got yours of March 3, 14, 21, 28 and Apr. 3. Mother's of March 3, 17, 24, and 31 and Duchess's of M. 7, 21, and 28. Quite right to take money from Cox for Badminton, though I was rather ragged by the move re sharing out. So glad you have heard from Miloradovitch. Do send him my love when you write and tell him I have read the copy of Boussa u ellups which he gave me with great interest. Tell him I hope he has not yet **"got the sign of old age"**.* [probably a reference to grey hair] *American Exp. parcel arrived recently. Please stop this now as with a new mess they are no more necessary. You are quite right to take the money for these off my account. In fact I think you ought to do so for all my parcels. How curious Duchess meeting a young lady who was at Gstaad the same time we were. I am afraid I don't remember her but I seem to remember the name. I hope the reports on our behaviour are as favourable as they should be. I have just had a letter from the late "Head", most interesting as far as it went but the last two pages were cut out by the censor! I am writing to him. Also, an excellent letter from Mrs. Chitty which I think I mentioned in my last. Snow has at last disappeared, and we are enjoying the spring weather rather a very thunderous attempt at it. It is however a great relief to be able to discard over coats, gloves etc. and resume a more rational costume. We are building a Tennis Court and a Polo pit and so had to get some exercise eventually. I have just come across a fellow called Wilson here in the Hampshire's whose people know Aunt Em very well and he has often seen her and spoken to her himself. He mentioned her to me in the course of an ordinary conversation without knowing I was a relation of hers, and it was most pleasing to hear what a great lady she is in the estimation of her neighbours. We had a long talk about her and Miss Canning and Moss Leigh. I said I would write and ask you to remember him to her when you write, and please send her my best love at the same time. So glad to hear good news of **Ellie and Cousin Jack**.* [Russia and Admiral Jellicoe] *I was rather nervous about the former's condition and news is of course lacking from other sources now. **Baba*** [probably the navy] *I hear is still rather unhappy, this is most annoying. Surely something can be done. Two parcels of songs have arrived recently and are being played with much success. Also some books which have gone off to the censor and not returned yet. Mrs. Macintyre's son* [2nd Lt David Hamilton MacIntyre] *is here in the Argyles and R.F.C. A very nice fellow who played cricket for*

Winchester v. Eton in 1915! Makes me feel quite old. I was going to act with him in a play here but that is now all off. Some Canadians have got an indoor baseball set, and I have been playing in the somewhat limited space till a few days ago. It is a most amusing game and when played by amateurs but with American colloquialisms great fun. I have not yet mastered the art of "pitching" "stopping" "bunting" etc. but hope to do so when we are able to play again. I hope you sent my message to Capt. Leech. [CJF] *Tell him next time you write that I think* **all my estimates were too high.** [A reference to his estimate of a date the war would end] *He may be interested to know that we are all well and that the Polo pit is in course of reconstruction, to the astonishment of many an intrepid bird man.* [this could be a reference to RFC officers] *My love to all with him and tell him we* **now consider rumblebelly the acme of "politesse".** [No information as to what this refers] *Write and ask Peskett about this. Please send me out a pair of Indian khaki puttees another pair of riding breeches to button on inside of the knee with continuations of light grey to fawn colour and strapping up at the side and not behind. I should think Hawkes had better make them. Cigarettes have arrived in good condition. I am just undergoing a course of minor operations with the local dentist, a strong and confident performer. Tell Duchess I accept her bargain re-the photos and will be taken as soon as possible, perhaps this week. The Sunday morning ones are no more possible, but one can go into the town under escort and have it done.* **Do you remember the gentleman's name who made enquiries about me at Burg?** [Herr Bulow *Letter 29*] *I wonder where he is now? Well I must close as I am orderly officer for the day in our mess and I must go and prepare the dinner. My meals, i.e. the meals I prepare are plentiful and simple. I am no fancy-cook! We are all well and determined to flourish!!*
Ever your affectionate son,

Brocas.

Letter 147

31st May 1917, Clausthal

My dearest Mother,
I fear I take up my pencil with the knowledge that I have no news. **All things here are very humdrum and we have none of the past excitements (!).** [possibly a reference to escape attempts] *Tennis has just started. We have one court built by the members of this camp last year and so we newcomers are naturally rather chary of playing on it. We are however building a new one*

*and really quite enjoy a severe spell of "navvy's" work. Two letters have come since my last to you Duchess's of May 6 and yours of the same date. Many thanks for them. I have passed on to Graves all your news re his father's visit. Letters are arriving badly here, which is most annoying. **J.S.B.** [no details] seems very happy so I expect he still would like to be in the North Sea. How amusing about Father and the rooks! Except of course for a Father. I seem to remember a certain worthy Bishop's remark when subjected to the same misfortune! We had a most successful little Empire Day dinner here to which we invited representatives of all the colonies and tried to "tie the knot tighter" if this is possible. The more news of **Ellie** [Russia] you can send me the better as I now get none from other sources. I am rather nervous about her. The following parcels have arrived. Nos. 179, 180, 181, and 185. Also, two from Holland. All most excellent. I fear I may sometimes not acknowledge parcels right as it is most difficult to do so. Other people sometimes get them for me and forget the numbers and so on. Did my letter asking for tennis shoes ever get to you? If not please send me two pairs of "New Wimbledon" shoes with hempen soles size 9 3/4. Please also send me a pair of brown brogues of about the same size. I think Gane would make them best. Also a pair of bedroom slippers just like the last you sent and one of those trench rain coats with a belt round them. We seem to get a full share of rain here one way and another. I have just written a P.C. to the late "Head" which I hope will reach him. I was much puzzled as to how to address him but eventually decided on "The Rev. Dr... and D.D. to finish up with. I hope this is correct. I am doing a lot of reading just at present and have just got hold of the most interesting book on Russia by Stephen Graham. Well's latest book about Mr Britling is quite amusing. We have at last got the Polo pit in action after a new lot of alterations. You can't imagine the difficulties of getting the slopes and angles right. We have to make the flooring out of stamped earth which is continually getting rubbed up and then the slopes have to be such as to make the ball come back the right distance away from the horse. All most complicated! I am afraid the seeds you so kindly sent are no good here as we have no gardens and it would be sinful to use any of our limited space for such a purpose. The mustard and cress however are duly planted and seem to be doing well. I hope your garden is taking advantage of the absence of ball games in it to produce an abnormal quantity of flowers. I hope also the Parks' garden flourishes. Well I must close. Best love to you all, and apologies for so poor a letter.*
Your affectionate son,

Brocas

Letter 148

13th June 1917, Clausthal

My dearest Father,
Several letters to answer since my last. Yours of Apr. 11, 18, 22, and 24 M's
of Apr. 7, 21, May 6, and 16, and D's of Apr. 22, 29, and May 6. All most
welcome. I am indeed sorry about the vagaries of my letters etc. to you. It is
most annoying and I hope will soon be rectified. Parcels 177, and 187 have
arrived and also 4 from Holland. All in most excellent condition. Please stop
Swiss bread and continue flour as we can now get it baked here. Have you
any more news of my regiment? We actually had a Vaudeville Entertainment 2
nights ago and I had to play Hawtrey's part in **"Q" by Stephen Leacox.** [A
farce in one act written 1915. A psychic story of the supernatural] *Most*
alarming. However it went off alright. Best love to you all.
Your affectionate son,

Brocas.

Letter 149

19th June 1917, Clausthal

My dearest Father,
So glad to hear that you have at last got a letter from me from this place. I
fear it has taken a long time. Your letters keep coming at intervals and I am
glad to say I have got quite a lot to answer by now. Since my last P.C. I have
got Duchess's of April 6 and May 13, yours of May 2 and 9, and Mother's
of May 13. All most welcome. You seem to be having quite a gay time with all
these weddings etc. It looks as if there would be hardly anyone left by the time
I return! So glad the "Earnest" photos have arrived safely. They certainly are
amusing and will be a good souvenir. We had a very successful little concert
here last Monday with a little one act play called "Q" at the end. It all went
very well but personally I am quite fed up with acting by now and don't intend
to do any more. Perhaps this winter! But who knows? Two parcels have just
arrived No. 183 ctg. tennis shoes which are most excellent and also a cap from
Hawkes. Please give Messrs. Hawkes my compliments and tell them I asked
for a cap, not an extinguisher! It is miles too big, so please don't pay for it.
Please ask Cator to send me a cap to wear with* blue *with a khaki
cover, not a forage cap like he sent me before. It is rather difficult
to explain. [probably because it was needed for an escape attempt] *I*
believe you have got an old Burberry of mine, if so please send it to **Mrs. W.**

Clark, Royal Irish rifles, Officers Quarters, Bhurtpore, Tidworth, Hants, [Possibly as payment for one lent for an escape attempt] *and say it is from me. Please also send me a "Trench raincoat". I believe cordine makes a good kind with a belt. Please send me also some more tinned meat and veg. (i.e. rations etc.) And also tinned fruit. I have spoken to Stirling here about his sister. He is a very nice fellow and* **we are both members of a small club which meets on Sunday.** [Possibly a reference to an escaping club] **(deletion by Censor)** *that is to say. Today we have had some really heavy rain, the first since the snow, which we hope will improve our new tennis court, which is still in course of construction. By the way that beautiful tennis racket you sent me, Aiseley Hexacon* [a make of tennis racket]*, broke the fourth time I used it and the experts here say that if you tell them this and lodge a forceful complaint they will send another free of charge. Will you please do this? It is really v. annoying. But if you can't get another out of them don't worry as I have purchased another from a fellow here. Major Morrison Bell has joined us here again and he and I are going to play together in the first tennis tournament.* **(deletion by Censor)** *I hope to get photographed soon but don't feel like it for the moment. We sent a P.C. to the Provost of Eton on the 4th of June which I hope will reach him. Do let me know if you hear anything about it. I hear Blake of my regiment has been killed. Please send me details and also other casualties if any. I do hope George is alright. No doubt he is having exciting times. Mother's letter of May 16 was full of news and most refreshing. We are told that walks are to start again soon which is a great boon. I heard today a parcel had arrived for me and so rushed down to the room to get it, only to find it was for R.F.G. Burrows (late of L.S.R.B.) Quite like old times but rather disappointing. Well I must end. My best love to you all and if you are cheerful and confident be sure we are none the less so here.* **"Bluff be d – d" is a very sound motto for "K.G."** [possibly a reference to an escape attempt by bluffing their way out]
Your affectionate son,

Brocas.

Letter 150

31st June 1917, Clausthal

My dearest Duchess,
I think it must be about your turn for a letter and so I will do my best to tell you all about everything. To begin with, we have just had a boxing competition (no, I was not competing). All the competitors were novices and so we had enough blood to glut the most savage barbarian. I officiated as second and so

attended the 'Beno' that took place after the event and have been persuaded (much against my will) to learn the noble art of self-defence. Please send me a pair of boxing gloves. **If you send them like parcel 151 they will arrive in the best condition.** [reference to maps and flash light refills in false bottoms of egg box sent 27 February 1917] *Since my last I have received parcel Nos. 183, 188, and 192. All as excellent as usual and what can one say more. Two letters have equally cheered me. Father's of May 16 and Mother's of May 20. E.C.G. etc. most interesting. Much interested in news of* **Lady Osler's friends,** * *so glad.* [Americans] *Books (Life of Napoleon etc) arrived but are still with censor. Many thanks. Cigarettes arrive safely as also eggs, of which perhaps one in twelve is broken, but handling is so rough I believe this is inevitable. We have just finished our second tennis court here and played on it for the first time today. It seems very good and as we have had best R.E.* [Royal Engineers] *advice during construction and have levelled and relevelled it an unmentionable number of times we hope for the best. It is now possible to get a game of three quarters of an hour very nearly every day. Squash rackets have arrived in excellent condition. I am sure you couldn't recognise me if you saw me now as I have grown side whiskers for a bit and they are really quite successful. Of course the local comedians find much amusement at my expense, but I think it is merely envy!! I am going to have my photo taken when they are at their best. So look out! After a spell of the most glorious weather it has suddenly turned quite cold here, but we have very little rain as yet. On the whole our existence remains as usual. We still keep church going and have a choir which is now of large dimensions, usually as big as the congregation. We are most fortunate in having a large number of distinguished pianists who are usually most willing to play when required. Our orchestra still continues under Sampson's direction and is really quite high class by now. So glad to hear enlarged photo of Duchess is on the way. What news have you of Dick Rawstorne? From some of the latest report he seems to have been fairing worse. Do tell me all possible news of Leech* [CJF] *and Co. I am most interested; is Walker still with him? I have had quite an amusing experience during the boxing i.e. running a* **Pari Mutuel.** [a form of betting] *Excellent practice for quick calculating etc. The funny thing is that owing to non-claimed tickets we are at present quite a lot of money up! However, I think this is too good to last! I have just read a novel called "Sonia"* [Sonia Between Two Worlds published Toronto 1917] *which I think you would like. It is by Stephen McKenna and really quite good. The first I have read for quite a long time! Well I must end. My best love to you all.*
Ever your affectionate brother,

Brocas.

*Americans [a note added by one of Brocas's parents]

Letter 151

19th July 1917, Clausthal

My dearest Father,
Three letters from you since my last card, yours of 30/V Mother's of 3/VI and
Duchess's of 10/VI. Glad to hear Wise's news, he appears to be one of the very
few satisfied ones there. The rope soled shoes are every bit as good as the India
rubber soled ones so please don't worry about the latter. At present tennis is
"off"! The following parcels have arrived Nos. 191, 194, 195, 201, 203 and
204 also two American Exp. (I think I thanked you for the one containing
sherry in my P.C. all excellent and entirely intact!) What a wonderful show
the O.E. dinner in France must have been. I see George and Alex were well
placed. Have you any news of my regiment? Where do I stand on the list of
subalterns? I have had no news for a long time. There are rumours of our
getting out of this to Holland. Praise God it's true, and the real old stagers
get a chance. You no doubt know more about this than we do, and any news
is most welcome. Meanwhile all is as usual here. I plug along at Russian and
Italian and though I make but little progress I keep them both going; you can't
imagine how one misses the French and the Russians. There is no occupation
in an all-English camp to really take the place of learning languages. One of
our room has been changed and we now have an R.N.R. Lieutenant Samble
by name, in place of Smyth Osbourn who was with us before. Did I thank you
for the photos? They are very good though not flattering of Duchess. However
accidents are bound to happen!! Please thank Sid for her excellent letter to
me. Most cheerful. Also for her photo. Alex and George must be having real
fun about now. (later) Your letter of June 13 just arrived. Thank you so much
for all the trouble you have taken re-balls etc. I fear it has not been easy. So
glad to hear such good news of Aunt Io and Bernard. I am sure the latter
could not improve on Miss Owen's and little Summer Fields. I have a few
requests. Please send me more tinned meat, not bully beef, but steak and kidney
puddings and **rations** [probably a reference to dry foods for an escape
attempt]. *Also more fruit and some galantines pâtés and vegetables. Please*
also send ideal unsweetened milk instead of the sweetened stuff. Please stop all
kinds of suet, etc. As we have no means of cooking it here also I have enough
soup for the moment. Please send me more soap. Did I tell you we had a Pierrot
show here a few days ago? Quite an impromptu affair I sang a song called
"Peru" (I'm Percy from Peru). The whole thing went very well indeed and it
was much easier doing it on the stage that in the old drill Hall at Friedberg.
I had a postcard from Peskett the other day in which he said he had heard
from Duchess and was writing to her. He never gives any news of himself,
but I presume he is at any rate better. Several books kindly sent by you have
arrived but they are still with the censor at Osnabrüch so I can't tell you which

they are yet. I am sure however that they will be excellent. Our spell of glorious summer weather has broken and we are now having it really cold again, much rain and wind. Very healthy no doubt but personally I prefer July hot. I have never seen such rain as we had the other morning. For a whole hour it came down in one solid stream. I should be most interested to see your garden in the Parks. I am afraid I have not done any gardening in captivity. Too slow a form of amusement for this kind of life. But I shall be most ready to dig it up for you. Please send me three pair of pants, cotton, white, like running shorts with the following measurements, waist 86cm. length from hip to above knee 50cm. seat 106cm. and also a leather waistcoat for which I enclose measurements, with long sleeves and not double breasted but flannel lined. Well my best love to you all,
Your affectionate son,

Brocas.

I fear this letter is even duller than usual.
Measurements for a waistcoat (rough) not chamois leather flannel lined.
> *chest 104cm. waist 84cm.*
> *seat (i.e. bottom of waistcoat) 102cm.*
> *sleeves, seam to elbow 34cm.*
> > *elbow to waist 26cm.*
> *back collar stud to bottom of v opening*
> > *in front 33cm.*
> *bottom of opening to bottom of waistcoat 32cm.*

Letter 152

30th July 1917

My dearest Mother,
Four of your precious letters since my last to you. Yours of June 9 and 17 and Father's of June 13 and 19. All as welcome as ever and I can't say more. The Dutch parcels have arrived once and were excellent. I couldn't think for the moment where they could have come from, but I think I acknowledged them; if not, I apologise. Golf balls have arrived and as we have at last been able to construct a small mashie and putting course, they are in great demand. I would love you to see us playing "ye olde and ancient game". The course consists of 6 holes, all of which cross and re-cross completely regardless of danger or anything else. The whole thing is on the slope of a small hill on which the camp is situated and is about the size of the school yard at Eton. However the fun is fast and furious and up to the present casualties have

been rare. *The second pair of rope soled shoes have also arrived and are most suitable, in fact I find them better than rubber as they are less tiring to the feet.* **Poor Ellie,** [reference to a set-back for Russia] *I fear all we can say as regards her is "worse much worse" to quote George Robey's song. So glad to hear that Duchess has not forgotten her cricket, though I fear bowling can hardly improve the fairy like forearm! Parcels No. 210, 201, and 202 and 204 have arrived. I may have acknowledged them before. The breeches and raincoat could not be better and the former are an excellent fit. By the time we go to Holland I shall be quite a smart officer again. Three books have just arrived from the Censor at Osnabrück. Rose's Napoleon 2 vols. and Marengo campaign. I shall read both as soon as possible. We are just going to start a tennis tournament, handicap doubles, I am playing with a Major Morrison Bell M.P. a delightful partner. We were going to play together at Friedberg but he moved to another camp and so we continue the partnership here. It seems very strange writing in ink again after so long a period. I could have done so before but hardly dared risk it and I fear this effort is far more successful!! Your parcels always arrive in excellent condition. I have no alarm on that score, and they are much appreciated by us. Good luck, and may they long continue so. Owen Price and I have started trying to compose a musical play to be acted here, at least he does most of the work and I sit by and try and put my oar in occasionally. It is most amusing as it means suiting the parts to the players and you find a leading lady who can dance and can't sing, or who can't enter R because the door isn't wide enough, or who must always play love scenes sitting down because her lover is several inches shorter than she is, etc. etc. I am sure Gilbert and Sullivan never had half so difficult a time. I have just been constrained to remove my side whiskers; people will go on with the same joke such a long time, I think I shall soon try an Imperial and see what they say to that!! Well I must end. Good luck and best love to you all and **may we meet soon in Holland or elsewhere.** [Probably reference to a pending escape attempt]*

Ever your affectionate son,

Brocas.

Please have enclosed cheque (£5) paid to my A/c.

Letter 153

My dear Sir,
Thank you very much for your letter of the 19th of June which I have had
great pleasure to receive the 7th VII. I am very glad to know your son is in good
spirit which he always was here in Mayence and gave us a good example. Till
now I did not get the sign of old age, but I am very frightened to get it. I am
very pleased to know that your son did not forget me in a such mournful time
and that he enjoyed my book. Thank you for your proposition to lend me some
English books but presently I am not in want of them. With kindest regards.
Yours very truly
N. Miloradovitch

I forgot to send to your son my love.

Letter 154

My dearest Father,
Since my last several letters from you have arrived, to whit those of 12-7,
18-7 and 8-8 also Mother's of 15-7 and Duchess of 22-7. You see the dates
are somewhat irregular! Sorry to gather that mine are not rolling up as well
as they might; your news is all most interesting as to Scouts, "joy rides" with
wounded, vegetables, Duchess' cricket etc. You ask if Oldfield came here from
Crefeld. No he did not. Only the senior officers did. Your enclosed letter from
Miss Canning just arrived. Very many thanks to her for all her excellent
news. I deeply appreciate her kindness in sending me so full an account of
life at Moss Leigh. Please tell Aunt Em that I fully sympathise with her for
not liking to write letters to be perused by the Censors. I have just had a
rearrangement of my corner here and put up most of the snapshots again. This
means preparation for the winter season, you see we are not quite so optimistic
here as you and Mrs. Estcourt appear to be!! I feel this really means we have
lost all confidence in hoping. We had a great affair a few days ago, the Regular
cavalry officers here (we are seven) gave an "at home" to the rest of the "eyes
of the army" (this has nothing to do with aeroplanes) and it was a success.
There were 3 Yeoboys, 6 Canadians, an Australian and a South African; it
was a most amusing evening, and I think I can say, even though a host, that

all enjoyed themselves. We have now entered on a regimental golf tournament and I am playing for the cavalry with a Major Bailey (12th Lancers). We are not very good but are quite confident. We have played three practice matches and lost them all easily. This only adds to our belief that our luck will change soon! I decided a short time ago to go out on walks on parole, a most difficult decision I consider, and they certainly are most excellent here. The country is quite pretty and all the most important hills have small view towers on the tops and some of the views are very fine. I have just read **Rose's Napoleon** *[The Life of Napoleon* by John Holland Rose published 1901] *with much interest and I'm at present doing quite a lot of reading. Mother's account of the cricket match England V Australia and S.A. is most interesting. What a kind thought to send it to me. I have received the following parcels, numbers 222, 223, 224, 225, and 228. Also Am. Ex. Co. parcels ctg. (1) tongues (2) ham (3) lots of tins. The cap has arrived and is the envy and admiration of all K.G's!! Such novelties led to much chaffing here as some people dress a bit, and others think those who do mad and vice versa! The Dutch parcels for the month have arrived and are excellent; also winters first 2 loaves, but they are, alas! bad! I know however this only happens occasionally and think it is worth while giving him a try. Tomorrow we are to witness an Indian play written and produced by people here. No mean undertaking. I saw the dress rehearsal yesterday I think it will be quite good. Please thank Miss Owen and Eleanor Butler for their kind letters to me and give them my best wishes. My sole requirements at present are a couple of ties, preferably fancy silk ones of a light fawn colour, two pairs of gloves, one lined and one for smart wear, to pull on and not button or clasp, and 6 pairs of socks equally light fawn colour and not thick.*
Ever your affectionate son,

Brocas.

Letter 155

19th August 1917, Clausthal

My dearest Mother,
The last mail brought me 3 most excellent letters from you and indeed I needed them. These possibilities of going to Holland are most nerve trying, and I fear one is rather apt to stake all on it coming off. So glad to hear how well Peskett is now, and also to have news of Hooper who always was one of the cheeriest and I am sure must be most useful at Mürren. I am very amused to hear you are no C.in C. girl guides in Ox'shire. I hope you don't wear a hat like that appalling thing Father wore on a certain visit to a Boy Scouts

camp we all participated in some years back! If so you and he must be a most awe inspiring pair when doing rounds or inspections together! Golf clubs etc. arrived in excellent condition and are now in great demand, especially the prehistoric niblick. Did this latter belong to Grandfather? Please thank Hedley for his kind letter giving account of you all. So glad to hear he is well again, give him my love and ask him to pass same onto his father and mother and Molly. The letters I am answering are yours of June 23 and 30 and Father's of July 4. I have received parcels Nos. 211, 212, 213, and 219. Also boxing gloves, cigarettes and 4 Dutch parcels. All most welcome, though home-made bread was alas mouldy, and No.211 (marked <u>"clothes"</u>) had lost all its contents on the way. Never mind, if you could see the state some of the parcels arriving here you would not be surprised at one of mine being broken and I believe this is the first; which is a real compliment to your packing! All the others arrived intact. I see Alban Hudson has the M.C. Well done he! How you must have enjoyed having Mrs. Fraser Mackenzie to stay with you. I am sure she was as cheerful as ever. Glad to hear Leo's hurts were not serious. **The Baba I referred to some months back was not the one you took him for. Don't you remember Uncle Edwards nickname?** [His nickname was 'The Commodore' (Jennifer Pearse pers. Com.) therefore Baba probably refers to the Navy] *All here is as usual. We get fairly good tennis and squash. I played Sampson in the local squash tournament this morning and got badly beaten. Hence I am now like a wet rag, as a small wooden court ill ventilated is no place for violent exercise this weather. I have great ambitions for Holland if we ever get there: No. 1 is to master the language "quam celerrime" (spelt right?) And after that to carry on with Russian and Italian. I think it ought to be fairly easy there, as one should get a certain amount of peace. I have at last discovered that in an all British camp real concentration is practically impossible and so I'm limiting myself at present to reading Military history. That Marengo campaign you sent me is most interesting. Can you please get me the others of that series i.e. Arcola, Teva and Waterloo? Some months ago you sent me some cough mixture* [was in fact whisky] *in a small biscuit box. I never looked inside the box which seemed closed till a few days ago, when I found the bottle, much to my surprise. Many thanks! When one comes to think of it time has really flown by pretty rapidly. This time three years ago I was in France and it really seems barely half that time. Gerald Crutchley has got Gareth's cap here, which of course removes all doubt. I fear it was a very good shot. Well I must end, my best love to you all.*
Your affectionate son,

Brocas.

Letter 156

23rd August 1917, Clausthal

Dear Bene,
It is sometime since I dropped you a line and I fear facilities for repeating my last are lacking. We hear rumours of a possible transfer to Holland. Pray God it's true. Yours truly is bored pretty stiff. Gerald Crutchley sends you his love. He is in great form, and we split a bottle or two most nights and talk of better days. We have now built a golf course on ground about as big as the garden at No. 9 and they tell me trench warfare is mere child's play compared to an ordinary afternoon's play here. We also get a little bad tennis here and some squash. I expect you are having a warm time of it. Good luck. Love to **Camac** [Alex], *I hear his hand is almost right again. Had an excellent letter from Sydney recently. So long,*

Brocas

Letter 157

31st August 1917, Clausthal

Gott strafe this nib!!

My dearest Father,
A great event. No less than seven of your letters arrive together and I have had a real field day reading them. To begin with, there are yours of July 25 and 27 (from Ewelme). How interesting about Mother's Demosthenian efforts. I have no doubt that her audiences sit as spellbound as the House did before great "Pitt", and I'm equally sure that her effects are gained without the stimulating juice that that hero found so essential!! I seem to remember an expedition to Ewelme with you to inspect Boy Scouts, but I'm a bit vague. How amusing about the golf clubs, but I fear it has given you a lot of trouble. They arrived in excellent condition. Mother's three letters of July 8, 22 and 29 and Duchess's of June 18 and July 8 the former enclosing 4 leafed clover. Neither of the Walkers are with us here. So glad to hear how well Arthur B. has done. Poor Duchess. Your snapshot of her is not complimentary. Very glad to get it, all the same, as also the other two of the garden. So glad Leo and Charles are alright. My respects to the Dr. and Mrs. Williams and the Alingtons when you next see them. The Duchess's cricketing career appears to be a really great one. How I should have liked to see her umpiring in the Parks. Georges letter from France seems well up to his old standard. I hope he takes all the good advice J.S.B. sent him on the matrimonial state. I have also just had a charming letter from Mr. Radcliffe

to whom I'm going to write a P.C. So glad that you exchange news with Mrs Showers. Stirling, and I and some other kindred spirits meet every Sunday evening over a glass of wine cup to discuss the affairs of the week. [possibly a reference to progress with a possible escape] *He got up an excellent Scotch show a few days back to which is about 40 of us went. Most enjoyable though I am afraid the "skirl of the pipes" appeals to me but little especially in an enclosed place! I had rather fortunate inspiration a few days back of arranging a dance in the dining hall. We decided to keep it secret and after an early dinner announced simply that the orchestra would play. We then cleared the tables away, and as soon as the orchestra started we began to dance "to beat hell" as they say in Canada. I was a little nervous about whether it would "catch on" or not, so had taken great care to get several couples to promise to start it off. Well it went down without a hitch, and in a quarter of an hour we had all ranks in the fray, not to mention all styles. Personally I started dancing man, with Crutchley in the pre-war nightclub style (now quite old-fashioned) and then danced lady, with a cavalry Major (real hunt-ball after supper style), a commander R.N. (heavy nautical style), and the local M.P., whose prime idea seemed to be if you bump hard you don't get hurt! I think we won!! Well we did this for 1 ½ hours and I have seldom been so tired or hot. Perhaps it is a sign of incipient barbed wire madness, but however it was great fun! If only you could have seen a certain colonel trying to Fox Trot. All concerned are deeply indebted to you for the good luck!** [Enclosed in parcel no 213 dated July 14 1917 and probably referring to a proposed escape attempt] *Well au revoir and by Jove, it looks more like a meeting now!* [almost certainly an escape attempt rather than just the prospect of exchange to Holland] *Best love.*
Your affectionate son,

Brocas

*Referring to extracts from newspapers sent in egg boxes with false bottoms. [Note added by one of Brocas's parents]

Letter 158

30th September 1917, Clausthal

My dearest Mother,
No less than three letters from you since my last and two from father. So I am indeed in luck. The dates of yours are Aug. 11, 18 and 26 and Father's of Aug. 1 and Sept. 6. The confounded vagaries of the post render it most difficult for me to remember what I had thanked you for and what not so please excuse

*repetitions. It must have been most interesting to have Mrs. F.M. with you
and Leo. Tennis racket, case of groceries, and case of 46 tins per Am. Ex. Co.
have arrived and could not have been better. I can't tell you how sorry I am to
hear of poor Leggat's death; one of the last left. At times it seems that it would
almost be better if all went, as meeting the few will bring back such a feeling of
missing the many. Never mind.*

Quotation in Russian? [no details]

*There's a nice little puzzle for Father and the Dean of Ch. Ch!! I think
George and I will have to give Mrs. Griffiths a solid silver cake after the war
to remind her of the pleasure hers always give. The only trouble here is that
they have become so famous that our mess is always doubly popular after I
get a parcel! So glad to hear Sandy's eczema is better. I feel sure a sojourn
here would quite cure him! Another lot of Mr. Koey's parcels has arrived
(No. 3), excellent as ever please thank him most sincerely from me. Of the
last 24 eggs he sent 23 were excellent and No. 24 "caused great amusement
by going off pop" when cracked. I fear I have rather disappointed you re-
photo but I have now decided to wait till Holland (?) for reasons I will
explain later. I gather from Father's letter that your stay at Buxton is over
and was a success. I am so glad as I had heard from my "spies" that you
would all benefit by a bracing change and now sincerely hope you have
done so. So glad to get news of the Sheffield's. I thought Molly was already
married. Sad about that. Here all as usual and the state of excitement makes
one rather jumpy.* [possible reference to an escape pending and why he
was making extra effort to get fit although an exchange to Holland was
also a prospect] *However I am re-reading Oman's History of England
as an antidote and also Napoleon's early campaigns. I have also begun to
try and get myself a bit fit by running at 7 a.m., playing 3/4 of an hours'
violent squash, and walking for at least an hour every day. We get good
walks about twice a week now, but I always think the pleasure of them is
spoiled by the clang of the gate on return! I have bought a pedometer, a most
amusing toy, grossly inaccurate. Would you please tell Hawkes to prepare
me a blue jumper with high collar (i.e. not to be born with a Roddy Owen)
and one pair strapped overalls, and Maxwell to make me a pair of parade
wellingtons. Please send these to me if Holland materialises.*

*Last night we had a most excellent impromptu concert as a farewell to some of
our number who leave us tomorrow, we hope, for Switzerland. Our local string
orchestra is now quite high class. We have also had another dance since*

[Pages missing]

Letter 159

8th October 1917, Clausthal

My dearest Mother,
A capital bunch of 5 letters since my last, yours of Sept 2 & 15 & Oct 7 &
Father's of Sept. 19 & Oct 10. Many thanks. Fruit arrived safe with golf clubs.
Duch's new job sounds excellent, hope she enjoys it. So glad F & D had a
good day at Harley House, have passed on June's? message to her brother. I
do hope your lumbago is better. So much in your letters to answer that I must
wait till I write mine. Gen. Bruce who is here asks me to send his kindest
regards thro' you to Mrs Max Müller whom he met in China. **Bad luck**
with egg boxes & cardboard do. [obviously the egg box ruse has been
discovered] *Please <u>discontinue</u>! Please send me a pair of snow boots. What rot*
these censors not allowing leather waistcoat thro'. I should like to meet some
of them! V. cold here!
Best Love

Brocas.

Letter 160

9th October 1917, Clausthal
[Written by Gerald Crutchley but initialled also by Brocas.
No recipient, probably to the Burrows family]

The auspicious moment has arrived to pen you a short epistle. Brocas and
yours truly find themselves in a room together and feel that you should be duly
advised of the fact. The size of the said room is about the same as the bathroom
at No. 9 we have to get up and go to bed by numbers trying to avoid the
"Sportsmen" who are apt to lie a bit thick on the ground. I was much grieved
to hear that the cricket world has suffered (1) by the loss of Wilkinson's good
length, finger, spin-round arm and (2) by the handicapping of Cartwright's
famous posterior boundary blow, as performed with effect of A.B. Stock. Our
regards, (M.C.) [probably Montagu Cartwright] *congrats and (finger)*
condolences to Alex.

G.E. V.C.
M.B.B.

Letter 161

My dearest Mother,
It is I believe an old adage that all things go in threes, and this is the third time
that I send you my most hearty good wishes for your birthday from captivity.
Pray God that next time paper and the pen of a most unready writer will not
be required to do this, but that the 15th of November will see us all united and
preferably at home. I write this in a positive hurricane of storm and rain in
my room which I went into a few days ago. It is a tiny little room for two, and I
share it with Gerald Crutchley, Scott Guards, one of the two pre-war friends I
have come across here. It is certainly a great boon to be with someone who was
a friend of all my friends before the war, and we have long talks about George
and Alex and the many others whom we knew so well. Please tell George
when you next write to him that we are indeed bowed down by grief to hear
of the irreparable loss caused to cricket by Alex losing his bowling finger! G.
will understand! Crutchley was of course with Gareth and has his hat here. I
don't think I mentioned in my last letter the great pleasure (and amusement)
the two photos of you and Father in uniform caused! Though the photo does
not include all Father's hat, I can remember it and I really think that in the
course of the last three years you might have found a deserving member of the
"poor clergy" who was in want of some such roof!! However "new times, new
(?) hats", I suppose. I suppose the correct thing to ask after the war would be
when we meet officially who salutes who first! You see one's environment begins
to affect one eventually! We had intended today to play hockey on one of the
tennis courts, it has turned out too wet an evening for that, so I shall have to
resort to a brisk hour's walk round the camp for exercise. So glad to hear you
paid the Brocks a visit and found them well. How wonderful Mr. B. is, still
driving about and enjoying life and I know his age is well advanced, though
as far as I remember it is kept a secret, isn't it? I hope you get into touch with
Neish and Peskett. I see a great many whom I know have got home from
Switzerland. One party left here recently for Heidelberg, we hope to eventually
take their places but do not know for certain yet. My latest occupation here
is a dancing class, as I think I told you. It has now grown to vast dimensions
and proves an excellent means of getting warm before dinner. It takes place
6-7 every day and it is most amusing to see some of the old stagers trying to
master the intricacies of the Boston and One Step. We hope to have another
evening dance soon in the Big Hall and I fear my lessons will have increased
the danger to the public weal as most pupils consider pace most necessary and
few can steer! We played the "Importance of being Earnest" again a few days
ago as a kind of stopgap since we had our caste nearly complete. It was a great
success in spite of only a week's rehearsal. I again appeared as Gwendoline,

and Crutchley played Cecily very well. It is said to have been better than last time at Friedberg. Well, my dear Mother again I send you my <u>*very best*</u> *wishes. Ever your affectionate son,*

Brocas.

Enclosed program of Earnest and also of an **Indian play** ['Dale Sahib of Dustypore' by Captain R D Davies Indian Army] *written and composed here.*

Letter 162

31st October 1917 5.30p.m., Clausthal

My dearest Father,
A line to you three at home on my natal day to assure you I have been thinking of you much, and I'm sure that "Gefangenschaft" comes under the same heading as "absence" in so far as it makes the "heart grow fonder". **(deletion by Censor)**. *Had a most cheerful day, and a birthday among so many old friends is the next best to one in the home circle, whatever the surroundings. To begin with, the members of my last room apparently went quite mad and serenaded me at 7.30. a.m. with some absurd song about sunrise, this with snow everywhere and icy cold. Hence I arose early! After breakfast a boxing lesson and then Pierrot rehearsals till lunch, then a walk, an extra rehearsal, a game of squash, tea and "me voici!" Certainly one of the advantages of a small room is the possibility of having it to oneself quite often. Most fortunately two letters from you, two parcels and an Am. Exp. Co. parcel ctg. the sherry all arrived today. Indeed a red letter day. The parcels were (1) bedroom slippers and puttees (2) Swiss bread. I have also received 236, 231, and 242 since my last. But parcels are arriving badly. I fear a leak somewhere! However we practically live on the hope of Holland though for the present it seems no nearer. As you see, winter is upon us in earnest.* **(deletion by Censor)**. *We are getting up a Pierrot show at lightning speed as we have now a lot of new arrivals here who will presumably take on the entertainments etc. when (?) we depart, and so we wish to show them what the "bow and arrow" men can do! Letters have been arriving well. Yours of Oct. 3. and Aug. 29! Mother's of Sept. 9, 23, and 30 and Duchess's of Sept. 12, 16, 23 and 30.* **(deletion by censor)** *Duchess's local news is always most amusing. I am indeed sorry for the **Osler's**, [Americans] a cruel blow. "Mais, c'est la guerre!" I wonder who was the wiser, Phyllis Thomson or her young man!* **(deletion by Censor)**. *Mrs. Leech has written to me again, and I'm going to send her a P.C. so glad to hear about K.M again. It is one of the places I most look forward to revisiting after the war. I felt so old myself this morning that on inspecting my face in the glass I decided to shave off my moustache. I*

did so forthwith! But then your letter arrived telling me off Aunt Em's 103rd birthday and I now feel quite ashamed of myself! She is really too wonderful for words. **(deletion by Censor)** *I hope you will meet* <u>him</u>* *someday, though he is such a giant I fear he would knock No. 9 over. "Till now I did not get the sign of old age, but I am very frightened to get it". I was his English professor and shall most certainly "tell him off for this" at the first possible opportunity. He was the man who, on being shown some sketches, of a senior British officer, said, "I am much admired to see your drawers!" This I am sure will not be good for Duchess! Price has just brought me the proofs of the programme in verse he has written for the Pierrot show. (I sing a song called "Archie" and he has written,*

> *"I know you will hear*
> *Of the terrible "Blocus"*
> *That the ladies have put*
> *Round the heart of poor Brocas!"*

Well you may be sure that I shall drink a glass to your very best health this evening and to our next merry meeting and may it be as soon as possible.
My best love to you all.
Your affectionate son,

Brocas.

I have just read O'Rourke's book for the first time. He ought to be shot!

Lieut. Miloradovitch. [* added by Brocas's parents]

Letter 163

24th November 1917, Clausthal

My dearest Mother,
No letters from you since my last, hence nothing to answer. Three parcels No. 243, one of apples and one from Jackson ctg. biscuits. Many thanks. Swiss and Winters bread arrive regularly. No more news about Holland: we still hope. This is not my Xmas letter but in case it should arrive too late, pray accept my best love and wishes by this. Also to Father for his birthday. I fear we may not spend it together. Better luck next time. We have snow here at last, very cold. So glad Con has D.S.O. Just received a letter from George. He seems well. Best love to you all.*
Yours affectionately,

Brocas
Con. Benson [* added by Brocas's parents]

Letter 164

30th November 1917, Clausthal

My dearest Father,
I feel like this is my most important letter of the year as it conveys to you all my heartfelt wishes for Christmas and also to you especially my wishes for your birthday. I must say I am disappointed at having to send you these from this place, but it really does look as if next time my abode will be more propitious. Today of course brings back many memories of happy days at Eton. We intended to have a small O.E. gathering here this evening, but the local Scotch are giving an exhibition of dancing etc., and as we are so few O.E's we have decided to celebrate founder's day instead.

Five letters from you since my last, yours of Oct. 17, 24, and 31 and Mother's of Oct. 15, and 21. All as welcome as ever and I can't say more. A most amusing letter from George has also arrived, and one from cousin Edith, written at Eton. I do hope Aunt Em's letter turns up. So glad to hear she is better. The Australian of our Cavalry "at home" was a fellow called Hunt and curiously enough he is in the Scottish Horse [Black Watch]. How he got there I really don't know! I fear you have rather an exaggerated idea of our walks here. They never attained the lengths you imagine they did. I fear few people but the "Englander" know what a walk is. __*Govare's pheasants*__ * [Zeppelins over France] *were certainly a magnificent "coup". Winters bread is a great success. I am indeed glad to hear Con. Benson has got D.S.O. What is he now? Parcels since my last include Nos. 246 and 248 and also one other home food parcel, number unknown. I am sure many don't turn up but of course know it is not your fault. We can understand it here. The home boiled tongue was A1, and also the eggs as ever. I think the tin boxes are the best for packing as they seldom get broken. Parcels of apples have also arrived and also three books which are at present in the hands of the censor. We had another most successful dance a few days ago, and it is certainly the best exercise we get here. One of my occupations at present is teaching the leading lady for the Pantomime to hold herself, dance etc. in a lady-like manner. A most difficult proceeding. This year's pantomime [Cinderella] is being done entirely by new captures, and it is really most gratifying to see the awkwardness of the beginner, and hear someone else told he looks a fool by the actor manager. We hear the Swiss party has crossed the frontier; perhaps only a rumour, but it is surely time. This should include Tom Estcourt, so his wife will be very pleased. Major Bailey should also be of the No. and I hope he will write to you. I have just been asked to sing at a concert here in a few days' time, and am trying to learn some songs. I hope Duchess is good at swift and breezy accompaniments, as those of my songs are real teasers, I believe. I am looking forward to hearing from him*

as his letter has not arrived yet. McGregor seems to have struck oil; others from his place give very different accounts. **Poor *Ellie***.** [Reference to Russian set-back] *I am glad I am no longer with any of her representatives. What must they be thinking! Did I tell you that Wilson has left for another camp? We miss him immensely. He was always a most cheerful companion. We had a most amusing "send off evening" for him. Well, again my best birthday wishes to you father, and my best Christmas ones to you all.*
Ever your affectionate son,
Brocas.

**The destruction of the Zeppelins over France.* **The Russians [Notes added by one of Brocas's parents]

Letter 165

17th December 1917, Clausthal

My dearest Mother,
My letter will follow tomorrow and this is only to procede it. Three letters from home since my last. Father's of Nov. 17, yours of Nov. 4 and Duchess's of Nov. 4. Many thanks. Also parcel No. 251. I fear clothes etc. have gone astray. Never mind. We produced "Tantalising Tommy" last night after a lightning spell of rehearsing of 3 weeks duration. So far from perfect, it went with a good swing. Account tomorrow. Sorry they took out the last programs. I have replicas. **Poor *Ellie*,** [Russia a reference to the Bolshevick revolution] *I fear she is done for! Oh for the whiff of grape shot! So glad to hear Malik is at it, my love to him!*
Best love to all.

Brocas.

Letter 166

31st December 1917, Clausthal

To Father,
Still ten more hours of this accursed year and I feel I could kick it out and should enjoy doing so if that would in any way accelerate its mournful pace. At any rate I am going to keep wide-awake till it has finally departed, out of sheer spite, and then pray God to grant us something better in the course of 1918. I apologise for this tirade, – ill expressed and commonplace; but to tell you the truth I am

feeling what is known as "fed up". Xmas festivities are over and the rather nasty aftermath of the first few days of quiet is much accentuated by the dreadful expectations, hopes and worries of a departure to a happier clime, this week? next week? some week?-? The first party has gone including Owen Price and the second goes tomorrow including Sampson and Cecil Graves. I shall be indeed angry if Sampson and I are separated, as we have been in a room together since Burg days, up to a few weeks ago, when I came in here with Crutchley and he, Crutchley, I and Alison (Coldstream Guards), who is an Australian, intend if possible to live together in Holland. I have again been having a few days in bed owing to a nasty bump on my old wound, but I'm now completely recovered and prepared for anything and everything. I went down the ice run here on skis for a bet, and negotiated the course up to the last corner, when I came an awful fall. Most annoying, as I ought to have done it! Just before this I went down with a passenger in a big bath, a most exciting ride. I believe these foolishnesses have been marked down by the authorities as barbed wire madness, and if so I ought to get to Switz. if Holland fails!! Well the Pantomime is over and was a great success, the new prince being most excellent in spite of my assistance. I really felt quite a Beerbohm Tree standing in the wings and watching the stage fright of the beginners!! Last night our mess gave a farewell musical evening and had a right cheery time. I can't tell you how sorry I am to think of some of these poor fellows here who have perhaps another year or more to run in this country. I know how I felt when the first lot of people went to Switzerland. (Excuse unfortunate change of nib). Four letters from you since my last. Mother's of Nov. 25 and Dec. 2. and Duchess's of the same dates. Welcome as ever: qui puis je dire de plus? Tell Duchess I am keeping up my singing with a vengeance, as I am sure learning songs and singing them is a most excellent exercise for the memory. I should think I learn about one a week. When I get to Holland I am going to send a list of those I want, as here I have hardly any music, and even the words originate mostly from other people's memory. I have also a couple of little recitations which I think you ought to like! I have ideas of trying to learn the piano for a bit in Holland, but must discuss this with you. How I wish I had done it when young!? I hope the mystery play was a success and I'm sure it was, under Father's management. We have now flooded both tennis courts here and skating is in full swing, though of course the space is limited. So glad to get your news of the last Swiss party. I hope they will not have the advantage of us for long. Parcel No. 248 has turned up and also the first two Danish ones, a great success. Bread also arrives well. Cecil Graves has promised to write to you as soon as he can from Holland, so you will probably hear from him before you get this. We had a tremendous carol singing on Christmas day. First of all some very hearty members of the community rose hours before any self-respecting lark would think of stirring and started off on Wenceslas, but whereas this worthy monarch is merely reputed to have had a peep, they retired somewhat smartly, this of course set off some

young comedians who tired of the chase and began singing on their own, they were also dealt with. And finally after church we gave them their money's worth and I believe it sounded well. We had a great discussion in the choir the other day as to whether the decani and cantores should stand i.e. on which sides. It was eventually decided perfectly simply that the former naturally stood nearest the Canting. Easy! Well perhaps this will be my last to you from here, but then again perhaps it won't. Anyway you may be sure I should be thinking of you and wishing you all luck tonight. God bless you all three.
My best love.

Brocas.

Letter 167

9th January 1918, Clausthal

To parents and sister,
My first line in 1918 naturally goes to you three at home to wish you Godspeed. We still await news of Holland and I am now tenth on the list in this camp, which ought to bring me into the next batch with any luck. Our latest amusement (?) is a so-called Cinema, of which we had the first exhibition a few nights ago. I have never seen anything worse. **(deletion by Censor)** *and am enjoying a good quiet read, the first in this camp.*
My best love to you all.

Brocas.

Letter 168

30th January 1918, Clausthal

My dearest Duchess,
We are enjoying a spell of most glorious spring weather, so balmy that I have spent the whole morning sitting outdoors without a coat. I fear this may mean bad times to come. No less than 5 parcels from you Nos. 253, 254, 261, 262, and 263, also eggs from Holland and bread as usual. All in excellent condition. Many thanks. I fear all clothes have been……. Lost (?) Never mind. I have enough to keep warm and cheerful.
Best love to you all.

Brocas.

Letter 169

31st January 1918, Clausthal

My dearest Father,

I have been putting off writing to you from day to day in the hope of being able to give you certain news of my prospective journey to Holland. At present however, we are still left in ignorance. We have had news from those fortunate ones who are already there and it seems that Bell and Humphreys, who as you may remember were my first acquaintances in captivity, and I will hold the unfortunate record of being the longest in Germany! Our latest amusement here is the Cinema which has now performed some three or four times. The films which have been exhibited up to date are without exception bad and I am sure none of them would have passed the censor at home! However we may get something better later. The best part of them from our point of view is that as the screen is put up in front of the stage a party of us go with our coffee and wine and sit on the stage in armchairs and so see everything in comfort though of course the wrong way round. I have just started a course of elementary electricity with an engineer here and so hope eventually to be able to repair a fuse etc. It is certainly a most interesting subject and my ignorance of it was previously quite complete. Two letters from you of Nov. 28 and Dec. 6 have turned up. Many thanks. So glad you still hear from McGregor he is certainly a very interesting man, whom I intend to see again after the war if possible. So glad you attended the Founder's Day service at Balliol. Stirling has not gone to Switzerland but to Holland, at least I believe and hope so! He certainly left here with that intention. Please tell Maxwell to send me spurs for my wellingtons. I shall certainly have to order all sorts of clothes as soon as I arrive in Holland as my wardrobe is practically non-existent. All the better for packing and travelling. I am writing to J.S.B. to congratulate him on being a proud papa, but I'm pretty vague about his correct address, so am trying J.S.B. R.N. Australia c/o Admiralty etc. I fear my last lot of correspondence has been rather insufficient, but really in the present state of chaos and confusion here I think I can claim forgiveness. I have been packed for a month in fear of a sudden call, and of course if I unpack we shall be sent off at once, and vice versa.
Best love to you all.

Your affectionate son.

Brocas.

Letter 170

Saturday 2nd February 1918, Clausthal

Enfin les bonnes Nouvelles? We depart for Aachen at 4 a.m. tomorrow morning, a most disgusting hour, but still beggars can't be choosers! We ought to crossover in about four days I think, and you will probably get a wire from me sometime before receiving this. In case not, please despatch all my kit to me immediately, civilian and otherwise. Letters from Duchess on bright blue paper just arrived containing beautifully worded tirade against alcoholism which I entirely agree with. My best luck to you all.

Brocas

12

Holland – Freedom

6 February 1918 – 18 November 1918

Brocas arrived in Holland on 6 February 1918 after over a month of agonising delays as he waited his turn. The first batch of officers had been exchanged and arrived in Holland on 29 December 1917. He was one of 96 officers in the fourth batch to be exchanged and he was told at the time that he and two other officers (Bell and Humphrey) held the unfortunate record of being the British officers held longest in Germany. The arrival record for Holland suggests otherwise. There were 24 others, most of whom were captured on 26/27 August 1914, who were on the same arrival list and had been prisoners for five more days. Brocas had been a prisoner for 1249 days. On arrival in Holland each batch of new arrivals was photographed as they were met at the station. In the photo which includes Brocas, one officer can be seen with a dog which presumably he had acquired as a POW. Those captured first, along with the sick and wounded, were the first to be exchanged.

His father, who arrived in Holland two days after Brocas, wrote an emotional account of their first meeting (*Letter 176*) in his first letter to his wife, dated 17 February 1918:

> *There are some moments in life it is only right to draw a veil over, & you know all. As to his looks he is simply splendid; decidedly taller & broader, face more decided & developed, but very handsome & still deliciously boyish, not a trace of deprivation about him, & nothing approaching to the 3 ½ years' difference I had expected. He was perfectly natural, quite charming in manner among perfect strangers (for we were a party of 6), & very smart in the blue evening kit which had arrived that day & fitted perfectly, boots & all. Of course I can't dwell on the sentimental side in a letter that has to be censored: you will fill that in. No trace whatever is left of his wound, & he could not look in better condition.*

This letter is the key to understanding and confirming much of what went on with the parcels from home and clarifies among other things,

Arrival in Holland of Fourth Party on 6 February 1918 – Brocas (circled). One officer is holding a copy of the Daily Sketch and on the right there is a dog.
Source: Burrows family archive

the circumstances of Brocas's capture at Néry; how the parcels with illicit escape items were received and how latterly things went wrong; and most importantly that Brocas had to destroy all but a few of the most precious letters he had received before he left for Holland.

His father wrote many letters home during his time in Holland and he described the arrival process in his letter to his wife of 26 February 1918 having not actually been present when Brocas arrived.

> *They actually got here at 10.30am on Sunday. They are met at the station by the Colonel in Command, his staff and a crowd of officers and brought in trams to a large room in the Café Burhoht? Where previously the high officials, the leaders of society, and we Y.M.C.A folk had assembled. We and the tea tables took up the lower half of the room; into the upper half the prisoners filed one by one, officers first lead by a grey-haired colonel in mufti…*

There were brief speeches and cheers *'the most touching to be heard anywhere…'* As the only parent present it is moving to read how his father described his own emotion.

> *… all the while you stood watching those upturned faces, wondering what thoughts they concealed or expressed, with that feeling John Inglesant expresses of not knowing whether you were really yourself or a dream-self, to full of suppressed emotion too be capable of utterance.*

Writing home, a month later on 5 March 1918, his father gave his general assessment of how internment had affected all the internees.

> *Both officers and men have lost all habits of church going and it will take a long time and much personal influence to make a change. On the other hand the conduct of all ranks is quite admirable, all things considered. There is very little drunkenness or excess of any kind and when you think of how tempting it must be to paint towns red after three and a half years of German repression, it says a great deal for English gentlemanliness.*

He went on to reflect on the sea change in the very social fabric of British life and particularly how the war had changed attitudes and social thinking. How the social classes had been re-defined as embodied in the new structure and nature of the British Army. Old 'colonial' life styles had been swept away on a world-wide wave of death and destruction.

> *It will be curious too to watch the meeting of the old army and new.*
> *Hitherto the "Contemptibles" have had it all to themselves. They have*
> *no conception what the new army is like. They themselves are not one*
> *jot changed from the type you and I know so well... They have been cut*
> *off since 1914 from all English intercourse, except a very few convenient*
> *newspapers. It is impossible for them to even guess at the changes that*
> *have taken place. They are of a pre-war England that is as dead as the*
> *dodo. A curious problem surely?*

That was astonishingly perceptive given it was written by the only
parent 'on the spot' and in the throes of the unfolding changes.
Whatever the outcome it would appear that Brocas went on to
embrace the changes and all the new challenges that life and the 'new'
army were to throw his way. It also worth noting his father's use of
the term 'Contemptibles' to distinguish the early exchanged POWs.
These being officers and men of the original British Expeditionary
Force up to 26 December 1914 when it was divided into the First
and Second Armies. The Kaiser had been famously dismissive of the
BEF, and allegedly issued an order on 19 August 1914 to "exterminate
the treacherous English and walk over General French's contemptible
little army". Hence, in later years, the survivors of the regular army
dubbed themselves '**The Old Contemptibles**'. No evidence of any
such order being issued by the Kaiser has ever been found but clearly
by 1918 the term was in regular use by the British and implied a certain
amount of pride in the achievements of the original fighting force.

Regarding the pending exchange, early as 30 December 1917
Brocas's mother had written her first letter to Holland hoping he
would be there soon, and it would be there for when he arrived. Brocas
wrote his first uncensored letter home on 9 February 1918. (*Letter
174*) He was clearly emotional, confused and understandably a little
angry and, as he later admitted, he still felt the restraint of the German
censors over him. He closed this letter with the words: '... *Tear this up;
it will make me sick to read it afterwards.*'

Fortunately, his mother did not tear it up as he requested and
kept it along with all the others she had received. The true awfulness
of his three and a half years in captivity began to be revealed in his
uncensored letters. Brocas was however, not a man to dwell on the
past although in an outpouring of emotion (*Letter 185*) he wrote
'May they die in thousands'. There are also several references to his
wanting to rejoin the fight and get his own back before the war ended.

However he soon began to savour his new-found freedom. He was quickly reunited with fellow officers many of whom had been with him throughout his internment and who had preceded him to Holland. A senior colonel commented to his father. (*Letter 180*) '*...Your son is of the best & we owe him a deep debt of gratitude for his high spirits, & the way he organised all our sports & theatricals.'...* and he went on to write '*All the senior officers I have met say the same, & the extreme niceness of them all to me is largely due to him...*'

His mother continued to send parcels to Holland, the first being on the 19 January 1918 in anticipation of his imminent exchange. These parcels contained mostly clothing and general necessities and only a few food items. The first parcel contained 1 warm vest, 1 warm pants (new), 1 sweater, 6 handkerchiefs, 1 pair warm gloves, 1 scarf, 1 warm pyjamas, and 1 packet of chocolate. After all it was the middle of winter. His mother was always ahead of the game and even in Holland, Brocas must have continued as one of the best, if not the best catered for British officer and ex prisoner of war. Two days later a second parcel was on its way via American Express. A deal case contained 23 clothing items, a mixture of military and civilian wear. On the 6 February 1918, the day he arrived in Holland, a box of golf clubs was also despatched via American Express. On 15 March, in readiness for the cricket season, parcel number 1 of that date contained his cricket bag, bats, pads and balls.

Parcels sent to Lieutenant M Brocas Burrows in Holland
(Sample list only)
30 December 1917 – 16 May 1918

DECEMBER 1917
TO HOLLAND

30th   *Sent my first letter to Brocas in Holland*

JANUARY 1918

19th	*No 1*	*1 warm vest, 1 warm pants (new), 1 (E.R.) sweater, 6 hdkf, 1 pr warm gloves, 1 scarf (Buxton), 1 warm pyjamas, 1 pkt chocolate*
21st	*No 2*	*1 Green scotch jug, 2 boxes soap, 1 tunic, 1 slacks (khaki), 1 grey woollen waistcoat, 1 coat, 1 knickers, 1 waistcoat (brown old Eton), 1 pr grey flannel trousers, 2 prs*

		white flannels, 2 flannel shirts, 2 striped shirts, 1 pr cream
		pyjamas, 2 vests, 1 pr pants warm, 2 prs khaki socks, 2 prs grey
21st	*No 3*	*P. post, 1 5lb box tea (Ceylon)*
		Acknowledged
22nd	*No 4*	*From Scheveningen, 2 tins biscuits (4lb) 1lb coffee,*
		toothbrush, shaving brush, manicure
		Acknowledged
25th	*No 5*	*Sponge, soap, shaving soap*
		Acknowledged

FEBRUARY

6th	*No 6*	*Box of Golf Clubs – American Express*
8th	*No 7*	*Biscuits, dates, <u>brushes</u>, book*
22nd	*No 8*	*Biscuits, books*
27th	*No 9*	*3 prs pants, 1 lb coffee, 1 book*

MARCH

15th	*No 1*	*Cricket bag, bats, pads and C.A. box*
15th	*No 2*	*1 large parcel, Flannel trousers and pants*
15th	*No 3*	*1 deal case (Am. Ex. Co.), shoes, Gillette, inhaler, papers*
		(S.M.B.) caps re Brocas
		(all addressed Brocas)
20th		*1 deal case magazines only*
22nd		*S.M.B. suit case c/o Warren, summer clothes, 4 Nelson's*
		History, magazines, newspapers and cuttings
		Deal case, slides Pompeii and Oxford and two lectures c/o Warren

APRIL

12th	*1 deal case magazines only*
16th	*1 suit case B's clothes, 6 evening shirts, 12 day-shirts, 18*
	white collars, evening dress suit, 1 white waistcoat, 1 sachet
	(love in the mist), neck tie

Brocas was at pains to point out to everyone he met, and who commented on 'how well they looked', that the POWs knew that this was due to the parcels they received from home and particularly those from his mother. (*Letter 179*)

> *…I meant to write a special letter of thanks to you for the marvellous manner in which you have always remembered me and sent me all necessities and in fact everything I asked for in Germany. Words*

Hotel Zeerust, Scheveningen c 1910 Source: Burrows family archive

*cannot express my gratefulness and I don't think anyone else ever got
so many or such excellent parcels from home…I don't think anybody
in England really realises how much the K.G. depends on his parcels
for his very existence. We do and are always most careful to explain to
people who remarked on our health that this is entirely and absolutely
due to the "old folks at home", God bless and keep them…*

Brocas was first billeted in the Hotel Zeerust, in Scheveningen, the
best of three hotels holding British officers, thanks to the effort of his
friend Captain Cecil Graves. He was soon joined by his father who,
from February until the end of June, took on the task of running and
re-vitalising the YMCA Hexham Abbey hut, a place which became the
centre of social life for ex-POWs during the time that his father was
running it. Initially, his father was the only parent who had risked the
journey to Holland to work in the hope of being with his son.

After the strangeness of the first few days of freedom, Brocas slowly
returned to normal and embarked on an energetic period of work,
socialising, dinners, dances, concerts and all manner of entertainments
and sporting activities as he continued to recuperate and rebuild his
life. He never lost his sense of humour and he was soon able to see
the more comic side of his new predicament. In his first long letter
home 10 February 1918 (*Letter 175*) he wrote: '…*The thick underwear
is magnificent, and if ever I am to be exposed to really heavy fire I shall
certainly wear it!!!…*'

He closed this letter saying he had his first ride on a horse on the
9 February 1918. The taste of fresh air and freedom must have been

Brocas with 'sickly grin' at Haarlem after being bowled first ball (Letter 201 18 August 1918). Playing against Mr Posthuma's XI Haarlem August 7 and 8 Source: Burrows family archive

overwhelming. '*...I went for miles along the beach quite alone, and then galloped the poor old hireling off his legs...*'

When his father was about to return home at the end of June 1918, in a letter to his mother Brocas summed up his pride and appreciation for all he had done. (*Letter 193*)

> *...I shall always remember as long as I live that mine was the one Father who really cared to run the risks and put up with so many annoyances in order to see his captive son at the first possible opportunity and I pray God it will help me to be a better man...*

Along with fellow officers and friends Brocas travelled widely through Holland with few restrictions. Sometimes for cricket matches, at other times for purely social outings. They were courted and feted by many a good Dutch lady whose aim was to catch a supposedly wealthy British officer for their daughter.

Brocas became bored with the noise and bustle of hotel 'life' and moved out of the hotel to shared digs with two other officers, Lieutenant Reginald Mosely and Lieutenant Hunter-Blair in 182 Riouw Straat, The Hague. He began visiting embassies and established connections in diplomatic circles with embassy staff with a view to utilising his language skills learned as a POW. He obtained a part time job at the American Embassy working as an interpreter. By June the commission tasked with negotiating the fate of the POWs was still deadlocked and the summer wore on with little prospect of returning home. Brocas rekindled his love of cricket. He was active both on and off the field organising and playing matches and tournaments. As well as competing on tennis courts and the golf course, he played two games of 'rugger'.

Brocas played numerous cricket matches as a representative for the POW XI, many of which were reported in local newspapers. In the closing match of the season, played on 7 and 8 September against a Netherlands XI, his score of 54 was the highest of the 213 for 7 wickets before heavy rain caused the match to be abandoned on the second day. He was caught in the cover five minutes before the close of the first day having hit two big sixes over the pavilion. Cecil Graves his close friend, did not bat, having taken five Netherlands wickets for 19 runs as the Netherlands were dismissed for 108. The match venue included a three-hour programme of music with an interval performed by The British

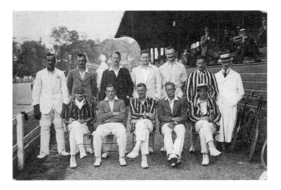

Back row: Greene, Foreman, Graves, Burrows, Henslow, Skeet, Robertson. (Umpire). Front row: Crutchley, MacBryan, Fowke, Tailyour, Caldwell – Haarlem, Holland August 7 and 8 1918 Source: Graves family archive

Military Band. At the close the teams retired to the Restaurant Royal in the Hague for an end of season dinner. Major Fowke proposed a toast 'To Cricket' and Captain MacBryan to 'The Netherlands Cricket Union'. The evening ended with a programme of music and dancing. In the averages for some of the 1st and 2nd class league matches in Holland, Brocas with an average of 42.75 was 3rd highest, scoring 342 runs in nine innings with a highest score of 142 not out. He was only bettered by MacBryan and his other close friend Gerald Crutchley who after the war went on to have a distinguished first-class career, playing 123 first class matches for Oxford University and Middlesex, averaging 22.46 runs. MacBryan played 206 matches for Somerset. After the war Brocas also played first class cricket for Oxford University and Surrey averaging 32.07 runs in 28 matches. Cecil Graves' 36.85 runs was 5th in the averages in Holland. In the team photo all except a Canadian, Greene, Tailyour who died in 1920, and Caldwell, played at least one game of first-class cricket.

As early as July 1918 (*Letter 198*) Brocas was beginning to contemplate 'where next', and his thoughts turned primarily towards Russia as a place where his recently acquired language skills would be of most use.

During this final period of internment, a world-wide pandemic of Spanish Flu was taking hold and in Holland, Brocas described it as *'positively raging here!'* He contracted it twice, the first time in August,

(*Letter 200*) when he was away for a cricket tournament. He was in bed for four days. The second time in late October, just before he was to return home, was not so serious.

In his final letter from Holland dated 4 November 1918, (*Letter 211*) just after his 24th birthday, his thoughts were firmly set on his next campaign and he closed with the following thought:

> ...*I am gradually dropping all ideas of cricket in Holland next summer and looking forward to shooting Bolshevichs instead!*

The Armistice came and went but he wrote nothing of this in a letter. Like so many, he was probably too busy celebrating and preparing to return home.

Brocas arrived back in England at Hull on Monday 8 November 1918 on the S.S. Willochra, 1556 days after he last set foot on English soil. After two days of assessment and debrief at Ripon Camp he returned home.

Final Note

A poignant hand-written note by Father concluded the diary of letters:

> "*Brocas and Marlow arrived safely at 8.30 p.m. (Wednesday 20th November 1918)*
>
> *And so ends the chapter.*"

S.M.B.

13

Holland – Freedom

6 February 1918 – 18 November 1918

The Letters

Letter 171

7th February 1918, Friedberg
To: Mrs Burrows, 9 Norham Gardens, Oxford, England

Dear Mrs Burrows,
I hope that your son is already interned in Holland and that at length he is free and happy, and you will be able to see him. I am glad for him. In a mournful situation as I am it is really a nice thing to know that a friend is happy. Please send him my love and tell him please how glad I am for him. No nearly 2 months I am at freed my God and to kill my time I intend to arrange a flower and kitchen gardens. I hope that this occupation will dispel a little my black thoughts and will help me not to grow old too quickly. In one of your letters you were so kind as to propose me to send some books don't you mind instead of books sending me some seeds for my Gardens. I am very sorry to bother you. I would like to have in my kitchen garden cucumbers, peas, beans, onions, potatoes tomatoes radish and turnip radish. Thank you in advance with kindest regards to you and Mr Burrows.
Believe me yours very sincerely,

N Miloradovitch

Letter 172

8th February 1918, Haag
Telegram to: Burrows, Norham House, Oxford

Arrived safely: send all kit to Heerengracht, 13 The Hague.

Burrows.

Letter 173

8th February 1918, War Office, Whitehall, S.W.
Ref. M.S. 3. Cas. /518a.

The Military Secretary presents his compliments to Mr. Burrows, and begs to say that the following report has been received at the War Office: -

2/Lieut. M.B. Burrows, 5th Dragoon Guards Prisoner of War arrived in Holland from Germany on the 6th February 1918.

C.C.L.

Letter 174

[No date but probably written 9 February 1918],
Hotel Zeerust, Scheveningen

My dearest Mother & Sister,
This is but a short note as I can't write yet. I don't think I have sat still for five minutes since leaving Germany. You can't imagine what it is; no one can unless he has been caged up for 3 ½ years, spat upon cursed and reviled by men and women, and then suddenly let loose among smiling kindly people who appear to sympathise, and even try to persuade you that they consider you a hero. Everything is strange, even wrong it seems; why no barb wire, no dogs, no men with guns? The only sentries I meet salute, kiddies say good evening; it all seems like a dream, and I could sit down and cry like a child if it were not that I was eaten up by one all engrossing "Hass" for those barbaric swine whose one idea and thought during three years has been to bully insult and annoy me. I suppose this is un-Christian; if so I hope it will pass. Perhaps, I know I ought to sit down and write you a long letter describing everything but, Mother, I can't and I'm sure you will understand why. In a few days I shall be "normal" (my compliments to Lord Newton) and then I will write you volumes. Fancy seeing father in a day or two! It seems incredible. Would that you two were coming also. However it will not be long now, but I could wait forever to see those brutes really beaten. How father has managed to get out, heaven only knows. He is wonderful, and from what I hear he's really wanted here. I wonder if he will recognise me. All who were with me at Torgau and have not seen me since say I have altered completely! Let's hope for the better. I am inundated with invitations, but I'm not going out yet. I'm going for my first ride tomorrow. Well goodbye, and God bless you both.
Ever your affectionate son and brother,

Brocas.

Tear this up; it will make me sick to read it afterwards.

Letter 175

10th February 1918, Hotel Zeerust

My dearest Mother,
I had hoped that father would arrive this evening but learned there is no news of convoy yet, at any rate it is only a question of days. I fear I shall be unable to meet him on the quay, but I've made arrangements with the Y.M.C.A. to inform me as soon as the ship arrives and I shall then meet all the trains. Well, the first rush of excitement is now over, and I am seriously examining my surroundings and trying to decide what to do. Needless to say all the pick jobs have been snapped up by various aviators and other non-descripts so it looks as if I shall have to content myself with ordinary routine work at first. I am sure it will be very good for me. What I want is some job at an embassy where I can use my languages, but nous verrons. I find my poor old memory is still rather dicky and have had to resort to a memo book for the time being. The first arrivals have been very kind to us "New boys", and we have been invited out all over the place; hence I have not even paid my duty calls yet. However I start off tomorrow. On Tuesday I am going to a reception at the Embassy, and on Wednesday to one given by the senior Russian Officer at Rotterdam. I have left cards at the Belgian Embassy, and informed them that their king is my colonel. I have spent the afternoon with Stirling, who is very well indeed and thoroughly enjoying life. On Tuesday afternoon I am putting myself in the hands of Pelham-Burn, and commissioning him to take me to call on everybody who should be called upon and known. Last night I went to a "club de danse" and had a most amusing evening. This however is supposed to be very secret, as dancing is not allowed here during the war. The Dutch people here are almost embarrassingly kind and one has to be saluting all day. They say the oi Torroi? are pro ally but the "four hundred" pro hun! If this is so the latter conceal their sentiments far better than the former, and I think we shall soon rectify that; at present we are all "regulars" (I don't mean to use the word in a snobbish sense but it is hard not to) and pray God I have a vague idea of how to behave even after 3 ½ years with barbarians, but I tremble to think what will occur when some of the later captures whom we left at Clausthal come here! George Graves had a magnificent bag of letters to present me from you on my arrival and I read them with the greatest avidity. At first I

thought father might already be here, but no such luck! Your wonderful lot of parcels also turned up yesterday, and you have really excelled yourselves in catering for my requirements. The "Blue" is quite a perfect fit, as also are the wellingtons. Tea is in great demand here, as also are biscuits and coffee. Please send me 1 box of sweet and 1 box of plain biscuits every week. Bread is very scarce. Don't forget to stop my bread going to Germany; this, just in case!

The thick underwear is magnificent, and if ever I am to be exposed to really heavy fire I shall certainly wear it!!! Do you remember the measurements I sent you for pants some months back? Would you please repeat them and send me three pairs? If you sent any to Germany I fear they were stolen, as also the woolly waistcoat; but I have quite enough warm clothes. The only other thing I require are the cigarettes, as you sent them to me in Germany please. I intend to stop smoking later but for the moment I feel I need a "soother" (!!) from time to time. Please tell Maxwell from me that the wellingtons were an excellent fit and order from him (1) a pair of very smart Field Boots with rubber things on the soles instead of nails and (2) a pair of brown gaiters to lace up the front. I see from your list that the parcel of clothes sent off on Jan.21 has not yet arrived. It is no doubt on this convoy. Mr. Koey invited me to dinner tonight but was taken ill and so has put it off. I have not had the pleasure of meeting him yet. This morning there was a service of welcome to the new arrivals in the English Church here, a most delightful building. The address was given by the local chaplain, and the things he said nearly made us all ill. I do wish these people would realise that we are not "Greek heroes" or anything like it, and that nothing they say will ever persuade us that we are. When one has rolled 3 ½ years in prison while other people have done ones work it rather hurts to be called "a saviour of Europe" by one of one's fellow countrymen. I really feel quite strongly about this. I hear the Germans at Rotterdam have been getting it hot! One has been killed already. I wonder if we shall meet any on Wednesday!! I met one, an officer, in a restaurant here the other night and think I managed to hold my nose higher than he did!! There were some shouts of "A bas les boches!" And so he left. I don't appear to have told you anything about my journey here, or this place, or to have answered your letters, but I have just rambled on and written you exactly what entered my old head. I will get down and write you an account of everything when I have digested it better. It all seems too good to be true. One of the greatest pleasures I shall have will be introducing my friends to Father when he arrives. I do hope he will take complete charge of the Y.M.C.A. here for a time, as I think the present men are pretty poor; perhaps I misjudge them. Well it is now 11.30 and I am rather tired so will close down. I still seem to feel the restraint of the German censor over me but this will disappear in time and then I should be able to tell you about things in general. My best love to the dear Duchess and to you, Mother.

Ever your affectionate son,

Brocas.

Did I tell you I had my first ride yesterday? I went for miles along the beach quite alone, and then galloped the poor old hireling off his legs, and so quietly home again!!

Letter 176

17th February 1918,Y M.C.A.,The Hague, Holland
[Reply to Villa Mess]

S.M Burrows to Wife

Well dearest,
If I write for a week I shall never get though half I have to tell you, but a beginning must be made. We got under way within half an hour of that last view of you both from the window as you went to catch your train, & steamed down the river to the Deeps (near the Downs) & anchored there by noon.We soon began to make one another's acquaintance. I shared a cabin (which on a P & O you would consider small for one) with three others: that man in the white Homburg hat, who is our intelligence officer at a certain town and was up at Magdalen; and two Americans, one an attaché at the U.S. Legation here, just out from America, & the other a most interesting man, the Director of the U.S. relief fund for Belgians in occupied territory. But I must not waste time on fellow passengers who are after all, transitory, or shall never get to the engrossing subject.We were to have sailed at 10:30 that night, & I turned in at 10 hoping to awake to Holland, slept like a top till 8 only to find ourselves as we were. The order had been cancelled at midnight, perhaps owing to fog & there we lay all Thursday till past midnight. It seemed very wonderful to be lying there hour after hour 25 miles from the land, absolutely unprotected, as were scores of other ships we passed, & absolutely immune. How it is done I do not know. At 12:30 we were off. I turned in in my clothes with my life belt beside me & slept till 8, to be awoken by a tremendous thud like shutting a monstrous iron door with a bang.We leapt from our berths on deck just in time to find that our destroyers had discovered a submarine a mile away from us; the thud we heard was the first depth-bomb they had thrown at her, & we saw them throw 5 more. Each sends up a mass of water the size of a house – a very fine sight in the dancing sunlight, & makes a most stupendous noise. Then we saw two of the destroyers circling about, apparently looking for oil and wreckage, & so the drama closed & we shall probably never know any more. We had minesweepers ahead of us through most of the danger zone &

so travelled very slow & did not reach territorial waters till 2. There we met the returning convoy, & our destroyers turned round & took them back to England as we were safe. We were at the Hook by 2:30 & I rushed off to wire to you & Brocas, caught a steam train to the Hague & left my trunk to follow by train. I was with a naval boy, such a nice fellow, & we decided we would dine at the Central Hotel & fetch our luggage afterwards & meet Brocas at the station as I had suggested to him by wire. I ran into Mr. Kooy (?) as I was depositing my handbag, & rushed round to the Y.M.C.A. office to see if Brocas had been there, found a most warm welcome (I had wired to them too) that Brocas was awaiting news of me on the telephone, which there was no delay in sending! We bade him to the Central at once, and all went over there to dine, & had hardly sat down when he came in. I won't write about that first five minutes if you don't mind. There are some moments in life it is only right to draw a veil over, & you know all. As to his looks he is simply splendid; decidedly taller & broader, face more decided & developed, but very handsome & still deliciously boyish, not a trace of deprivation about him, & nothing approaching to the 3 ½ years' difference I had expected. He was perfectly natural, quite charming in manner among perfect strangers (for we were a party of 6), & very smart in the blue evening kit which had arrived that day & fitted perfectly, boots & all. Of course I can't dwell on the sentimental side in a letter that has to be censored: you will fill that in. No trace whatever is left of his wound, & he could not look in better condition. He & I went off in a fiacre to the station for my trunk, & then to Scheveningen, while the others went by train, & so we arrived at this delightful 'Villa Mess' on the sea front which has been taken by the Y.M.C.A. as a hostel, & which will be my home while I am here. It is at present inhabited by Mr. Clapperton (whose wife, you may remember, I went to see in London), Miss Randall (a helper) & her brother Captain Randall who came over in the second batch & is also a helper. I found a most comfortable room prepared for me, & everything very nicely done; & Brocas is as free in the house as I am. Next morning, I went with Clapperton to inspect the vast new 'Hut' I am to be in charge of, & on to the Hague to attend a meeting of helpers, but by 11:30 I was free & ran back to Brocas' hotel, the Zeerust on the sea front & only ½ mile from this villa or less. He wisely moved to it from the Royal – or rather Cecil Graves contrived it for him before he arrived & it could hardly be nicer. He has a very good room on the first floor with Captain Moseley whose face you know from those Friedberg photos & his luggage all came through, & several of our parcels have reached him already. It is a smaller hotel than the Royal with much better accommodation, & a far better position. We then began to talk in earnest, & never stopped till 10:30 that night. I despair of ever telling you a tenth part of all he said, & can only jot it down disjointedly for of course we rushed from topic to topic regardless of date & order. But before I begin to report his talk, which perhaps will take some letters to get through, let me tell you what a real pleasure it was to meet the many men we have heard of through Brocas; Cecil Graves among the first, such a nice looking, attractive fellow, Leech [CJF], Sampson, Moseley, Usher, Smyth-Osborne, the Heberden's friend; Horn & Rogerson of the Cavalry & Eton, & a heap of others. I spent a charming half hour with Stirling, delivered the watch. In case I have not time to write to all the parents by this mail, would you let Mrs. Graves, Mrs. Leech & Mrs. Showers know that their boys are in perfect health, quite charming & quite comfortable? I have also had a long talk with Wise: will you tell Mrs. Parker he is in excellent form. Let me here, as an interlude, tell you how to send letters to me quickest. Put your letter into an envelope addressed:

Per favour of Foreign Office
Mr. S.M. Burrows
Y.M.C.A.
c/o The British Legation
The Hague
Holland

Do not stamp that envelope, but put it inside another addressed

Mrs. S. Clapperton
Y.M.C.A. Headquarters
Tottenham Court Road
London W.1.

& put a penny stamp (or more according to weight) on that envelope. There is no regular day it will reach me, but probably two days later. Now for a little of Brocas' talk. He never was wounded in the groin at all as the War Office said. At the Battle of Nery he had two horses shot under him, & got a bad fall each time. He got hold of a third horse, but was almost done, on the top of 10 days terrific work, & his C.O. told him to go and lie down for an hour & get a little sleep if he could. He lay down face downwards on his arms, & his orderly was told to hold his horse; but the orderly too was done & went to sleep, the horse was restive & trod on & kicked the back of his head & inflicted a very nasty wound. He was practically unconscious until two days after he found a German peering over him in bed in the Field Hospital. He must have lost a lot of blood, as the first bandage was only partially successful, & he must have been bleeding for at least three hours until the doctor got at him. The celebrated postcard in German was, as Byrne decided, written entirely by him. On the way to Germany he temporarily fell into the hands of some decent officers, one of whom, a Dutchman, asked what he could do for him. Brocas had that old

postcard in his pocket, scribbled it off & asked the Dutchman to post it which he evidently did.

One up for Holland! Campion's story about the capture of the German officer was a fable, or rather a mix-up. It is true that Brocas & the two men with him were told on the second night that they were to be shot next morning, but that was cancelled. The story probably arose in connection with Rogerson of the 15th Hussars, whom I have just met. He did not capture an officer, but jumped out of the train in a tunnel on the way up, was captured, & put up against a wall to be shot, with the rifles actually levelled, when a German General came up & said: 'What are you shooting this officer for?', was told, & said, 'You cannot do that, put him back on the train', and here he is, but his nerves are still very much the worse for wear, poor chap. I am sorry to say Campion has been killed since.

When you hear what happened to the parcels, or rather to the covers, the marvel is that he was able to acknowledge any at all. But the contents got to him better than we thought, though latterly things went wrong, & the poor woolly waistcoat never arrived. Your false bottoms & their contents were the joy of the whole camp, only equalled in reputation by Lizzie's cakes, which eclipsed Buzzard & Fortnum. He clean forgot about that code (Begin-end), & never noticed any of our messages, or used it himself. The uncensored letters were sent inside the woodwork of carved frames by the French, a most ingenious contrivance too lengthy to describe. They all got in, but there were not many of them, so ours are precious. Brocas has managed to keep a lot of interesting souvenirs, programmes, photos, signatures, small presents, & the more precious of his letters, e.g the first he got for (from?) us that were on him when he was wounded & are still bloodstained. He wisely burned the bulk of them before he left. He has got every one of the snaps we went him, good & bad, & they were invaluable to him. Please tell Lizzie, Ada & Jacques that he particularly enjoyed the two or three (e.g. Boy Scouts & Guides at tea in the garden) which contained their likenesses. It was such a dream like feeling to be going over them all again with him; in fact I have been pinching myself frequently the last three days to make sure I am awake. I really think I had better close the letter now. It is already outrageously long, but I know you will forgive that under the circumstances. I am starting a second letter to the Duchess today. No sign of Sandy or Mary* whatever so far. Brocas & I cabled to you yesterday. You mustn't expect long letters from him at present. You can imagine what it means to these fellows to be free, & how impossible it is to settle down to anything just at first. That will soon pass, of course. Will you note that Brocas' address is Hotel Zeerust, not Royal? But as Stirling is in charge of the post, his letters are sure to reach him, however addressed. Will you please send me another bath towel, a packet of Gillette razor blades (Martyr keeps them),

& some polish for brown boots? I hope my cable as to tobacco was clear. My brand is called 'Smith's Glasgow Mixture', & I like it best in the red ¼ lb tins if procurable, but the yellow would do. Hopkins of G.T. Jones & Co., 14. High Street, would help you, & if that tobacco is not to be got, I would take whatever he sends. I seem to be making a great fuss about this, but the fact is English tobacco became unprocurable here just before I arrived, & yet one wants it so badly, to be able to offer a 'fill' to the men you are talking to – a highway to friendship. So if you double my order you will do no harm. More of me personally in my next.

Yr. loving Jack

The Germans * [note added later after the letter was typed]

Letter 177

18th February 1918, Gravenhage

Telegram to: S.M. Burrows, 9 Norham Gardens, Oxford, Engd.

Arrived Hague. Met Brocas at once. He is in splendid form and perfectly well.

Burrows.

Letter 178

As previous

Telegram to: S.M. Burrows

Father arrived safe and well we have hardly stopped talking.

Brocas.

Letter 179

20th February 1918, Hotel Zeerust

My dearest Mother and sister,
At last I feel I can really write you a coherent account of things in general. I have been trying to for some days, but simply haven't dared trust myself to pen and paper!

Firstly and most importantly of all, Father is here in the best of health. He has already got a real hassle on the Y.M.C.A, and we all see that in spite of all difficulties and opposition he intends to make the thing hum, and will do so. It is a very difficult task, as the people here seem to have forgotten that they are dealing with officers and men of the old army and not with imbeciles and children. Then again none of us have appreciated the present day excellence of the Y.M.C.A., and so we are all very apt to look askance on an organisation that seems to want to patronise us. If it were not for Father I am sure there would have been serious trouble here about it. But of course he understands, and all my friends among the officers here have explained the difficulties which have arisen before he came. You see, they sent out two people to run the show who, no doubt most excellent fellows, we're not quite "it", and so there was bound to have been trouble. As it is, all will be right and the one cause of concord will be Father. Voilà. You can't imagine what pleasure it has given me to introduce all my friends to him. Not that he has had time to meet them all yet, but he now knows nearly all the special ones, and I think must be thoroughly tied up as to names, regiments etc. To meet some 50 new faces and hear some 50 new names in about five days is indeed bewildering. As I told him when he arrived, I had determined not to expect him here till I actually saw him. One has become such a fatalist after 3 years of waiting that nothing surprises one either way, and one gets to accept practical certainties and possibilities, and then doesn't think any more about them till they take place. I eventually got a telephone message at about 6.30 one evening to say he would arrive at the Hague at 7.44. so I rushed up to change, and while in the middle of this operation got another message to say he had already arrived, and was awaiting me in the Hotel Central. So I rushed down there and we met in the big restaurant, after almost exactly 3 years and six months. Whether he would have recognised me or not if he had seen me in a crowd, I don't know, but I don't think he has changed in the slightest, or that the strenuous work he has been doing has aged him a bit. I don't think I have ever seen him better or more cheerful; and certainly his throat outlasted mine in talking capacity; we started in right away, and have carried on at every meeting up to date without a break. The first two days we were together practically all day, and at the end I could hardly talk at all! You can understand from this that it is a physical impossibility to write down all my various experiences, and they must wait till we meet and I can tell them to you. I have been able to clear up various mysteries re-early days, and no doubt Father has passed these on to you. He is now hard at his work and I have a job too, so of course we have to fit in our meetings now; but never fear, we shall see a great deal of each other, and one of the fondest memories I shall have all my life will be that of his affection to me, shown by his taking all the risks and coming out here to take on this very strenuous and difficult job in the hopes of being with me. He is the only parent who has done it and you may be sure that I shall do all in my power to see that he wants for nothing and is comfortable as far as I can arrange, for your sake and mine.

Well, up to the present life has been one mad whirl of amusement, everybody has been immensely kind. Russians, Belgians, French and Dutch and of course one's own people; then again I have re-met all my old Torgau Friends after three years, and we have all dined each other and talked till we were hoarse; then I have had shopping to do and calls to pay and official luncheons and "soirées" to attend, and so you see I have been as full up with engagements as anyone can be. However it is all great fun after prison! Yesterday father and I lunched at the Embassy; previously I had been for a ride from 9-11, and had visited my N.C.O's 11-12; at 3 o'clock we separated, and he went to the hut and I went to Ryswith to meet a party of Spaniards at the house of the Spanish naval attaché. Then I came back and dined out with some friends, left them at 10, and went to a dance and have some music with a Belgian family, and got home about 1 am. This was really quite an ordinary day, so you can see that when, after a fortnight of this, I am extremely well and fit, my health has not suffered from the hardships of captivity. My share of the entertainment at the Belgians was to recite the hymn of hate in German which they had never heard before! I am hoping shortly to get a job here which will make me use my languages; at present I am helping look after the N.C.O's, but as they are mostly men of many years' service and experience this job is not very arduous. Tomorrow Father and I are going to pay more calls in the afternoon, and I am lunching with him at his hostel. I meant to write a special letter of thanks to you for the marvellous manner in which you have always remembered me and sent me all necessities and in fact everything I asked for in Germany. Words cannot express my gratefulness and I don't think anyone else ever got so many or such excellent parcels from home. I am writing this here because if I want to start keeping separate subjects for separate letters I should never finish writing. I don't think anybody in England really realises how much the K.G. depends on his parcels for his very existence. We do and are always most careful to explain to people who remarked on our health that this is entirely and absolutely due to the "old folks at home", God bless and keep them. I am writing specially to Mrs Griffiths. I will now try and tell you something of our existence here. There are three hotels, the Royal (holding about 200 officers), The Rauch (100) and the Zeerust (100); more will be taken later as officers come out of Germany. The hotels are not yet full and we have only about 50; this is far the best hotel, right on the sea, enough sitting space and quite decent rooms, excellent food, and most of my quieter friends are here, the noisier ones are at the Rauch, just across the road, so I can join in when I want to. Except that we are supposed to be in the hotel by 12.30 every night, we keep what hours we like, breakfast from 8 – 10. Lunch 1-2 and dinner 6.30-8 being meal hours. We at present have to wear uniform, but this will be modified later I expect. Games are sadly deficient, and nothing has at present been done in that direction. There is however riding of a sort to be got, and of course lots of walks etc. We exchange salutes with Dutch officers, and on the whole friendly relationships exist, and we are assured that the khaki invasion is looked upon with pleasure by all. The restaurant keepers at the Hague have certainly nothing to complain about! Prices here are enormous, but I appear to have enough cash in hand to afford myself a small "bust", and am going to do so!! The theatres are nothing very great, but I have seen quite a decent French play and attended a Dutch Music hall. Everyone stares at one where ever one goes and the poor highlanders have a wretched time, everyone being curious as to what they wear underneath!! If you have any questions you wish me to answer, put them down on paper and number them and I will do my best. I should certainly not have adopted this mode of procedure if Father had not been here. He gives me an excellent report of your healths, and I am indeed glad to get it. Well, I will write again very soon and tell you more. My best love to you both.

Your affectionate son and brother,

Brocas.

Letter 180

20th February 1918, [no address]

Dearest Duchess,

I am going to begin Chapter II to you by jotting down to or three minor facts about the boy. **That famous air-cushion has survived everything, & was of the greatest use, especially in hard railway carriages.** [it was never obvious why this was specifically requested] *So has the 'flea-bag'. He is very well off for clothes, & can get anything here. He has got at least three wrist watches, & his two cigarette cases & silver matchbox, & all the photos he hung in his various rooms. One result is that I am better known by sight than I expected. He has really done very well as to letters, not only from us but from others. The tea arrived all right & is now in his room. We will arrange about its use. His teeth are to be seen to by the dentist Rilot (?) told me of. There is nothing much wrong with them. He packed all his books before departure but had to leave the package behind in the hope that it will follow after. His acquisition of languages is most refreshing. I can answer for his French, & the senior officers are full of praise of his other*

*linguistic acquirements. I interviewed the senior Colonel in command yesterday in
the way of business & when he knew who I was said, 'Your son is of the best & we
owe him a deep debt of gratitude for his high spirits, & the way he organised all our
sports & theatricals.' All the senior officers I have met say the same, & the extreme
niceness of them all to me is largely due to him. I particularly like all his intimate
friends, who seem as if they could not do enough for either him or me. We owe great
gratitude to Cecil Graves for getting him into the Zeerust Hotel at once. There
is simply no comparison between it and the Royal.* **The story of his various
efforts to escape is really too funny for words.** [A reference to several
escape attempts and being funny suggests they involved some sort of
disguise, trickery or just pie in the sky attempts] *I hope in time I shall get him
to write it all down, but that must wait until the first month of excitement is over.
Between us we shall soon get to know all the people we want to know in the place,
so there will be plenty of varied society, & there are lots of theatres, cinemas etc., &
in spring & summer there will be any amount of tennis & cricket. He is awfully
nice in coming to see me every day & twice a day, though I want him to be as free
as possible to knock about & see his friends. He nearly always looks me up at the
Hut at tea time & spends an hour there. Nothing could be more charming than our
relationship. I hope we shall go to H.C.* [Holy Communion] *on Sunday together
to return thanks. Of course, this is all a private page for the family only. I am going
on the next page to give you a more public review of affairs in case it interests others.
I am waiting for him as I write, as we are just off to lunch together at the Embassy.*

S. M Burrows (not signed)

Letter 181

9th March 1918, Hotel Zeerust, Scheveningen

My dearest Mother and Sister,
*I fear I have not written to you as I should have, but I have set aside tomorrow
as a real "letter day" and intend to send you a real good screed. This is merely
to announce it, and in case the convoy should start off suddenly without it.
Yesterday father and I were photographed, and the results which arrived today
might have been worse. You should have them as soon as possible of course, and
also some snapshots if they come out. I am at last settling down to a serious
existence here, and beginning work on Monday. I am going to do Italian and
Dutch, and have just returned from lunch at the Italian embassy, where the
ambassador introduced me to the lady who is to teach me. Father and I meet
every day either at his hut or here, and we always lunch here on Sunday. His
hut is now a wonderful affair, and one and all laud him to the skies what he
has done and is doing there. He now is thoroughly muddled up as regards us*

all, as my friends all introduce themselves to him and he hasn't a chance of knowing who's who!! He is always "at home" to me for tea at the hut and the teas are so plentiful and good that my figure is suffering grievously. I am just beginning to get to know some of the people here, and it is really a most amusing society, and the number of languages one talks in the course of a day is appalling. Tonight Father has a concert for 300 N.C.O's, and I am going with 7 others to hand around refreshments and entertain the ladies behind the bar. I won't say I wish you were both here because I don't think you would like it much, but I wish you could just see our life for a day or two. What it will be like in summer one only knows. This place is apparently a second Trouville and absolutely packed even in wartime! The weather is now lovely, and I was most annoyed to miss my ride today. The horses are too awful for words. But it is great to get on anything again. I have received several letters from you and will answer them tomorrow. Clothes are excellent. Well au revoir till tomorrow. Your affectionate son and brother,

Brocas.

Father is in the best of health and so am I.

Letter 182

18th March 1918, Hotel Zeerust, Scheveningen

My dearest Mother and Sister,
I am indeed ashamed of my slackness in writing to you, it is quite inexcusable. But really for the last month I have hardly known where I am and have seemed to be doing something all day and yet doing nothing. However I think I am beginning to settle down at last and so shall be more regular in future. I hardly dare think of this possibility of your coming out; it seems too good to be true. Oh! If it can only come off, what a time we shall have! You would of course have lots of work to do, but I'm sure you would find it interesting, and then in your spare time we could really enjoy ourselves. There are lots of very nice people here, and I am just beginning to know them all; in fact I am becoming quite a society man for the moment and enjoying it. Your delightful letters keep coming in, and Father has shown me yours to him so I am au complete with your news. Well as regards local news, Father is considered quite the hero of the place and deservedly so. He has simply done wonders, and his hut is now an unqualified success. Crowds of N.C.O's there all day, and also lots of officers, and you can't imagine what this means. The officers' room has been found far too small and it's going to be doubled in size and even this won't be big enough, and the one salient

fact of it all is that if Father had not been here to get it going, hardly an officer or N.C.O. would have frequented it. You see the Y.M.C.A. was never popular in the old army. Last night we had a great St. Patrick's Day dinner to which both Father and I were invited as guests, and it was a most excellent evening. Quite an informal dinner with the orchestra playing Irish tunes, and we ended up by dancing. I have started working at Italian with a dear old lady here whom I was put onto by the Italian ambassador. This afternoon we were shown the Italian war films on the cinema, and they are certainly very good, though somewhat dower in parts. Tonight I am having a quiet night for once and intend to go to bed early! As tomorrow father and I are going to the opera, "Louise". I went to "Manon" here a few nights ago and it was mostly good, though the men's voices were poor in the extreme. Well, I must close but will write again very soon. Father and I are both in radiant health and spirits and live on the hope that you may be able to come out here and join us. We have been photographed and the results are passable. My best love to you both.
Your affectionate son and brother,

Brocas.

Letter 183

26th March 1918, Zeerust

My dearest Mother.,
Once more I begin to try and write you a letter, but you can't imagine the difficulties of doing so. There ought to be so much to write about and yet there really isn't. No convoy has arrived recently, so I have no very late news of you, but the last I got was most excellent. Well, I am gradually settling down to a more ordinary life and starting work. Italian is in full swing, and I am shortly going to try to get employment at their embassy here. The next problem is whether to stay here or go and live out, a very difficult one indeed. I have been looking at rooms and flats, and saw some yesterday which tempted me a great deal. The advantages are, that one is away from one's brother officers with whom one has been so long, one is quieter, one avoids this hotel life, and also one is free from stupid little restraints and annoyances which are bound to exist when senior and junior officers are billeted together. Also most of these rooms are away from Scheveningen, which will doubtless be hopelessly overcrowded in summer. The disadvantage is the expense and the fact that one may eventually be short of food if one lives out. I can't decide at present! Well, I have been going out a lot and really enjoying life in a mild way. Society here is quite amusing and very mixed. Father and I had to great afternoons calling.

The first time we ended up at a reception at the American Embassy and the second time at the Serbian Legation. One is beginning to notice far too much khaki about, and though the local inhabitants like it at present they will end by hating it all right. Father is in great form, and his hut is an unqualified success. Twenty of our officers gave refreshments to 300 N.C.O's during a concert there on Saturday, and everything went without a hitch. Sorry to hear you have had no luck re your coming out here. I dare not think about it, it seems too good to be possible, but still --!! We are going to get up for a game of Eton football here in which Father is going to play! Wonderful! Please order me an Eton Football from Mat Wright. Goodbye and good luck to both of you. Most affectionately,

Brocas.

Letter 184

8th April 1918, Hotel Zeerust, Scheveningen

My dearest Mother,
Rumour has it that a convoy will start very shortly, so I again take up the pen to try and give you some more details of our life here. Firstly we are all very well, Father especially so and full of work. It is a long time since we have had news from you excepting telegrams, but we know from them that you flourish. Nervous times these, but I must say I am most optimistic and see no reason for anxiety yet. You can't think how awful it is to sit here and be out of it all. One feels it more than one did in Germany, I think, because one is quite comfortable and everyone is nice to one, and this gives one time to think. I see the cavalry have had a go again. I wonder if this means my regiment. Father's hut is flourishing more and more every day, and it is all entirely due to him. You can't imagine how strong the prejudice against the Y.M.C.A. was in the old army, and all this has got to be lived down here, and it is no easy job. There have been concerts in the hut every night, each time for 300 N.C.O's, and these are always packed and most popular. He and I have been twice to the opera together and it was most enjoyable. The opera is practically all there is here in the theatrical line, and, though not very good, is extraordinarily cheap, and so I am making the most of my time and have already seen, Bohème, Butterfly, Manon, Louise and the Magic flute; not bad for a start. Do you remember taking Duchess and me to 'Butterfly' at Oxford years ago? I quite remembered the plot here, though that was about all. I appear to be doing an extraordinary amount of society work here, and it is really most amusing, though it hardly bears description in a letter, especially as a letter may be censored now-a-days. Father likens the place to an Indian hill station, and I should imagine that the metaphor was just right. Last night I supped with some delightful Americans

called Kirke (Mother and son). He is first secretary here and was previously in Berlin. After supper we danced and had a really cheery evening. Mrs. Garrett the American ambassador's wife is a most charming and original woman, a really first class singer and full of go. She is at present trying to persuade me to go on a colossal bicycling trip with her, 45km!! I am rather doubtful about it. On Wednesday we are going to play a game of Eton Football and I am trying to collect 22 O.E.'s. No easy job, especially as most of them have not played for ages. There are about 40 of us here altogether, and of course more arrive with each batch. A new batch arrives tomorrow ctg. 76 officers. So glad to hear George and Alex are all right. Have they been in this affair and if so where? A rumour has just come in that a convoy has arrived; if so I will finish this in hopes of catching the out-going one and write another on receipt of your news. My best love to Duchess and to you. Ever your affectionate son,

Brocas.

Letter 185

14th April 1918, Zeerust

My dearest Mother and Sister,
You really are the most wonderful correspondents in the world. After spending the morning reading your letters to me I have spent up to now (5 p.m.) reading yours to Father, and most interesting they all are. You absolutely put me to shame, but I fear I have been most neglectful of writing to you. I can't tell you how glad I am to hear of your excellent health not only from yourselves but from others who have written to me about you. I long to hear an account of Duchess' adventures on the land. I am sure she will enjoy it and the open air life will make her a positive amazon. The four photos of you and George are most excellent. He certainly looks exceedingly fit. I hear Father is rather discouraging your coming out here. It is certainly a very difficult question, as so much hangs in the balance. I can't tell you how I long to see you both and this would be such a priceless opportunity for us to really see a lot of each other and have a really good time. I am sure it would do you both a world of good, and Duchess would really get a little gay life. I am afraid they would try and work you very hard, but from all accounts you are used to that. On the other side, there is the risk of the journey (which I personally don't think great), the expense and always the chance of something unusual happening and my being sent home either on leave or for good. Who knows! You must certainly be very smart if you come!! The parcels on this convoy have not yet been distributed, but I will write again as soon as they are. I am afraid the cake, plum puddings and turkey did not arrive in Germany while I was there. Of course they may have turned up after my departure, and if so they were no doubt much appreciated. I

fear nevertheless that it is far more probable that the Hun stole them. I am finding it very difficult to settle down to anything serious yet, but it has got to be done. I feel an awful slacker doing nothing when all of you are working so hard. I think I am going to ask the Italian ambassador to give me a job in his Embassy, but I am rather shy of doing so. The last two nights we have been shut in our hotels after 6 p.m. owing to the strikes. A confounded nuisance as we might have had a most amazing time. As it was, the night before was most exciting and I will tell you all about it later. I am really very sorry for the poor people here, as they see us all going about the place and enjoying ourselves. I know we are living on their food and they of course are short. However, I don't think that they are hostile to us at all. The police and military are not very clever at keeping order and rather excite the crowd than otherwise. Two delightful letters from Aunt Io and a French one from Bernard, whom I will endeavour to answer in that language. Also a very kind letter from Aunt Io's mother who is I suppose technically speaking my great aunt! How very kind of her to remember me. Please also thank Mrs Griffiths for writing me such a charming letter. I hope she is flourishing and managing to keep you all well-nourished, in spite of the food restrictions.

Father is still quite wonderful and doing more work than anyone here. All the same he is in the best of health and spirits, and we are both optimistic re the present push. I more so than he, I think. Once the first rush failed I have had no more qualms, and the reports have really been quite humble and have lacked almost completely that bombastic boasting which is always inserted when they consider a victory in sight. May they die in thousands! Last Wednesday we had a great game of Eton Football. 20 of us turned out and it really was great fun, though dreadfully fatiguing after such a long time without practice. Father very kindly gave us all tea after the game, and we felt so much the better for it that we are going to get up another for next Wednesday. We are also going to make arrangements for a dinner on June 4th. I am hard at work studying Buchan's 'History of the War'. Not at all a bad work to get an outline from. I expect by this time you have got the wonderful photos! How do you like them? Any news of the Regiment? My best love to you both and thanking you a thousand times for your magnificent letters,
Your affectionate son and brother,

Brocas.

Letter 186

17th April 1917, Hillehom, [Post card to Mother]

Father, Gerald Crutchley and I are spending a day in the bulb country and I write you this from the bar room of the local pub while the other two are playing billiards – we have had a great day in the country mostly by tram so far – return this evening – all very well – Father received your wire last night – please send congrats to George – cricket bag has arrived – best love to you all.

Brocas.

Post card of 17 April 1918 from Hillehom, Holland Source: Burrows family archive

Letter 187

5th May 1918, Friedberg
To: Mrs Burrows, 9 Norham Gardens, Oxford, England

Dear Mrs Burrows,
How am I to thank you for your most gracious attention, which is much more valuable to me than all the kitchen and flower gardens in the world. Your letter was to me that kind of strength, which makes forget all the distress. I am a poor hand at expressing my feeling on paper, but I should like to do so. You told a true thing, that the word held still much, that is good for me. I have understood after your letter, that it holds too much for me – sincere friendships. Be so kind

as to send to your son Brocas, my love. Kindest regards to Mr Burrows.
Believe me your very sincerely,

Nicolai Miloradovitch

Letter 188

6th May 1918, Zeerust

My dearest Mother and Sister,
I am very ashamed of myself for not having written to you for so long and in future I am going to try and bombard you (Trou fever?) to make up. It is even more difficult to write from here than from Germany. Formally in G. there was nothing to do and hence nothing to write about. Here there is lots doing but nothing of surpassing interest. I am at present busily engaged in arranging a 4th June dinner – a tremendous undertaking, as the difficulties of getting food, arranging for a room and then inviting everyone, are vast. Prices must be so high that I fear some will be frightened off. Then I am doing secretary to one of the cricket teams for the league matches, and hope any day to get a job in the H.Q. office here. So at last "je me sens occupé". I have been living a somewhat wild life up to the present and think I have entirely chased all remembrances of K.G. out of my head. I am now seriously settling down and going to live out in "Digs" with two friends, Moseley and Hunter-Blair, the latter a relation of Mrs Rawstorne of Roche Court. We have got a little flat in a quite decent quarter of the Hague, I have decided to risk possible starvation in preference to this wretched and costly hotel life, where one's soul is not one's own. We have started cricket and I have had several "nets" and find I can still see moderately straight in spite of all. How you would laugh if you could see me as a society man here! Last night I went to a dance with some people called Guasalaga. Mr. G. is the Argentinian Minister here. It was most amusing. The attachment of D.G. after one's name and a pair of spurs to one's heels proves an irresistible attraction to the mamas of unmarried and ugly daughters here, and it is really quite amusing to be chased! I don't think it will spoil me. All these people think that the English officers are fabulously wealthy, and so "voila". However, I don't think you will ever have to welcome a Miss Hook of Holland as Madame Brocas. One good lady here thinks she has firmly hooked me for her daughter, and gives me some very good dinners in consequence. I wish you could see the daughter. Father knows her and the mama! Another old lady is trying to get off with him I think, and attacks him violently whenever she meets him. I always see his face fall about a metre!!

Really the work he is doing here is most wonderful, and he now thinks of returning in June. What the Y.M.C.A. will do heaven only knows. To attempt to explain on paper what he has done would be an insult, and all I can say is that he has achieved what I candidly considered an impossibility, i.e. turning a thoroughly unpopular institution (with the old army) into a roaring success. One sees officers who have always scoffed at the Y.M.C.A. as they knew it, going to tea there every day now, and the reason of course is that instead of the usual Y.M.C.A. man they find a perfect gentleman who does his very best to entertain and look after them. "Je ne peux plus dire". Your last batch of letters to him gave me great pleasure and really were excellent. He showed me your wire today re Alex – most excellent. He ought to be safe now. George's rise is certainly remarkable. To what is it due? Things seem to be going alright now in the west. You can imagine how nervous we have been all this time. One feels it much more here than in Germany, because one is better in health, stronger, and feels one is doing nothing to help in any way. I think we shall get back before the end. "Nous verrons". I hear Mrs Graves is expected daily. How I wish you and Duchess were coming too, but I think it is better not. The meeting is not so very far ahead. Well goodbye and good luck to you.
Your affectionate son and brother,

Brocas.

Letter 189

Friday, 182 Riouw Street, The Hague

My dearest Mother,
The reason of this outburst is that we arrived here* and took over last night. At present the chaos is indescribable! No pens or ink have come with our things, so I am reduced to pencil and heaven only knows where my writing paper is packed. I suppose, however, things will unravel themselves eventually. It is all great fun and we are thoroughly enjoying ourselves. Fortunately the corporal in my regiment, who is my servant, is an ex head boots and is in his element. We are entirely in his hands. You can't imagine the pleasure of enjoying comparative peace and quiet and having a "pied à terre" entirely one's own after all this time.
* i.e. the new flat. [a note added by his mother]

Later.

One of the great ladies of the town has just been in to help us put our flat in order and I suppose has succeeded. She has certainly turned everything upside

down and sent us lots of flowers, which I am finding it v. difficult to avoid upsetting. We hear rumours that a convoy may start at any moment, so I am hustling this along in order to catch the mail. Your letters are just beginning to arrive from the last convoy, and I will wait till the lot have arrived before answering. We have just finished dinner, and I am sitting in my pyjamas and a dressing gown in the drawing room, on the sofa. Both my "flat mates" are out for the evening, and I am finishing this before going round to see father. The street is always absolutely quiet and it seems almost uncanny to me!! At the moment I am fearfully busy, as I am running an Eton dinner for June 4th, a Cricket group, and the Athletic sports which we are preparing for July. It is great fun, but requires a lot of bicycling, and in this hot weather is most fatiguing. It is piping hot today. We have had one thunderstorm which caught me properly, and even now it is hardly supportable. A remarkable change after Clausthal! Another party came through last night from Germany, ctg. several friends of mine. The treatment there seems worse than ever. It really is disgraceful, and all so unnecessary. Please excuse this scrawl, but I am sure you will understand what getting up a new ménage means. Father is well as ever and I think his work is slightly less, as his helpers are getting to know their jobs better. It is still, however, enormous, and we all wonder how on earth he manages it. Well, my best love to you and to Aunt Io and Bernard.
Your affectionate son,

Brocas.

Letter 190

20th May 1918, [No address]

My dearest Mother,
After my last appalling scrawl to you I feel I owe you another letter as an apology. Well, nothing much has changed since then, excepting that we had a grand game of cricket yesterday, the first match of the season. It was only a nominal match v. Haarlem, but as only three members of the Haarlem Side turned up, we gave them eight officers and had a great game, finally winning by one wicket on time, thanks to Gerald Crutchley making 48 not out. I only got 5 runs but had some grand exercise in the field and got thoroughly sunburnt. Last night Father and I dined with a **Capt. and Mrs. Reynolds** *at the hotel they are living in. He is a most charming fellow and a great friend of mine; in fact I used to make my efforts to escape with him in captivity.* [His name does not appear on any lists for Mainz Friedberg or Clausthal] *His wife has just arrived and seems equally nice. Tomorrow night Father and I dine with Mrs Graves and George G. so we are having quite a great time. He came and had*

tea with us in the flat today. Originally two of the great ladies of the place were coming but couldn't at the last moment. Hence we had a tea "de luxe". I don't think I told you about my adventures at the Sergeants dance last Wednesday. It was really most amusing. Of course I arrived fashionably late and had had my partners selected and reserved for me by my soldiers servant, Corp. Marlow, 5th D.G. who was also Master of the Ceremonies. I fear he had paid far too much attention to my instructions re-the beauty of the selected "damseuses", and had entirely forgotten that when beauty cannot dance her girations are apt to prove fatiguing to her pilot. This, coupled with the fact that none of the ladies spoke anything but Dutch tired me to such an extent that I had to leave before I had originally intended to. However I managed a Valeta, a Larinka, 2 Waltzes and a barn dance, complimented the orchestra, drank a bottle of beer to the health of the Group Entertainment Committee and departed, hot, blown and thankful, but with a certain sense of having done my duty and earned my nightly sleep. As a result of my so-called success in the dancing world, I have to sing a song at a concert on Wednesday next! I have just discovered that I have got slightly mixed up with the paper but will continue, as they tell me paper is getting scarce. Please excuse. Your letters are simply splendid and give immense pleasure. You all seem rather pessimistic, I think, re-affairs in general, but "nous verrons". Duchess appears to be a regular "land hog" – if I may be permitted to translate a mere vulgar motorism to the all enthralling occupation of harrowing potatoes. The hours seem long certainly, and I am glad to see that she is not busied in watering or weeding. These were the two abominations that kept me from a semi horticultural existence in Germany. I don't think I shall ever go on the land – the streets perhaps!! So sorry to hear of Aubrey Tennyson's death. He was one of the best. The time parcels take to arrive is most annoying and really rather disconcerting. However one is used to such things. Well I will close and go to bed. My best love to you.
Your affectionate son,

Brocas.

Letter 191

My dearest Mother,
Another short line to tell you some more of our doings. We have just had a most aristocratic tea party – our 3 selves – Mrs. Huitveld – the Norwegian minister's wife, Mrs Kirk, the mother of the American First Secretary, and Mrs. Booth, the wife of our second military attaché. Mrs Kirk brought us a most magnificent basket of hydrangeas, and so with our other flowers the

sitting room looks a positive conservatory. How I wish you could see it! The tea party went off very well, and our landlady is very pleased that we are bringing such fashionable society to her house! Last night I went to a "house warming" given by Gerald Crutchley and Capt. Sampson, who have taken a flat together, and we had a most cheery evening with singing, dancing etc. I was made to sing down a "Recorder", a most frightening ordeal, and the machine was far from complimentary to my vocal powers! However it caused great amusement! The flat these two have taken is right at the far side of the Hague, which is a nuisance. Last night for instance we had to walk back and of course got caught in a storm. It is a good half hour walk too! The night before I sang in a group concert, quite an amusing show. One of the N.C.O's here is a fellow called Cheeseman, who appeared on the Music Hall stage before the war and is quite first class. He was performing, so I was in good company! Tonight I am going to an Empire Day concert at the Y.M.C.A. hut. I believe Sir Walter Townley is to preside and of course Father is running it.

Later.

Just back from the concert; it was a great success and Sir Walter was in excellent form. Tomorrow I am making my tennis debut of the season and have fears of being horribly stiff after it.

You can't imagine the joy of this flat. Here I am writing in pyjamas and a dressing gown with a room entirely to myself. One co-occupant is asleep and the other out for the evening. In the hotels the hubbub just about reaches its height about this hour and one can't do anything. We were rather afraid about the food here at first, but up to the present it has been very good indeed, the only eccentricity is cheese for breakfast, but one soon gets used to even this!! Next Tuesday Father and I are going to see some American war films at the Embassy which ought to be very good. He is coming to dine here first which will be quite an excitement! Well I must close. My best love to you and Duchess, Your affectionate son,

Brocas.

Many thanks for cable and at the same time bicycle – a most useful present – now that one has got over the dislike of seeing officers in uniform on these machines. Everything is now half an hour nearer!

Autograph list of the old Etonians who attended the O.E. tea party at the Hexham Abbey Hut, Scheveningen, June 4th, 1918.

———

NAME	HOUSE AT ETON	REGIMENT
Lt. V.G. Style	A.C.G.H.	Coldstream Guards
Maj. B.G. Van De Weyer	F.C.A.L.	Scots guards
Maj. Walter Trefusis	S.A.D.	Scots guards (att. R.N.D.)
Capt. Sir F. Fitzwygram Bart.	R.W.W.T.	Scots Guards
Capt. C.F. Hargreaves	I.H.A.	East Lancs att. Army Signal S'vice
Lt. J.C. Rogerson	J.H.M.H.	15th Hussars
Lt. T. Chaloner	C.H.A.	
Lt. J.F.E. Goad	P.L.V. & A.C.R.W.	K.R.R.C.
Capt. W.A. Worsley	A.A.S.	The Yorkshire Regt.
Lt. K. Rawson-Shaw	R.P.L.B. R.F.A.	att. R.F.C.
Capt. G.F. Connal Rowan	A.A.A.	A & S Highlanders
Capt. J. Houldsworth	P.W.	Gordon Highlanders
Capt. G.S. Rowley	R.S. de H.	Grenadier Guards
Capt. J.D. Bibby	P.V.B.	IVth Hussars
Capt. C.W. Norman	E.I.	IXth Lancers
Capt. J.B. Noel	A.A.S.	K.O.Y.L.I.
S.M. Burrows	K.S.	
Lt. Guy Horne	P.W.	XIX Hussars
Lt. M. Brocas Burrows	L.S.R.B.	5th Dragoon Guards
Capt. C.F. Scarisbrick	H.F.W.T.	The Royal Scots
Capt. J.C. Leech	F.L.V.	8th Hussars att. R.F.C.
Capt. C.C. Schneider	J.M.D.	Sherwood Foresters
Lt. R.G. Harvey	H.B.	Suffolk Regiment
Lt. C.A. Gladstone	H.M.	General List att. R.F.C.
Lt. C.F. Harman	K.S.	Middlesex Regiment
Lt. F. Huth Jackson	S.G.L.	Royal Sussex Regt. Att. R.F.C.
Lt R.F.G. Burrows	L.S.R.B.	The Manchester Regiment
Lt. M.B. Hope	H. Br.	60th Rifles
Lt. F.H. Bevan	H.M.	Intelligence Corps
Capt. N. E Baxter	S.R.J. & H.F.W.T.	Hampshire Regiment
Capt. Hon. A.A. Fraser	L.H.W.	3rd Gordon Highlanders

Letter 192

12th June 1918 , 182 Riouw Straat, The Hague

My dearest Mother,
I have been hoping daily to receive my tappal but there are no signs of it yet so
I will send you a short line before it arrives and answer it afterwards. I spent
the afternoon today with Father watching the cricket. I should have played,
but each side thought I was playing for the other and so I fell between two
stools. However, I don't much mind. Tomorrow I am going with Father and
a party of N.C.O's from Oxford to inspect the Peace Palace and F. is giving
us tea after it at the Hut. Then in the evening comes a great dinner which
ought to be most amusing, and then a party should arrive from Germany ctg.
some 70 officers. It will be most amusing to hear their stories, as no doubt the
Huns have been spreading some remarkable tales about their successes. The
Commission is hard at work trying to decide our fate, and we hear now that
they have reached a deadlock. Quite possible, I should think. The chiefs i.e.
Cave, Newton, and Belfield, had tea with Father at the hut yesterday and
were very pleased with the work there. We are wondering whether they noticed
a peculiar emptying of the officers' room on their arrival. What a splendid
letter the Duchess's last was! And what a great existence for her. She will be a
positive back-woodsman by the time I return, and able to twist me round her
little finger. Of course her existence must be a trifle lonely I expect, but we will
make up for that later. I am enjoying an evening of complete solitude in the flat
tonight, as one of the occupants is away at Amsterdam and the other has gone
to a cinema and then is going to a dance. My Italian teacher came and gave
me a lesson here this morning. She is a charming old lady and her only fault
is that she talks so much I never get a word in edgeways. I usually go to her,
but on Wednesdays she gives a lesson to a young lady who lives opposite and so
comes onto me afterwards. The aforementioned young lady and her family are
rather a difficulty. Their sitting room looks straight into my veranda-bedroom
and I almost invariably forget to draw the lace curtains I fear my toilette is
often somewhat public! I frequently wake in the morning and find myself being
gauged upon by several pairs of eyes. Most embarrassing. We are still much
enjoying the flat and I have got my books out at last and I'm doing more
work. Father is as wonderful as ever, and absolutely untiring in his efforts for
all. Well I must close. My best love to you and Duchess to whom by the way I
wrote yesterday. Also to Aunt Io and Bernard.
Your affectionate son,

Brocas.

Letter 193

28th June 1918, 182 Riouw Straat, The Hague

My dearest mother,
A splendid letter from you dated June 2 has just rolled up. Many thanks for it. It is the only one from home that arrived by the last convoy. It really seems dreadful to think that Father is really off home again. We shall miss him most frightfully here – all of us. He has made the Hexham Abbey Hut such a centre of our existence, and this in spite of deep-rooted prejudice against the Y.M.C.A., which most of their representatives out here have no idea how to tide over; though he leaves his work in very able hands, those of Mrs. Graves; it will not be the same, and I really think his departure will cause a fundamental change in the life of a great many of us. However, I am very glad that he is going back to you, as whatever he may say most of his work here was grossly unworthy of him and of a most annoying kind, and I know he has been worrying less Aunt Em's death should take place and leave a lot of complicated business to you in his absence. It has been most delightful having him, and I feel I can never express my appreciation of the risks he ran and the trouble he took to get out and see me immediately on my arrival. To really meet and talk to one of one's own kith and kin, and more especially one's own Father, on finishing 3 ½ years captivity means more to the ex-prisoner than any of you can imagine. What his impressions of me are I, of course, can't guess. He has struck me in a somewhat difficult time, just re-finding my feet and remembering that I have a position in the world. But I am sure he has made allowances for this and I am indeed glad to have got this job at the American Embassy before his departure so that he leaves me with the assurance that I have a serious occupation and one that may lead to something. I shall always remember as long as I live that mine was the one Father who really cared to run the risks and put up with so many annoyances in order to see his captive son at the first possible opportunity and I pray God it will help me to be a better man.

These last few days have I feel been rather uncomfortable ones for Father as he has been expecting to be off almost hourly, but we have seen a great deal of each other. Last night we dined at the Villa Mess and went round to spend the evening with a great friend of mine and his wife who has just arrived. Previously we had to pay a couple of calls and had tea at the H.A. Hut. The day before we dined with the Graves's at their hotel and went to a very serious concert where an old gentleman called Lamont – of Scottish origin – play the piano with considerable success, though perspiring freely. The orchestra also treated us to part of Tannhaüser. The night before F. dined me at the Kurhaus and we went to the "Follies" – a troupe of pierrots formed by interned R.N.D. men from Groningen, who proved exceedingly bad, though they are exceedingly popular with the Dutch here and do a great deal of good for various charities. Last Saturday after dining with me here at the flat we went to the boxing at the "Zoo" – a curious place to hold a boxing competition. It was not very good. Hence you see we have been having quite a great time these last few days.

The news of Duchess is first class and I will certainly drop her a hint re "Fliegers", my experiences being mostly unpleasant in that direction. However, one of the most important things is that she would have a bit of gay life and enjoy herself! Aunt Em is really wonderful and I fully expect to see her on my return. My best love to Aunt W. and Bernard. I am writing Duchess a letter which I hope will equally catch this convoy; meanwhile my love to her. The same to you, and I'm happy to think that as regards Father – my loss is your gain.
Ever your affectionate son,

Brocas.

Letter 194

29th June 1918, 182 Riouw Straat, The Hague

My dearest Mother,
I have just got back from saying goodbye and seeing the last of Father in Holland, and I will tell you all about our last day at once. We met at the Hague station at 12.10 this morning. I very nearly missed the train owing to the fact that I found myself on an appallingly crowded train which took 40 min: to complete a journey which should have taken 25. However, I got it, and after his farewells to the other Y.M.C.A. people who had come to see him off we steamed away to Rotterdam, where we arrived shortly before one. There we had a certain amount of trouble re-luggage, and eventually got off to lunch at about 1.30. After an excellent meal at a restaurant – where we were fortunately undisturbed by any of the local Germans, though we saw several of them walking about – we went off to the consulate to get passes viséd, etc., this proved a somewhat tedious job but we eventually got through it by 3.30 and returned to the station where we had tea and caught the 4.20 train to the Hook. I went as far as Schiedam – they won't let us go further as the Hook its self is a fortified area – and there we parted.

So ends a very happy though somewhat curious chapter of our respective existences, and I must say that when I think that there was at one moment a chance that he might become a K.G. because he came here, I am very glad he is safely out of it. [a concern that Germany might win the war and Holland would also come under German jurisdiction] *God grant him the best of passages home. I am wiring to let you know of his departure and possible arrival on Monday. I am dining this evening with Gerald Crutchley and Allison, who I hope will help me to forget that I have got that same feeling of an unfillable void that I had that evening at Aldershot in August 1914. Good-bye, good luck,*

Your affectionate son,
Brocas.

Letter 195

8th July 1918, 182 Riouw Straat, The Hague

My dearest Father,
Just a line before leaving for Groningen for the cricket. The week has been comparatively uneventful, except for the most startling announcement of the engagement of Ivan Hay of the 5th Lancers to Olga Lentrum! I absolutely refused to believe it till I met Ivan face-to-face last night and he confirmed it. She must be a good forty if not more, and he is not yet 34. Another engagement is also announced between a fellow called Russell and a Dutch girl! So the wickets are falling fast!

We play our league match A and B on Friday and, of course, it resulted in a draw; a bad windy day and a hopeless game. We got 300 for about 6 and then got 4 of them out for 170. This in 6 hours hard cricket. We should need 30 hours to play it out. I was at Schiedam again the next day after our parting, when we defeated the local team with great ease. My return journey from the parting was disastrous, as not only was H. Randall, worse than usual, but Willem Stirum also got into our carriage and attempted to be facetious all the way home to the intense amusement of H.R., who laughed without stopping. I fear I was somewhat unappreciative.

On Saturday I was invited by a Russian Colonel, Pavloff, to hear a rendering of one of Tchaikovsky's Trios in the Vieux Doulen, and jolly good it was.

No letters from this convoy yet, but a priceless lot of papers – Westminsters, Fortnightlies, etc., etc. – which I have devoured with great ability. In Mr Radcliffe's letter which I read through I see he mentions a Sgt. Booth whom he would like to know about. I will see to the matter. I hear there is chaos in the hut and we have to stand in Q's for our change already. Poor Mrs Graves, she

says she will never forgive you for going!! She can't stand Clapperton. I hear
also that other ladies are following Miss Houldsworth's example!! What a life!
Will write from Groningen. My best love to you all.
Your affectionate son,

Brocas.

Am taking Baedeker with me!!

Letter 196

12th July 1918, 182 Riouw Straat, The Hague

My dearest Mother,
I got back from Groningen yesterday evening to find quite a tappal awaiting
me, including three first class letters from you dated June 9, 16, and 20, and
also one from Duchess which I am answering direct to her Grace!
The Groningen stay was an unqualified success. We left here on Monday
at 4.30 and got there about 10.30 having dined on the train. I had a long
conversation with a Dutch horse-coper who had been in the States, and he
gave me much information re-opinion of his class on the war. We were met at
the station by officer i/c games and taken to the hotel, where we were introduced
to Mrs Williamson and had a substantial supper. This lady is the Dutch wife
of a fellow called Archie Williamson who was a great friend of mine at Oxford.
She is most charming and I should think the marriage is a real success. He
was a very wild devil formerly but seems to have changed a lot, and they seem
very fond of each other and she has picked up English extremely well and is
determined to become thoroughly Anglicised.

We started playing at 10.30 the following day in the camp. This camp is a
disgrace, and this is entirely due to the men in it. They have been there some
years and have done nothing towards making it decent. The cricket ground
was partly sand and partly un-mown grass, and all the men were slovenly
dressed and seemed most undisciplined. We were all disgusted. We batted first
and made 408 for seven wickets and then declared. I got 78 badly. We then got
four of them out for 59 before closing at 6 p.m. We went to a "Revue" in the
camp at 8 p.m. after dinner at the hotel. This review was appallingly bad. No
wonder they think the Follies good. Then there was the prize-giving for the
Sports. Mrs. W. presented the prices, and the Commodore, by name Henderson,
made a speech. We were introduced to him and I had a long talk with him, but
not enough to judge him. I have heard him much reviled but his ideas seem
sound. They were starting "Flu" in the camp and had some 60 cases, which

was worrying though. The next day we dismissed them twice for 165 and 209 and so won by an innings. I don't think they have been beaten before, so that should do them a lot of good. I then dined with the Williamsons, Gerald Crutchley and MacBryan, and afterwards we had a good old-fashioned singsong in the hotel to the annoyance of the local Dutch. There was some big agricultural meeting on, so all the rooms were full and Crutchley, MacBryan and I had to share one originally meant for one! We caught a train at 8.45 back – very crowded as all the trains are – and got back about 2. At Givolle I was joined by Father Wrafter, the R.C. padre, who had been visiting Urk and was most talkative. He is a most unconventional and amusing old man. He had a most delightful time at Urk, in the camp (punishment for N.C.O's offences), and with the local Dutch who are apparently most primitive and wear full national costume always.

I got back here to find my leave to Arnhem granted, and so I go off there on Monday till the 22nd. On Sunday we play the Hague C.C. at cricket on the home ground. I am very busy with my American work and have hardly been out today. We seem to be doing well in Albania.

I have heard no more scandal from the Y.M.C.A. ladies, but I believe some people have been having words with S.D. I met the namesake today but could get nothing out of him. He was very worried about some lamp, so I let him be!

I will try and write again before going to Arnhem. I am very fit and well. My best love to you all.
Your affectionate son,

Brocas.

Please tell Father Tom Marshall was at Groningen, up for the match from Leuuwarden. He sends F. his salaams. They don't care for L. much, nothing to do but sailing and batting. Marshall is running the Y.M.C.A. there, and was taking Bailey down to lecture. The latter was also at Groningen for a night – very bluff and hearty. My best love to Father.

Letter 197

18th July 1918, Menthenberg, Arnhem

My dearest Mother,
The first letter from this convoy has just arrived here and I was right glad to get it. It is dated June 30th. I have just had a letter from Lady Parker with news of the regiment, and will answer it, and also call on the people you mention, though I have never heard of them even. We heard yesterday that we are to be allowed home – it seems too good to be true. I expect this will be about December. I know nothing about it yet and shall hear nothing definite till I get back to the Hague on Monday. This is a charming country house about 2 miles from the town and we are having a most delightful time. The family consists of M. and Mme. Scheidius and her daughter by her first marriage with Caton Woodville. The guest are Mlle. Miteleven, the Rumanian ministers' daughter, Capt. Usher and myself. The ménage is entirely à l'anglaise, and Mme. is a delightful hostess. She has a bad reputation for wishing to affect a marriage for the daughter, but I have told her I am engaged so I am not worried! Our host is Dutch, but most charming. He is unfortunately pro German, and was in the Dutch diplomatic corps all over the place. We have been playing tennis and golf; watching the Dutch Tennis Championships which are on here, and dancing. Tonight we go to a ball and again on Saturday. So you see we are very gay. The great point is that we are begged to do whatever we like, and if we want to be alone can be so. They are extraordinarily kind, and I think I entirely misjudged them when I met them previously.

No particular news to give you; our journey was amusing, as I got caught by a wonderful old lady who talked solidly to me from Utrecht to Arnhem, and had been all over the world and told me the most wonderful tales to the intense amusement of the rest of the carriage.

Well I must end; we are just off to town to buy some films for a camera, then back to dinner at 7.30, and so to dance. I have just looked round the stables; they are most delightful. More later. Best of luck to you and father. Hope you flourish. My health is A1.

Brocas.

Our cricket match on Sunday was drawn v. Hague C.C. We got 274 for 6 and they got 70 for 1; then it rained: I got 74 not out.

Letter 198

20th July 1918, Menthenberg, Arnhem

My dearest Father,
A short line to you on a rather important subject. I am rather well situated here for hearing rumours from Hun sources – 3000 Huns in the town; and my host a friend of many of their officers. They affirm that the new agreement will permit us to fight anywhere except on the Western front. This seems to me a bit too optimistic. If so, I suppose Mesopotamia or Palestine would be best, but I fear this may not be allowed. However, I think it may be possible to get to Russia. I know nothing, but if there is to be a show, it strikes me as a place where I can be of most use. I know the Russians fairly well and have done my best to study both them and their language by books and intercourse. Now what I want you to do please is to find out what possibility there is of my getting some staff or interpreter job in any fighting that may take place there. I cannot believe that we are going to allow Russia to be turned into a German province without striking a blow. Unfortunately my knowledge of soldiering is nil practically speaking, and I should have to go through a lengthy course before doing any training – if this is what they intend to use us for. Hence, it seems to me possible that the quickest way I can get into the show again is to get a job through my Russian. If this is possible I will work it all up again and be ready for anything immediately on return. Sorry to trouble you again but it may be a small chance to 'make good'.

We are having a great time here, and I am making some very nice Dutch friends of the old Dutch type. We went to a dance in a beautiful old Dutch castle last night and are dancing in the town tonight. Tennis very dull.

Well, my best love to you all, and I shall be much obliged if you will fix this up for me; if there is a chance, just cable me, YES, and I will understand. Vinogradoff might help. Au revoir.
Your affectionate son,

Brocas.

They say perhaps September. I return Hague on Monday.

Letter 199

24th July 1918, 182 Riouw Straat, The Hague

My dearest Mother,
I got back from Arnhem on Monday evening after a most delightful week,
and I feel ten times better for the change. I have been frightfully busy since
my return, and this is the first moment I have had to drop you a line. I hope
to write you a full account of the visit tomorrow. Tell father that the eldest
Neuerberg girl has got engaged to one Clark – the man who was always with
her! One other fellow has been caught since I was away, but I don't know his
name. Otherwise nothing to report. Much better news from H.A. Hut. Was
there for tea today, and Mrs G. has got the best of Clapperton. I'm going to a
big Caledonian Ball tomorrow – dreadful show – bagpipes; dancing etc. On
Friday am singing at sailors group concert – shall probably be entertaining
Joe and Doris!! Played tennis with Mrs Garrett today, and am bathing with
her tomorrow! My first bathe of the year. I'm not looking forward to it much
– very windy and not too warm. Poor Tzar – dead again. I believe finally
this time. Russians in mourning. Parcel arrived today. Biscuits No. 1. Many
thanks. Re news of exchange. Please find out if there is any chance (if Russia
possible) of getting out of England on any job – diplomatic or military, and if
so what country. We know nothing here and you will probably hear first. What
about India? Well I must close. My best love to you all and I will write a more
coherent letter as soon as possible.
Ever your affectionate son,

Brocas.

Letter 200

26th July 1918, 182 Riouw Straat, The Hague

My dearest Mother,
I had a very busy day yesterday and not a moment to write. Then came the
Caledonian Ball in the evening, and so this is my first moment. Well re our
stay at Arnhem. We arrived on Monday 15th at about 5 p.m. I was with a
friend of mine Capt. Usher of the Gordons. It was v. hot so we decided to go
into the restaurant and have a drink before bicycling out to the Menthenberg
where we were to stay. We sat down comfortably for about ten minutes, and
then the station master came in and asked us if we were staying with Mme.
Scheidius. We said yes, and he told us that she was waiting for us. Imagine our
consternation. However, we explained, and she very kindly forgave us. They
have a remarkable four wheeled pony cart which holds six people in three rows,

and luggage as well. In this we and our little all were driven out to the house about 3 miles. Here we met our host – a Dutchman with German tendencies I fear, but anyway a most charming and amusing man, late diplomat. Miss Mitileneu daughter of the Rumanian minister, and Mme. Scheidius' daughter by her first marriage. – Miss Woodville. They were all awfully nice to us and begged us to do exactly what we liked. We had two very peaceful days. It was very hot and thundery, which we spent chiefly in the lovely garden. The garden is glorious, masses of roses and carnations though these latter are poor this year owing to lack of coal for heating. The whole garden was laid out by Baron de Pallandt and his present wife (late Mrs. Van Loon) and he is apparently very artistic and a great gardener. The de Pallandts then lost their money and had to sell the place, and Scheidius bought it. There are lovely stables and though there are only 3 horses there at present they intend to get many more after the war. One day we played a round of golf on their local 9 hole course which is quite decent and well kept, and we also played tennis on their private court. The Arnhem Tennis week was on of course and we saw quite a lot of good tennis. The owner of the courts at Arnhem is very anti-German and flatly refused to allow any Germans to play on his courts. When we arrived he received us with open arms, complained bitterly that so few British came to Arnhem, and begged us to play on his courts whenever we wanted to! From Thursday on we danced every night and had great fun. There are some most charming people round Arnhem, and considering their supposed leanings towards Germany they received us extremely well. I think their sentiments are chiefly controlled by fear. Arnhem is so near the German frontier. There are 150 German officers there and of these only two are received in society or seen anywhere.

6th August.

Well, I hadn't a moment to continue this before Saturday when I had to go to Amsterdam for the day to play cricket. I left this meaning to finish it on Sunday evening. Hardly had I got to the Hotel Pays Bas at Amsterdam when I began to feel extraordinarily ill, and so went to bed. Next day I was worse, had to give up all idea of cricket and sent for the doctor who immediately diagnosed this malady as this Spanish disease, gave me odd medicines and told me to keep my bed till further orders. So there I was and there I remained until Thursday. I was very comfortable and the hotel servants treated me very well. On Thursday the authorities began to worry so much about my prolonged absence that I returned and took to my bed here. I am now completely recovered again and very fit. Everyone is getting this sickness here, and it is no joke while it lasts, but comes and goes very quickly. One feels rotten and has a high fever and gets a sore throat. I had meant to see a bit of Amsterdam on Saturday, but needless to say did not. I hear a convoy has just arrived, and in fact have

got a copy of the weekly Times from it, but nothing more at present. I hope to go to Haarlem on Thursday for a week's cricket. At present the weather is too fearful for words, perpetual rain, and if so I don't expect we shall get much play. No more news of repatriation but more people are expected from Germany. Great excitement here because Miss Woodville has got engaged to be married to Capt. Graham-Watson of the Royal Scots. Several comedians have sent me condolences because I was staying with them before the event. I have of course tried to convey the correct congratulations etc. I pity them both and this is not "pique"! I went through the cases of books sent to Father c/o Y.M.C.A., and selected a few for personal perusal and sent the rest to the huts. I am sending you a model of the 'Iron Duke' [HMS *Iron Duke* a British battleship built 1912] *that I had made at Groningen. I really think it rather good. I have been trying to look up something to send you for some time but it is very difficult to find anything here and these nick nacks from Groningen are at any rate supporting home industries. Tell Father I have passed on all his news to people here and all are most grateful. It really is most kind of him to have taken so much trouble. Tell him I misread his letter first time through and read "Burrows' wife" for "Barrow's wife"!! I thought he was being facetious! And referring to Mrs. G. D.! Baroness de Brienen met Mrs. Houldsworth at Major Lyster's wedding a few days ago and said "I see you are well enough to attend social functions but not to work – go home by next convoy!" This is a very good story even if not true. Mrs. Reynolds has got bad blood poisoning in her hand and is temporarily laid up. Mrs. Graves and son very well and the hut apparently flourishing. Tennis courts not yet ready and we are not going to play any more cricket there. The ground is not worth playing on. We have made arrangement to play all matches at Haarlem, which is much nicer. Moseley has gone away for a fortnight with Sampson to Overeen near Haarlem where I shall meet him, and Hunter-Blair is laid up, having recently damaged his "tendon Achilles". I fear he will be in bed for some weeks; he did it hurdling in some sports at Clingendaal during the Red Cross fête on August 4. I like the news from France; we seem to be regaining confidence. I am getting up a big concert for the Group to take place on August 27. Well I must close. I will write to you shortly from Haarlem. How should I address letters to Lady Parker? What on earth was she?*
My best love to all,
Your affectionate son,

Brocas.

PS. I enclose some photos I took at Arnhem, not very good I fear.

Letter 201

18th August 1918, 182 Riouw Straat, The Hague

My dearest parents,
Just back from Haarlem after a most delightful cricket week, to find the rest of your mail awaiting me. I shall answer it all tomorrow in detail and also send you an account of the week. All is as usual here, and I am quite glad to get back as our "pub" at Haarlem was none too comfortable and crowded out with commercial travellers. Davy Hunter-Blair is much better and can hobble about now, though I fear he will not be right for some time. MO. [Moseley] is still at Overeen with Sam [Sampson]. I went and dined with them there. It is a delightful little village quite near Haarlem and yet entirely out of the rush. I am very busy for the moment, as besides my work for the Americans I am getting up a concert for my old group and also arranging a cricket dinner and big 'Test Match' here for the beginning of September. I went to the "hut" today and found it nearly empty. I am told today was exceptional, but even so I am sure that things are not going well. I will try and collect details and send them to you. Many thanks for your letter of advice and re India. All most sound, and I am really going to get down and do some work now. I fear Hindustani is a difficulty here but may be possible. Anyhow I could soon pick it up again. News seems v. good except for our exchange. Had a row with a Hun at Zaandfort. He is manager of a restaurant there and his waiter tried to cheat me. I sent for him and gave him socks in my best German before an appreciative crowd of Jews and his fellow countrymen, and I told him I would see no English or French (!) come near his place again if he didn't sack the waiter – which he did on the spot. No doubt the waiter is back by now, but still it was v. amusing! My Spanish flu has quite gone. Gerald [Crutchley] has had it and is not quite well yet. Everyone seems to get it here and some of the men are quite bad. I **am sending you a photo of myself after being bowled first ball at Haarlem, a dreadful ordeal to have to pay the photographer at such a moment, but you will see that I managed a sickly grin!!** *[see photo page 247] Well I must close. My best love to you both.*
Ever your affectionate son,

Brocas.

Letter 202

16th August 1918, Zaandfort

Post Card to Father

Friday – Gerald and I here for lunch after innings victory over Netherlands at cricket. G. got 100 I got 0! Thanks from G. for letter – he will write – Returning Hague Sunday when will send you full account of cricket week – Grand weather – intend to bathe in sea! Best love to all.

Brocas

Post card from Zaandfort 16th August 1918 Source: Burrows family archive

Letter 203

20th August 1918, 182 Riouw Straat, The Hague

My dearest parents,
After a somewhat violent morning arranging for a group concert and a big cricket dinner, I settle down to try and give you a concise account of my movements during the past few days, and to answer your letters to me. Well the cricket week at Haarlem started on the 8th Thursday, with a three-day match P

of W "A" v. "B". This should have been a really good match, but unfortunately owing to Spanish sickness no less than 6 of our side "B" were unable to turn out, and so it resolved itself into Henslow, Gerald and I trying to play the whole of "A", and of course we got badly beaten by an innings. We had absolutely no bowling, and Gerald had to bowl 44 overs and I 36! This in boiling hot weather. On Sunday I heard the mail had arrived here from the convoy, and so dashed back here for an hour or two, but only to find that most of mine has not yet come. It had arrived in the hotels but not been distributed to "livers out". I went back to Haarlem on Sunday night, and on Monday we began our match v. the R.N.D. we got them out for about 150 (I forget exact scores) and then made 280. Then they made about 230 and left us 100 to get in an hour, and we got them in 45 minutes. I had quite a good match, getting 5 wks and 43 and 39. This lasted Monday and Tuesday and then on Wednesday and Thursday we played the Netherlands or rather as representative an XI as could be collected. We dismissed them for about 150 and then made 380. Gerald and Fowke each getting hundreds and MacBryan 50. In their second knock they again got about 150, and so we won somewhat easily, but they were very sporting about it and have asked us to play them again, and so we are arranging a match on the Teutoon-stelling terrein for the beginning of September. The week as a whole was an unqualified success. I forgot to mention that the last match on Friday and Saturday was a mixed XI v. N.C.O's and men from Groningen which I stayed to see. It was won by the mixed XI very easily. I think we have done a lot of good for cricket in Holland, and this I am sure is good propaganda. The crowds were never exactly large, but range from 2 to 3 hundred every day, and they were very appreciative. Gerald and I bicycled round the neighbouring country and saw the sights. It is certainly a glorious part of Holland, and if we are here next summer I shall try to go and live there. We went to the local seaside resort Zaandfort, but found it full of Germans and Jews. Overeen was very nice and quiet, and so was Bloemdaal. Both really country villages. Several officers are living around there and seem very happy. I came back here on Sunday to find lots of letters and lots of stuff from the Americans and so I'm now hard at work. My "Pelmam" books have also arrived, and we three are starting the course on Thursday. It looks promising.

Re local news. There is nothing much happening. The Botterills are just back, the Younger's have been back sometime. Mrs. Younger appears to be the leader of the ladies who refuse to return. Mr. Huitvelt the Norwegian minister is away on holiday, and Aguerra, the Spaniard has returned to Spain. A new American military attaché has arrived, Col. Davis; and one or two budding English diplomatists. I doubt their ripening much! Most of the Dutch people are still in the country, and very wise of them too. Scheveningen is too awful for words, and the Hague is dreadfully lowering. One feels it like a lump of

lead on one's back as soon as one returns. This evening I am going to sit for a Russian sculptor who appears to think that I must look ferocious when charging "à cheval", and wishes to "sculpt" me in that attitude! Rather nerve trying! Tomorrow we have a cricket match v. Schiedam on the Teutoon-stelling terrain, and next Tuesday an extra special concert for the group which I am getting up. I will send you a program. Did I thank you for the French books? They arrived and are excellent. Davy [Hunter-Blair] *is hard at work at Spanish and I am very glad he has got such a good occupation during his enforced lying up. His leg is much better, but he won't be normal for another month. Booth's case in hand for Mr. Radcliffe. I hope Mother is by now quite recovered. It was indeed time you went home if she was over working like that. Duchess wrote me a stinker re marriageable Fliegers. So I appear to have put my foot in it there all right!! In your letter of July 21, you mention a chill Mother recovered from. I hope it was not a bad one. So glad you are having a really peaceful holiday. Your accounts of Duchess make me mad to think that I cannot be with her now and see her work etc. It must be great. I am very sorry to hear you are sending Bernard to* **Big Summer Fields and not Little Summer Fields** *first.* [Prep schools] *Of course it is nothing to do with me, and when I was at little S. I didn't like Compton at all, but I know now that he was the man who made the most impression on me of all private schoolmasters, and the whole atmosphere of "Little S." for a short time is excellent, and also by changing schools after a year or so a schoolboy gets a wider view of school customs and other schoolboys, and so must gain in originality of ideas and independence. I should strongly advocate a year at Little S., just as I had before going to the bigger one. Incidentally B. would get much more individual attention at Little S. as regards games as well as work. Do you tell Aunt Io this from me. Your letters of advice do me an immense amount of good and I am trying to follow them closely. So glad India and Russia afford possibilities for a career. I think we are going to be made to do some military work here. The American work goes well and they are giving me much more interesting stuff to do. Now I have passed all your messages, I think, and will have another run through in case I have missed any out. All are most thankful to you for your kindness. We have now settled down to a very quiet life in 182, all three of us and what with Pelman and our various other occupations are very occupied. No more breakfasts in kimonos etc. Early rising at 7.30 is now the order. Well I fear the mail is shortly off and so will close what I fear is a somewhat disconnected rigmarole. I will write better and more often in future. My best love to you both.*
Your affectionate son,

Brocas.

Letter 204

28th August 1918., 182 Riouw Straat, The Hague

My dearest mother,
The first letter from this convoy has just arrived, and from you, so I sit down
to reply forthwith. It is dated July 14, and so is very late in turning up. You
write it in bed, and I'm glad to say that the letter announcing your complete
recovery preceded it. I do hope your well-deserved holiday has been a success
and that you have really rested. Sorry to hear of the accidents to the Duchess's
Fliegers. They must certainly want all relaxation possible, to act as an antidote
to weed pulling. Very glad to hear of the success of Aunt Io's theatricals. I
remember her and Thyra acting in the garden at Drove ages ago. I forget
what the place was, but believe there was some Morris Dancing before it, or
in the entracte. People have gone on board for the convoy today and rather
a lot of our friends are included, particularly Mr. and Mrs. Garrett (off for
six weeks to fix up some things for American P's of W) and Mrs. Huitveldt.
Mrs Wyndham also returned home, as do Misses Allom and Kirkaldy, whom
Father will remember. Many marriages are taking place about now and I
am attending one on September 5th. A Miss Burns to Captain Maclean
of Ardgour; reception at the Legation afterwards. I don't think much of the
fiancées from England. I have only seen one with anything like decent looks.
No more engagements for the last week but I fear rumours that two girls,
one Dutch and one Belgian, who work in the local Red Cross office, are both
unofficially engaged to officers. Ivan Hay's people are said to have refused to
allow his marriage with Olga Leutrum. Last night I got up a concert for the
Cavalry group, and we had all the great people there. It was quite a success,
and I think they appreciated the change from an ordinary sing-song concert.
I enclose the program. Afterwards we had supper and some more music, and it
really was a most amusing evening. We appear to be asserting ourselves at last
on the front. [Western Front] *We hear tonight of the capture of Nesle.* [about
30 miles north of Néry where Brocas was injured] *I had a most exciting*
day defending it in '14! I wonder how much is left of it now. The manicure set
has arrived and is most serviceable. I shall hope in future to keep my nails
fairly decent. Winter seems to be starting already and it is very cold today,
so much so that I blankly refused to play cricket! I am very busy with my
American work and Pelman, and I'm finding the latter very useful. I am also
reading various books on the sins of our late hosts, etc. We certainly make good
propaganda out of it, but I don't find it very convincing on the whole. Well, I
will say au revoir. My best love to you both.
Ever your affectionate son,

Brocas.

Letter 205

31st August 1918, 182 Riouw Straat, The Hague

My dearest Father,
A most amusing thing has just occurred which shows off the magnanimity
of the British diplomat abroad at its best. Do you remember the telegram we
ask Trefusis to send of June 4th to the headmaster of Eton and about which
we never heard anything more? Well, today I get an enormous envelope from
H.B.M. Legation containing a colossal sheet of notepaper on which is written
an official letter requesting me to forward at my earliest convenience the sum
of money to cover cost of despatching same telegram, as H.B.M's Legation
presumes this was sent at my instigation!! I have not yet decided whether
to send them the money in copper coins, or whether a cheque would be more
suitable. I think on the whole the latter! (Sampson paid me a visit at this
moment re-orchestra for cricket dinner and requested me to send you his love.
He is very well and he's just back from a stay in the country). You ask why
Jervis resigned from B.E.F. He allowed a rather stupid article to be published
about Gen. Friedrichs during his (the latter's) stay here for the conference.
He got hauled over the coals by Graeme Tomson for this, and so the matter
ended. But several days later Dennis very stupidly wrote to him and told him
not to publish such articles again. Result a considerable amount of mutual
recrimination, and Jervis's resignation, as he refused to have anything more to
do with the Y.M.C.A. This was followed by the resignation of most of the rest of
the staff, and now the Y.M.C.A. have appointed some other people, and most
of us have stopped taking in the paper. Dennis has done another peculiarly
unfortunate thing in appointing West, whom you may remember, to introduce
all lecturers and take the chair. This of course is quite enough to diminish the
attendance at lectures by 50%. Things in the H.A. Hut certainly don't go well,
and the old lot have entirely stopped going there. I go occasionally to see Mrs
Graves, and never meet anyone I know. Most disappointing after all you did,
and the popularity it attained under your direction. Force has had Spanish flu
and has been sent to Leuwarden I hear. The Villa Mess is now full of lecturers
and Mrs Graves tells me they are a truly remarkable crowd. Exceedingly
rough. It is quite true about Mrs. G. and Mrs. H. and the latter was dancing
Highland dances last night! The former is I believe rather ill, but the latter is
a damned fraud and ought to be publicly dealt with on return. She is quite
worthless, and is entirely in the hands of Mrs.Y., whom you will remember, and
with whom she and her husband are now living. I hear this latter lady is the
cause of all the trouble and can quite believe it. Did you ever find out about
Mrs. Bedingfeld who wrote to me from Brighton? Never mind if it is a difficult
job. So glad to hear mother is getting better and that you are both really resting.
I'm sure that is what you really want. We hear most disheartening news about

the treatment of repatriated officers. One wrote the other day and said he would much rather be back in Switzerland. This sounds rather hard. Here the cricket season is drawing to a close. We play our last league match tomorrow and on the whole I am not sorry. The weather is already getting rather too cold for fielding, and I'm not looking forward to the "Test Match" on the 7th and 8th. I don't know what to do for exercise in the winter: perhaps Rugby Football. Fancy the Duchess being 21 in December! What shall I give her as a birthday present? Please suggest something. I fear the chances of our all being together by then are somewhat small. No advance seems to be being made at all. However I hope we don't climb down about the Chinese Germans.

Well I must close. With Best love to you both.
Ever your affectionate son,

Brocas.

I think I gave you 2 n's last time. Sorry.

Letter 206

20th September 1918, 182 Riouw Straat, The Hague

My dearest Father,
Just a line to let you know that Sampson has passed the Commission and goes off today to England. He has been very ill, and we eventually persuaded him to go up, and they passed him like a shot. He has promised to write to you and give you latest news etc. We shall all miss him a great deal here. Nothing much of interest going on. I went over to Nordwyk for a dance on Wednesday evening. Great fun. All the Dutch people retire there for the summer, and it is a delightful quiet seaside resort. Good golf course and decent tennis. If we are here next summer I shall certainly try and get there. Unfortunately there are many Germans there, but they don't appear much. We danced from 9pm till 4 am. A Miss de Kuyper had a birthday party and so we had gymkhanas etc. I was most effusively greeted by old Countess Stirum, who could not have been nicer. Why I don't know, as I have never called, and have been most unlucky as regards cutting her in the street. Davy Hunter-Blair is still at Clingendaal, and Moseley has gone to Rotterdam to see Sampson off, so am alone in the flat and getting down to a good day's work, which must include a birthday letter to Aunt Em. If convoy rumours are correct this should reach her just about in time. Affairs generally seem to be going well in the various theatres of war and diplomacy. Most people are getting very optimistic here. I may be going to get

a job on the British News Staff as translator. I think it might be useful to get some experience of newspaper life, as the Press is such an important weapon these days. The British news has assumed a much more influential position nowadays and is most ambitious. I may have told you of this in my last. I have offered to learn Dutch if they want a Dutch interpreter. Pray heaven they don't.

Well, I flourish and hope you do. My best love to you both, or is it not all three at home now?

Ever your affectionate son,

Brocas.

PS. What shall I give Duchess for her 21ster?

Letter 207

26th September 1918, 182 Riouw Straat, The Hague

My dearest parents,

A priceless letter from each of you has just arrived, and so I will just acknowledge them on the spot. The amount of trouble you have taken for me, Father, is phenomenal, and I positively blush when I think of my unworthiness of it all. I am weighing up all your advice and results of interviews etc. and trying hard to decide on what to do. At present I am still far from a decision, and so will write about it. Russia certainly seems the biggest temptation. Everything must be built up again from the very beginning, and that certainly should give scope for all kinds of things. So glad the ship gave pleasure. [a model of HMS Iron Duke] *I fear it is a mere "bagatelle". I have been seeing a lot of the most delightful lady Mrs. Kirke, and helped her yesterday with her big tea party to introduce the wife of the new American first secretary, Mrs. Bliss, to the "monde diplomatique". And the most amusing performance. The new lady is most charming and very beautiful. Certainly the Americans choose their diplomatic women well. I think our representatives are somewhat jealous. I am writing to Mr Radcliffe re Sergt. Booth, whom I have interviewed. Moseley is at Apeldoorn and Hunter Blair at Clingendaal, so I have the flat to myself and I am enjoying a really quiet time. We now have an old Dutch gentleman living underneath us, quite tame. Our latest innovation is dinners from Mme. Haas herself instead of the restaurant Smaan. She is a first class cook and really taken an interest in us now. Marlow has turned out trumps, and completely runs the household with great success. He is shortly to appear in mufti as a "gentleman's gentleman". My letter to Aunt Em unfortunately missed the mail, so I will cable on the 29th. Grand news from everywhere. Had a long talk yesterday with the American military attaché, Col. Davies,*

D.S.O., who was with Allenby. He is a cavalry man himself, and most capable and charming. He thinks it <u>the</u> success up-to-date, and expects colossal results. I was dining with friends at Doulen. He was at table next to me on the left, and on the right was the German Mil. Attaché with one of the Turkish Secs. We talked very loud. Well my best love to you both and Duchess.
Ever your affectionate son,

Brocas.

PS.
I should think Duchess has had more than enough grubbing by now. Glad she is stopping!

Letter 208

12th October 1918, 182 Riouw Straat, The Hague

My dearest parents,
As usual an excellent mail from you for which I thank you heartily. We are certainly living in exciting times, but personally I cannot attain the general height of optimism. The Dutch are all immensely pleased, and are sure the war will be over by Christmas. Praise God, it isn't. If it is, the Hun will never really experience its horrors; and what's the use of beating him unless he does? So thick skinned a nation can only be persuaded by the lash laid on really hard! Surely this "Leinster" atrocity [sinking by torpedo of The Leinster, a Royal Mail Steamer on 10 October 1918 near Dublin] *will open people's eyes. I don't believe Max of Baden is speaking for himself at all. He is merely a mouthpiece, as are all the German pressmen for the moment. I really believe that if we advance much more and peace does not come, these Dutch will decide to come in and finish off the war! At present they are rather obsessed with the idea of a peace conference here, and making a lot of money and getting a lot of kudos out of it; but they have sent their army to Brabant and if they get something for nothing they won't hang back long. How I hate them! Everyone is very disturbed and excited and it's a confounded nuisance.*

I have just had a very sad letter from my first Russian teacher, a Lt. called Puische, who is still in Germany having a dreadful time. He had had no news of his people in Petrograd since 1917, and as they were always rather mixed up in politics of a rather advanced order he fears the worst. He is a friend of the wretched Miliukoff, and is the man who sent so much important news back to Russia re-treatment of prisoners. I think I told you about this. I was going to Amsterdam today, but have postponed my visit for a bit, as we have a spell of fine weather which is really exceptional now. I am playing Rugger this afternoon, the second time this year; the first time I sprained my thumb and got kicked most violently on the shin by a small but determined full back, and so I'm quite nervous about today! The local inhabitants are much amused by the game, and roar with laughter at the scrum or a good tackle!

So glad to hear you have had a "Full house weekend". I hope it was cheerful. You must be very glad to have the Duchess back again, and I hope she has not got "farmers knee" or "labourers' leg" or any such like complaint due to too much bending or hard work. Mrs. Graves has left, and what will become of the H.A. Hut now? Heaven only knows. The present so-called leader oughtn't to be allowed to sell bacon in a grocery store. Tell George from me that Portman is going strong. He only arrived from Germany just as Father was going home. Again ever so many thanks to father for his trouble re Russia! I am working hard at it here with Colonel Pauloff. The fellow who had a disagreement with a tram here was a Lt. Martin in the York and Lancasters. He was most unfortunate, got his stick caught in his heel and was thrown off just as a tram was passing. No one's fault. He got badly mauled and died painlessly some three days later. He never knew he was dying and had no pain. The tram was badly bent. Many thanks to Duchess for her letter which I am answering. Best love to you all. Your affectionate son,

Brocas.

Letter 209

My dearest parents,
I fear it is ages since I last wrote to you and feel duly ashamed. It is not from lack of good intentions, but chiefly owing to another slight go off "Spansche sickte", which is positively raging here. I am however quite recovered today. Everybody has been most kind, and my sitting room is a mass of flowers of all kinds! Mrs. Kirke has kindly sent me a set of cushions for the flat as a birthday present, so we shall now be very cosy indeed. Marlow has given me a copy of the regimental crest which he worked in captivity, and I shall have it put on a cushion! This evening I am having a quiet celebration with Gerald, Martin-Thomson and Stott. Mo is unfortunately ill with the fashionable ailment, and is in bed at the Kirke's house, they having very kindly insisted on his going there, and Davy H.B. [Hunter-Blair] cannot get in from Clingendaal. Anyhow we shall be cheery, and with any luck I think I ought to be a free man by my next birthday.

I am not writing you your birthday letter by this convoy, Mother, as I expect there will be another in about 10 days' time which should hit on the day exactly, but in case I miss it I send you all best wishes in this screed as from one "birthdayer" to another! **I have got an awful shock for you in the way of a present which I am sending home with the next lot of repatriated.** [No details] *So be prepared!!*

Well, excuse so short a line, please, and I will write again tomorrow. My best love to you all and be sure my thoughts are much with you!
Ever your affectionate son,

Brocas.

Letter 210

31st October 1918, Sgravenhage
Telegram to: Burrows, Norham House, Oxford

Twenty-four and flourishing. Best love to all.

Brocas.

Letter 211

4th November 1918, 182 Riouw Straat, The Hague

My dearest Mother,
With this poor effort of pen on paper go my best and most heartfelt wishes to you for your birthday. As you say of mine, it is the fifth since we have seen each other, and, God grant, the last. I am taking big risks in writing to you so late, my luck has been with me so far in hitting off the day, and I have a certain amount of inside information and so hope for the best. If this arrives too late please forgive, and remember that the intentions were of the best. I am sending you a real shock as a birthday gift! It was well meant, but I fear the result is disappointing. Nevertheless I shall be thinking of you much on the great day and having a small party in your honour at the flat.

Many thanks for the birthday telegram to me, and also to Aunt Em for sending me one. Birthday letters have arrived Aunt Io, to whom my best thanks. You were all most accurate in your shooting, which doubled the pleasure and excitement of "l'anniversaire".

Many thanks for the cheque. I am much puzzled as to what to get.

As regards things here. We have got it really cold at last, which is much preferable to the rainy muggy autumn we have been having. There has been a fearful amount of "flu", and among the Dutch it has been very serious. We have had one or two serious cases, but on the whole have got off lightly. I have quite recovered from a slight touch, and Moseley is now well again and back at the flat. Gerald hopes to get home with the next "Commission" for nerves, and I should think has a very good chance. Davy Hunter-Blair is still at Clingendaal but much better and able to walk without crutches. I have just had a charming letter from Mr. Radcliffe in answer to mine about Sergt. Booth. To answer your letters. I did not know that anyone had arrived to take over the H.A. hut. If so, I must mistake him for one of the Belgian carpenters. He certainly does nothing and all still bewail Father's loss. I never go there now, nor do Gerald, Mo, George Graves or any of the old lot.

So glad to hear D. is singing etc. The more the better. How I wish I could get home for her 21ster.

Aunt Em's letter was marvellous! I have little doubt that I shall see her again on return. I will make immediate enquiries about the five racing men at Nijmegen and let you know by cable. There is a lot to be said for and against. Of course they are a bit short, and perhaps stable boys find jobs a bit scarce, but if you once help one – !

Father's last letter was an absolute record October 23 – November 2. I am glad Molly's nuptials were a success, but what a pity she has chosen a fellow like that! I thought there must be something fishy from her letters to me. So full of his eulogies! However!!

Excuse this scrawl but we have a fire in the sitting room and I'm writing this in a real luxury curled up on the sofa. Alison and Cumming are expected shortly, the former to talk over "important business" (heaven knows what) and the latter to dine. I think they must have heard that we have just got in some new sherry!

Well, as you say, it really looks as if the captive will soon be home. I am gradually dropping all ideas of cricket in Holland next summer and looking forward to shooting Bolshevichs instead!

My best love to you all three and every good wish to you, mother, for our last celebration of your birthday with me in "jug".

Ever your affectionate son,

Brocas.

Letter 212

Telegram: Monday 18th November 1918
Post mark, Hull, England.
Arrived on S.S. Willochra (ICRC record R 51957)

Arrived safely. Going to Ripon camp for a day or two. Will wire time of arrival. Don't meet me at station. Hope bring Marlow.
Best love,

Brocas.

Letter 213

20th November 1918
Telegram: No address
To: Burrows, Norham House, Oxford

Hope arrive Wednesday about eight. Please arrange room for Marlow for night. Don't meet or wait dinner. Best love.

Brocas.

Final Note

[Hand written note by Father to end diary of letters:]

"Brocas and Marlow arrived safely at 8.30 p.m. (Wednesday 20th November 1918)

And so ends the chapter".

S.M.B.

14

Murmansk – Another Campaign

21 January 1919 – 14 October 1919
A Final Campaign – Parcels and Letters

The Murmansk Expedition, also known as the North Russia intervention, the Northern Russian expedition, or the Archangel campaign, was begun in early 1918 in order to prevent Germany from withdrawing her forces from the Eastern Front after the Russian Revolution and the subsequent disintegration of the Russian army. It was also to deny Germany the use of Murmansk, the only year-round ice-free port in Northern Russia, as a submarine base from where she could attack allied shipping. Manpower was in desperately short supply after the slaughter of the previous four years and so it is not surprising that Brocas was ordered to leave for Russia after barely two months at home and after four years in POW camps and internment in Holland. As a fluent Russian speaker, he was extremely valuable – neither General Maynard who was head of the Murmansk Expedition nor General Ironside spoke the language and probably only a very few of the other officers and none of the rank and file did.

After arriving back at Oxford on 20 November 1918, Brocas received notice of his appointment to General Maynard's staff on 21 December 1918 and he was ordered to leave for Russia on 24 December but through a mistake made by the War Office, he missed his steamer and returned home. It would be his first Christmas with his family for five years. On 20 January 1919 he received a wire ordering him to leave on 21st. The ship was the S.S. *Stephen* with 200 officers on board and in Brocas's opinion, *'vile accommodation'*. Some Russians were also on board – a bad lot mostly chucked out of England for various misdemeanours. They arrived at Murmansk on 31 January 1919. He wrote home soon after describing his first dramatic encounter with Russian subterfuge:

> *It is a desolate place and the Russians sullen and Railway Workers, who were Bolshevik at heart, invited the allied officers of the Murmansk*

front force to a dinner at Soroka, the intention being to poison all the
officers at the dinner & initiate a Revolution. The plot was discovered
& the Workers were obliged to give & pay for the dinner nevertheless
under armed supervision. The two principal organisers of the dinner
being exiled immediately afterwards. (executed?)

During these first few months his mother continued to support Brocas
with parcels, although with less rigour than during his internment.
She sent mainly essential items for his comfort together with a few
luxuries. A final parcel, 6lbs of figs, the 636th since October 1914, was
sent on 6 May 1919 and was the last of over 2800 items.

List of Parcels sent to Brocas in Murmansk
17 April 1919 – 6 May 1919

17th April	*1 flat deal case, 1lb chocolate biscuits, 1lb plain chocolate, 1 forage cap, 3 linen pants, 2 prs sheets (twill) 2 pillow cases, 1 pillow, 1 bottle eau de cologne, 1 bottle gargle, badges 5 D. G., 3 artex vests, 3 pants, polish for boots and buttons 1 small deal case groceries :- currants, raisins, dates, almonds, sweets, toffee, oil of cloves*
23rd	*1 parcel photos – Jock*
24th	*1 pillow, butter, muslin, propaganda photos*
24th	*2lbs chocolate (vidal)*
2nd May	*1 bottle King Green*
6th	*6lbs figs*

February 1919 was spent at Brigade HQ Kem, where Brocas tried to
establish good relations with the locals. In March he received orders
to attach himself to HQ Second Murmansk Infantry at Shueretskaia
as British Liaison Officer. Here the few remaining Russian officers
were trying to form the Russian army of the North destined to take
over the entire Murmansk front when the allied forces were recalled.
No easy task as they had revolted twice and murdered their colonel.
At this time, he was promoted to the rank of temporary captain. On
arrival, Brocas was assigned a soldier servant and when summoned to
meet the commanding officer, left orders for his kit to be unpacked
and dinner to be prepared for him on his return. After having had
to imbibe too much vodka with the usual endless toasts, he returned
to find nothing had been done as far as unpacking and dinner were
concerned. He found the soldier asleep in the kitchen, yelled at him
and was joined by the C.O.s adjutant who had come to invite him

to dinner. Nothing happened until the owner of the boarding house intervened – apparently the man was Karelain and spoke no Russian. A Russian speaking substitute, Stepan, was found and proved fairly satisfactory. Brocas had only just managed to stop him putting on his, Brocas's, best and hitherto unworn uniform and parading in it in front of his friends.

On 13 May 1919 they advanced south with a column of 160 Russians from the newly formed 2nd Northern Rifle Regiment. They were due to attack a garrison of 40 at Yalozero and then 150 Chinese at Povenets. On 17 May they occupied Povenets and a few days later on 24th they were off to attack the enemy in the rear and try to encourage the peasants to rise behind him. On 25 May, with a party of 10 men, Brocas landed on the Sunga Peninsula, and by his energetic action against the Bolsheviks covered the landing of a Russian battalion. This being the action for which the Military Cross was recommended by Major-General Maynard. On other occasions he also showed similar gallantry and ability to command. On 30 May he wrote home from Maselskaya Stansia:

> *Just back for a few hours from a trip behind the enemy's lines where I have been raising a counter revolution & generally annoying the foe in rear. A most amusing pastime and I was most successful. I am extraordinarily well tho' rather tired as my journey here started with 10 versts on horseback then 50 versts in a rowboat by night, avoiding enemy steamers, then another 10 versts on horseback and 30 versts in a Brewery car. The Russian forces here are now in full array & we are gradually withdrawing our own.* [a verst = just over 1 kilometre]

None of his letters home in June survive but in July 1919 he wrote: '*the populace has got wind of our impending departure and are quite desperate in some places.*'

On 16 July, quartered comfortably in Shunga, he enjoyed a duck hunt.

> *Two of us were in a motor boat with my old 12 bore and a rifle. Two kilometres from the coast we found an aged eider duck, chased him for 20 minutes until he was dead beat & then shot him amidst loud cheering from front line trenches which stretch down to the lake at that point.*

On 23 July he wrote home:

My dearest Parents,

Again, I seize pencil to write you a fleeting line re things here in general. Since my last I have journeyed along the whole line from Lake Onega to Unitsa visiting the various Russian troops. At Unitsa I was shelled out of my quarters and arrived just in time for quite an amusing little fight nearer home. Things are now pretty well fixed up on the front and I had hoped to go for a week's rest but now the officer working with me has gone sick and I have got to take over his job temporarily. Hence, I am leaving soon for …… where I fear I shall have to make my HQ. However, nothing is settled yet and I hope to be able to stay here. I am trying to persuade the Russians to move their HQ here but they seem to consider it rather too exposed. We have just started the rainy period here and it is coming down in torrents. Someone has just stolen my pencil so I must carry on with another. A most curious party has just arrived from the front line. First and foremost an ex Russian officer condemned to death by the Bolsheviks five months ago – he has been hiding in the forest ever since and has only just managed to escape; then secondly a family of real gypsies, the gayest dirtiest set of ragamuffins you ever saw, without a care of any sort and ready to dance and sing at any time of day or night. There is one little boy who I am thinking of taking on as a body servant. I shall be able to purchase him for a few tins of bully beef, so that will be quite cheap, but in order to wash him I shall have to use all my soap supply, so I am not quite sure whether it is worth it.

Things don't seem to be moving very fast out here but there is a chance that I may get home at the end of September for a short spell of leave and I think my job here will finish by the end of November – (this letter is between ourselves). Our affairs with the Russians have been going badly and now in official circles they are hardly on speaking terms and this is why I have to go back to HQ for a bit. A most unpleasant job but fortunately the worst offender on our side is ill and I have managed to have their worst offender sacked. As you will see intrigue has a lot to do with our life here and things are rendered much more difficult by the fact that so few of us here speak any Russian and so few of the Russians speak any English. I am literally the only regular officer out here who is fluent! Disgraceful isn't it? I applied for interpreter's pay but it was refused as I have passed no examinations. I pointed out that I had put my country's needs before my own cash but that failed to soften their hearts and so I am the poorer but 'qu'importe'!

We had the pleasure of capturing the Bolshevik O.C. Front yesterday – as soon as I heard of it I galloped down to get hold of him but only arrived in time to hear the volley that terminated his existence. G.H.Q. are as usual furious and I have received a frantic telegram. My reply is let them come and rescue prisoners themselves and somehow, I don't think they will.

I have got two wonderful recipes for you Mother, one for a drink called 'Kvass' rather like old English mead – very cooling and refreshing and the other for a kind of red currant wine. We abound in berries of all kinds here and I eat stacks of them, whortleberries, wild strawberries, raspberries, red and black currants and numerous others whose English names I don't know. It is a great blessing to touch something like fruit again after so long an absence from it.

We had a great tragedy here recently – our pride of the lake and one and only warship 'HMS Jolly Roger' blew up and went to the bottom with the loss of five men. Hence the enemy has again got control of the sea which increases my supply difficulties tenfold as my boats have to add blockade running to their other sports. Unfortunately, nights are becoming fairly dark again so they will have more chance.

I read Col. De Maiers' letter with great interest – his book should be most entertaining as he is undoubtedly a very clever man but I doubt its having a very big sale, as it seems to me our colonies are going to give us all quite enough to think about without our worrying too much about Siberia. I see the Cavalry is much to the fore in Russia now. Gough with the Esthonians and Briggs with Denikin. More later.

Your affectionate son

Brocas

On 30 July 1919 he wrote from Medvedja Gora: '*They have made me a temporary Major with pay and allowances and I have been inflicted with the Cross of St. Anne – a Russian order.*'

And again, on 26 August 1919 from Medvedja Gora he wrote powerfully of his deep concern and distress at letting down and deserting the Russians whose cause they had been supporting:

My dearest People,

I am feeling at present exceedingly like a fish out of water. Gen. Lord Rawlinson has arrived and announced the sad news that we are to leave this country and the Russians, whom we have been straining every nerve to help and support – to their fate. What does this mean to them? It means the massacre and annihilation of many thousands of poor simple peasant folk by the paid bands of Finns, Chinese and other Bolshevik mercenaries who will be sent to clear up after we have gone. Had we been trying our hardest to let these poor people down we could not have done it more thoroughly. For months a large number held aloof from us here – not being certain of our eventual intentions. In this manner they hoped, in the event of an allied evacuation to avoid destruction by the Bolsheviks. A short time ago new British forces began to arrive – owing to the occupation of the Shunga peninsula. A large number of volunteers joined the ranks of the Russians, and so finally nearly all those who though they wished us well, had been 'sitting on the fence' – threw in their lot with us. This is quite recent history and now as I look back on it all, I feel like the small boy at school who has been caught by his fellows 'sneaking'. We have made these poor folk show their hands and now we are cold-bloodedly, traitorously deserting them. I know we all know why! But how can you explain it to the people here? God knows what will happen. Most of the dirty work has been done. Watts Crawford and I have laboured since April and now we really have got some Russian forces and if only these could be supported a few more months everything would be well. The enemy is tottering and a few more shrewd blows would affect his fall. As it is we are going to erect a line of defence a few miles in front of our present position and then tell the Russians to occupy this as best they can and calmly say goodbye! I have applied to be allowed to go on leave and then come back and see it through. I am sure I could help somehow but I am told the chances of this being permitted are infinitesimal – I am really quite heartbroken about it all and so few people here understand or even wish to understand the real situation. If we could only have occupied Petrozavodsk and given them a large recruiting area and a decent forward base for the winter, they might save themselves but as it is? You will hardly believe me when I tell you that the original intention appears to have been to leave here almost without informing the Russians. Thank heaven we have got this changed.

Well I see I have inflicted you with four sides of my grievance, but it has considerably improved my temper which has recently been unbearable! I caught a nasty chill recently and then had a go of 'Medvedja Gora fever' a disease akin to dysentery and said to be largely caused by inhaling large quantities of sand which abound here. I have however completely recovered and have come in here to make final arrangements for a big affair tomorrow night. We are going to land a party of about 200 men miles down the coast of Lake Onega at a place where the enemy H.Q and stores are reported to be. I am going with about 150 Russians and we are to be supported by about 50 sailors in case of need. We are going to land in row boats by night and attack at dawn. The garrison is said to be composed of about 200 Finns, who always put up a good fight. It should be quite entertaining if only the weather holds good. I hate these expeditions when it is wet...

It is apparent that they continued their mission in to September and Brocas was in the thick of it. For his actions he was award a DSO and the citation by General Maynard read as follows:

For gallant and able leadership of a landing party on the night of 13th-14th September, 1919. He took his party of 120 men across 15 miles of Lake Onega, this part being in the hands of the enemy, landed them near Vate Navolok, 21 versts in rear of the enemy front line and captured the garrison of this place. He then took his party on to the railway west of Vate Navolok, and by his skilful dispositions greatly assisted the column operating on the railway.

With that, for Brocas, this exciting and hectic, but troubled few months in Russia, was about to end, but not without implications some 25 years later when Stalin would have the last word.

15

Life After the War

15 October 1919 – 17 January 1967

On 14 October 1919, Brocas arrived back in Oxford from Murmansk. He re-joined his regiment at Colchester on 8 November. In January 1920, instead of taking what would have been his first holiday since 1914, he came back to Balliol for the Hilary term to pass an exam in French literature that would give him his degree. On 22 March 1920 he satisfied the examiners and on 22 April, the university published the names of the successful candidates including Burrows Montacutus B.

At the age of 26, Brocas was enjoying his first ever taste of social life outside the officers' mess and as a first-class cricket player and amusing company, he was overwhelmed with invitations.

On 10 March 1920, he went to Buckingham Palace to receive his DSO and MC. He was finally promoted Captain on 1 May 1920 but it was not all regimental and academic work that year. On 2 July, he played for the Eton Ramblers against the Staff College making 204 runs. Then on 29 August 1920, having been granted leave for the duration of a tour to America, he and the rest of the 'Incogniti' team played against teams at several locations including Philadelphia – he also played for Surrey County.

On 1 October 1920, he was appointed Adjutant O.T.C. and on 31 August 1922 Officer of Company of Gentlemen Cadets at R.M.C. Sandhurst. In the College Magazine for Christmas 1924, he recorded his failed attempt to escape from Mainz in the spring of 1916. On 22 January 1925, he joined the Staff College as a student and graduated on 21 January 1927.

On 22 February 1927 he embarked on HMS Neuralia at Southampton for India along with 99 officers, 1200 men and sundry women and children. They arrived on 15 March 1927 and he took the troops to the 4/7 Dragoon Guards at Sialkot and then travelled to Risalpur on the North West Frontier to join the 5/6 Dragoons. By 5 April 1927 he had already taken part in a skirmish with a local tribe, the Shinwari from Afghanistan. He played polo for the first time and soon became addicted, starting with a stable of three government horses, two chargers and a polo pony. There was also pig sticking, cricket, tennis, squash rackets and a busy social life.

On 28 April 1927 he was off to Sangar Equitation School, a journey of a thousand miles. His horses had been sent on a few days in advance to get the stiffness out of their legs. The course was for senior officers and it was the colonel's idea that Brocas should be given an opportunity to fill up some of the large gaps in his knowledge of equitation. He was already aware that in India 'graft & influence' play a far bigger role than at home, and he was anxious to make the right contacts to advance his career. He had been kept very busy. *'I have been learning my job ... my career so far has been a 'cart before the horse' affair & my ignorance of the duties of a cavalry regimental officer is monumental'*.

By 10 July 1927 he had given much thought to his future and had decided to apply for a staff job in India for three or four years in order to make some much needed money to enable him to get married – out of the question at the moment given his financial situation. On 26 October 1927 he accepted an appointment as 2nd grade officer at Delhi where he was chosen to accompany Field Marshal Birdwood, Commander in Chief India, on a week's troop inspection to Jubbulpore and then to Gorakhpur to unveil the Gurkhas war memorial. He didn't know why he was selected for this honour which caused *'much heart-burning among the A.D.C.s and satellites.'* He was also told that the Chief of General Staff had something promising for him when he returned. He forewarned his parents of *'possible complications of a most pleasant nature'* which he would reveal in his next letter. This was the first hint of his engagement to one Nancy Singer, granddaughter of the sewing machine manufacturer, but for whatever reason they never married.

On 1 January 1930 he wrote to his parents with amazing news. He had been offered what was the plum of all staff jobs – Brigade Major – 1st Cavalry Brigade, Aldershot. He was going to try to come home as early as possible and fit in a spell of learning his new job before the wedding. On 4 June 1931, when playing for the Old Etonians against the 1st Eleven, he met Molly Le Bas, sculptress daughter of Jersey business man Edward Le Bas. They were married on 5 April 1932. He was promoted Major on 2 November 1933. On 24 February 1935 he was appointed General Staff Officer II in the Department of the Chief of the Imperial General Staff – War Office. They moved into a flat in Brook House, Park Lane where their daughter, Jennifer, was born in 1936.

George VI's coronation was 12 May 1937. Brocas, since 1 January 1936 a Brevet Lieutenant Colonel, was the most junior of five gentlemen allotted to Generalfeldmarschall von Blomberg, Minister for War and Commander in Chief of the German Forces. After the coronation, he took von Blomberg on a tour of military & naval bases including his own regiment 5th Inniskilling Dragoon Guards. On 19 May 1937 he dined on board the Avisos 'Grille' – Hitler's yacht which was docked at Southampton. With war a mere two years away and already threatening, it seemed a strange decision to allow this German to view our military and naval bases.

One day at the War Office that year, he was asked by a senior officer for his help. Someone had been chosen as the new Military Attaché in Rome but had just been caught in flagrante delicto with the wife of a fellow officer and there was going to be a big scandal. It did not seem suitable for someone with that reputation to be so close to the Vatican and did Brocas have any suggestions for a replacement. He did – himself. A fluent Italian speaker apart from all his other qualities, he was an obvious choice. So, on the 18 May 1938 he was promoted to Colonel and appointed Military Attaché to Rome and Durazzo Albania. Then on 23 July 1938 he was also appointed Military Attaché to Budapest at the same time.

On 11 January 1939, Prime Minister Chamberlain visited Rome. If Brocas ever felt that he had failed in his mission to persuade Mussolini to choose the allies as opposed to the Germans, he was exonerated in a 1983 paper written by the Italian historian, Rosaria Quartararo. Mussolini saw Chamberlain's visit as a crucial opportunity for obtaining British mediation in Italy's quarrel with France and for increasing Anglo-Italian commercial contacts so that Italy's political and economic dependence on Germany could be gradually reduced. It was up to Chamberlain, Miss Quartararo maintained, to respond to Mussolini's overtures – Chamberlain did not.

On 27 January 1939, their son Richard was born in Rome and they received 46 letters of congratulation, 11 telegrams and 18 bunches of flowers from home, abroad and Rome. An indication of their wide circle of friends and their popularity. One letter from Major General Roger Evans writing from the Headquarters of the Mobile Division in Andover had a suggestion. *'I congratulate you on your diplomacy – it only remains to christen him Benito and the entente cordiale will be firmly cemented.'* Luckily this was not acted upon.

In April 1939, Molly, the children and Nanny left Rome. Brocas
was granted local rank of Brigadier on 9 November 1939 and left
for England on 16 May 1940. He relinquished his appointment as
Military Attaché on 19th and also the local rank of Brigadier. The
next day he was appointed Commander 1st Motor Machine Gun
Brigade, Colchester and acting Brigadier. On 1 December 1940 he
was appointed Commander 9th Armoured Division, Guilsborough,
Northants and granted rank of Acting Major General. A panda's head
was the insignia of the regiment and the cap badge. On 1 December
1941 he was appointed temporary Major General and on 20 March
1942 was appointed Commander of the 2nd Armoured Group and on
15 October 1942, Commander of the 11th Armoured Division, during
which period he led Brocforce (named after him), comprising the
9th East Surrey Regiment, two companies of artillery and a pioneer
battalion. On 15 January 1943 he was promoted Major General with
seniority from 17 November 1941. His second son, Michael, was born
on 16 January 1943. On 21 August 1943, he was appointed temporary
commander of the 8th Corps and appointed Acting Lieutenant
General. On 9 November that year he relinquished command of
the 8th Corps and on 6 December 1943 that of the 11th Armoured
Division. Then on 14 February 1944 he was Commander of No. 30
Military Mission Moscow and assumed the appointment on 30 March
1944. His office was at No 34 Skatertny Pereulok. He left seven months
later at Stalin's request.

It seems clear that he should not have been sent there in the
first place. A newspaper article announcing his appointment had
the headline: *'"Wanted" man now an envoy. Lt. Gen. Montagu Brocas
Burrows on whose head a big price was once put for his activities in Russia,
is going to Moscow as head of the British Service Mission. The time he was
a wanted man was 25 years ago during the Murmansk campaign when,
as a subaltern, he was given the task of organising peasants on the side
of the White Russians.'* On 6 June 1944 news of the allied landings in
France was broadcast throughout the Soviet Union. There were scenes
of tremendous excitement in the streets. A statement by Lieutenant-
General Brocas Burrows, commander of the British military mission
and Major-General J.R. Deane, commander of the American military
mission was read on the Moscow radio, followed by a speech in
Russian by Lieutenant-General Burrows. The National Anthems of
the three allies were then played.

On 9 October 1944, Winston Churchill flew to Moscow to discuss the final defeat and control of Germany and the future of a liberated and independent Poland. Brocas was at the airport to greet him with other dignitaries. On 14th there was a Command Performance at The Bolshoi Theatre and afterwards 'we had a most interesting and successful military discussion at the Kremlin. Stalin had with him Molotov and General Antonov. Mr. Averell Harriman, the then American Ambassador brought General Deane. '*I had Brooke, Ismay and General Burrows, head of our Military Mission in Moscow.*' So writes Churchill in Volume VI of *The Second World War*. There is no mention of Stalin asking him to remove Brocas from the country.

Stalin once implied that being rude to the Russians in the presence of Soviet eavesdroppers was as grave a breach of diplomatic manners as being rude to them in person. When the Soviet Union requested Brocas's recall, Harriman asked Stalin for the reason to which he replied "We don't mind being called inefficient but we don't like being called barbarians". In the British Mission's office, 28 hidden microphones were found two months later. Also, Stalin knew that the Red Army was the only force in the USSR capable of overthrowing his dictatorship. In 1937 he had had eight generals executed for supposed treason. Brocas had arrived with a letter he had been told to deliver to a senior soviet general but attempts to do this were constantly frustrated – hence his outburst. Also, the fact that he was a fluent Russian speaker, unlike his opposite number at the American Mission, General Russ Deane, would have told against him. Translators are carefully briefed to toe the party line and non-Russian speakers can't communicate directly with anyone, which suits dictators very well.

Brocas left Moscow on 2 November 1944 arriving back at Northolt on 6 November 1944. On 5 January 1945 he was appointed General Officer Commander-in-Chief West Africa where he was in post for just over a year arriving back in England in March 1946. Molly was told that she could only accompany Brocas to Africa if she found a job to do out there so she joined the Red Cross. On their way out, they stopped in Rome to visit Sir Noel Charles, the British Ambassador and his wife. Brocas retired on 25 July 1946, he was transferred to the Regular Army Reserve of Officers and granted the Honorary rank of Lieutenant General. So ended a remarkable career which spanned two world wars and began 32 years previously when a 19-year-old boy, fresh out of school and without rank or distinction, sailed to France to serve his country. He finally ceased to belong to the Regular Army Reserve of Officers on 31 October 1954, his 60th birthday. That year, the film *White Christmas* with Bing Crosby and Danny Kaye had been released. It included a song entitled *'What can you do with a general when he stops being a general? What can you do with a general who's retired?'* It was a song which his children picked up on and according to his daughter they sang to him rather irritatingly. No doubt he would have brushed it off with a smile.

Brocas died on 17 January 1967 at the age of 73. The day before he asked if it was his son Michael's birthday, and so hung on for another day so as not to cast a shadow on future birthdays. A brave, kind and noble man to the end and an enduring example for his descendants and all who knew him.

'And so ends this book!'

Medals and Honours of Montagu 'Brocas' Burrows:
Military Cross
Distinguished Service Order
1914 Star, British War Medal
WW1 Victory Medal
Mentioned in Despatches (London Gazette 11 June 1920)
Order of St. Vladimir of Russia 4th class
Order of St. George of Russia 3rd class
Order of St. Anne of Russia 3rd class
Commander of the Order of the Crown (Granted by H.M. the King of the Belgians)

Brocas, approximate date 1946, Source: Burrows family archive

List of items sent in parcels to Brocas 1914 – 1918

Item	Torgau	Burg	Mainz	Friedberg	Clausthal	Holland	Total
CLOTHING							
Aertex pants pr		2					2
Aertex vest		2					2
Badges			4	1			5
Bath slippers pr			1				1
Bath towel			1				1
Black and white under woolly			1				1
Boot laces	2	10	1				13
Boots (Newmarket) pr			1				1
Boots pr	1		1	1			3
Braces pr	2						2
Breeches pr	2		1		1	1	5
Buttons				1			1
Canadian gloves pr	1						1
Cap			1		2	2	5
Cap (khaki)						1	1
Cap cover			1				1
Chain set			1				1
Cigarettes box	1	2					3
Cricket sweater white			1				1
Cricket white flannel trousers						2	2
Cricket white flannel shirt						2	2
Dressing gown				1			1
Felt boot slipper		1					1
Flannel belt	1	1					2
Flannel shirt	1						1
Gaiters pr	2						2
Gloves pr	2		1				3
Gloves pr warm						1	1
Gloves pr lined parade				1			1
Handkerchiefs	25	36	14	10	2	6	93
Hats (felt)						3	3
Helmet			1				1
Jacket					1		1
Jaeger blanket	1						1
Jaeger boots pr			1				1
Khaki handkerchief	1	3					4
Khaki shirt	4	1	3	3			11
Lappells			1				1
Long drawers pr	2						2

Item	Torgau	Burg	Mainz	Friedberg	Clausthal	Holland	Total
Long suspenders			2				2
Military waistcoat	1						1
Mittens pr	1			1			2
Neck ties		4		2	1	1	8
Overcoat		1					1
Pants Pr				5		7	12
Parkin					1		1
Pouch (5 DG's)					1		1
Puttee stockings			1				1
Puttees		1	1		2		4
Pyjamas	2						2
Pyjamas (warm)						1	1
Pyjamas (cream)						1	1
Pyjamas thin			2				2
Raincoat					1		1
Scarf	1	1	1			3	6
Scarf khaki			1	1			2
Service cap			1				1
Shirt collars (white)						18	18
Shirts (day)						12	12
Shirts (evening)						6	6
Shirts (striped)						2	2
Shirt collars	1	1	6	3			11
Shirts (thin)			2		2		4
Shirt Thick				1			1
Shoes						1	1
Shoe laces		2	1				3
Shoes Brogues		1	1				2
Shoes tennis			1				1
Shorts cotton					2		2
Slacks				2	2		4
Slacks (khaki)						1	1
Slippers jaeger					1		1
Slippers warm				1	1		2
Socks cashmere pr			1				1
Socks pr	9	12	10	4	4		39
Socks (khaki)						2	2
Socks (grey)						2	2
Socks silk pr			1				1
Spurs & chains			1				1
Stockings pr		2	2	1			5
Suitcase of clothes (unspecified)						1	1
Suit (complete) grey/brown/blue						3	3
Suit (black)						1	1
Suit (evening dress)						1	1
Summer Clothes (unspecified)						1	1
Suspenders		1		1		1	3
Sweaters				2		1	3
Taffeles collars		4	4				8
Taffeles shirts		3	2				5
Thick pants	2	2					4

Item	Torgau	Burg	Mainz	Friedberg	Clausthal	Holland	Total
Thick vest	5	3		3			11
Tie		1					1
Ties silk		3	4				7
Trousers blue flannel pr			1				1
Towel	1		2				3
Trousers		1				1	2
Trousers grey flannel prs				2		1	3
Tunic and badges			1			1	2
Uniform button set			1				1
Uniform tunic OTC	1						1
Vermelli			1				1
Vest Jaeger	2	2					4
Vest long sleeved cashmere				1			1
Vest (warm)						1	1
White woollen gloves	1						1
Woolly helmet				1			1
Waistcoat (grey woollen)						1	1
Waistcoat (brown – Old Eton)						1	1
Waistcoat fleece					1		1
Waistcoat (white) £40						2	2
Waistcoat woolly	2						2
Clothing subtotal	**78**	**103**	**86**	**49**	**25**	**92**	**433**

NECESSITIES

Item	Torgau	Burg	Mainz	Friedberg	Clausthal	Holland	Total
Bath Olivers			7				7
Bone Fork		1					1
Bone spoons		14	2				16
Bromo pkt		1					1
Brushes						1	1
Candles (Lux)				2			2
Cardboard plates		11	7				18
Cleaner (brown and white)				1			1
Cooker primus				1			1
Cooker refills				2			2
Flashlight refills				1			1
Flypapers			1				1
Grey army blankets			4				4
Hair oil		1					1
Hot water bag				1			1
Inhaler						1	1
Keatings powder		2	1				3
Leather folding case fitted from Selfridges			1				1
Love in the mist (sachet)						1	1
Luminous watch 27 Feb 1917				1			1
Maps in egg boxes 27 Feb 1917				1			1
Nail brush		1					1
Nail cleaner		1					1

Item	Torgau	Burg	Mainz	Friedberg	Clausthal	Holland	Total
Ointment					1		1
Pencil		6	5				11
Pillow			1				1
Pillow cases			3				3
Portmanteau						1	1
Razor blades (pkt)					1		1
Rubber air cushion			1	1			2
Shaving Brush						1	1
Shaving soap sticks			1		2	1	4
Shaver (gillette)						1	1
Small despatch case			1				1
Soap (unspecified but some Jerebone or Yellow)		3	12	26	5	3	49
Solid methylated spirit			2				2
Sponge						1	1
Table clothes				2			2
Tooth picks pkt							0
Toothbrush		1					1
Toothpaste					1		1
Twill sheets			4				4
Vermin powder (fleas)				2			2
Necessities subtotal	0	42	49	45	10	11	157

SOCIAL

Item	Torgau	Burg	Mainz	Friedberg	Clausthal	Holland	Total
Bridge markers			1				1
Candles					11		11
Candles and lanterns				1			1
Candles cake					1		1
Candles (coloured for lanterns)				1			1
Candles (lux presumably lighters)					12		12
Chess set		1					1
Crackers box				1			1
Cricket bag/bats/pads						1	1
Cricket balls			13				13
Cricket balls rubber (red)			22				22
Cricket leather guards				1			1
Cricket shirt			2	2			4
Cricket stump bat			1				1
Dominoes		1					1
Gramophone record set			1				1
Golf clubs returned then sent again					1		1
Golf clubs (box)						1	1
Heather				1			1
Kamplite					4		4
Pack of cards			2	1		1	4
Paint box		1					1
Pantomime things				1			1
Photo Aunt Em			1				1
Photo Duchess enlarged					1		1

Item	Torgau	Burg	Mainz	Friedberg	Clausthal	Holland	Total
Photo Duchess in brown case				1			1
Photo Leggat				1			1
Ping pong balls (box of 12)			36	36			72
Pipe			2				2
Prints in roll					1		1
Racquet				1			1
Racquet badminton				1			1
Racquet gut				1			1
Squash racquet bats					1		1
Tennis balls (box of 6)			1	1			2
Tennis shoes returned				1	2		3
Tennis shoes sting soles					1		1
Tikka camera		1					1
Tikka kodak films		1	1				2
Tinsel box					2		2
Tobacco tins		6					6
Social subtotal	0	11	83	54	35	3	186

BOOKS MAGAZINES ETC

Item	Torgau	Burg	Mainz	Friedberg	Clausthal	Holland	Total
Books (unspecified)						2	2
Prayer book		1					1
Bible		1					1
Burberry catalogue			1				1
Music			4				4
Songs				2			2
Operettas			2				2
Book Ansell's				1			1
Book Bags of Chivalry				1			1
Books Browning Tennyson Byron			3				3
Books *Cranford, John Ingleshant, Lorna Doone*			3				3
Book Italian *The Women in White*			1				1
Books Italian			2				2
Book French		3	2				5
Books Russian			2				2
Book Hindustani manual			1				1
Book *Inside of the Cup*			1				1
Book *History of 5th D.G.s*		1					1
Book of songs (Agnes)			1				1
Books *Anna Karenine 2 vol*			2				2
Book Russia History		1					1
Book Fletcher's History		1					1
Book *Peninsular War vols 1 and 2*, Oman			2				2
Book Browning			1				1
Book Scot			1				1
Book Beaconsfield			1				1
Book Carey			1				1
Books 3 vols Everyman's			3				3

Item	Torgau	Burg	Mainz	Friedberg	Clausthal	Holland	Total
Books Stage plays			1				1
Book *Peninsular War vol 3*, Oman			1				1
Book *Peninsular War vol 4*, Oman			1				1
Book *Illustrated Record*, Lang			1				1
Book of plays			1				1
Book *Spanish Armada*, Trocedas			1				1
Book *Essays on Men*, Stevenson			1				1
Book Motley Vol II			1				1
Book *Essays on literature*, Frone			1				1
Book *In the Hands of the Enemy*, O'Rorke			1				1
Book 1st Vol. *Rise of Dutch Republic*			1				1
Book Stonewall Jackson				1			1
Book Life of Napoleon					1		1
Book Life of Havelock			1				1
Book Daffrein			1				1
Book Wellington			1				1
Book Nelson's History						4	4
Book Management of Horse				1			1
Book *Wisden Almanack*		1					1
Autograph book			1				1
Eton chronicle					3		3
Weekly Times					1		1
Old Etonians dinner					1		1
Eton v Winchester cricket report					1		1
Cricket Letter from Buxton					1		1
Magazines and newspaper cuttings						2	2
Slides of Pompeii and Oxford						1	1
Lectures						2	2
Books subtotal	0	9	49	6	8	11	83

FOOD AND DRINK

Item	Torgau	Burg	Mainz	Friedberg	Clausthal	Holland	Total
Almonds and Raisins lbs	5	5					10
Apples doz.		3			1		4
Apples box			4		2		6
Apricots (tin)		3			1		4
Asparagus (tin)	1		5				6
Bacon joint and rashers		4			2		6
Beef corned					2		2
Beef roast (Edgar)			2				2
Beef pressed			1				1
Beans baked		4	2		4		10
Biscuits (tins size not specified)	3	20	15		2	6	46
Biscuits 4 lb (tins)						2	2
Biscuits (wheat meal) lbs	3	1					4
Biscuits cheese		1					1
Biscuits cheese (tin)		1					1
Biscuits chocolate		1					1
Biscuits digestive		2	1				3

Item	Torgau	Burg	Mainz	Friedberg	Clausthal	Holland	Total
Biscuits ginger			2	1			3
Biscuits Jacksons					1		1
Biscuits large assorted H & P			4	2			6
Biscuits lbs		5		6	1		12
Biscuits Marie					1		1
Biscuits Petit beurre			7	1			8
Biscuits savoury		2	2				4
Brandy					2		2
Brawn		1	1				2
Brawn (Boars head)			1				1
Bread (A & N)		1					1
Bread (tins)		10	1	35	26		72
Butter 1/2 lb tins twice a week from 25/7/1915	ongoing						0
Butter lbs			30	37	30		97
Butter puffs (box)		1	5				6
Butterscotch					1		1
Café au lait		2		11	7		20
Café au lait deal case with 2 large tins					1		1
Cake		6	30	39	42		117
Cake Christmas 7lbs				1			1
Cake (Dundee)		1					1
Cake (ginger)			1				1
Cake (Lizzie's)		3	14		1		18
Cake Birthday			1		1		2
Cake Easter 5lb				1			1
Cake with false bottom 'Good luck' 30 June 1917			1				1
Cake to Miloradovitch				1			1
Cereals (deal case)						4	4
Cheese assorted (tin)			1				1
Cheese Danby			3	2	2		7
Cheese lbs or tin (size not specified)		6	5			1	12
Cheese 8lb tin				1			1
Cheeses Dutch		2					2
Cherries (tin)			1				1
Chocolate Bournville nut		2					2
Chocolate slabs or bars		15	29	7	9	1	61
Chocolate with enclosures and good luck 14 July 17					1		1
Chocolate Whitley's vanilla pks			13				13
Chocolates – box of Fullers for Easter			1				1
Chutney (jar)			1		1		2
Cobb nuts			3				3
Cocoa (Bivonae) (pkts)		33	4	1			38
Cocoa (tins)			2	18	16		36
Cocoa and milk			1				1
Cocoa essence			3				3

Item	Torgau	Burg	Mainz	Friedberg	Clausthal	Holland	Total
Coffee lbs				3		5	8
Coffee (Russian) tin	1						1
Chicken (presumably potted)				2	1		3
Cream (tin)			8				8
Custard birds					2		2
Dates (box)			1	1	1	1	4
Dripping		3					3
Eggo (tins)			14	12			26
Eggs (doz)			19	18	33		70
Eggs dried				1			1
Figs pkt			1				1
Flour bag				1			1
Flour 7lb tins				3	1		4
French beans (tins)			6	2			8
Fruit parcel			1	2	1		4
Fruit dried					1		1
Fruit tins					12		12
Galatine Turkey			1				1
Golden syrup (tin)		1					1
Groceries (Twining) random then 1st of month				10	5		15
Haddock			1	3			4
Ham (half)			1				1
Ham				4	1		5
Ham (York)			1				1
Ham & chicken			4				4
Herrings (tin)		2		5	8		15
Herrings in tomato (tins)		2	10	4	7		23
Honey lb				3			3
Jam Pineapple with dyes				1			1
Jam Tiptree lbs or other			25	26	14		65
Jam Tiptree with compass				2			2
Jam Wilkins box			1	1			2
Kippers				7			7
Lemonade				5			5
Lemon squash (tins)			2	7			9
Lemon squash powders			12				12
Lime juice bottle					1		1
Linseed (tin)			1				1
Lobster (tins)		2					2
Macaroni lbs			4				4
Macaroons (tin)		1					1
Mango chutney (jar)			1				1
Mackerel					1		1
Margarine lbs			1	2	3		6
Marmalade (tins or lbs)		4	22	5			31
Milk Nestles			25	1	1		27
Milk				30	23		53
Milk unsweetened					1		1
Milk ideal					1		1
Milk tablets					1		1

Appendix I

Item	Torgau	Burg	Mainz	Friedberg	Clausthal	Holland	Total
Mince pies			12	12			24
Mustard & Cress seeds (pkts)			7		2		9
Mustard 1/4 lbs			5	2			7
Mutton chops			1	3			4
Nuts lbs			2	1			3
Nuts Walnuts lbs		1					1
Oranges			12				12
Oxo (small tins)		1	1		6		8
Parsnips			1				1
Pâté of chicken		1					1
Peaches (tins)			2				2
Peas (tins)			15	15	9		39
Pepper 1/4 lbs		3	16	2			21
Peppermints (tin)			2				2
Piccalilli pkt			1				1
Pineapple chunk (tin)			3		1		4
Plum pudding		1	1	2	2		6
Potted meat		11	39	19	14		83
Potted meat with whisky				1			1
Potted beef steak with wire cutters				1			1
Potted pheasant lbs		2	1				3
Prunes lb			1				1
Pudding Apple				3			3
Ox cheek				2			2
Quaker oats (pkts)			8	8	5	3	24
Rolled oats lbs						3	3
Raisins lbs				10	1		11
Rations (Army)				15	18		33
Rice lb			2	14			16
Rusks (tin)		2	1				3
Salmon (tin)		1	7	7	2		17
Salmon cutlets (tin)			2				2
Salt lbs		3	7	4			14
Sardines (tins)		17	51	20	23		111
Sausages thin Captains lbs			2				2
Sausages (tins)			4	10	10		24
Sausages Reford lbs		4	8				12
Scotch buns pkts			3				3
Shortbread (tins)		4	10				14
Soup (Chivers) box		1					1
Soup (pkts)		8	2	5	5		20
Soup consommé with maps				2			2
Soup (squares)			2	1			3
Soup (tins)			9				9
Soup (turtle) pkt		2					2
Soup scotch broth (tin)			1				1
Steak and Kidney pudding (tin)			1				1
Strawberry jam Tiptree lbs		9					9
Sugar castor lbs			4	8			12
Sugar lbs		2	4	15	19		40
Sugar lump lbs			5	5			10

Item	Torgau	Burg	Mainz	Friedberg	Clausthal	Holland	Total
Sugar demerara lb				1			1
Sugar maple lb				1			1
Suet					4		4
Sultanas lb			1				1
Tea 1/4 lbs			3	16	7	12	38
Tea 5lb box from Scheveningen						1	1
Tin of Toffee		1	3	1	2		7
Tomatoes (tin)			1				1
Tongue (lambs) (tin		1					1
Tongue (Ox) (tin)		10	17	12	8		47
Veda Bread (loafs)			48	7			55
Veal and ham pâté					3		3
Vegetables (box)					1		1
Wine (case)					1		1
Whisky bottle of Scotch						1	1
Food and drink Subtotal		200	705	580	420	40	1945
Total All Items	78	365	972	733	498	157	2803
Total period of Days	84	139	398	267	318	275	1481
Total Parcels	12	71	220	176	123	27	629
Days per Parcel	7	2.0	1.8	1.5	2.6	10.2	2.4

HARRODS PARCELS – ITEMS INCLUDED IN MAIN LIST (TO MAINZ)

Peaches (tins)	2
Apricots (tins)	2
Cherries (tins)	2
Fruit parcel	4
Lemon squash powders	8
Cream	3
Flypapers	2
Biscuits (tin)	1
Biscuits Petit Beurre	1
Biscuits assorted lunch (tin)	1
Castor sugar lb	1
Almonds & raisins lbs	3
Sardines	1
Sauces & pickles	1
P.C. Crisps H & P (tins)	2
Total	34

Item	Torgau	Burg	Mainz	Friedberg	Clausthal	Holland	Total

ITEMS SENT TO PRIVATE MCGREGOR (MAINZ)

Item	Total
Biscuits (tin)	1
Sardines (tin)	6
Sausages	1
Dripping 1/2lb	1
Cake	1
Cheese	1
Milk (tin)	2
Veda bread	2
Tongue	3
Soap	1
Shirt	1
Vest	1
Sweater	1
Socks	1
Heather and groceries from Pitlochry	1
Total	24

PARCELS SENT 'DIRECT' BY OTHER COMPANIES BUT CONTENTS INCLUDED MAIN ITEMS LISTS (SOME SENT VIA AMERICAN EXPRESS)

Item	Torgau	Burg	Mainz
Harrods	8	1	
Selfridges	1		
Twining	26	20	6
Tiptree	3	1	
Greenwoods	1		
Coopers	3		
Jackson butter twice weekly			
Hawkes			
Maxwells			
Lillington			
Fortnum & Mason			
Cator			
Blackwell			

Some of the parcels were sent from the following locations on holiday etc.

Folkstone	Harrogate
Malvern	Barcombe
Kinnersley	Pitlochry
Buxton	

Schedule of Names

Alex (Alexander Camac Wilkinson) – A first cousin and Etonian lost his bowling finger (nick name Camac) – dined with Brocas, George, and Leo page before Brocas's departure for France in August 1914

Alington – became Head at Eton during the war

Alison, James Stuart Irvine – Lieutenant Coldstream Guards – b 1.1.1895 Sydney (Australian) – Captured/wounded 29 October 1914 Ypres – POW Aachen Clausthal Holland – planned to live together with Brocas Crutchley and Sampson in Holland – reputedly from a very wealthy family

Allenby, Edmund – General 5th Dragoons Guards – one of most successful commanders of WW1

Ansell – Lieutenant Colonel 5th Dragoon Guards killed in action 1 September 1914

Armitage, Edward Leathley – Lieutenant RFA b 26.4.1891 d 24.11.1957 Captured 26 August 1914 Le Cateau – POW Torgau Burg Magdeburg Holland cricketer and later Hampshire CC

Bailey, Percy James DSO OBE (South Africa where seriously wounded) – Major 12th Lancers b 2.12.1873 d 1.2.1947 London – Captured 6 September 1914 taken Maubeuge (Hospital) – POW Crefeld Villingen Heidelberg and at Clausthal where he was Brocas's golf partner in tournament – exchanged to Switzerland 5 November 1917 Chateau d'Oex – son of Sir James Bailey of Baileys Hotel

Bailey, W. – Private – No details

Barker, Gordon – Lieutenant Connaught Regt. – Captured 26 August 1914 Le Grande Faye – POW Torgau Burg Magdeburg Halle Saale – Brocas knew him at Torgau and they ate sausage together

Barlow, Nelson William – Major 1st Hampshire Regt. b 4.12.1870 Monagyr Bengal – Captured 7 September 1914 Senlis France – POW Torgau Mainz Friedberg Heidelberg and Switzerland (Mürren)

Balfour – Captain and Adjutant 5th Dragoon Guards – married late 1914 – not POW

Barnardiston, Samuel John Barrington – Major Suffolk Regt. b 1875 Ireland d 1924 – Captured 26 August 1914 Le Cateau – POW Torgau Fort Zinnia Burg Halle (Saale) Weilburg Clausthal – taught book keeping – Holland 2nd batch – final rank lieutenant colonel – well known Suffolk family from The Ryes Little Henny nr Sudbury – father also military Colonel Nathaniel Barnardiston – wife Lady Florence Barnardiston daughter of 4th Earl of Dartmouth

Belfour, Okay Algernon – Lieutenant Royal Engineers b 18.10.1882 Staines – Captured 25 August 1914 Mons/Le Cateau – POW Zinnia Torgau Burg Magdeburg Augustabad Holzminden Holland – possibly Corporal AO Belfour alias Prof A O Belfour MA of Eton, Christchurch, Oxford and Queens University Belfast – he acted as interpreter at Torgau

Bell MP, Morrison Arthur Clive see Morrison-Bell

Bell, Joseph A.D. – Captain Army Service Corps – Captured 1 September 1914 Ermenonville – POW Zossen Torgau Clausthal 1916 with Lieutenant LG Humphreys – was one of the two British officers with Brocas at Zossen

Bene or Buns (Bene or Benning Cartwright) Cartwright, George Hamilton Grahame Montagu – Lieutenant Coldstream Guards i.e. George Cartwright nephew of Brocas's mother – later rank of major and on cricket tour to USA with Brocas 1920

Benning – see Bene probably living with family November 1914

Benson, Constantine Evelyn (Con) – Lieutenant Grenadier Guards awarded DSO pre-November 1917

Benson, F.R. – Probably Shakespearean actor knighted in 1916

Benson, Rex – died pre-Sept 1916 Bernard – Son of Brocas's Uncle Edward Burrows therefore Brocas's cousin

Bingham, Edward Barry Stewart – Commander HMS *Nestor*, Royal Navy b 26.7.1881 Bangor Castle Co. Down – Captured 31 May 1916 Skagerrack, Battle of Jutland awarded VC knew Conrad Jenkins at Dartmouth – POW Mainz Friedberg Holzminden probably Holland retired as Rear Admiral 1932

Blackburne, C.H. – Lieutenant Special Reserve 'C' Squadron 5th Dragoon Guards – attended to Brocas when he was injured at Néry still with regiment 17 September 1916 at Oeuilly (by which time regimental diary has him promoted to Captain) and wrote to Brocas's parents 6 February 1915 from home address The Chantry, Chichester

Blake – 5th Dragoon Guards killed pre-June 1917 but not on a list up to 19 September 1914

Boger, Robert E. – Captain RFC – Captured 5 October 1914 Peronne – POW Torgau, Burg, Mainz, Clausthal Osnabrück Wahmbeck and Holland 6.2.1918 4th batch with brother Lieutenant Colonel DC Boger CO 1st Bn Cheshires – captured at 24 August 1914 Audregnies

Booth – Sergeant was interviewed by Brocas in Holland no details

Boswell – presumably wounded or killed pre-Aug 1916

Bradbury, Edward Kinder – Captain 'L' Battery RHA d 1.9.1914 age 33 at Nery awarded VC – son of Judge James Kinder Bradbury of Altrincham, Cheshire

Brown, William – Lieutenant RFC b 31.1.94 Giffnock Rhuallau Scotland – Captured 23 April 1916 Famyout (Tamjant) – POW Friedberg – in orchestra – Clausthal Holzminden

Bruce, Gen – POW at Clausthal see Knight-Bruce

Burrows, Richard F.G. – 2nd Lieutenant Manchester Regt. b 22.8.1893 Manchester in orchestra – Captured 26 August 1914 Le Cateau – POW Mainz Clausthal Holzminden and Holland – late of LSRB Eton

Butt, Thomas Bromhead – Lieutenant KOYI/Yorkshire Regt. b 20.4.1892 London – Captured/ seriously wounded 26 August 1914 Le Cateau – POW Torgau, Burg and on first exchange to Switzerland 29 May 1916 – he knew Major Yate VC who escaped Torgau and was killed under dubious circumstances – his letters re the above at IWM

Caldwell, James Arthur – Lieutenant 19th Manchester Regt. b 9.6.1888 Salford – Captured 23 July 1916 Guillemont – POW Gütersloh Crefeld Ströhen Holzminden Holland – cricketer

Camac – (see Alex) had damaged hand

Campbell, William Macleod – Captain 2nd Suffolk Regt. – Captured/wounded 26 Aug 1914 Le Cateau – POW Halle Saale Burg Weilburg Mainz Friedberg – in tunnel gang Friedberg – escaped from a train with Lieutenant Philip Godsal Ox and Bucks LI 20 March 1917

Campion – Possibly in 5th Dragoon Guards – told fabled story to Brocas's parents of capture of German officer but since killed – ref Lieutenant Rogerson

Cartwright H.A. – Captain Middlesex Regt. – wrote *Within Four Walls* published 1930

Cartwright George Hamilton Grahame Montagu (See Bene) – 2nd Lieutenant 5th London Regt. (T.F.) Lieutenant Coldstream Guards wounded 2 May 1915

Chance, William Hugh Stobart CBE – Lieutenant Worcestershire Regt. attached RFC b 31.12.1896 d 1981 from Linden Malvern – POW Captured 14 September 1916 Bortou due to engine failure – not wounded – POW Osnabrüch Stralsund-Dänholm (Denmark) Clausthal Edinburgh – in 1912 cricket team at Eton with Brocas and at Old Etonians dinner at Clausthal 4 June 1917

Cheeseman, Frederick William Henry – NCO Bandsman 4th Bn Royal Fusiliers London Regt. b 7.5.1886 – Captured 23 August 1914 Mons – POW Sennelager Crefeld Fürstenberg Holland 7 May 1918 – real name Fred Gwyn who appeared on the music hall stage before the war and performed in Holland concert

Chetwynd-Stapylton,
B.H. – see Stapylton

Chidson, Montagu Reany –
Lieutenant RGA attached to RFC
b 18.4.1893 London – Captured
28 February 1915 Werwisq – POW
Friedberg Ströhen Clausthal
Holzminden and Holland 6th Party

Clark, Walter – Lieutenant
Royal Irish Rifles b 4.8.1872 –
Captured 26 August 1914 Caudry
– POW Burg Mainz Friedberg
Crefeld Ströhen and Clausthal
probably 'Clark' in Holland
engaged to eldest Neuerberg
girl – no details although he may
have been already married

Cox & co – bank used by army

Crutchley, Gerald Edward Victor
– Lieutenant 1st Scots Guards b
19.11.1890 Chelsea d 17.8.1969 St
John's Wood London – Captured/
wounded right shoulder 25
January 1915 nr La Bassée taken
Lille hospital – POW Osnabrüch
Wahmbeck Clausthal 3 February
1917 (date taken from menu) –
knew Gareth Freeman-Thomas
and had his cap which confirmed
Gareth was shot in head – shared
tiny room with Brocas at Clausthal
– one of two pre-war friends at
Clausthal – split a bottle or two
most nights and talked of better
days – Holland 25 February 1918
6th Party – played a lot of cricket
– Hull 18 November 1918 S.S.
Willochra and home 3 December
1918 (Newspaper article) – Father
Major General Sir Charles
Crutchley Lieutenant Governor
The Royal Hospital Chelsea – after
the war had a successful career
as first class cricketer for Oxford
University and Middlesex playing
in 123 matches retiring in 1932

Cumming – in Holland
with Brocas no details

Curran – no details

Davenport, John Archibald
– Captain 2nd Bn Lancashire
Fusiliers b 14.8.1878 London d
1938 – Captured/wounded 26
August 1914 Hautcourt – POW Laz.
Braunschweig Torgau Burg Mainz
Friedberg Clausthal Holland – they
were friends of the Burrows family
and he helped produce 'The Torgau
History of the European War'
held at National Army Museum
https://discovery.nationalarchives.
gov.uk/details/r/N16445018

Davidson, Charles D. –
Lieutenant South Wales Borderers
b 2.11.1884 London – Captured
20 April 1916 Loos – POW Mainz
Friedberg Clausthal Holland

Davies – Colonel DSO – probably
Colonel (Brevet) Price-Davies
April-November 1918 Special
Employed – met and had long
chat with Brocas and American
military attaché in Holland

Davies, Ronald Despart —
Captain 127th Baluchistan
Light Infantry Indian Army
— Captured/wounded La
Bassée pre 3 February 1915 —
POW Wähmbeck Osnabrüch
Clausthal Holland (6th batch)
– composed a play at Clausthal

Dennys, Kenneth George
Gordon – Lieutenant Somerset
Light Infantry – Captured/
wounded left elbow and thigh 18
December 1914 Ploegstert Wood
nr Le Quesnoy – POW Lille
hospital Darmstadt hospital Mainz
15 June 1915 on first exchange
to Switzerland 29 May 1916

Dick, R. – presumably Rawstorne see below

Duchess (Agnes Burrows) – Brocas's sister

Dugmore, Wilfred Leslie Radcliffe – Captain CO 'C' Coy 1st Battalion Cheshire Regt. b 26.7.1879 Guernsey d 28.2.1932 – Captured 24 August 1914 Audregnies POW Torgau Fort Zinnia then Fort Brückenkopf Burg Magdeburg Augustabad Holland – extensive diary of time at Torgau and Burg

Edward (Edward Le Bas) – Brocas's uncle

Elliot, William Grenfell Riversdale – Lieutenant 1st Battalion Cheshire Regt. – b 17.4.1892 India d June qtr. 1978 Worthing – Captured 24 August 1914 Audregnies POW Torgau Burg – Tunnel gang at Friedberg with Grinnell-Milne – Clausthal Holland

Estcourt, Thomas Edmund (Escott) – Captain Royal Scots Greys b 27.4.1881 Newnton, Tetbury – Captured 5 September 1914 Rebais – POW Burg Mainz Friedberg (attended St Andrews Day dinner 1916) Heidelberg – wife visited Brocas' parents – exchanged to Switzerland November 1917 – also known as Sotheron-Estcourt

Fairweather, Ian – 2nd Lieutenant 1st Battalion Cheshire Regt. b 29.9.1891 Bridge of Allan Scotland d 20.5.1974 Brisbane – Captured 24 August 1914 Audregnies – POW Torgau Burg, Mainz (escape attempt with Brocas) Friedberg (escape attempt with Grinnell-Milne brothers) Ingolstadt Fort

IX Freiburg Crefeld Ströhen Saarbrücken Holland Hull – rejoined British army in India in WW2 – in later life considered by many to be Australia's greatest modernist painter living the life of a minimalist non-materialistic recluse and wanderer

Fletcher, Reggie – Etonian died pre-January 1916

Flower, Lord Albert – impersonated by Brocas in Friedberg in a potted version of a play by Chekhov

Force – Had Spanish flu in Holland – no further details

Forman, Humphrey P. – 2nd Lieutenant South Wales Borderers b 26.4.1888 Repton d 21.5.1923 Bangkok – Captured 14 May 1915 Ypres – POW Quedlinburg Burg Fürstenberg Holland – cricketer Holland and played two first class matches for Cambridge University and one for Somerset in 1910 – at Burg 'Olympic Games' held in May (presumably 1915) 30 British officers won against 770 Russian French and Belgians – he was 2nd in the half mile and 3rd in the quarter mile behind Hunter-Blair

Fowke, Gustaves Henry Spencer – Major/Captain 1st Gordon Highlanders – b 14.10.1880 Brighton d 24.6.1946 Wansford – Captured 24 October 1914 Auberge/Antwerp – POW Mainz Augustabad Fürstenberg Holland 17 April 1918 cricketer with Brocas – arrived Hull 18 November 1918 SS Arbroath and played first class cricket for Leicestershire and army between 1899 and 1927 by which time he was well over 40 – captained the county

**Freeman-Thomas, The Hon.
Gerard Frederick (Gerry)** –
2nd Lieutenant 1st Battalion
Coldstream Guards b 3.5.1893 d
14.9.1914 age 21 on list of missing
9 July 1915 and memorial La Ferte-
sous-Jouarre – son of 1st Viscount
Willingdon, of Ratton Willingdon
Sussex – Eton with Brocas in
1912 cricket team – his father was
later 13th Governor General of
Canada 1926 and 22nd Viceroy
and Governor-General of India

**Gareth (Hamilton-Fletcher,
see Hamilton-Fletcher)**
– Scots Guards KIA

Gaston, Page – probably a
French POW at Burg who
received parcels for British and
details of British casualties etc

George (See Bene) – 1st cousin
to Brocas also at Eton – dined
with Brocas, Leo Page, and Alex
before departure for France

George, Theodore – Captain,
Suffolk Regt. b 29.10.1914
– Captured 26 August 1914
Le Cateau – POW Mainz –
birthday party with Brocas
– Friedberg and Clausthal

Gerry (See Freeman-Thomas)

Gethen – no details

Gibson – no details

Gilet, Lieutenant – Belgian officer

Godsal, Phillip MC – Lieutenant
Buckinghamshire and Oxfordshire
LI – POW Torgau Mainz escaped
with Captain W M Campbell
from train from Friedberg to
Clausthal and made it to Holland

Gordon, William Eagleson VC
– Colonel Gordon Highlanders
b 4.5.1866 d 10.3.1941 Hindhead
– Captured 26 August 1914
Bertrix while 2nd in command
to Lieutenant Col Neish they
were covering the retreat of 3rd
Division from Le Cateau and
Neish did not want to retreat
without orders – Gordon saw the
danger and Gordon exercised
his right to take over command
after a furious row (according to
the official history) but it was too
late – most of the battalion was
either killed or taken prisoner
including Gordon himself – POW
Torgau Burg – left February 1915
probably for Lazarett Berlin/
Lazarett 1 Magenleid early 1916,
and whilst, 'in a condition of great
weakness,' he was exchanged
for the Prussian Prince Salm-
Salm in a deal controversially
brokered by King Alfonso of Spain.
https://www.britishempire.co.uk/
forces/armyunits/britishinfantry/
gordonsgordon.htm

Gough – Sergeant 'C' Squadron
5th Dragoon Guards – visited
Brocas's parents on 3 October
1914 and gave the account
taken down by and presumably
typed by them – wounded
Salbonniere 8 September 1914

Gower, Erasmus William –
Captain 2nd Battalion Royal
Munster Fusiliers b 5.3.1885
Killgoran, Pembrokeshire
– Captured 27 August 1914
Etreux – POW Zinnia Torgau
Burg Mainz May 1916 Friedberg
Augustabad Holzminden
Holland – his wife became
chief cook at the YMCA hut

Graham-Toler, Leopold James –
Lieutenant/Captain 4th Battalion

Middlesex Regt. b. 18.12.1888 Co Tipperary d 9.6.1938 – Captured 23 August 1914 Mons – POW Torgau Magdeburg Mainz (birthday party for Captain George 29 October 1915) Ströhen Holzminden and Bad Colberg – brother of 5th Earl of Norbury

Graham-Watson, Alexander James (Fitz James) – Captain 3rd Royal Scots b 30.4.1892 Edinburgh – Captured 27 August 1914 Cambrai/Le Cateau – POW Blankenburg on reprisal list 25 April 1915 Halle Saale Cüstrin Augustabad Heidelberg Holland 3rd batch 22 January 1918 (engaged to a Miss Woodville in Holland August 1918) Hull 18 November 1918

Graves, George (Cecil) MC – Captain 2nd Battalion Royal Scots MC for work at Le Cateau b 14.3.1892 Kensington d 2.1.1957 West Cults, Aberdeen during WWI family living at Outran Lodge Aylsham Norfolk – Nephew of Sir Edward Grey Foreign Secretary therefore on reprisal list 25 April 1915 – Captured 27 August 1914 Bertry – POW Torgau (telegram of 24 October 1914 from American Secretary of State) Burg 13 April 1915 sent to Magdeburg prison as reprisal for treatment of German submarine crew Weilburg Halle Saale Mainz Friedberg (prominent member of orchestra and theatre property man) Clausthal shared room with Brocas – Holland 2nd batch – wrote letter to Brocas's parents 2 April 1917 – Graves's father visited Brocas's parents – mother went to Holland and took over running of Hexham Abbey Hut when Brocas's father returned home and ran it until October 1918 – Holland prodigious cricketer

with Brocas, Crutchley and others (see photo) later played one first-class match for MCC in 1920

Greene, Gerald Elliot D. – Lieutenant/Captain 'D' Coy 3rd Canadians b 10.4.1888 Toronto – Captured 24 April 1915 Ypres – POW Bischofswerda Crefeld Holzminden Holland cricketer – mentioned in *Three Years a Prisoner in Germany* by JC Thorn

Grey, Sir Edward – British Foreign Secretary in 1914 and uncle of Captain Cecil Graves (see above) to whom he left his family home, Falodon Hall, Northumberland

Grinnell-Milne, Douglas – Captain RFC b 20.7.1886 – Captured 16 May 1916 Lille – POW Friedberg (member of tunnel gang and escaped with Fairweather and brother Duncan Grinnell-Milne September 1916) Crefeld Ingolstadt

Grinnell-Milne, Duncan – Captain RFC b 6.8.1893 London – POW Friedberg June 1916 wrote *An Escaper's Log* Tunnel gang Friedberg (member of tunnel gang and escaped with Fairweather and brother Douglas Grinnell-Milne September 1916) Ströhen and Saarbrucken – no mention of Brocas

Haig, Alfred E. – Major 2nd Kings Own Scottish Borderers b 3.6.1866 – Captured/wounded 26 August 1914 Le Cateau – POW Fort Zinnia Torgau Fort Brückenkopf Torgau Burg Halle Salle Augustabad Holzminden Holland 22 January 1918 and finally Prince of Wales Hospital England

Halliley, William Goodenough
– Naval Officer Sub Lieutenant
b 6.6.1882 Bedford d 12.12.1943
– Captured 31 May 1916 North
Sea – POW Friedberg chief
seamster and had many relations in
Ceylon – Clausthal prominent in
theatricals – after war Commander
of Destroyer HMS Norseman

Hamilton-Fletcher, Gareth
– 2nd Lieutenant Royal Scots
(Grenadier) Guards d. 25 January
1915 age 20 remembered Le
Touret Memorial France – Eton
in 1912 cricket team with Brocas

Hamilton-Fletcher,
Mrs – Gareth's mum

Harrison, M.C.C. – Major
Royal Irish Regiment –
wrote *Within Four Walls*

Hartley – Awarded MC no details

Harvey, Douglas – ex
captain of tutors at Eton

Harvey, Douglas Lennox – 2nd
Lieutenant 9th (Queen's Royal)
Lancers d 3.1.1914 age 22 fag
master at Eton – son of Edward
Douglas Lennox Harvey of
Beedingwood Horsham, Sussex

Hawkes & co (Hawkes)
– Clothing suppliers

Hay, Ivan Joseph Lumley
– Lieutenant 5th Lancers b
31.10.1884 Sligo 3rd son of 20th
Earl of Errol – Captured 26 August
1914 Le Cateau – POW Burg
Osnabrück Crefeld Clausthal
Holland – one of 39 officers placed
under arrest 25 April 1915 for
sinking of a German submarine
– engaged to Olga Lentrum in
Holland but family refused to allow

marriage – family Seat Woodbury
Hall, Everton, Bedfordshire

Hedley – Army – wounded pre-7
March 1916 in good health by 11
April 1916 – a family relation

Henderson – presumably
wounded or killed pre-Aug
1916 – not Ian below

Henderson, Ian MacDonald –
Captain Gordon Highlanders/1st
London Scottish – Captured/
wounded 31 October/1 November
1914 – POW Mainz 18 August
1915 – shared room with Pelham-
Burn and was helped a lot by
Captain Usher who massaged
his leg for three months for an
hour a day and who was also an
organiser of games with Brocas and
others – interned in Switzerland
29 May 1916 with first group of
32 Officers to be transferred

Henslow, Edward Lancelot Wall
MC – Captain 2nd Wiltshire Regt.
b 19.3.1879 Mere Wilts d 12.3.1947
Salisbury – Captured 24 October
1914 Reutel – POW Holzminden
Holland and cricketer with Brocas
played one first class match for
army in 1912 final rank lieutenant-
colonel – 1926 Commandant Army
School of PT Aldershot and has
Henslow room named after him

Hill, Maurice – 2nd Lieutenant
5th Dragoon Guards wounded
1 September 1914

Hooper – POW transferred to
Mürren – Brocas described him as
one of the cheeriest – no details

Horn – Cavalry and Eton
in Holland met Brocas's
father – no details

Houldsworth, J. – Captain Gordon Highlanders in Holland also visited by his sister

Howey, John – 2nd Lieutenant Bedfordshire Yeomanry attached to RFC – POW at Mainz, Crefeld and then transferred to Chateau d'Oex Switzerland 21 April 1917 – friend of cousin Eustace Burrows

Hudson, Alban – awarded MC – no details

Humphreys, Lionel George – Lieutenant Army Service Corps b 23.5.91 Aldershot – Captured 9 September 1914 Ermenonville – POW Zossen, Torgau Burg Mainz helped organise games – Friedberg Augustabad Holzminden – with Major Bell was one of two other British Officers with Brocas at Zossen

Hunt – Australian in Scottish Horse (Blackwatch) – POW at Clausthal

Hunter-Blair, David W. – Lieutenant Gordon Highlanders b 22.7.1894 Glasgow helped organise games – Captured 27 August 1914 Bertry – POW Torgau, Burg Fürstenberg Holland – One of 39 including Cecil Graves placed under arrest 25 April 1915 while at Burg as reprisal for treatment of German submarine crews in England – at Burg, (Olympic Games held in May presumably 1915) when 30 British officers won against 770 Russian French and Belgians – he was 1st in the mile the half mile and the quarter mile (source: Hunter-Blair War book newspaper letter no date sent by Brigadier from Naval and Military club) – damaged an achilles tendon in sports in

Holland – arrived Hull on S.S. Porto 22 Nov 1918 with Duncan Grinnell-Milne and J C Leech – played rugby for Gordons – retired with rank of lieutenant-colonel

Hutchinson, Cecil K. – Captain Royal Scots attached 1st Coldstream Guards b 10.4.1877 – Captured 25 January 1915 La Bassée – POW Friedberg Clausthal Switzerland 27 November 1917 with Captain EA Jackson and others – according to Brocas was at Friedberg possibly only temporarily – Clausthal designed golf course 19 January 1918 transferred to Heidelberg then Mürren Switzerland – same regiment as Gareth also at Eton and runner up Amateur Golf Championship 1909

Jack (Bovill) – 1st cousin of Brocas – lived in Australia December 1914 – later in action when he came over and joined the British Navy and parents visited Brocas's parents on several occasions

Jackson, Eric Archer – Captain 'C' Company 1st Battalion Cheshire Regt. b 28. 6. 1880 Hawkhurst – Captured/wounded 24 August 1914 Audregnies – POW Paderborn Halle-Salle Burg Fort Zorndorf Augustabad Fürstenberg Fort IX Ingolstadt Holzminden Heidelberg Switzerland (Mürren) – four escape attempts from different camps – father of the author

Jackson, Sydney Charles Fishburn DSO – Lieutenant Colonel Hampshire Regt. b 21.4.1863 near Colchester – Captured/wounded thigh and heel 26 August 1914 Nauroy (Le Cateau) – POW Cologne, Torgau Burg Mainz took church services – March 1917 via Villingen interned

Chateau d'Oex Switzerland – liked hunting golf and rowing

Jellicoe, Sir John Rushworth – Admiral in charge of Battle of Jutland – a distant cousin of Brocas b 5.12.1859 Southampton – created Earl Jellicoe and Viscount Brocas of Southampton on 1 July 1925 d 20.11.1935 buried St Paul's

Jenkins, Conrad – Lieutenant Royal Navy HMS Warspite d 24.12. 1916 age 22 or 25 buried Kirkwall Cemetery – son of Prof Charles Frewen Jenkin Chair of Engineering Science University of Oxford – Brocas knew of death 12 January 1917 *Letter 129*

Jervis, Henry S. – Captain Royal Munster Fusiliers b 14.4.1878 Weston-Super-Mare – Captured 27 August 1914 Etreux – POW Torgau Burg Mainz Friedberg (in Cinderella) Augustabad Holzminden Holland manager of YMCA printing press – Prince of Wales hospital England with nerves 31 August 1918

J.S.B. (John Bovill) – Australian cousin of Brocas who joined the Australian Royal Navy

Keene – no details

Knight-Bruce, John Horace Wyndham – Lieutenant/Captain Warwickshire Regt. b 29.10.1885 Bethnal Green d 31.8.1951 – Captured 26 August 1914 Haucourt 14 km west of Le Cateau – POW Hospital Duisburg with Lt Sampson Torgau (where he stayed because he was sick when others went to Burg) Clausthal (Wildmann approx. 7km from Clausthal) Chateau d'Oex Switzerland

Lamble, Arnold Edwin B. – Acting Lieutenant Royal Navy Reserve SS Appam – b 1890 Edmonton Middlesex – Captured 15 January 1916 by German raider Moewe in the Atlantic – POW Clausthal (shared room with Brocas) played Dhobie (washer woman) in *Dale Sahib of Dustypore* September 1917 and town crier and royal trier on of shoes in Cinderella December 1917 – Holland 18 April 1918 R51301

Lawton – POW at Clausthal Nov 1917 – no details

Le Hunte, John Legh – Captain Hampshire Regt. b 11.8.1886 Herefordshire d 14.5.1974 Chelsea – Captured 26 August 1914 Clery/Le Cateau – POW Burg, Mainz Friedberg Clausthal Heidelberg Switzerland – father governor of South Australia 1903-1909 and Trinidad and Tobago 1909-1916 – while at Mainz received slightly improved facilities because his father had treated some German prisoners well in Trinidad – learnt Russian with Brocas at Mainz and shared room him and Captain Peskett (Lincoln's) Captain Usher (Gordon Highlanders) Lieutenant Fairweather (Cheshires) Lieutenant Walker (RFC) Lieutenant Younger (RFA) Lieutenant Sampson (Royal Fusiliers) and a parrot

Leech, John Cyril – Captain 8th Hussars attached RFC – Captured Douai – POW Burg Mainz Friedberg Holzminden not at Clausthal – arrived Hull on S.S. Porto 22 November 1918 – old Etonian

Leech, Cecil John Farran – Captain/Adjutant Royal Field Artillery b 25.4.1882 d 1952 Dublin

– Captured 26 August 1914 Le Cateau – POW Mainz Friedberg Augustabad – 10 June 1920 as major awarded MC – brother William John Leech well known Irish painter – with Lieutenant Colonel CF Stevens Major ACR Nutt and Lieutenant JET Younger (See Younger) at Mainz http://www.bristol2014.com/assets/files/articles/150224-Manuscript-V113-LOW.pdf

Leechman, Colin – 3rd Hussars probably died 23 September 1914 (ICRC record)

Leggat, L.C. – Eton in 1912 cricket team with Brocas, killed during the war

Leigh, Austin – died pre-30 April 1916

Lindop, Victor Somerset Erskine (Erskine-Lindop) – Captain RFC/Prince of Wales Leinsters Regt. b 1891 d 1978 Jhansi, India – Captured Peronne/La Ferte POW Halle Salle (with Captain EA Jackson) Burg Mainz Friedberg (The Queen of the Fairies in Cinderella Xmas 1916) – 1927 a squadron leader

Lizzie (Griffiths) – The Burrows' cook

Loder-Symonds, William (Willie) – Lieutenant Wiltshire Regt. b 19.8.1886 Hinton Waldrist d 30.5.1918 Thetford in flying accident – Captured 27 August 1914 Courtrai – POW Torgau Halle Burg, Mainz, Friedberg, Magdeburg, Limburg, Ströhen, Aachen, Holzminden – successfully escaped to England – news of his escape noted by Brocas's father 5 March 1918 stating that

L-S had refused exchange to Holland and had been moved to a distant lager (POW camp) arrived in Holland 7 March 1918 (noted by Brocas's father)

Lyster (Lister) Phillip G. – Possibly Major P.G. Lyster RFA or probably Captain/Major George Douglas Lister Royal West Kent b 3.9.1874 Yorkshire father Rev Canon Lister Newcastle-on-Tyne – Captured 23 August 1914 St Ghislain – POW Torgau Burg Mainz Friedberg Clausthal Heidelberg – helped organise games at Mainz with Brocas, Usher, Humphreys and Sampson – married while in Holland July/August 1918 and Captain CG Graves was best man

MacCulloch – died no details

MacGregor, Albert – Private, 8035 Kings Own Royal Lancaster Regt. b 24.8.1888 3 Clarke Street, Ashton-under-Lyne, Manchester – Captured 6 September 1914 Compiègne Brocas's orderly/servant as POW Zossen Torgau Burg Mainz – later transferred to Soltau

MacIntyre, David Hamilton – Argyles Regiment and 2nd Lieutenant AFC b Sydney – Captured 9 July 1916 Beaulencourt – POW Gutersloh and Clausthal – played cricket for Winchester v Eton in 1915

MacBryan, John Crawford William (known as 'Jack') – Lieutenant/Captain Somerset LI b 22.7.1892 Bath/Box Wilts d 14.7.1983 Cambridge – Captured 26 August 1914 Le Cateau – POW Burg Augustabad Furstenberg Holland (3rd Batch 22 January

1918 R51078) – played cricket at Groningen with Brocas and One Test match for England 1924 also MCC and 206 first-class matches for Somerset

Maclean, Alexander H. – Captain 2nd Argyle and Sutherland Highlanders b 1.12.1880 Calcutta (from Ardgour) – Captured/wounded 26 August 1914 Le Cateau – POW Torgau Burg Blankenburg Crefeld – married Miss Burns in Holland 5 September 1918

MacNeal – accompanied Col. Neish to Annarad Japoorah

Madan, Geoffrey – wounded pre-30 April 1916 probably brother of Nigel Madan

Madan, Nigel Cornwallis – Lieutenant 8th Battalion King's Own (Royal Lancaster Regt.) presumably d 2.3.1916 age 27 – 2nd son of Falcon Madan 94 Banbury Rd Oxford – educated Eton and Christ Church Oxford – commemorated Memorial Menin Gate

Marlow, William – Lance Corporal 3750 5th Dragoon Guards from near Rugby wounded and missing 26/27 August 1914 Attras – POW Hameln, Soltau – Brocas's servant in Holland (Master of Ceremonies at function) – arrived Hull 18 November 1918 on SS Arbroath same day as Brocas and arrived back with Brocas at parents' house in Oxford 20 November 1918

Martin, George Charles Russell (probably) – Lieutenant York and Lancaster Regt. attached Sherwood Foresters Regt. –

Captured 20 October 1915 Lille – POW Crefeld 1915 Holland d 12.9.1918 hit by tram and died 3 days later – son of Captain George Martin C.B.E (R.N.) White Cottage Saltwood Kent

Martin-Thomson (Tomson), William John – 2nd Lieutenant RFC From Ramsgate – Captured 10 July 1916 Mametz wood? – POW Gütersloh Clausthal (in Charley's Aunt cast list December 1916 /January 1917) arrived Holland 16 May 1918 R51402 – enjoyed Brocas birthday celebration 31 October 1918 with Crutchley and Stott (letter to his mother from Crutchley dated 6 March 1918 source: Catherine Ashmore, granddaughter)

Massy, Bertie Errol – Captain 1st Battalion Cheshire Regiment b 1.11.1883 Tenby – Captured 24 August 1914 Audregnies – POW Torgau, Burg Mainz Friedberg Holzminden – married in Holland June 1918

McDonald, Alistair – on list of missing January 1916

Miloradovitch, Nicolai – Lieutenant Russian Army – POW at Mainz – Brocas's Russian friend and teacher who gave two volumes of *War and Peace* to Brocas which are still in the family – wrote several letters to Brocas's parents – possibly related to Count Mikhail Andreyvich Miloradovich Governor-General of St Petersburg 1813 and his Grandson Andrey who became Governor of Little Russia (Ukraine)

Molly (Molly Burrows)

Mon – Friend of Brocas pre the war

Mont – died Pre-September 1916 – presumably a gunner

Montgomery, Joseph – Captain 7th Dragoon Guards b 3.7.1879 Hertfordshire living at Ifield Hall, Sussex – Captured/wounded 24 August 1914 Wiheries – POW at Torgau Halle Magdeburg Burg Friedberg Clausthal Holzminden Holland – spoke and studied Italian with Brocas

Morrison-Bell, Clive Arthur MP – Major 1st Scots Guards b 19.4.1871 Newbus Grange Durham/London d 16.4.1956 – Captured 25 January 1915 Quinchy nr Le Bassée same battalion as Gareth – POW Blankenburg Friedberg Crefeld Clausthal (Brocas's tennis partner) Heidelberg Switzerland – Baronet 1923 and MP until 1931

Mortimer-Phelan, William Charles – Captain RFC b 14.10.1895 Brasted Kent – Captured 23 April 1916 Fanpoux nr Arras – POW Mainz Friedberg (in orchestra) Clausthal Holzminden Holland and Hull with Brocas 18 November 1918

Moseley, Reginald Anthony Deane (Referred to as 'MO') – 2nd Lieutenant Royal Munster Fusiliers b 15.5.1891 d 1979 London – Captured/wounded 27 August 1914 Etreux – POW Torgau Halle (with W Loder-Symonds D Wise and EA Jackson) Burg Mainz Friedberg Augustabad Holzminden Holland shared room with Cecil Graves and then digs with Brocas and Hunter-Blair – 1931 Major (local lieutenant-colonel) Royal Scots – final rank Brigadier

Neish, Francis Hugh – Lieutenant-Colonel Gordon Highlanders b 1863 d 15.2.1946 – Captured 27 August 1914 Bertry – POW Torgau, Magdeburg, Mainz, Heidelberg and Switzerland

Nettlefold, E.J. – Lieutenant B Squadron 5th Dragoon Guards Special Reserve one of two brothers – Wounded 16 September 1916 near Chavonne when a shell exploded close by killing two men

Nettlefold, J.H. – Lieutenant B Squadron 5th Dragoon Guards Special Reserve one of two brothers

Newman – Sub Lieutenant RNAS in room with Brocas at Friedberg possibly Lieutenant Harry Alexander Newson Royal Munster Fusiliers – Captured 3 September 1914 Etreux – POW Torgau Burg Mainz Friedberg

Newton, Lord – no details

Noel, John B. – Lieutenant and later Captain KOYLI b 6.4.1891 – Captured 26 August 1914 Le Cateau – POW Torgau Burg Magdeburg Gutersloh, Crefeld, Holzminden and Holland – Old Etonian

Nutt, Arthur Charles Rothery DSO – Major RFA b 19.3.1873 Kensington d 21.6.1946 Dorset – Captured/wounded shot through throat 26 August 1914 Le Cateau – POW Torgau Burg Mainz (at birthday party for Captain George 29 October 1915) Friedberg Clausthal Wurzburg Heidelberg and interned Switzerland 27 November 1917 – Invented the Nutt (artillery) Miniature Range – final rank lieutenant-colonel

O'Rorke, Benjamin G.
– Chaplain to the Forces –
Captured 29 August 1914
Landrecies – POW Torgau Burg
Magdeburg – wrote *In the Hands
of the Enemy* published 1915

Odiaux, Felix (probably) –
Captain 32nd Infantrie French
– Captured Mauberge 20 August
1914 – POW Torgau in next
room to Brocas in Mainz

Oldfield – POW at Crefeld
and presumably not a senior
officer – no details

Page, Leo – friend probably Eton
dined with Brocas George and
Alex before departure for France

Pelham-Burn, Herbert Lachlan
– Captain Gordon Highlanders
b 21.3.1891 London d 13.5.1927
– Captured 27 August 1914 Le
Cateau/Bertry – POW Mainz
Friedberg Clausthal Holland –
mother wrote to Brocas's parents
about plans for escape from
Friedberg – married Captain
Younger's ex-wife 1923

Peskett, Reginald Frank –
Lieutenant later Captain 2nd
(Feb 1915) Lincolnshire Regt.
– Captured 9 September 1914
Noyon – POW Torgau Burg
Mainz Friedberg and Switzerland
February 1917 PA 8291 – one of
Brocas's first English-speaking
fellow POWs – later Major

Phillips – killed pre-13 March 1916
– Great friend of Brocas at Eton

Picton-Warlow, Ivor (later
Picton-Turbervill by deed poll) –
Captain 1st Gordon Highlanders
b 15.11.1881 Brighton d 9.3.1957
– Captured/wounded forearm

27 August 1914 Caudry/Le
Cateau – POW Halle Saale (with
Captain EA Jackson) Augustabad
Fürstenberg Clausthal Aachen
Holland (3rd Batch) Hull –
married in Holland 27 August
1918 – final rank lieutenant-colonel

Portman, Guy Maurice – Captain
8th London Regt. b 4.8.90 Dorset
– Captured 22 May 1916 Vimy –
POW Gutersloh Crefeld arrived
in Holland after 1 July 1918

Price, Owen – Lieutenant Duke
of Wellingtons Regt. b 15.5.1893
Teddington – Captured 24
August 1914 Wasmes (Mons) –
POW Mainz Clausthal where he
composed a musical play (Pierrot
Show) – Holland with Brocas
became a sub-editor of 'British
Empire Fortnightly' a magazine in
Holland and assistant manager of
the YMCA printing press under
Captain Jervis of Munster Regt.

Radcliffe, Douglas – December
1914 was off to war a friend
of Brocas no details

Randall, Harry Cohu – Captain
HQ 1st Battalion Cheshire Regt. b
2.12.1887 Guernsey – Captured 24
August 1914 Audregnies – POW
Torgau Zinnia and Brückenkopf
Burg Mainz Gütersloh Crefeld
Holland – visited by sister who
helped run YMCA Hexham
Abbey Hut with Brocas's father

Randall, (Miss) Maria Louise
– b 1882 Nurse and brother of
Lieutenant/Captain HC Randall
1st Bn Cheshire Regt. – she
went to Holland and helped run
YMCA Hut with Brocas's father

**Rawson, (probably Rawson-
Shaw K.)** – Lieutenant RFA

attached RFC – Brocas's fag at Eton on list of missing January 1916 but in Holland on Old Etonians tea party list

Rawstorne, George (George R or 'Dick') – Eton in 1912 cricket team with Brocas

Reynolds, Thomas – Captain Royal Yorkshire Light Infantry (2nd KOYLI) – b 5.3.1887 Edgemoor – Captured 26 August 1914 Le Cateau – POW Fort Zinnia Torgau Burg Magdeburg Gütersloh Crefeld Ströhen Holland 5 January 1918 Hull 17 November 1918 (same list as Fairweather) – great friend of Brocas as POW and he used to try to escape with Brocas possibly from Burg or Torgau – dined together in Holland with Mrs Reynolds – also referred to by Brocas's father as in 17th Lancers

Righton – Army no details

Robertson, George – Captain 6th Battalion Scots Fusiliers (Gordon Highlanders?) b 13.1.1875 St Andrews – Captured 25 September 1915 Loos – POW Gütersloh Crefeld Ströhen Holzminden Holland cricket umpire

Rogerson, John C. – Lieutenant 15th Hussars – Captured Busigny taken to Maubeuge jumped a train recaptured and put up against a wall to be shot – reprieved by a German General – POW Halle Saale Burg Fürstenberg Holland met Brocas's father – traumatised and had bad nerves – arrived Hull 16 November 1918 SS Stockport also at Eton

Rose-Troup, John Montgomery – Captain The Queens's Regt. b 1890 d 1967 – Captured 31

October 1914 Ghelvelt 1st Battle of Ypres – POW Weilburg, Bad Coburg – wrote several war poems including one specifically for Captain C G Graves at Weilburg entitled 'March 4th 1916' – Clausthal shared room with Brocas

Russell, Charles – Lieutenant Duke of Cornwalls Light Infantry b 10.2.1896 West Maitland N.S.W. Australia – Captured 21 October 1914 La Bassée – POW Gnadenfrei Mainz Crefeld Holzminden Holland (4th party with Brocas) became engaged to a Dutch girl July 1918

Troup, John – see Rose-Troup

Samble – See Lamble (incorrect spelling in original transcript)

Sampson, Frederick A. – Lieutenant 4th Royal Fusiliers b 8.11.1890 London d 26.11.1966 Bury St Edmunds – Captured early September 1914 Bertrix – POW St Vincents Hospital Duisburg (with Captain Knight-Bruce) Torgau Burg Mainz Friedberg Clausthal Holland not a great cricketer and batting number 10 for MCC v The Rest in Holland – scored 0 – helped organise games at Mainz – shared room with Brocas at Clausthal where he was in charge of string orchestra in theatricals.

Sclater-Booth – Major 'L' Battery RHA wounded at Nery

Showers – in Holland met Brocas's father

Skaife, Eric Ommaney – Captain 1st Bn Royal Welsh Fusiliers b 18.10.1884 Chichester d 1956 unmarried – Captured 19 October 1914 Menin – POW Danholm

Friedberg Clausthal (shared room with Brocas) was also at Holzminden Aachen Holland – later major 1918 lieutenant-colonel 1929 and military attaché in Moscow 1934-1937

Skeet, Challen Hasler Lufkin known as 'Hasler' – 2nd Lieutenant 12th Royal Fusiliers b 17.8.1895 Oamaru NZ d 20.4.1978 West Tytherly Hants – Captured 28 September 1915 Vermelles – POW Gütersloh Fürstenberg Holland cricketer and played first-class cricket 1919-1922 for Middlesex and Merton College Oxford – solid bat and 'great fieldsman of his time'.

Slessor – Captain and family friend pre the war

Smith, A.L. – Elected master presumably at Eton

Smyth-Osbourne, John Greville – Captain 1st Bn Royal Welsh Fusiliers b 27.7.1886 Stapleton Bristol d 1979 Newbury – Captured 21 October 1914 Zonnebecke – POW Crefeld Bad Colberg Hann Münden Ströhen Clausthal (shared room with Brocas) Holzminden Holland 4th Batch 6 February 1918 (with Brocas) Zeerust Hotel – final rank major

Sotheron-Estcourt, Thomas Edmund see Estcourt

Stapylton, Bryan Henry (Chetwynd-Stapylton) – Major 1st Battalion Cheshire Regt. – Captured 24 August 1914 Audregnies – POW Torgau Burg Clausthal (active in theatricals) Holland

Stirling, Archibald – Lieutenant/ Captain 2nd Bn Argyle & Sutherland Highlanders b 29.11.1885 Garten Stirlingshire – Captured 26 August 1914 Le Cateau – POW Gütersloh 9 Dec 1914 Cöln 30 Dec 1914 Wahmbeck 5 June 1915 Clausthal (member of same club as Brocas that met on Sunday evenings possibly escape club? to discuss affairs of the week over a glass of wine) Holland via Aachen 15 January 1918 2nd batch 28 January 1918 (ICRC R51067)

Stirum, Willem – both he and Countess Stirum probably local Dutch

Stiven, Ronald Walter Sutherland – Lieutenant/Captain Royal Scots Fusiliers – Captured 23 August 1914 Mons – POW Torgau, Burg Mainz died in captivity 15 September 1915

Stott, John – Captain 5th Dragoon Guards b 10.6.1878 London – aviator – Captured 12 September 1915 Colencourt – POW at Mainz (briefly summer 1915) Crefeld Ströhen and Holland approx. 26 April 1918 – Brocas's best man

Sydney (Wilkinson) – Alex Wilkinson's sister – spent quite a lot of time with the Burrows family in Oxford

Tahourdin, Victor Richard – Captain and Adjutant 1st Battalion Cheshire Regt. b Apr qtr. 1881 Windsor Castle – father was chaplain to Queen Victoria hence name d 1948 Bramdean Hampshire – Captured 24 August 1914 Audregnies – POW Torgau Fort Zinnia and Brückenkopf Burg Mainz Friedberg Heidelberg Switzerland (Montreux) –

reputed to have shaved in Champagne in Paris on the way home when repatriated

Tailyour, George Forster Hercules – Major Royal Field Artillery b 31.8.1876 Emberton nr Olney Bucks d 1921 in command of Royal Artillery Brigade Colchester – Captured 26 August 1914 Le Cateau – POW Torgau Mainz Friedberg Clausthal (studied or taught mathematics to Captain Graves) Holland in 2nd batch 5 January 1918 – cricketer

Talbot, Neville – Awarded MC probably wounded pre-March 1915 no details

Tennyson, The Hon Alfred Aubrey – 4th Bn Rifle Brigade – d 23.3.1918 age 26 Pozieres Memorial France – Son of 2nd Baron Tennyson of Farringford, Freshwater Isle of Wight

Tennyson, Lionel – killed pre-September 1916 possibly The Hon. Harold C Tennyson d 29.1.1916 HMS Viking

Thomas, Gerry Freeman (See Freeman-Thomas) – on list of missing 9 July 1915

Thompson, Albert George – Lieutenant-Colonel RAMC – Captured 12 September 1914 Montigny POW Torgau Burg Mainz

Toogood, Cecil – Major 1st Lincolnshire Regt. b 31.3.1870 Cheltenham – Captured/wounded through neck and shoulder 23 August 1914 or 26 August 1914 Charleroi/Troisvilles – POW Brunings hospital Paderborn Torgau Burg Mainz Friedberg

Heidelberg (sent back from Constance) Crefeld Ströhen

Townley, Sir Walter – President of the Y.M.C.A. Advisory committee in Holland with his wife

Tweedie, Gerald Scott – Major 2nd Royal Scots b 24.11.1874 Peebles – POW Torgau Magdeburg Mainz Clausthal (secretary of entertainments committee) Holland – from well-known Tweedie family of Quarter

Usher, Charles Milne DSO OBE MA – Lieutenant/Captain 1st Gordon Highlanders b 6.9.1891 London d 21.1.1981 – Captured 27 August 1914 Bertry – POW Burg Mainz Friedberg Clausthal and in Holland with Brocas went to Arnhem together – massaged Captain Ian Henderson's leg for three months for an hour a day and was also an organiser of games with Brocas and others – later colonel in Gordon and Sutherland Highlanders 1939 DSO Dunkirk – played rugby 16 times for Scotland and also fenced for country – wrote book *A History of the Usher Family in Scotland*

Wainwright, David – Naval Officer Sub-lieutenant HMS Nomad b 8.9.1894 Teddington – Captured 31 May 1916 Skagerrack – POW Mainz Clausthal November 1917

Walker, Ronald – RFC b.1.4.1897 brother of Eric also aviator – Captured 25 August 1916 Bapaume – POW at Friedberg Augustabad

Walker, Eric George, Sherbrooke – Captain RFC b 4.7.1887 London – Captured 7 July 1915 Douai – POW Mainz Friedberg (shared room with Brocas and attempted to escape) Ströhen Furstenberg, Augustabad Holzminden

Wallace, William Berkley – Lieutenant Colonel Suffolk Regt. b Peona India – Captured Ypres – POW Mainz Friedberg – went to hospital to recuperate 20 March 1917 – invented charger holder for magazine rifles (Enfield Lock) and applied for patent 1906

Ward – escaped before April 1916 from a train near Swiss border and made it back to England possibly with Champion – visited Brocas's parents

Watson, Graham Alexander James (Fitz James) – See Graham-Watson

West, Cecil Harley L'Estrange – Lieutenant/Captain Royal Dublin Fusiliers b 20.11.1890 Dublin d 8.7.1951 – Captured/wounded in hand 27 August 1914 Clary – POW Burg Mainz Friedberg (signed July 1916 entertainment programme at Friedberg with Fairweather) Holzminden Holland 4th batch – married in Holland 26 November 1918

Wiggett, A. – 2nd Lieutenant Kings Royal Rifle Corps – Wounded and missing 9 March 1916 France – not at Mainz 30 April 1916 but ICRC card records death 15.3.1916 at Asette? Anette?

Wilfred, T. – no details

Williamson, Archie – great friend of Brocas at Oxford and Brocas met his wife while in Holland

Wilson, Robert Eric – Captain 3rd Hampshire Regiment b 19.1.1891 – Captured 2 September 1916 – POW Gutersslöh Osnabrüch Clausthal Stralsünd Danholm described by Brocas as a most cheerful companion immensely missed and was given 'an amusing send off evening' from Clausthal – knew Brocas's Aunt Em

Windram, G.H. – Private no details

Wise, Douglas MC – Captain Royal Munster Fusiliers, b 18.11.1879 Caraghlen – Captured 27 August 1914 Etreux – POW Torgau, Halle Saale (with Captain EA Jackson) Burg, Mainz Friedberg Augustabad Holzminden Holland 4th Party – Hull on SS Willochra 18 November 1918

Wynwood – no details

Younger, John Edward Talbot CBE nick name 'Sam' – Lieutenant RFA b 2.11.1888 Auchen Castle Langshaw Bush Moffat d 1974 – Captured 26 August 1914 Le Cateau – POW Torgau (in choir) Burg (where he became choir master with Brocas one of that choir) Mainz Friedberg Clausthal (taught Brocas Hindustani) and shared a room with Brocas at Mainz and probably member of the escape team – Holland 2nd batch – mother was one of the wives to visit – Final rank Major General CBE in Army and founded Army Ski Association and The Army mountaineering Club. Father possibly Sir William Younger 1st/2nd Baronet of Auchen Castle, Langshaw Bush, Moffat of Youngers Brewing family

Bibliography and Sources

Burrows, Montagu, *The Life of Edward Lord Hawke* (1883)

Burrows, Montagu, *The Family of Brocas of Beaurepaire and Roche Court* (1886)

Burrows, Professor Montagu, *Worthies of All Souls* (1874)

Cooksey, Jon and Murland, Jerry, *The Retreat from Mons 1914: North* (1914)

Evans, A.J., *The Escaping Club* (2012) Edition

Roche Court and its former owners. Paper read by Miss Skinner Hist. Tripos (Cantab) 13.06.1914

Harrison, Major M.C.C. and Cartwright, Captain H.A., *Within Four Walls* (1930)

Grinnell-Milne, Duncan, *An Escaper's Log* (1926)

Hamilton, Lord Ernest, *The First Seven Divisions* (1916)

Diary of Captain W.L.R. Dugmore, Cheshire Regiment (1918)

Horsfall, Jack and Cave, Nigel, *Mons 1914* (2000)

Jackson, Paddy, 'IF' (unpublished, 2020)

Jackson, Paddy, *To a Prison in Paradise* (unpublished, 2018)

Jackson, Robert, *The Prisoners 1914-18* (1989)

Lewis-Stempel, John, *The War Behind the Wire* (2014)

McKenna, Stephen, *Sonia Between Two Worlds* (Toronto 1917)

Oman, Carola, *An Oxford Childhood* (1976)

Roberts, Claire (ed.), and Thompson, John (ed.), *Ian Fairweather – A Life in Letters* (Australia: Text publishing, 2019)

O'Rorke, B.G., *In the Hands of the Enemy* (1915)

Simpson, Frank, *The Cheshire Regiment: The First Battalion at Mons and the Miniature Colour* (1929)

Terraine, John, *Mons – The Retreat to Victory* (1960)

Watson, Philip, *Audregnies* (2019)

https://grandeguerre.icrc.org/en/File/Search

http://www.worcestershireregiment.com/wr.php?main=inc/whs_chance_7

https://www.friendsofthesuffolkregiment.org/operation-legacy/archives/03-2017

Lieutenant J.E.T.Younger RFA at Mainz POW camp on the way to collect his parcels in 1916 Source: Michael Younger from Younger family archive

Index of Military Personnel

World War One – Key dates

4 August 1914	Britain declares war on Germany and begins mobilisation
9 August 1914	First British troops move to France
10 August 1914	Brocas and 5th Dragoon Guards move to France
23 August 1914	BEF first contact with the enemy at Mons
24 August 1914	The Retreat begins
2 September 1914	Brocas injured at Néry and taken prisoner
9 September 1914	Allied forces finally halt German advance
14 September 1914	Brocas at Zossen POW camp
28 September 1914	Brocas at Torgau POW camp
26 November 1914	Brocas at Burg POW camp
7 May 1915	German submarine sinks 'The Lusitania'
20 May 1915	Brocas at Mainz POW camp
31 May 1915	Battle of Jutland
28 August 1915	Italy declares war on Germany
6 April 1916	USA declares war on Germany
15 June 1916	Brocas at Friedberg POW camp
1 July 1916	Battle of the Somme begins
27 August 1916	Romania enters the war
24 March 1917	Brocas at Clausthal POW camp
15 May 1917	Zsar Nicholas II abdicates
14 August 1917	China declares war on Germany
17 September 1917	Russia declared a republic
15 December 1917	Russia signs armistice with Germany
6 February 1918	Brocas arrives in Holland
4 March 1918	First case of Spanish Flu in USA
1 April 1918	Royal Air Force founded
21 March 1918	Germany begins their final offensive
17 July 1918	Zsar Nicholas II and family executed
26 September 1918	Allied Forces begin final offensive of the War

4 October 1918	Germany formally requests armistice
	USA demands Kaiser abdicates
	USA demands Gemany withdraws all
	forces from occupied territory
11 November 1918	Germany signs armistice at Compiègne
18 November 1918	Brocas arrives back in England at Hull
21 January 1919	Brocas sent to Murmansk as part of the
	Russian campaign
15 October 1919	Brocas arrives back in Oxford and re-joins
	his Regiment
17 January 1967	Brocas died
3 October 2020	Germany made final reparations payment
	for WW1

Wahmbeeck , 14 octobre 1915

Jules De Boeck

*Officer POW's at Wähmbeck POW camp in 1915 with Lieutenant G.E.V. Crutchley
Scots Guards fifth in the line from a sketch by Jules De Boeck a Belgian fellow POW
Source: Catherine Ashmore from Crutchley family archive.*